SHIP "AKBAR" OF BOSTON, CAPTAIN LAMSON

From a painting by Charles R. Patterson

The Making of a Sailor

or

Sea Life Aboard a Yankee Square-Rigger

Frederick Pease Harlow

DOVER PUBLICATIONS, INC.

New York

Published in Canada by General Publishing Company, Ltd., 30 Lesmill Road, Don Mills, Toronto, Ontario.

Published in the United Kingdom by Constable and Company, Ltd.

This Dover edition, first published in 1988, is an unabridged and slightly corrected republication of the work originally published as Publication Number Seventeen of the Marine Research Society, Salem, Massachusetts, in 1928. Most of the illustrations have been placed back to back in the present edition.

Manufactured in the United States of America
Dover Publications, Inc., 31 East 2nd Street, Mineola, N.Y. 11501

Library of Congress Cataloging-in-Publication Data

Harlow, Frederick Pease.

The making of a sailor, or, Sea life aboard a Yankee square-rigger.

Reprint. Originally published: Salem, Mass. : Marine Research Society, 1928.

1. Harlow, Frederick Pease.   2. Voyages and travels. 3. Seafaring life.   I. Title.   II. Title: Making of a sailor. III. Title: Sea life aboard a Yankee square-rigger.
G540.H35   1988   910.4'5'09034   87-30595
ISBN 0-486-25613-8 (pbk.)

PREFACE

HAVING made several voyages at sea, a number of friends have asked me to write a description of sea life in the '70's, aboard a deep-water ship. It is a difficult task to perform with due regard for the proprieties of speech. In those days swearing was prohibited on some ships but on others the conversation was decidedly obscene. It was my misfortune to sail in a ship of the latter class and I am afraid if I picture my experiences one-half as true to life as I found them on board the *Akbar*, the Board of Censors will "clap a stopper" on my yarn and those who might wish to know something of "high life" aboard ship would still remain in ignorance. For how can one describe the petty rows and the language used while shortening sail without including the swear words that Jack has been accustomed to use all his life? Can you imagine a row between two greatly excited men who used only psalm-singing words to end an altercation? You certainly cannot. Neither can a true description of life aboard ship be told at a prayer meeting.

Having kept a journal, during voyages, for my own information, I have now taken incidents from it and included many of the expressions used on board ship, but have disguised the names of individuals in some instances. The following account of my first deep-water voyage may be accepted as a faithful description of life on board an American sailing ship fifty years ago. I wish to thank Miss Dora L. Peakes of Edgartown, Mass., for inspiring me to write this yarn, and twice over to thank my wife, Gertrude G. Harlow, and her sister, Mrs. C. May Hudson of New York, who "took the wheel" and steered me clear of shoals.

CONTENTS

ILLUSTRATIONS

The Making of a Sailor
of a Sailor

THE MAKING OF A SAILOR

CHAPTER I

GOING TO SEA

LONG before I left high school I had made up my mind to become a sailor. Three of my brothers were in the merchant service and there was nothing else for me to do for we all took to salt water like ducks. My grandfather, on my mother's side, was a sailor and had commanded vessels, both in the merchant service and the whaling industry. In fact he was a Tartar from the old school.

It was told of him that his order was law aboard ship and on one occasion when they had lowered for whales and had struck and made fast to a big bull, from which they were obliged to cut loose on account of a gale arising, the whale-boat returning to the ship with the men in a dejected mood because of their ill luck, my grandfather, who was pacing the quarter deck, became very unreasonable and began to find fault with the officer in charge as he came alongside, addressing him as follows:

"Mr. Davis, who cut the line after you had made fast to that bull?"

"I did, sir," replied the mate.

"What in hell did you make fast for if you knew you couldn't hold on to him? What do you think I am out here for; sailing the ship on a pleasure trip at the expense of the owners?"

"I did what I considered the best for all, sir. The sea is rising and it would be impossible to tow him back in this sea," said the mate.

"The sea be damned! Couldn't you hold on and ride out the squall? We could have picked you up after the squall had passed."

"You'd play hell doing it," said the mate, as he reached

for the block of the davit fall to hook it into the ring in the stern of the whaleboat, which was about to be hoisted out of the water.

"What's that you say? Do you dare to answer me in that manner, you — — — —!" And working himself into a passion he seized a harpoon and jumping on top of the rail, drove it with all his force at the mate in the whaleboat below.

The mate, bending over with the block in his hands, showed a pair of shoulders and a back equal to any humpback whale, certainly a good mark for the skipper. No doubt he may have thought he was harpooning one, for he was heard to exclaim, "Heave your iron!" as he hurled it at the mate.

The harpoon, true to his aim, entered Mr. Davis' oilskin jacket just below his shoulder blade, but the whaleboat, at that moment, took a sudden lurch, causing the mate to lose his balance, and throwing up his arm instinctively to catch himself, as he was thrown against the gunwale of the boat, the harpoon glanced from his shoulder, passed under his arm and came out underneath, through his oilskins in front, doing no damage except to spoil an oilskin jacket. So great was the force with which the harpoon was thrown that it not only passed through the mate's oilskins, but it went through the bottom of the boat, as well, going the whole length of the shaft, clear to the hitches, where it was temporarily held by the cedar boards.

The mate, surprised by the attack, failed to hook the block in the ring; but not so with the man in the bow. His hook was fast and when the wave receded, the bow of the whaleboat was hung in the air and as the stern settled the men were thrown aft, in a heap, spilling two men into the sea. On the next wave, the block in the bow was unhooked and the two men were pulled into the boat with great difficulty. The stern of the whaleboat had drifted away from the davits and the harpoon, dangling from the bottom of the boat, was soon playing havoc with the lapstreak boards as she rolled back and forth in the sea.

The skipper, seeing that the iron was about to be released from its holdings, sang out: "Now, don't lose that harpoon! Some of you get a move on you and catch it before it gets away!"

One of the sailors jumped for the iron, as it was working through the boards, but in his haste he was thrown against it by the roll of the boat, which was now half full of water, and it dropped out of sight into Davy Jones's locker.

Another extemporaneous speech in unprintable language followed the disappearance of the harpoon and each man would have received more than his share if the condition of the boat had been any different. As it was, they were reviled because the harpoon was lost.

It was a lucky thing that the whaleboat was dancing a jig when the harpoon was thrown or I might have been a descendant of a murderer on the high seas.*

Did I run away from home to go to sea; or was I knocked down with a club and dragged all over the barn floor for refusing to milk the cows? No! I never was knocked down at home, for my father was a Methodist minister, preaching in the Thames Street Church at Newport, Rhode Island, and he lived his life as a minister of the gospel should. I had the best of homes and my parents did everything they could to make home pleasant. Instead of bringing his boys up to be sissies, my father impressed on us that hard work of the right sort killed no man. "Do not pick a quarrel. Keep out of it, if you can, but if you are forced to fight, see that you win. In other words, whatever you do, do well."

He did all that he could to make me understand that there were better things on land for me to follow than going to sea, but to no avail. Finally, seeing that nothing else would do, he gave his consent with a "God bless you," saying, "We'll see what we can do for you."

When I was thirteen years of age, my oldest brother, who was mate of the ship *Windward*, while on a voyage from

---

* My grandfather was Capt. Isaac Winsor of Duxbury, Mass., and the last ship that he commanded was the *Claudius*, 527 tons, built at Medford in 1836.

Seattle to Portland, Oregon, was caught in a gale off the mouth of the Columbia River, in a southwester, with two other vessels. A towboat came out from Astoria to take them in and picked up the *Windward* first, taking her in over the bar where they dropped anchor just south of Sand Island. There the towboat left them to go out again in an effort to pick up the other two ships.

The wind was increasing every minute until it reached the velocity of a hurricane and the towboat and ships had to stand out to sea in order to keep away from the coast. In the meantime the *Windward* began to drag with all her anchors out. A very high sea was running and could be seen to break over Sand Island, towards which they were fast drifting. In order to save the ship from destruction, the masts were cut away. This relieved her and she rode out the gale and was afterwards towed up to Portland and fitted with new spars and rigging.

While stepping the mizzenmast, the old stump, which had been hoisted out and laid on the deck of the after house, started to roll as the ship listed under the strain of the new mast on the dock, for the sheers were rigged for the occasion aboard the ship. The old mast rolled from the blockings, through the monkey-rail on the house, and caught my brother in some manner and broke both of his legs. So badly was one leg mangled that amputation was deemed necessary. They took him to a hospital but the shock was so great that he only lived a few hours after the operation.

One of his last letters, written home, said: "Do not let the boys follow the sea. At best, it's nothing but a dog's life." But we didn't heed the advice and it was not long before we were all on board ships, endeavoring to find the pleasures afforded by the sea.*

* My brother, Julius I. Harlow, was mate of the *Windward* at the time of his death and was to have been placed in command of the ship upon her arrival at San Francisco. He was a deep-water sailor of the first order having doubled Cape Horn in the following ships: in January, 1859, in the clipper ship *Kingfisher* of Boston, Captain Kimball Harlow, and also on her return voyage in July following; the ship *Samuel Robertson* of Fairhaven, Capt. John R. Tabor, in April, 1860, Boston to Honolulu and

Ship "Claudius," 527 Tons, Built in 1836 at Medford, Isaac Winsor, Master. From a Chinese painting in the possession of Frederick Pease Harlow.

NEWPORT, RHODE ISLAND. From a lithograph by J. P. Newell, published in 1870.

My older brothers, after returning from some long voyage, would tell of the hardships encountered and admonish us never to follow the sea for a living, yet I took particular pains to observe that they didn't remain ashore for any length of time before they were off on another voyage and so I judged there must be something very fascinating about the life. Like John Alden, I soon decided that I would see for myself.

While not a big, husky fellow, I was of an athletic build and took part in all kinds of sport, from turning handsprings by the block to sparring and wrestling by the hour. Having been instructed in the "manly art of self-defense," to take punishment and stand up under it, on many an occasion they had me going; but I only welcomed it for I knew it would toughen me for the work I was about to enter into.

I was taught navigation at home and how to use the sextant and could "shoot the sun" in a saucer of molasses in the back yard and reckon the "day's work" before I had ever been "outside."

We had a sailboat at our disposal and my brother and I sailed the Narragansett, from one end to the other, exploring bays and inlets, and many a hard blow were we in, so that reefing and knotting were not entirely new to me. In fact, we had a royal yard slung in the attic of our house, which we could raise and lower, bend a sail, clew up, and furl,—in fact, brace the yard the same as one could on any vessel. Here, I learned to put a "harbor furl" on a square-sail. On one occasion my brother gave me a lesson in furling, in a heavy head sea, that I never will forget.

We were in the attic one afternoon, with a friend, when

the return voyage in November; the ship *Jennie W. Paine* of Gardiner, Maine, Capt. Wm. Cowell, in September, 1861, New York to Callao, and the return voyage in January, 1862; the ship *Golden Fleece* of Boston, Capt. John L. Manson, in November, 1862, New York to San Francisco, and the return voyage in July, 1863; the ship *California* of Boston, Capt. Henry Barber, in September, 1864, New York to San Francisco; the ship *Grace Darling* of Boston, Capt. Nathan P. Gibbs, in June, 1866, San Francisco to New York; and again in the ship *Golden Fleece* under Captain Wilcomb, in August, 1868, New York to San Francisco.

we lowered the yard and clewed up the sail ready for furling and I was "sent aloft" to take it in. As I stepped on to the foot-rope, he let go the braces and calling our friend to take the other side, first one and then the other would pull and yank at the braces, while I was being swung from starboard to port, bringing up against the backstay at one time and stopped with a "round turn" the next, for they did their best to shake me off the yard. I stayed with it until the sail was furled. While making the end of the gasket fast to the tye, they cut the strap in the jaws of the yard and my brother sang out: "Watch her roll! Hang on, for I'm going to show you how she behaves in a chop sea." Did she roll? Did she pitch? You should have seen those fellows work at the braces while I was being swung from one side of the attic to the other. As for me! Well! They said my eyes stuck out so far that you could have knocked them off with a club and I guess they were correct, for I have furled many a royal when the good ship was rolling and pitching, but never experienced anything like the sensation on that royal yard in our attic.

When the strap was cut I was on the port side. My weight, of course, sent everything to starboard. A royal yard is not slung like a trapeze. The lifts from the yardarm do not run perpendicularly but diagonally to the pole of the mast above, and as gravity seeks its level, it was a pretty hard thing for Mr. Gravity to keep the line of direction inside the base, with those boys at the braces.

As I slid to starboard, it was a queer sensation. A yank at the port brace didn't help matters. Bump! I went into the mast and bouncing off,—away to starboard I flew. "You want to be a sailor, do you?"—Biff! And I got it on the other side. "You'll get it rougher than this, outside. Watch her dip." Then both of them caught hold of the yardarm and swung me forward fully ten feet. Back I came with a rush, and brought up "All standing" against the mast. So great was the impetus that the blocking at the bottom of the mast carried away and the wind was entirely knocked out of me and we "All came down with a run."

Luckily, I didn't break an arm or a leg and with the exception of a skinned elbow and having the breath knocked out of me, I got up from the mix-up and walked around the attic, viewing the remains very much as a gamecock would after knocking out his victim and looking for more worlds to conquer—slightly disfigured, but still in the ring.

My brother complimented me on staying with it to the last and further said, "I guess you'll do." It wasn't much to say, but the way he said it put more confidence in me than I had ever felt before and I awoke to a sense of realizing that I was fitted for the sea right then. That evening I again broached the subject to father and seeing my determination to go he finally gave his consent.

It was my ambition to become a deep-water sailor and to start out at once on a long voyage, but father argued that it was better to make a short trip first, because in a short voyage, if you don't like the sea, you are not tied down so long; on the other hand, if you decide to follow it for a living, having learned the ropes, etc., you can ship in the next vessel as an ordinary seaman, at a better wage.

Living next door to us was a sea captain by the name of Winslow, whom I had been talking with that day. He had been sailing in coasters all his life and was part owner as well as skipper of the schooner *David G. Floyd,* then in the coal trade, running between Newport and Philadelphia. She measured about three hundred tons and was one of the smartest schooners on the coast at that time. Captain Winslow was a typical "Down East Yank." He loved his ship as he did his wife and never grew tired of telling about the good qualities of his "schoonah," as he called her. On the last trip he said he had passed every sail in sight from Philadelphia to Newport and he had yet to see the "two-stickah" that could pass him, for he could show his heels to many of the large three- and four-masters hailing from Taunton, that had already made records.

This race was still fresh in mind when father convinced me it was better to make a short voyage first and it didn't take much persuasion when he asked me if I wanted him to speak to Captain Winslow, and if so, we would go together that evening. I readily consented.

The Winslows were very neighborly with us, in fact, Mrs. Winslow was quite a prominent worker in the church and when the captain was ashore he would accompany her regularly. He had the reputation of being a kind-hearted man ashore but was simply "hell" afloat.

Living with the Winslows was an old sailor who was not quite right in the "upper story." His mind at times was a little unbalanced. He had sailed with the captain for years and had been in the *Floyd*, prior to his accident, from the time she was launched.

One night, in a heavy gale, he fell from aloft, striking his head as he fell into the mainsail, which broke the fall and saved his life. He was unconscious for hours and struggled between life and death for months, finally regaining his strength but remaining mentally weak. The captain took pity on the poor man and gave him a good home in the family.

As we were ushered into the room that evening and shook hands around in the accustomed fashion, father took occasion to address the sailor who was also an attendant at the church.

"Good evening, John! I haven't noticed you at church lately. Have you been sick?"

"No-o, Brother Hahlow, I never felt better. I just got tired of the Methodists an' I wanted a change. No-o, I'm an Episcopalian naow."

"An Episcopalian, John! When did this happen?"

"Oh-h, some little time! Some little time! Brother Locke is a great man. A fine preacher. Didja ever hear him, Brother Hahlow?"

"Oh, yes! He is a very earnest man and a great speaker, John."

"You bet yer damn life he's a great speaker! You ought t' hear him pray! Gee! You're not in it when 't comes t' prayin'. Why-y Brother Hahlow, he'll give ye cards an' spades an' leave ye so far behind you'll look like a shadow, for when it comes t' prayin' he c'n beat ye prayin' all t' hell."

"Oh! Oh! John!" Mrs. Winslow exclaimed. "I hope you will excuse it, Brother Harlow."

"Don't let it worry you, Mrs. Winslow. I enjoy a good joke as well as any one." Whereupon we all joined in a hearty laugh at father's expense.

It was arranged that evening that I should make a trip in the *Floyd,* due to sail in two days, but before we left the house Captain Winslow impressed on my mind that I should not expect any favors from him while on board the schooner.

Then father reiterated that in making this voyage I must rely on myself to get along with the captain and crew, saying, "You will of course make your headquarters in the forecastle, for you can't expect to live in the cabin, and I do not want you to go to Captain Winslow with any petty annoyances that may come up, for the captain can't take your part while you are with the crew." This was said for the captain's benefit and I found out afterwards that father talked over the whole matter again the next day, with the captain, telling him to make it as disagreeable as he could for me, so that when I got home again I would be content to stay there.

I left the captain's house a happy boy. At last my dream was to be realized and I considered myself very fortunate in obtaining a situation so soon in the fastest schooner sailing out of Newport.

The captain wanted me to report the following day and upon getting home my dear old mother, with tears in her eyes, helped me get my things together for the trip, giving me a little advice as she thought of some little article that would be of service to me and tucking it away in the corner of my sailor's bag where she knew it would be found. It was in the wee small hours of the morning before I went to bed and what little sleep I got was interrupted by a very realistic dream that followed me through the night. One moment I was going aloft to shorten sail and the next I was crowding on sail while racing with the big three- and four-masters from Taunton,—only to awake and find it all a dream.

The morning sun finally awakened me and I was up bright and early. There was no sleep for the rest of the family and we had an early breakfast so that I was ready long before the appointed hour. I was to meet Captain Winslow at ten o'clock, at the landing on Swinbourn's wharf, and half an hour before I bid my parents an affectionate farewell. Shouldering my sailor's bag, brother Will went with me to the wharf. It is needless to say how I got there, but I didn't hire an express wagon. No! I proudly walked the streets to the wharf, for I felt like a sailor and wanted to act like one, carrying my bag as I had often seen others go aboard their ship.

The *Floyd* was anchored in the bay, just northeast of the Torpedo Station, and was to have sent a boat ashore to meet us, but we could see the longboat under the quarter and knew they had not left the schooner.

Captain Winslow was not far behind us and soon appeared. As he approached he said "Good morning" to us both and going to the end of the wharf, stood on the cap-log and immediately began waving his hat at the schooner. His signal was answered and soon we saw two sailors jump into the longboat and it wasn't long before they were at the landing.

The cook, who pulled one oar, came ashore to get some meat for dinner and the captain agreed to wait for him. I put my "dunnage" into the boat and the captain and I both got in to await the return of the cook.

Captain Winslow was a typical Yankee skipper. He didn't believe in spending any money for a launch to carry him back and forth to his schooner so long as he could use his longboat. Blow high or blow low it was all the same to him. As he stepped into the boat he introduced me to the sailor.

"Fred, this is Bill. Bill, Fred is goin' aout with us on this trip as boy, d'ye understand? Anything he wants t' know abaout th' schoonah you c'n show him an' I guess he'll need a plenty of showin'."

I shook hands with Bill, who was a year or so older than I. He was tall and slim, with light hair, smoothly shaven, showing a tanned face from the tropics. I found out afterwards that he was a native of Barbados, W. I., and claimed to be a son of the Governor living at Bridgetown. I asked him how long he had been on the schooner and he replied, "About two months." As he didn't seem inclined to carry on the conversation I took my seat on the after-thwart.

That morning the wind was blowing pretty strong from the west. A large cat-rigged fishing boat took up all of the space at the head of the landing and our boat lay under the lee of the fishing boat, alongside of the landing, taking up the rest of the room.

A whistle from a large steam launch entering the slip, caused us to look up. I read the name *Dauntless* on the bow, and knew she belonged to James Gordon Bennett, for I had seen the *Dauntless, Madelene* and *Nimbus,* all big schooner yachts of fame, anchored just out of Brenton's Cove, a few days before.

James Gordon Bennett, dressed in white flannels of naval cut, stood in the stern-sheets and waving his hand, shouted:

"Get that boat out of there. We want to land!"

I took up an oar and standing astride a thwart was about to shove the stern of our boat away from the landing, when Captain Winslow thundered out:

"Drop that oar! I'll tell ye when t' move this boat."

So astonished was I at receiving such an imperative command from Captain Winslow, that I dropped the oar where I stood and the handle struck the captain across the knees and the knuckles of his left hand. I was so startled that I stood like one petrified, for I had never heard a voice in that tone addressed to me before. I forgot to apologize and probably would have gotten more had I attempted it. As it was, he reached down for the wooden bailer at his feet and the next thing I knew, I saw him in the act of throwing it at me. So sudden was his movement that I had no time to dodge, but turned halfway around and got the full force fairly in the most fleshy part of my anatomy.

"You damn little fool!" said he. "If ye're goin' t' be as clumsy as that aboard th' schoonah, I don't want ye 'round!"

I turned to Bill, who was holding a turn of the painter around a cleat on the landing and shaking his sides, but not laughing aloud, and saw from the expression of his face and the sneer from the curl of his mouth, that I'd get no sympathy from him; in fact, he looked disgusted.

Realizing that I was "getting in bad," I hung my head in shame and sat down on the thwart greatly humiliated. The blood rushed to my face and I sat there blushing like a schoolboy. Looking ashore, I caught my brother's eye. He also seemed to enjoy the situation I was in and no doubt it reminded him of a similar incident on his first voyage at sea.

In the meantime the launch was drawing nearer and I was brought to my senses by a second call from Bennett.

"Move that longboat over to starboard and let me land! There's plenty of room for us both!"

"You go t' hell, Gawd damn yer! You don't own this wharf, nor th' landin'. Go hunt another berth, for I'll b' damned ef I'll move my boat."

By this time the launch was almost upon us and although the engine was reversed the wind was bringing him in faster than he had figured. One of the sailors stood up in the bow with a boat-hook in his hand and so did Captain Winslow in our stern.

"If you attempt t' stick yer boat-hook into my boat, I'll break yer jaw!" said the captain.

The way the launch was coming in there was nothing else left for the sailor to do; either he must stick his hook into our boat or have the launch smash into us. He arose to the occasion by putting his boat-hook against our gunwale and throwing his whole weight on the handle in an effort to stop the launch. Captain Winslow at once struck the sailor's hook a mighty blow, breaking it in two, and the sailor, having all his weight on the hook, fell headfirst into the water and went completely out of sight. The launch passed over him and he came to the surface on the other side, where he was pulled in by his shipmates. Bill and I put our shoulders against the stem of the launch to stop her, but she hit us amidships and smashed through the gunwale, cutting a gap clear to our keel.

Our boat began to fill and the captain began to curse at his misfortune, calling Mr. Bennett all the pet names in the dictionary as he leaped ashore. I rescued my sailor's bag before it got very wet and scrambled ashore after the captain. Bill was already on the landing, having jumped just as the launch struck us.

On the launch, two sailors were holding the man who fell overboard. He was as much excited as Captain Winslow. "Let me go, I tell you!" said the sailor. "I'll punch his head!" "Keep quiet," said his shipmates. "Don't make a fool of yourself before Mr. Bennett. Shut your mouth!" and soon he was quieted. After the captain had ranted about the landing he finally asked: "Who's goin' t' pay fer this boat, I'd like t' know? Why didn't ye take another landin' when I told ye to? This is a hell of a way t' come into a landin'."

"Why didn't you get your boat out of the way when you saw us coming in?" replied Mr. Bennett. "This landing will accommodate three launches like this."

"By Gawd, I didn't hev t', I tell ye! Ye could hev taken airy one of th' wharves above an' ye wouldn't hev smashed in my boat ef ye'd done it. What'll ye dew abaout this damage? Goin' t' pay me fer it?"

"I do not think anyone is to blame but yourself, captain, and if you had moved your boat at first there would not have been an accident here."

"I want t' know!" said the captain, with a sneer. "Ye don't mean it naow, dew ye? Let me tell ye somethin'! Somebody is goin' t' pay fer this 'ere boat an' it won't be C. H. Winslow. Put that 'n yer pipe an' smoke it!"

"Now my good man, this is only a trifling matter and not worth mentioning. What do you consider the amount of damage done?"

"Not worth mentionin'? Ye bet it is worth mentionin'! Haow d' ye think I'm goin' t' git aboard my vessel in this boat? It's clean knocked out of commission an' past redem'-shun. Damn it! Don'tcha see I've got t' sail for Philadelfy in th' mornin' an' another boat'll cost me a hunder'd dollars?"

"I think you are putting the figure a little high, captain.

If you will set a fair price on the damage done I will be willing to pay you what it is worth to have the boat repaired."

"Repaired, be damned! I've got t' have a boat to-day t' take my crew aboard the schoonah."

"Now, captain, I am willing to pay you for the damage done, but I will not buy you a new boat," and taking a wallet from his inside pocket, Mr. Bennett opened it and showed it filled with bills. The captain upon seeing the money stopped talking and, stroking his beard, began to meditate.

"Here is seventy-five dollars, captain. Your boat can probably be repaired for half the amount and if you think you can be satisfied with the amount, take it and keep it."

Captain Winslow was a true Yankee and a trader by instinct and seeing his chance to make thirty-five dollars was not long in making up his mind to take it, but he didn't like the idea of giving in too quickly and while wondering what next to say, Mr. Bennett again asked, "Will you be satisfied with this amount?"

The question was right to the point and the captain answered, "Wa'al mebbe so-o," still hesitating and wondering how he could ask for more. But Mr. Bennett was satisfied and jumping from the launch to the landing he put the bills in the captain's hand and without saying another word turned and walked up the wharf without looking to the right or left.

There was a merry twinkle in the captain's eye as he put the money in his pocket, for he knew he was being well paid for the damage to his boat, and telling us to await his return he followed Mr. Bennett up the wharf in search of another boat. Then the sailor who had received the ducking came to life again and called to the captain.

"What are you running away for? You know damn well if you stayed here I'd punch your head. Come back and I'll put a tin ear on you! You dasent do it!"

The captain paid no attention to him and his shipmates again succeeded in quieting the man as the captain moved out of sight. My brother came down to the landing to view the wreck and I went over to where he was standing and said, "Not much of a longboat is it?"

"Oh, that can be easily fixed! I see you have got a warm captain! What did you color up so for? Why, you looked like a Duxbury b'iled lobster, your face was so red. I'm afraid Cap'n Winslow will be a hard man to get along with, but never mind, Fred; I don't think he is a man that will show partiality, so just remember that you are not the only pebble on the beach. What he will say and do to you, you'll find that he will do the same to all and you can console yourself with that idea."

These were words of comfort and I had occasion to think of them many times afterwards.

The captain had been gone about half an hour when the cook appeared at the gangway above, saying: "Bring your oars an' dunnage 'round t' th' next wharf. Th' cap'n's got a boat over there."

Bill took the oars and I shouldered my bag and we all walked around together. Bidding my brother good-bye, I followed the others into the boat and taking an oar helped pull back to the schooner.

Not much of anything was said and on reviewing the incident of the morning I was far from being in a jovial frame of mind; in fact, there was a lump in my throat that I could neither raise nor swallow and on reaching the schooner I seemed to have been forgotten. I sat in the boat thinking Bill would help me with my dunnage, but after making the painter fast in the boom-stopper bail in the rail, he vanished and I had to climb on deck and take an end of a rope and go over the side into the boat again and make it fast to my sailor's bag and then go on deck again and pull it over the rail. After landing it the mate came up from the cabin and asked if the bag belonged to me, to which I answered, "Yes."

"Oh-h, I see! You're th' other man. What vessel didja leave?"

"I have never been to sea, sir. Captain Winslow agreed to take me as boy on this trip," I answered.

"The hell, you say! Funny he didn't say sunthin' t' me.

Hold on! I'll go an' see th' cap'n," and turning on his heel he walked aft while I took the rope off the bag and awaited his return.

The mate was a man about forty-five years of age, six feet tall, of dark complexion and wore a heavy mustache. He was of the Nova Scotia type and hailed from Providence, Rhode Island, where he had lived for twenty years, sailing from that port in steamers and schooners. He was a thorough sailor, when fully aroused to the occasion, but was a little inclined to take things easy. He didn't believe in working too hard and frequently said, "Never do to-day what you can do to-morrow." Consequently the schooner was not always looking as neat as the captain could wish. It didn't seem to me that the mate had hardly got inside of the cabin before he appeared again and called:

"Hey you! Come aft! Th' cap'n wantscha."

I went into the cabin, which was entered from the after end of the house, through a companionway directly in front of the wheel and leading directly into the cabin below. The captain's bunk ran fore-and-aft, on the starboard side, and the mate's bunk was across the room on the port side. There was no partition in the cabin and in the center of the room was a common dining table spread with a checkered red and white table cloth. The accustomed bench in front of the bunks was covered with red plush cushions. In the forward end the captain had his desk, where he was seated when I entered. I stood with my hat in hand, waiting for him to speak. He opened first one drawer and then another as if he were looking for something. Finally he wheeled around in his chair and spread out a large sheet of paper on his desk which proved to be the ship's paper.

"Here, sign yer name on this line! I told yer father that I'd pay ye ten dollars per month, but I don't believe yer worth it. There are plenty of boys that'll take yer place for less an' ef yer wants t' sign for eight dollars th' job's yourn. Otherwise ye can go ashore."

I bit my lip and said nothing, signing the paper as he directed. While I was greatly disappointed at the turn of affairs, yet I would have signed for a dollar a month had he asked it, for it was too late to back down then. I felt that I was worth more, but was in no position to demand it and so left the cabin. The mate told me to take my dunnage into the fo'c'sle and I saw by his looks that he, too, was disappointed in me and taking my bag under my arm I walked forward feeling more like crying than anything else as I went below in the forecastle.

CHAPTER II

LEARNING THE ROPES

THE forecastle was just abaft the foremast and instead of its being a house, such as most of the modern schooners have, the deck was raised from the foremast, aft, about fifteen feet and flush with the rail. The galley, on the port, and the forecastle, on the starboard side, extended below the deck to the between-deck beams, which gave us plenty of room. We entered below, through a double-companionway with sliding hatch overhead for each and separated by a soft-pine partition, running fore and aft, made of inch ceiling boards which had dried out so much in places that one could see what was going on in the galley, and when things were cooking on the stove we got the full benefit of the odor as well as the smoke which percolated through on its way across the bunks and up the companionway to the air above.

It had just struck eight bells as I went into the forecastle and the cook, having started his fire afresh, was warming up stew and hash for dinner. It was a kind of greasy smell that greeted me as I went below. In a way it wasn't new to me for I had been in almost every galley and forecastle of the regular schooners running into Newport, and from listening to the stories at home, of forecastles my brothers had been in, I took it for granted that this one was all right.

The forecastle was about eight by ten feet in size. There were two bunks, one above the other, on the partition next to the galley and two bunks, one above the other, running athwartships on the bulkhead, forward. Bill was lying down in the lower thwartship bunk, smoking a clay pipe. I had been fully instructed never to take a bunk running athwartships, if I could help it, and so wondered why Bill had taken one of this kind, for any sailor with any experience whatever knows how inconvenient they are when the vessel is running before the wind, in a heavy sea, for when the vessel rolls, one minute you are on your feet and the next you are standing on your head. So putting the bag down and making a survey of things I asked,

"Which bunk shall I take, Bill?"

"Take that one over there," pointing to one of the fore-and-aft bunks. "I don't want you over my head," said he, without looking up. He had acted rather strangely in the longboat and I tried to make myself believe it was his manner towards a new acquaintance, so untying the lanyard from the neck of my bag, I proceeded to unpack. The odor from the galley reminded me it would soon be dinner time, so I ventured to ask another question.

"What time do we have dinner, Bill?"

"Oh-h, go ask the cook."

This was said in an irritating manner and not liking it I turned and looked him in the face and said: "What have you got against me, Bill? You have scarcely answered a civil question to-day."

"Well, if you want to know, I'll tell you, damned quick! You're coming here to take the place of a man and you are nothing but a boy, robbing a good sailor of his job. There are only five men aboard this schooner. The captain, mate, cook, myself and you. We ought to have seven and instead of getting two more sailors—what do you know about a schooner anyway?"

"I can learn, can't I? Didn't you start as boy when you first went to sea?" I asked.

"Yes, but my case was different. There were plenty of men to do the work when I started. This schooner is short-handed. Do you see those extra bunks? This schooner used to carry two more men, but the captain is so stingy and mean he wants to pay for the ship on every trip. He's so stingy he won't buy mooring lines and we haven't enough to tie her up at the wharf, so he anchors out here to save wharfage and lines. When we're out to sea he carries on till the last minute and when he has to shorten sail, believe me, boy! you'll have to work some or I miss my guess. Hell! I'm going to leave her!"

Just then the cook called out, "Dinner, boys!" and Bill

said, "You go and get it," addressing me for the first time voluntarily.

I knew most of the duties of a boy aboard ship and went to the galley as ordered, but I didn't like Bill's manner and reasoned he might have gone with me on my first trip; on the other hand, I didn't expect him to. Our dinner was warmed-over stew, potatoes, onions, dry hash and a pot of coffee. I had to make three trips before I got it all for I was new at the business. I set it down on the bench in front of Bill's bunk and he immediately sat on the other end and began to eat. There was no table in the forecastle and only one bench so I stood up and helped myself and sat down on the edge of my bunk to eat. Bill had a flying start on me and was nearly finished before I began. Neither of us volunteered a conversation before he had finished, and, lighting his pipe, he said, "Boy, when you are through, take these dishes to the galley," and then rolling into his bunk, he picked up a magazine and began to read without paying any attention to me whatever.

I carried the dishes into the galley and came back and was busy fixing up my bunk until the mate called us at two bells (one o'clock). Going on deck I began my first work as a sailor.

"Here, boy," said Mr. Cardiff, the mate. "Connect this hose to the handpump and we'll wash her down." After I had made the connection I stuck the suction hose out of the side mooring chock into the water below and sang out, "All ready, sir!" I think he was surprised that I knew how to do it, but I had seen them wash down decks on other schooners and although I had never done it I knew how it was done. The mate looked over the side to see if everything was all right and being apparently satisfied said, "Heave away."

I worked the pump-brakes back and forth several times, but could bring no water. Bill was on the forecastle-head, with a broom, and the mate held the nozzle of the hose waiting for the water to come through. Finally I stopped heaving and looked around for a bucket of water, but there was none in sight.

"What's th' matter, there? Heave away, boy," said the mate.

"She's pretty dry, I guess! Wait till I get some water to pour on the valve," I said. The mate dropped the hose and came aft, and, looking over the pump, which was connected up all right, sang out to Bill, "Git a draw-bucket from under th' fo'c'sle-head an' bring some water here."

Bill got the bucket and standing on the rail, abaft the fore rigging, lowered the bucket over the side without making the bucket-rope fast. The schooner was light and the bucket-rope was not long enough to reach the water and as the rope slipped through his hands he paid no attention to the length of the rope and before he knew it the end went through his hands and the bucket dropped into the water.

"Naow, you've played hell, haven't ye?" said the mate.

"Get me a boat-hook!" said Bill, as he stood there watching the bucket drift along the side from the force of the wind. I didn't know where there was a boat-hook, except the one in the longboat on the other side. I stood by the main rigging, under the fore boom, which had been swung over to starboard, the sheet being made fast to a pin in the rail beside me. Throwing the coil over the side, I jumped over the rail and slid down the rope to the water and as the bucket drifted to me I put out my foot and caught the bail and drew up the bucket-rope and made it fast to the fore sheet. Then bracing my feet against the side of the schooner I walked up the side, pulling myself up hand-over-hand to the rail above and then drew up the bucket. There wasn't enough water in the bucket to wet the pump, so I bent the bucket-rope to the end of the fore sheet and dipped up a full bucket.

The mate took it from me and I coiled the sheet up again on the pin and by the time I finished the mate had the pump working all right. I was kept pumping for two hours and thought my back would break before the deck was finished. Bill was kept busy with the broom, scrubbing the coal dust from the deck and the paint work about the stanchions, and I think I must have lowered the water in the bay from the amount that passed through that pump. The mate used plenty of it and I kept the stream running, wondering all the time if anyone would ever relieve me. While standing on the plank of the pump, working the handles back and forth, all alone, I began to ponder and came to the conclusion that the captain would certainly watch every move I made for some time to come, for it was quite evident that he was none too well pleased with his new boy. The mate, no doubt, was of the same opinion, for I was a green hand taking a sailor's place and no doubt that was why he was making me stay at the pump so long.

Bill had shown what he thought of me, during the dinner hour, by telling me to my face I wouldn't do, and I remembered that he was talking to the cook as I hoisted my dunnage aboard, showing conclusively that he had told him all about the incident in the longboat when I dropped the oar on the captain's hand, for the cook had said nothing to me when I went after the dinner. This resolved itself into one grand total, that all hands, including the cook, were taking me to be a "Joskin," for their manner showed it. What was I to do? Quit? Not by a dog-goned sight! I then thought of the royal yard, at home, in the attic. Did they shake me off? No! They couldn't do it, and I'll live to show these schooner-sailors that I'll make good on this trip.

I was getting warm, and the sweat fairly rolled down my face. Pretty soon the mate came near and there was a quiet smile on his face.

"What's th' matter, boy? Ye look warm," he said. "Wa'al, it's good fer ye! Good fer ye!" I ventured to say, "It's a pretty warm day, I guess," and wiped my face with my sleeve. He said nothing more, but took the hose aft on the poop. Bill helped by keeping it free from kinks. While they were washing the deck, back of the cabin, I could catch a word now and then from their conversation. "Sticks to it pretty well,—do outside,—blow—plenty to do,"—so I knew they were talking about me and evidently the mate was wondering what they were going to do when outside in a blow. I shut my mouth and grinding my teeth said, half-aloud: "I'll fool you all. I won't be sick. I can't afford to be sick," and pumped till I had raised several blisters on my hands. I thought they never would finish with the hose; but everything has an end and at last came the welcome order, "That'll do th' pump, boy."

What a relief to my poor, soft hands. I stood away from the pump and, taking off my hat, wiped my face and head with my handkerchief and looked at my hands, which were beginning to smart, for the skin was off in several places. The mate was evidently watching me for he said: "Take this swab and go over all the white paint work. Draw yourself a bucket of water an' begin with th' stanchions an' taffrail. When that's done, go over th' mouldin's on th' cabin. It'll soften yer hands. That'll keep ye busy till four bells" (six o'clock). So saying, he took Bill forward where they were busy the rest of the afternoon.

I was glad to be left alone and glad to get a change of work. Although awkward with the bucket and swab, yet I made pretty good headway towards the last and when four bells struck I had only one side of the cabin to do. The mate looked over my work and found no fault with it, but he said, "I guess you'd better stay with it till ye finish, for we won't have eny time in th' mornin'," and leaving me alone he disappeared in the cabin.

It took me about half an hour to finish the cabin and after wringing out the swab and rinsing out the bucket, I took them forward under the forecastle-head. When I came out, the cook, who was watching me, asked: "Are ye through? If so, carry the supper into th' fo'c'sle."

He gave us a nice supper of steak and onions, vegetables and hot biscuits and a pot of tea. My afternoon's work certainly gave me a good appetite and I ate a heavy meal. Bill said nothing to me as usual and finishing his supper he lighted his pipe and threw himself into his bunk.

"When you're through, boy," he said, "take the dishes into the galley and come back and clean up the fo'c'sle."

The forecastle certainly needed it for it was very dirty and after taking away the dishes I looked around for the broom and dust pan. Not seeing any in the forecastle I asked, "Where do you keep the broom and dust pan?"

"Where do you suppose we keep 'em?" he answered.

I had never been told just where they were kept so I looked in all the corners and even in the bunks.

"What in hell are you looking for?" said Bill, with a sneer.

"Why-y, I can't find the broom."

"You don't suppose you're going to find it in my bunk, do you? Go get the deck-broom under the fo'c'sle deck!" he ordered, in a disgusted tone of voice.

I went, as directed, and found the broom, but failed to discover anything that looked like a dust pan, and so came back and gave the forecastle a thorough sweeping, removing the rubber boots, shoes and slippers from the floor and putting them in the spare bunk over mine and sweeping the old newspapers, sticks, etc., in a heap ready to carry out.

"Have you seen the dust pan?" I asked Bill. "I don't see it under the forecastle deck."

"You little dumb-head! It's a wonder you don't ask for a carpet-sweeper. Go get a shovel!"

I obeyed like a whipped cur and after getting the shovel swept it full of papers, etc., and started for the companion-way where I hit the casing of the door with the corner of the shovel and spilled most of my load on the steps and the deck below.

"Where do you think you are? In a barn? Why didn't you bring a pitchfork from the farm along with you? You'd be more handy with it," said Bill.

"Well, that was clumsy in me, wasn't it? I'll sweep it up though," said I.

"Clumsy! Why that's your name," said Bill, with a laugh. "Hello, Clumsy! That's a good name for you. I guess I'll call you by that name."

I tried to take it as a joke and laughed with him over it; but it was not a hearty laugh, for he gave me a look as much as to say, "It's no laughing matter for you, boy." I finished the sweeping in silence and as the forecastle seemed a little close, I went on deck for some fresh air, but principally to get away from Bill. Here I walked the deck as I had seen others do and wondered if they all walked because of an uneasy mind. Finally, I got interested in the running rigging. Captain Winslow said I could ask Bill for anything I wanted to know about the schooner. "Will I ask him? I should say NOT!" I began to pull first on one and then another rope to see where it led to so that I might become familiar with the working of the vessel. The twilight had begun to settle down when Bill put his head out of the forecastle and called, "Here, Clumsy, come and light the fo'-c'sle lamp."

I said to myself: "I wonder if that's my work? I guess it is all right for I'm the boy"; and answered him: "All right! Have you got a match? I haven't."

He handed me a match as I passed him, taking good care not to give me any more room than the law allowed. In fact he didn't budge as I squeezed by.

"The next time, don't ask me," he said. "You'll find matches in the matchbox behind the stove. When it's empty, go to the cook and fill it and see that you keep plenty of matches in it."

This was rubbing it in a little too strong. If he had been five or ten years older, I suppose I should have thought nothing of it, but such talk from him and he only a few months my senior and a sailor living and eating in the forecastle with me, I must confess it went against the grain and the blood rushed through my veins to a fever heat when I saw that he was using me as a lackey. I tried to forget it, realizing that I was only the boy and in order to get along with him I must take a certain amount of his abuse.

Striking the match and taking off the chimney, which looked as though it had never been cleaned, I found the lamp empty. Instead of asking where the oil was kept, I took out the lamp and carried it to the cook.

"What's th' matter? Lamp dry?" asked the cook. "Gee! You'll have t' git another lamp t' see this by. Here, take a dipper o' water from th' kettle and pour it in yer hand-basin. Put plenty o' soap in th' water an' rench it aout well," after which he filled the lamp from his oil can.

Thanking the cook I explained that this was my first voyage and hoped that I wouldn't have to bother him so much after I had "learned the ropes."

While I was lighting the lamp for Bill, the mate came forward and looking into the forecastle said, "When ye git through with that lamp, come on deck an' we'll put up th' ridin'-light." Going on deck he showed me where the side-lights were kept and bringing out the riding-light explained that it would be my duty to keep the lights filled and trimmed.

"Now, I'll show ye haow to make the lamp fast in th' riggin'," and taking the lanyard in his hand and making it fast to the shroud he asked if I knew the name of the knot he used.

"Yes, sir!" said I. "That's a rollin' hitch, sir."

"Haow didja know it was a rollin' hitch? Thought ye said ye had never been t' sea."

"So I did, sir! But my brothers are all sailors and they taught me most of the knots and splices at home."

"Can ye splice a rope?"

"Yes, sir."

"I want t' know! Can ye make th' ridin'-light fast in th' riggin'?"

"I think I can, sir," and taking the lamp by the lanyard, I went up the rigging about fifteen feet, letting the lamp hang down far enough so that the heat from the flame of the wick couldn't set fire to the hemp rigging. All of which had been taught me at home. As I came down the ratlines to the sheer pole, he said, "That's all right," and walked aft.

The cook was sitting on the door-sill of the galley, with his feet on deck, smoking a corn-cob pipe in an effort to cool off in the evening breeze. As I jumped down on deck to go below, he spoke to me.

"This 'ere air feels awful good t' me after bein' in that hot galley. Say! Ain't yer father th' preacher at Thames Street Church?"

"Yes," I said.

"I was introduced to yer brother Wiley up at th' maarket some little time ago. He's been t' sea ha'n't he? Understand he went a-whalin' wunst. Is that so?" said he.

"Yes, he was on the brigantine *Lizzie J. Bigelow* of Provincetown. A regular hell ship, he said. Do you know my brother Will? He's just in from the West Indies and was on the bark *Neptune* of Boston."*

"No-o, I never met him. Haow many brothers hev ye got?" And so we talked. It was nearly nine o'clock before he went below and in leaving me said: "I guess I'll turn in for I've got t' git up at one bell (4.30) in th' mornin' t' git youse fellers yer coffee. Ye know we've got t' heave up anchor first thing."

I began to feel a little more comfortable than I had and was glad that the cook had shown a disposition to be friendly, for it had been drilled into me that I must keep on the good side of the cook unless I wanted to go hungry. Soon after being left alone I decided to follow his example and went below and was about half undressed when the mate called from above:

"We've got t' keep anchor watch to-night, boys. Who's got th' first watch?"

"I have," said Bill.

"Why in hell don't ye keep it then?"

"I've just come down to get some tobacco."

"Look hea', Bill! When ye lie, lie so ye won't git caught. Whatcha think I've been a-doin' of all this time? Asleep, an' snorin'? No! by Gawd! When ye come on deck, I wantcha t' stay on deck, an' ef I ketch ye goin' b'low ag'in I'll make ye stand anchor watch in th' proper way. You're worse than an

* The bark *Neptune*, 493 tons, was built at Portsmouth, N. H., in 1870. She was sold to Portuguese owners, at Lisbon, in January, 1897. In 1874 my brother was in the bark *Hazard* of Salem. She carried a main skysail and was a fast vessel having been in the slave trade at one time. Will told me the ring-bolts, in the between-decks, to which the slaves were shackled, were still in her. She was lost on Old Man's Shoal, off Nantucket, February 14, 1881, and carried seven of the crew down with her.

old sailor! The easier I make it fer ye th' more ye want t' rub it in. I don't have t' split th' anchor watch if we *are* short-handed."

Bill went up on deck and the mate gave me instructions regarding my duties in which he said it was very important, above all things, to keep awake while on duty and look out for river pirates who might come alongside during the night, in a rowboat, and steal all the running rigging on the pinrail. If it came up foggy, I must ring the ship's bell every half-minute or so, and also strike the bells every half-hour, to give the time through the night; and if I had any trouble I must call him, explaining that I could always find him in his "room," which was the first bunk on the port side as I went into the cabin. After assuring me I would have no trouble with the vessel on account of the fine weather he left as abruptly as he came.

To those unfamiliar with the working of sailing vessels, a few words of description will not be amiss here.

The anchor watch is kept on larger vessels, by one man, through the night, and is usually from 8 P.M. to 6 A.M. On the *Floyd* there were only two men before the mast and it was the custom to divide the watch between them. One man was on deck from 8 P.M. till 12 (midnight), when he called the other and the second man kept the watch till 6 A.M.

During the day the mate took care of the vessel, but if there was any work to be done both men were on deck.

When at sea, the watch is divided into the starboard and port watches. The captain takes the starboard and the mate the port, each taking a man, except the cook, who stands no watch, but has all night in. In addition to his duties as cook he is called upon to man the windlass or to help shorten sail, if his services are actually needed. As Bill was in the starboard watch I was taken in the mate's, or port watch. These watches were of four hours duration, beginning at 8 P.M. and changing at 12 (midnight), 4 A.M., 8 A.M., 12 (noon) and 4 P.M.

From 4 P.M. to 6 P.M. and from 6 P.M. to 8 P.M., are two short watches called dogwatches. This is necessary in order

BARK "HAZARD" OF SALEM, 337 TONS, BUILT IN 1848. LOST ON OLD MAN'S SHOAL, OFF NANTUCKET, FEBRUARY 14, 1881, FAMOUS FOR HER FAST VOYAGES. From a painting in the Peabody Museum, Salem.

NANTUCKET STEAMER "ISLAND HOME," OFF COTTAGE CITY. From a photograph made about 1890.

to change the watches into seven out of the twenty-four hours, instead of six. Otherwise, if the mate took the port watch, from 8 P.M. to 12 (midnight), he would have those same hours every night; but by instituting the dogwatch it shifts the watch every night. Not much of any work is done in the dogwatches, as a rule, but in the morning watch, from 4 A.M. to 8 A.M., the men are turned to at 6 A.M., beginning the day's work by washing down the decks, which generally takes till seven bells (7.30) when the watch below is called for breakfast, and at eight bells (8 A.M.) they come on deck and the morning watch goes to breakfast and sleeps till noon.

The hour at sea is not spoken of as half-past eight, or nine o'clock, but instead, the time is denoted every half-hour by tapping the ship's bell, which is a stationary bell hung on a frame or harp. From the clapper hangs a neat lanyard of square or round sinnet, worked in white cotton cord and about six inches long, by which the man striking the hour grasps and pulls the clapper against the side of the bell with a sharp jerk. One tap for the first half-hour, two taps for the second and so on until eight bells have been struck. This ends the watch and with the beginning of the new watch the first half-hour is marked by one bell again, thus:

8.30 P.M. strike one bell: Ding.
9.00 P.M. strike two bells: Ding-ding.
9.30 P.M. strike three bells: Ding-ding, ding.
10.00 P.M. strike four bells: Ding-ding, ding-ding.
10.30 P.M. strike five bells: Ding-ding, ding-ding, ding.
11.00 P.M. strike six bells: Ding-ding, ding-ding, ding-ding.
11.30 P.M. strike seven bells: Ding-ding, ding-ding, ding-ding, ding.
12.00 P.M. strike eight bells: Ding-ding, ding-ding, ding-ding, ding-ding.

Sailing vessels usually have two stationary bells. The smaller one is just abaft the wheel and fastened to the wheel box, while forward, fastened to the beam at the break of the forecastle-head, amidships, is a larger one.

The ship's clock also strikes the bells and it is placed where the man at the wheel can see and hear it. It usually hangs in the companionway leading into the cabin. The helmsman watching the time, upon hearing the clock strike, repeats the number of bells by striking them on the small bell behind him. Then, any member of the crew who is near the large bell, forward, immediately taps the same number on the larger bell. In big ships, where a lot of discipline is displayed, these bells are answered by the lookout who sings out, according to the number of bells struck: "Three bells, and all is well. Lights burning bright, sir!"

Jack, in the forecastle, never asks, "What time is it?" but, "How many bells have gone?" If, on turning in at midnight, he is awakened and hears the big bell strike one, he knows at once that it is only 12.30 A.M.

During my first night aboard I think I heard every bell, because it was a strange sound and my quarters were not like my own spring-bed at home. I hardly got asleep before Bill called me. It was fifteen minutes ahead of time and I was on deck before he struck eight bells.

Nothing occurred to break the monotony of the night watch and it is needless to say I kept awake. Had there been a sparrow alight on the jib-boom-end I think I would have known it, so impressed was I with the importance of my duties as a sailor keeping anchor watch.

I heard the cook's alarm clock at one bell (4.30 A.M.) and he was soon stirring around building a fire. At two bells he called us for coffee.

It is a custom aboard sailing vessels to serve a pot of coffee before the men go to work. Some vessels serve it a half-hour before turning to. On coasters, the coffee is served with sugar, but on deep-water vessels, black strap, or molasses, is boiled in the coffee and it is surprising how one learns to like it and if the cook is not as generous some mornings as others, old Jack is there with a kick just the same. No bread or meat is served with the morning coffee, but there is always plenty of sea-biscuit, *i.e.*, pilot-bread, in the bread barge, which is a square box about 12 x 18 inches long, in a handy place in the forecastle.

At three bells (5.30 A.M.), the mate came forward, saying, "All hands heave up anchor." The *Floyd* didn't have a patent windlass. It was the old-style, wooden barrel, under the forecastle-head, which was worked above by shipping the windlass-brakes into the brake-beams and heaving up and down by hand.

There were two windlass-brakes or bars. Each bar was fitted with a wooden handle, not unlike the handles on a hand-car on the railroad, and they worked the same way, only the windlass didn't turn as fast.

Bill and the cook took one side and the mate and I worked the other, the mate keeping watch of the chain as we hove in the slack. When the chain was up and down or right over the anchor, ready to break it out from the bottom, he sang out to the captain, who was walking the poop, "Chain short, sir!"

"All right! Get th' mains'l on her, Mr. Cardiff."

"Aye, aye, sir! That'll do th' windlass, boys," said the mate, and taking us aft, the captain having already taken the gaskets from the sail, we proceeded to hoist it. The mate, having a deep voice, started to sing out, "You-hay-yah, O-ho-you," etc., as we hoisted now the throat and then the peak halliards, until we raised the sail as far as we could. I entered into the spirit of it with all my energy, pulling upon the halliards with all my strength. By the time we went to the jig-halliards, the blisters on my hands from the pumping of the day before had broken and when I took a turn under the bull-cleat and over the pin, and grasped the halliards, holding on with my feet braced, as the mate and Bill swayed off, the skin rolled back in the palms of my hands. It was all I could do to hold the turn, the pain was so great, and when the sail was finally set there were one or two patches of skin off from the inside of my hands, showing signs of bleeding; but I stuck to it and was glad when the mate finally said, "Belay!"

"H'ist the fo's'l, Mr. Cardiff," said the captain, and we went through the same proceedings with more misery for me. The wind was blowing lightly from the northwest and after setting the foresail the captain said,

"Break out th' jibs, Mr. Cardiff."

"Break out th' jibs, sir," repeated the mate, and turning to me said: "Boy, git aout on th' jib-boom an' take th' gaskets

off'n th' jib an' jib-tops'l. Do ye know what the gasket is?"
I saw Bill laugh and wink at the mate as I turned and answered, "Yes, sir."

"Very well! Let's see haow quick ye c'n do it."

It was smooth water and I had climbed all over schooners,
out to the jib-boom-end and to the truck of the masts, so I
knew how to get out.

Bill's sneering laugh made the blood run again to my face
as I jumped over the bow and worked myself out on the
foot-ropes. I must confess that I didn't break any records
while taking the gaskets off or making them up, but I did
the job and was back on the t'gallant fo'c'sle deck by the
time the jibs were up. Then we went back to the windlass
and soon broke out the anchor, when the mate called to the
captain, "Anchor's aweigh, sir!" while we kept on heaving
away until the stock of the anchor was out of water and up
to the hawse-pipe before he gave the order, "Avast heaving."

We scarcely drifted in the light breeze and the mate
pulled the jib to starboard, which swung the bow to port,
and we finally gathered headway, with the captain at the
wheel, and slowly made our way to the southward of Goat
Island. Hooking the pendant of the fish-tackle into the ring
of the anchor and taking the fall to the capstan, we had it
cat-headed as·we were off the Beacon. I watched every move
Bill made in going down the chain to hook the pendant into
the ring of the anchor, for the chain was foul of the stock,
and by the time the anchor was fished and the flukes over the
rail, where we secured it with the shank painter, I knew I
could do the work as well as Bill.

As we rounded the bell buoy off Fort Adams, the captain's
voice rang out again, "Set th' tops'ls, Mr. Cardiff."

"Set th' tops'ls, sir," repeated the mate. "Boy, jump aloft
an' shake out th' fore tops'ls. Do ye think ye c'n do it?"

"I think I can, sir," I replied, and jumped into the fore-
rigging, while Bill was sent up the main. He was on the
cross-trees before I reached the futtock-shrouds. I had seen
gaff-topsails set on the yachts in the harbor and while I had

never been aloft to loose one, yet I had been thoroughly
drilled in the work and knew that the foot of the sail must
go to leeward of the peak halliards and that the tack must
trim down on the weather side of the jaws of the gaff. I rehearsed this in my mind as I went aloft and was thankful for
a light wind and smooth water on my first trip aloft; besides,
the topsails had been furled on the port side and as we were
on the starboard tack all I had to do was to unhook the sheet
from the throat-halliard block and fasten it to the clew of
the gaff-topsail. Some schooners do not unhook the sheet
while lowering the gaff of the foresail or mainsail, but Captain Winslow took advantage of anything that would save a
rope-yarn and didn't propose to have his gaff-topsail sheets
worn out by sawing them through the sheave in the gaff-end.

I watched Bill, at the main, to see whether he took the
gasket off before picking up the sheet and was relieved to
see him go down to the jaws of the gaff and so I followed
suit. Instead of finding sister-hooks in the end of the sheet,
as I had been instructed, I found the end was fitted with a
bight which was tucked through a ring and slipped over a
double "wall and crown." It puzzled me at first, but by following the rope out to the end of the gaff, with my eye, and
pulling on it, I found it to be the rope I was after.

Getting back to the cross-trees I was again puzzled to find
the clew of the sail, for it had been covered up. Looking
across to the main, they were hoisting the topsail already,
and I had started up the rigging first. Then I began to sweat
blood, as it were. I was afraid to take off the gasket for fear
the sail would blow out and get away from me. "What will
I do?" I said to myself. Finally it dawned on me that there
was only a light breeze blowing and I could easily pick up
the sail if it did blow out, and making fast the sheet to the
shrouds I took several turns off the sail being careful not to
take the gasket entirely off. Then I went back to the sail
again and followed the leech down to the clew to make sure
everything was clear. This took a lot of time, for, believe
me, I took no chances of falling and hung on like a leech.
Just as I slipped the bight through the clew and over the

knot, the mate called out: "Well, what's th' matter with ye up there? Goin' t' sleep? How much more time d' ye want?"

I looked again at the main and saw that the sail had already been set and Bill was making his way down the rigging and was nearly to the sheer pole and I had not yet taken the gasket entirely off the sail. I moved with caution, sweating great beads of perspiration, and when I took off the last turn, the sail rolled out and the breeze filled it out in front of me like a big balloon. "What if the sheet is foul?" I asked myself, getting away from the sail and grasping the topmast shrouds.

"Are ye ready up there?" called the mate, and with fear and trembling I answered, "All ready, sir. Hoist away."

Fold after fold shook out as the mast-hoops slipped up the mast. The halliard running through the block above was music to my soul as I saw the sail being stretched and when at last they began to sheet home I saw for the first time that everything was clear. Oh, joy! What a sense of relief! And as it was my first attempt it was indeed gratifying.

I felt the schooner heel over under the new stretch of canvas and surveying the topsail just set, I thought it the finest-setting sail I had ever looked at. The wind was getting stronger as we sailed down past the Dumplings and holding firmly to the topmast shrouds, I gazed about, looking at the main topsail and then down at the wake of the vessel just beginning to show white as the schooner gathered headway, with Captain Winslow at the wheel. Looking over the land, I saw Fort Adams as I had never seen it before. Then looking ahead, I saw the deep blue sea in the distance, dotted here and there with sails shining brightly in the morning sun. Castle Hill was off the lee bow and right ahead was a big four-master, bound in, scarcely a half-mile distant, with everything set and drawing finely with her beam wind and standing as straight as a major, for she was loaded down to the scuppers. Looking below, the jibs were spreading out like the tips of huge sea gull's wings fluttering over the water, bearing us on to the approaching schooner. The little streak of white foam, showing at her bow, was like the pearly white teeth of a maiden's mouth. It was good to look at and certainly a beautiful sight. Beyond was the blue sea and soon I would be with the other schooners, riding the long swell of the ocean, and I wondered how it would affect me on a large schooner like the *Floyd*.

When fourteen years old I had made a trip as passenger on the old side-wheeler *Island Home*, from New Bedford to Nantucket, where many were seasick, but I hadn't been affected by the roll of the steamer. I had caught tautog in my sailboat, off Brenton's Reef where the ground swell was pretty high, and had caught blue-fish while sailing in a stiff breeze between Castle Hill and Hull's Cove, also in the ocean swell; but this little "outside" experience was as nothing to what I was about to enter and so I wondered what effect the rolling of the schooner would have on me while rounding Point Judith. The wind was off-shore so I knew there would not be much of a swell, but if I should be sick there would be no living with Bill.

All this flashed across my mind in a second and gritting my teeth I said, half aloud: "No sir! I won't give in to it! I'll show you all that I am worth more than eight dollars per month," and taking a last look at the surroundings, I sat on the cross-trees and swung my feet to the ratlines below. By the time I reached deck, the four-master was off our lee bow and I read the name *P. F. Butman* on her bow. She was a new ship, so the mate said, and one of the fastest on the coast. She certainly looked like a huge yacht, with her bright spars and sails and it seemed a shame to load such a fine vessel, down to her scuppers, with a big deck-load of dirty coal. In those days, American vessels were not marked with Lloyd's, Bureau Veritas or American Bureau of Shipping Plimsoll marks and the skippers in the coal trade often loaded their vessels to the sheer streaks.

I have seen many a schooner come in with her decks awash while making fast to the coal bunkers, and the *Butman* was one of them. She looked like a rail in the water sailing by and all hands, including the cook, stopped work aboard the *Floyd*, as she passed us within a stone's throw, to comment on her sailing qualities; but Captain Winslow broke up the conversation by giving the mate orders to set the staysail. This sail was set from the deck. The wind was blowing a little stronger and the *Floyd* heeled over nicely under full sail for the open sea.

"We'll straighten up th' decks afore breakfast; an' boy, when you've et, ye c'n turn in till eight bells," said the mate. Then showing me how to hitch a coil of rope to a belaying-pin, he went aft and took the wheel, relieving the captain who went below to eat his breakfast. Bill finished coiling up the rope he had started, leaving me to finish the rest, and went to the galley for breakfast. I coiled up all the ropes on the main-deck and started to coil up the peak halliards of the mainsail when the mate called to me, asking where Bill was.

"I think he is getting his breakfast, sir," I answered.

"You go for'ard an' tell him I want him."

"Aye, aye, sir!" I replied, and going to the forecastle I called to him, "Say, Bill! the mate wants to see you."

"What th' hell does he want now? Can't he let a fellow eat his breakfast when it's hot?"

"He asked me where you were and I told him you were eating breakfast."

"What th' hell did you tell him that for? You might have known he would want me." We both walked aft; he went to the mate and I proceeded to coil up the halliards.

"Did you want me, sir?" asked Bill.

"Yes, I wantcha! Didn't I tell ye t' straighten up th' decks first?"

"I didn't hear you, sir," said Bill.

"Wa'al ye hear me naow. Git over there an' coil up th' throat halliards an' don't go t' breakfast till I tell ye. I want these decks cleared afore ye git aout o' sight. Naow, I've been a-watchin' of ye fer some time an' I notice ef there's a chance fer ye t' git aout of eny work ye'll dew it, ye lazy lout, but I'm goin' t' stop it right here, by Gawd!"

It was my time now to laugh, but I turned my back so Bill couldn't see my face. I had felt all along that he was taking advantage of me and my spirits arose as I threw lay after lay into the coil on deck before me, and sore as my hands were I threw out the kinks of the rope with new life which seemed to lessen the pain, for I gloated in the call-down given Bill by the mate.

After the ropes were coiled up he told us we could get our breakfast and I was glad to give my hands a rest. Going forward I bathed my hands and face in cool water and went below where Bill sat in a sulky mood.

I was pretty thirsty from the morning's work and poured out a pot of coffee and putting it to my lips, said, "Gee! this coffee is none too warm, is it?"

"Serves you right, damn it!" said Bill.

"I didn't have anything to do with it," said I.

"If you hadn't told the mate I was eating my breakfast, I would have been on deck long ago."

"What's that to do with the coffee? I couldn't have been here before and if you had waited until the ropes were coiled up we would both have had our coffee hot," I answered, getting more confidence in myself.

"Now look here, Clumsy! Don't talk back to me; if you do you'll get your mother's monkey into trouble. So close your trap, for I haven't time to argue with you; I've got to take the wheel. See that you sweep up before you turn in," and going on deck he left me alone. I felt my blood boil as he left and my hands shook so I could scarcely hold my knife and fork while eating my breakfast, but I had plenty of time to cool off and I was glad he left as he did, because, had the conversation continued much longer, one of us might have had occasion to regret it.

Finishing my breakfast I swept the crumbs from the floor and took the dishes into the galley. "What's th' matter with Bill?" asked the cook. "Did th' mate give him a jawin'? He wants t' look out or th' mate'll put a tin ear on him, an' ef he don't behave himself 'round here, I'll dew it myself."

"Oh, he wasn't feeling any too good, I guess," I replied. "He seemed to think I was to blame for getting him on deck again, but I didn't have anything to do with it, did I?"

"Oh-h, tell him t' go to hell. I wouldn't pay any 'tention

to him. He ain't worth a pinch o' snuff," said the cook, and looking at his clock he continued, "Ye'd better turn in an' git some sleep, young feller, ye might need it afore mornin'. When ye're aout t' sea ye never knows what minute ye'll be called, consequently, git all th' sleep ye c'n when ye have a chance."

"Yes, I guess you're right. I think I'll take your advice," and leaving him I went below and turned in. I was pretty tired from the morning's work and by the time I got into the bunk I could feel the long ocean swell, which soon rocked me to sleep. It seemed only a short time before Bill called me, at eight bells, for dinner, and jumping from my bunk I found I could scarcely stand for the schooner was rolling in the trough of the sea.

Going on deck I found we were becalmed and the schooner was rolling back and forth in the swell with no headway. Off the starboard quarter the land looked familiar and I called to the cook, below, asking him if it weren't Point Judith.

"Yes," said the cook, "we haven't made much headway this mornin'. Wind went daown off th' P'int. I thought ye'd be thro'in' up by this time. Feel like eatin' agin? Yer dinner's ready ef ye c'n eat it."

I assured him that I still had my appetite and ate bountifully of the mutton stew and curry and rice.

At one bell I was called to relieve the wheel by Bill, who seemed to have lost his grouchiness since the mate gave him a calling down. Never having steered a vessel with a wheel I went aft with fear and trembling. The mate stood outside of the cabin door and I walked up to him and told him that I had never steered a vessel, but if he would stand by and give me a few pointers I thought I could manage it.

"Ye won't have eny steerin' t' dew. Just hold th' wheel till th' breeze comes, then it'll be time enough."

Captain Winslow was standing at the wheel as I went aft. "Hello! ain't ye sick yet? Ye seem t' stand it pretty well," said he.

"So far I'm all right, sir," I replied.

"Keep her west, ef she'll steer."

"Keep her west, sir," I answered and the captain walked to the weather rail. "By th' way, ye don't know haow t' steer, d' ye?"

"I have never steered with the wheel, sir."

"Can ye box th' compass?"

"Yes, sir."

"I want t' know! Let's hear ye."

"Nothe, nothe by east; no-nothe-east, nothe-east by nothe; nothe-east; nothe-east by east; east-nothe-east; east by nothe; east," and so I kept on to the last quarter, ending: "Nor-nor-west; nor by west, nothe."

"Where didja learn it?" he asked, and I told him about studying navigation at home. I was surprised that he talked as much to me as he did and was more surprised when he pointed to the "lubber's-mark" on the compass box and explained how to bring it in front of the point on the compass.

"Here comes a little breeze. She'll have steerage way, bum by, an' I c'n show ye." With the coming of the breeze the sails filled again and the schooner gathered headway slowly while the captain stood by and put her on the course.

"Naow, d' ye see, ef th' mark swings t' lu'ard of th' p'int, pull her back again and ef she comes to, too fast, why, just shove her over a couple o' spokes, an' ef she don't move at that, give her a couple more, an' as soon as she begins t' swing, put yer wheel back where ye had it at fust or she'll keep ye a churnin' yer whole trick at th' wheel."

He watched me for a while and being apparently satisfied that I would not get him into any great trouble, went below to his dinner. With the light breeze, I had time to experiment with the wheel and before long I had mastered the art of keeping the schooner on her course. The mate came aft several times and asked me if I was having any trouble, always taking a good look in the binnacle as he walked past the wheel to leeward; but I assured him that I could keep her straight as long as the wind didn't blow any harder. Instead of blowing harder it finally died out altogether and left us rolling in the ocean swell. The hot sun beating down upon the water was reflected back in our faces and I soon felt the effect on my neck and arms. The big fore-and-aft sails swung back and forth and the sheets were hauled flat down; the staysail was lowered to the deck and the gaff-topsails triced up. The sails flapped with the swinging of the gaffs, from side to side, while the jaws at the mast creaked that monotonous tone, peculiar to its own, with every roll of the schooner, and there I stood at the wheel fighting my best to overcome the nausea I felt coming on. Was my stomach weak or strong? I smiled a sickly smile when I thought of the poor seasick lady on the steamer, who, after vomiting, was asked by the purser if her stomach was weak, when she aroused herself sufficiently to look at the other passengers hanging over the rail and replied, "No-o, I seem to be throwing as far as any of them."

I didn't dwell long on the scene and giving the wheel a spin to port kept it going, hard up and hard down. Anything, to keep my mind from the present situation. Finally I heard someone whistling, as if calling for a dog, and looking forward I saw the mate raise his face from the work of coiling up ropes and looking towards the land, he kept whistling softly. He was whistling for a breeze.

I had often heard that old sailors wouldn't allow any whistling on board ship, for they were a superstitious set and claimed that any whistling would certainly bring on a gale, followed by bad luck; but whistling for a breeze on Long Island Sound, I concluded must be different. I had supposed that this ancient custom was obsolete, but the longer I went to sea the more I saw how superstitious the sailors were, as a class.

The unlucky number 13; beginning a voyage on Friday; failure to break the bottle of champagne by the sponsor at a launching; animals or persons dying aboard ship; rats going ashore from the vessel, etc., were all forebodings of ill luck to the sailor. But the mate kept up his whistling until he came aft to relieve me at four bells.

On taking the wheel he looked at me and asked: "Haow

d' ye feel by this time? Feel sick eny? Ye seem t' stand it purty well in this swell."

I assured him that I was all right and asked if there was anything forward that I could do.

"Nope, jest keep handy 'bout th' decks, that's all. Ef ye were in a big ship ye would be kept busy all day, but we don't aim t' dew nothin' more'n we hev t' aboard this craft."

I walked forward, feeling all puffed up at my ability to keep on the upper side of seasickness, so far, but I was "spitting cotton" just the same. I had been told that a person confined in a warm room where he could see garments swinging back and forth on the walls would get seasick quicker than anywhere else; but if one could look out of a window, away from these swinging objects, he would be less susceptible. The best medicine was to get on deck, in the center of the ship and fill your lungs with plenty of fresh air and briskly walk the deck. So I determined to follow the latter advice at once by walking from the forecastle door to the mainmast and back. I had only made one trip when the cook appeared in the galley door, evidently anxious to see what condition I was in.

"Haow are ye feelin', Fred? Sick yet?"

"Not yet," I answered, "but don't know how soon I will be though."

"Oh, ye're all right. A boy that c'n eat mutton stew like ye did, won't be sick."

I left him and walked to starboard, to get a good look at the land and take another good drink of fresh air, for the thought of the mutton stew had a lifting power in my stomach, with a firm hold, and I had all I could do to shake it loose.

Upon reaching the rail I felt a little breeze in my face and opened wide my mouth, drawing in all the ozone I could swallow; but whether it was the breeze or the order from the mate, that followed, that prevented me from losing my dinner, I am unable to say—but enough, I didn't lose it. The mate, feeling the same breeze, sang out: "Slack away th' jib sheets, boy! Let 'em all go for'ard."

I was mighty glad he gave the order for it gave me something else to think of; anything to relieve me from the sight of those tall masts swinging from one side to the other.

"Aye, aye, sir!" I answered and ran forward as directed, giving the headsails plenty of slack. The breeze came from off the quarter, but it was hardly strong enough to fill the sails. The mate had swung the mainboom to leeward, but it swung back and forth as the schooner rolled.

"Come aft, boy, an' hook th' boom-tackle on th' mains'l."

"Aye, aye, sir!" Coming aft I saw the boom away out to leeward, but before I got the tackle-block in my hands, the sail had swung clear back to windward.

"Watch her when she rolls an' hook it in th' strap when she comes back, boy."

I tried to do as directed, when the boom came over again, but only made a sorry attempt, nearly falling overboard as I reached for the strap.

"Here, give it t' me! Mind th' wheel," and taking the block from my hands he succeeded in hooking it as the boom swung back again. I watched every move he made; saw him take in the slack of the tackle; and also how he made the boom fast to leeward. Coming back to the wheel he said: "Yer hav'n't got yer sea-legs on yet. Feel sick, eny?"

"Not very much," I answered, whereupon he gave a short laugh.

"Wa'al, don't give in t' it. D'ye see what whistlin' fer a breeze does? I never knew it t' fail ef ye keep it up long enough. Naow, d'ye s'pose ye c'n ease off th' sheet an' hook th' boom-tackle on th' fo's'l?"

"I think I can, sir."

"Go ahead an' try 't." I saw he was still smiling when I went forward and I said to myself: "I'll fool you, old man. I'll hook the block in the strap before I ease off the sheet." Taking the block from the rail I found that I didn't have slack enough to reach the boom by ten feet, and wondered why tackles were not cut long enough to reach across the vessel; so there was nothing left for me to do except to slack away the fore sheet.

Slacking away, the sail began to flap with the roll. The boom lifted and I was nearly pulled through the sheet-block and the sheet slipped through my sore hands taking off what little skin remained from the morning's work. So quickly did the sheet slip through my hands that they fairly burned. It was only for a second, but in that short time I had something to show for it. My hands were simply raw. This little incident seemed to knock all the seasickness out of me, for after I had made the sheet fast around the cleat my hands needed more attention than my stomach. But I took up the block and hooked it in the strap, sore as they were, and finally succeeded in pulling everything taut as I had seen the mate do with the mainsail. Before I got back to the sheet, the mate called out,

"Give her a little more sheet, boy."

"Aye, aye, sir!" I don't think I ever had anything smart quite so much as when I again picked up the fore sheet to slack away. My hands were all covered with blood and everything I touched showed the stains of blood.

"That'll dew th' fore sheet, boy," said the mate. "Make fast."

"All fast, sir," I answered, and then I had to haul taut the boom-tackle as before. I had no sooner made all fast when another order rang out. "Sheet home the topsails."

Gee! This was more than I had bargained for as I knew I must put all my weight on the topsail sheet in order to stretch the clew to the gaff-end. I dreaded to touch another rope, but I was there to be a sailor, so wrapping my handkerchief around my right hand, I protected it somewhat; but before the sail was sheeted home my hands were so numb that I had scarcely any feeling in them. Going aft to the main, I was still pretty careful, but managed to set the sail. The mate saw the handkerchief wrapped around my hand and asked if I had hurt myself, but I answered him it was nothing and proceeded to coil up the ropes. The gentle breeze gave the schooner steerage way and she didn't roll quite so much, but the mate's mind was never at rest, for he wanted the staysail set.

"Go call th' cook, and ast him t' help ye set th' stays'l."

"Aye, aye, sir!" Oh, how I dreaded to pull another rope and I shuddered as I answered him. Calling the cook, as directed, he was soon on deck and noticing the blood-stained handkerchief asked, "What's th' matter with yer hand?"

I told him how the fore sheet had slipped through my hands taking the skin off because I was unable to hold it.

"Don't it hurt?" he asked.

"It might be worse," I answered, trying to smile.

The staysail had been lowered to the deck and was loosely rolled up on the main hatch. The cook took the halliards at the fore and I took the main. It is needless to say the cook got it mastheaded before I did and coming aft gave me a hand, for I could hardly pull a pound my hands smarted so.

After the sail was set he said: "Come t' th' galley an' I'll fix ye some brine. There's nothin' so good t' heal up yer hands as salt brine, right off o' beef, or pork."

He brought up a pan of brine that he had dipped from a barrel of beef and told me to "stick" my hands right in and let them soak.

Taking the handkerchief from my hand I plunged them in as directed and immediately pulled them out, dancing about the deck in pain. The saltpeter in the brine was more than I could stand and I begged the cook to pour some fresh water over them to relieve the pain.

"Don'tcha dew it! Don'tcha dew it! Stick 'em in ag'in. It's th' best thing in th' world for ye. Come on! Souse 'em in ag'in!" he implored.

The pain subsiding somewhat and urged by the cook, I set my teeth firmly together and plunged in again only to jump about the deck as before. Then he took my soiled handkerchief and after saturating it in the brine with another cloth he wrapped up both hands. "There! naow ye'll find yer hands'll soon git well. This is th' best thing that ever was fer sore hands."

He was probably all right in what he said, but the remedy was worse than the disease. I kept the bandages on, however, for the rest of the watch, but it was all I could do to stand it.

There was nothing of interest that happened during the afternoon and evening except that we held the breeze, which grew stronger in the afternoon. I took the wheel in the second dogwatch. The sea was comparatively smooth and the schooner, heeling over, clipped it off at a lively rate. It was no trouble to keep on the course for she steered like a yacht, yet I had to "mind my eye" on several occasions when she swung to.

Although my hands were very sore I thoroughly enjoyed the trick at the wheel and was proud to think old King Seasickness didn't catch me in his net. On first taking the wheel I was bothered by giving too much wheel. When the bow sunk in the swell, the lubber's-mark in the compass box would swing to windward and I would throw over the wheel too far. Then the stern settling would throw it the other way and I found myself pulling her back too much, with the result, just as the captain said, that I was churning away all the time and instead of the schooner's running about wild, she was simply balanced on a big wave, amidships, which finally left her giving way to another.

The trick at the wheel is noted for day-dreaming, for the man at the wheel is forbidden to talk and unconsciously one's mind is continually picking up things that have happened during a lifetime. The sun, setting in the west, was a beautiful sight and I wondered how the tropical sunset could possibly be any grander. From the sunset, I pictured myself in the tropics and sailing in the trade winds. Then again, to the back yard, with sextant in hand, "shooting" the sun and studying navigation at home, and so the hours flew by until I saw the side lights being put up in the fore rigging, red light to port and the green light to starboard. This brought to mind the

Rules of the Road at Sea

When both side lights you see ahead
  You port your helm and show your red.
For green to green, or red to red,
  Is perfect safety, go ahead.

And when upon your port is seen
   A stranger's starboard light of green,
There's not so much for you to do.
   For green to port, keeps clear of you.

At All Times

When in safety and in doubt,
   Always keep a good lookout;
Strive to keep a level head,
   Mind your lights and heave your lead.
Two close-hauled ships upon the sea,
   To one safe rule must each agree;
The starboard tack must keep his luff,
   The port,—bear off.

We had passed Race Rock and were well into Long Island Sound at eight bells. Going below I immediately turned in and lost no time in getting to sleep. It seemed an awfully short time to eight bells (midnight) when Bill awakened me with a rough shake, saying, "Come, pile out of here; we're going to tack ship and the mate wants you on deck." I jumped into my clothes and hurried on deck, but didn't see anything exciting that required immediate attention. It was a beautiful moonlight night and we were sailing "By the wind," on the starboard tack, in a very light wind. Bill had raised the clews of the gaff-topsails, ready to come about, but the staysail was still drawing. A few minutes later the mate came on deck, rubbing his eyes and stretching. He opened his mouth with a yawn, looked aloft and to windward, and stretching again, said: "Wa'al-l, I guess we'd better lower th' stays'l. Lower away, for'ard!" Bill let go forward and I pulled the sail down with my poor sore hands. Then we came about and ran up the staysail again before Bill went below.

"That'll do fer ye, Bill," said the mate. "Fred, jump up aloft an' shift over th' fore-tops'l tack."

"Aye, aye, sir!" I answered. This is considered one of the worst jobs on a schooner, when it is blowing, unless it be to furl it. Both are bad enough. In shifting over the tack it is unhooked and must necessarily be thrown over the spring-stay and hooked into the clew-iron again. I was glad that I had had the opportunity of being on the cross-trees in the daytime for I knew just how the tack and sheet led and, although it was in the middle of the night, we had a bright moon, so I had no trouble except from my sore hands which prevented me from making any time; but the wind was light and I got through pretty well.

I took the wheel at four bells (2 A.M.) and soon afterwards the mate lowered the staysail and came aft, saying: "I think I'll try t' put her about. I'll take th' wheel an' ye c'n go for'ard. When I sing aout 'Hard-a-lee,' let go th' jib sheets an' make 'em fast t' lu'ard."

The schooner scarcely had headway enough to come about and I waited some time before the mate gave the order. At last he sang out, "Hard-a-lee!" I let go the sheets immediately and not waiting for her to swing, jumped to the other side and pulled the sheets to windward. When we came about at midnight there was more of a breeze and she came about so quickly that she filled away on the other tack at once, with breeze enough to carry the jibs past the stays, and Bill and I had to step lively to pull the sheets down. But now, the schooner scarcely having steerage way and knowing how quickly Bill and I had worked before, it didn't occur to me to watch the vessel come to, consequently, the schooner was at a standstill with not a sound to be heard. The monotony was broken by hearing the mate coming forward and when he saw the jibs to windward, he exclaimed: "I'll be good Gawd damned! Who ever heard of jibs bein' hauled t' wind'ard in a wind of this kind! What'n hell are ye doin' of eny way? No wonder she wouldn't come abaout. Naow shift those sheets over, damned quick, an' we'll fill away an' try it ag'in!" and with a disgusted air he went aft while I worked with my smarting hands harder than I did before in bringing the sails to windward. The next time I used my head and watched the schooner get a good full and when the mate sang out, "Hard-a-lee," I let go the sheets and waited till she was well on the other tack before hauling them to leeward, for there wasn't wind enough to carry the sails over the stays without help.

As she slowly gathered headway on the new tack, I was sent aloft to shift the tacks over again, which in my mind was entirely uncalled for; but having pulled off a "bone-head" with the jibs I took it gracefully. On regaining the deck eight bells were struck, which relieved the watch and my aching hands.

At seven bells (7.30 A.M.) I was called for breakfast and going on deck saw that we were being towed by the towboat *E. H. Coffin.* The cook told me that we would soon be up to "Hell Gate," the worst stretch of water on the whole eastern coast.

"Hell Gate" is a narrow place in East River, between Long Island and Manhattan. It is the passage between Ward's and Randall's islands, that is properly called "Hell Gate." The tide from the Sound, into East River and back from Sandy Hook into East River, through to the Sound, was so great in early days that this stretch of water, from the ebbing and flood-tides, caused a millrace of seething whirlpools and eddies which not one out of fifty vessels could sail through, so it is said, without being thrown upon the rocks and damaged more or less.

These obstructing rocks and ledges were eventually removed by blasting, the last of them disappearing in 1885.

I took the wheel at eight bells, just before going through "Hell Gate." Captain Winslow was on deck and stood by me as we entered the passage. With every swing of the bow, as the tide rip surged against our side, he was there to issue an order to port or starboard the helm. In fact, he stood on the other side of the wheel, practically steering the vessel through.

It was a beautiful Sunday morning and after passing the penitentiary we began meeting excursion boats from New York, loaded to the guards with passengers. From four bells (10 A.M.), I was a free agent and spent my time at the rail watching the shipping as we passed through East River and while going down the harbor past Governor's Island, for we were still in tow on account of there being little or no wind. Excursion boats of all descriptions were coming and going and I answered many a waving handkerchief with a swing of my cap as they passed.

CHAPTER III

THE CLOSE CALL IN THE NIGHT

WE CAME to an anchor in Sandy Hook, about noon, on account of no wind, leaving the foresail and mainsail standing but furling the jibs. Hauling down the jib we parted the downhaul, on account of it being so rotten, and I was sent out on the bowsprit to haul the sail down.

After furling the jibs we had our dinner of soup, roast beef, vegetables and plum duff. I had heard so much about plum duff that I was curious to taste it. Instead of boiling it in a bag, this was steamed in an oval-shaped tin mould. It was a mixture of cake and pudding, seasoned highly with spice. Instead of being white as I expected, it was the color of spice cake, almost as dark as gingerbread. It was served with hard sauce and I liked it very much.

It was a hot, sultry day and the sun beating down on the deck made the heat almost unbearable. The only cool place I could find was under the foresail where I laid down and was soon fast asleep. I must have slept an hour or more when I was awakened by Bill throwing water over the deck in an effort to cool it. Seeing me awake, he said, "I think it will be cooler below, now that I have thrown some water around." Not long after I went below, and laid down in my bunk. I hadn't been there long before I fancied I could hear a drop of water on my pillow but on putting my hand over the spot couldn't locate anything wet. neither could I see anything as it was quite dark under the upper bunk. Spat— and I would feel again.

"Bill," I said, "There seems to be a leak overhead. I can hear water dropping somewhere around my pillow. Does the deck leak over this bunk?"

"No-o, not that I know of," said he.

Then I felt it drop on my hair above my ear, but putting my hand up I could feel no moisture. Then it came on the rim of my ear as if a drop of water was running down. Instinctively I put my hand to my ear with the same result. Finally I felt it on the back of my hand and putting it up to the light I saw the fattest bed-bug that it had ever been my fortune to discover. If this had happened off Point Judith, when I was feeling so seasick, I certainly would have needed a strong stomach right there. Lighting the forecastle lamp I began a search in my bunk. Under the pillow and along the seams of the mattress the bugs fairly lay in windrows. The bunk-boards and ends and the ceiling between the galley and the forecastle, in the cracks, were simply alive with them, big and little. My pea-jacket, hanging against the bulkhead, had a row of the prettiest beads under the lapel of the coat that one ever saw and instead of all being of uniform size there was an assortment of all sizes, even down to eggs, and I had only been aboard the schooner two days!

"What's the matter, Fred? Have you lost anything," said Bill.

"No! I've found all that I was looking for and more too."

Bill laughed as I answered him. "Yes, they are pretty thick in that bunk. I gave it up for this one and God knows this bunk is no paradise."

"What are we going to do?" I asked. "Has nothing been done to exterminate them?"

"Oh, yes! The cook gave me a lot of insect powder and a squirt-gun to blow into the cracks. I used it once but the bugs ate it all up and came out of their holes licking their chops and looking for more, so I gave up in disgust. You ought to see the arena the cook has on his table. He has made a frame which slips over the edges of his cake-board and placing this on the table, he goes behind the range and catches a cockroach; then, taking a straw from the broom, he runs it up and down in the cracks of the bulkhead, back of your bunk, chasing out the bugs until he secures a lively one. Then placing the two in the center of the board, with their heads together, he sics 'em on. You'd naturally think that the cockroach would eat the bug up, but believe me! the bug is there with bells.

"The first time I saw the fight I nearly laughed my head

off. I was talking to the cook one Sunday afternoon when I saw him with a straw in his hands poking the bugs about the board. 'What have you got there?' I asked. 'Come down and see,' said he. 'How much will you bet on the bed-bug that he can lick the cockroach?' 'Oh, I'll bet the cockroach can lick the bed-bug,' said I. 'All right! It'll cost you twenty-five cents to come in,' said the cook. I put up the money and the cook said, 'Ready! Go!' keeping their noses pointed together with the straw. The roach finally got mad and jumped on the bug and stuck his beak in, but the bug rolled over on his back and caught a leg of the roach and working himself up under his breast, tried to get a half-Nelson on him. The roach would draw up first one leg and then another in an effort to pry the bug loose and sometimes all his legs would be working at the same time. It was sure a comical sight. His legs seemed too long and there was no way in which he could bring two feet in a position at the same time so as to shake off the bug which held to it like a bulldog holding a shaggy cur by the throat. Finally, getting a vulnerable spot on the roach, he fairly sucked the life out of him and I lost my quarter. If it wasn't so late we'd ask the cook to give us an entertainment this afternoon."

"No doubt it would be amusing," said I, "but instead we'd better get a can of insect powder and get busy."

On going to the galley and asking the cook for the insect powder he only laughed and said, "Good Gawd, boy! ye can't do nothin' with that. The only thing to kill 'em is a smudge. We tried it in Philadelfa last month but it didn't do no good. Guess it wasn't strong enough." Notwithstanding what he said I put in the rest of the afternoon sprinkling the forecastle in every place I thought needed it, but the smell was so strong that I had to take my bedding on deck for the night.

There was nothing of interest to relate while we lay at anchor in Sandy Hook. Not a breath of wind for two days and we scarcely did any work at all. Monday morning the mate took me out on the jib-boom and showed me how to reeve off the new jib downhaul, which was my first attempt at sailorizing; but aside from that we did nothing but the customary washing down decks.

On Wednesday morning, bright and early, we finally got a westerly breeze and heaving up the anchor sailed down the coast with all sail set. That afternoon Captain Winslow put out a blue-fish line, while I was at the wheel, and was fortunate enough to catch a fine, large blue-fish which made a meal for all hands. While we had plenty of meat yet the change was more than acceptable for supper.

Towards evening the wind backed around to the southward and eastward and began to blow. A large black cloud sprang up from the southeast, bringing rain and a big ocean swell.

"Take in yer jib-tops'l an' kites, Mr. Cardiff. Glass is 'way daown an' we may have a nasty night," said the captain.

"Take in the jib-tops'l, sir!" answered the mate.

We ran forward and hauled down the sail, as well as the flying-jib which we furled and then hauled down and clewed up the gaff-topsails. I was sent up to take in the fore, while Bill handled the main.

My hands were not as sore as they were the last time I went aloft, but the higher I got the more the schooner rolled. Bill was on the cross-trees before I was halfway up the rigging and I found that I was holding on tighter as I neared the cross-trees. Pulling myself up I clung to the topmast shrouds while the sail flapped about in front of me. The wind came in puffs, stronger and stronger with the rising sea, while the schooner heeled over to an angle of 45 degrees. I could feel the mast bend under the strain while I attempted to smother the wind from the flapping topsail. The roll to windward and the pitching of the schooner forward, threw the sail full of wind; but rising on top of the next wave, the sail was whipped around forward of the mast and around my head as I clung to the topmast shrouds. The next roll then carried the sail back, scraping across my face and pulling my cap from off my head. It circled high above the sail only to be caught by the wind which swept it far away to leeward where it finally dropped into the white-capped waves. I worked at a disadvantage because I hardly had my sea-legs on; besides, I took no chances in letting go my hold on the topmast rigging. By pulling and hauling blindly on the sail I nearly succeeded in spilling the wind from it when a big sea carried me high in the air and the schooner diving forward, a gust of wind caught the sail and tore it from my grasp, at the same time turning my finger-nails back. I let go my hold and the whole sail blew out to leeward again. I used to wonder why it was that sailors were so gifted in swearing; but when this sail got away from me —I acted just like a sailor.

Looking across to see how Bill was getting along with the main, I was surprised to see him finished and nearly on deck; then away to leeward we swung and I held on all the tighter. The deck of the schooner seemed a mile to windward and dipping in her nose she threw the spray high over her bow as she plowed through the water. Everything about the vessel was one streak of white foam. It was my first gale at sea and I was aloft to take in a sail that was getting the best of me.

With the wind came the rain, making the sail still more difficult to handle and the rigging harder to hold on to. Every roll to windward was followed by a pitch forward and a flap of the sail. The creaking of the jaws of the fore-gaff, below me, as it swung around the mast and the quiver of the mast, vibrating as the wind whistled through the rigging, was a new experience. Realizing that I was in a precarious position and must get the sail in, I made another attempt. Grasping it again and tugging away I felt the topmast bend and sway from side to side until I was sure it would carry away. There was a strange vibration to the sail that shook my arms as I struggled to take it in, which I couldn't account for. Another dip to leeward and I saw the cause. The captain, at the wheel, was keeping the schooner into the wind and so shivering the leech of the foresail, which flapped back and forth with a crack when too near the wind, shaking the foremast from truck to the keel. This relieved my mind and leaving the cross-trees I climbed up the ratlines of the topmast shrouds where I could use my weight against the sail as well as my feet and legs. Then taking a turn around the sail with the gasket, I gradually smothered the wind from it and although I didn't give it much of a "harbor-furl," made it fast to the masthead where it outrode the gale.

I don't know how long I was aloft, but when I reached the deck the mainsail was being lowered and I hurried aft to lend a hand. With the help of the cook we soon took it in. Then we reefed the jib and close-reefed the foresail. I watched the mate very carefully while he passed the weather earing and when all was fast all hands pulled away on the reef-points, to leeward, to stretch the band along the boom as much as possible while the earing was passed through the cringle in the leech of the sail and around the boom-end. Then taking a position beside the mate I knotted the reef-points, with the rest, under his watchful eye. Everything being knotted satisfactorily, we hoisted the reefed foresail and hove to for the night, putting the schooner on the starboard tack, which, while drifting, would take her offshore. It was nearly two bells (9 o'clock) in the evening before I was told to go below and, being wet to the skin from the rain and spray that continually dashed over the rail, I lost no time in getting to the forecastle and taking off my wet clothes. It was all I could do to stand there and I really didn't know how much the schooner was rolling until I got below. The dim light from the forecastle lamp cast a phantom shadow across the deck as the coats swung away from the bulkhead, and standing in the middle of the forecastle I could almost touch either side as the schooner rolled back and forth.

Pulling off my wet clothes I rehearsed in mind the incidents of the last two hours on deck and aloft with a satisfaction that gave me all the confidence of a sailor and I felt quite at home and able to combat with anything that might come up in the future. Tumbling into my bunk I found it impossible to lie in a comfortable position, but by bracing my back against the bulkhead and drawing up my knees against the front of the bunk and holding on with both hands, I soon wedged myself in and in this position slept till eight bells, when I was called.

It was still blowing and raining and as it was my lookout I dressed in oilskins and rubber boots. We were still hove to on the starboard tack and riding a heavy head-sea which caused us to roll unmercifully. I hadn't been on deck more than an hour when I raised a light right ahead.

"Light ho!" I called; but it was blowing so hard I had to go aft to the mainmast before I could make myself heard.

"Where away?" answered the mate.

"About two points off the weather bow; a red and green light, sir."

"See if yer side-lights are burning," said he, and I hastened forward as directed and found everything burning all right. Presently the captain appeared at my side, evidently called by the mate.

"Are yer side-lights all right?" he asked.

"Yes, sir," I replied.

"Then why'n hell don't he keep off? In my room under the wash-bowl ye'll find a flash-light. Run quick an' git it," he ordered.

I found the lamp and was soon at his side. This flash-light or flash, as it is nautically termed, was about the size of a quart measure and made of tin. A wire extended from the cover into the bottom of the lamp, to which a bunch of waste was fastened which was submerged in either alcohol or turpentine. The waste was pulled out of the lamp by a straight wooden handle fastened to the center of the cover on the outside and at right-angles with the cover. Lighting the waste and holding it above one's head, the cover acted as a basin to catch the dripping alcohol, insuring safety to the man against fire while waving the torch.

We lighted the torch under the forecastle-head and the captain ran forward waving it frantically above his head, but the steamer, which it proved to be, kept right on her course heading directly for us. Brighter and brighter grew the lights to windward as she approached. We could even smell the smoke from her smoke-stacks.

"That's a Baltimore steamah. They nevvah altah their course fer nobody an' they don't give a damn ef they sink us," exclaimed the captain. The steamer was now getting dangerously close and he sang out:

"Hard daown yer hellum, Mr. Cardiff! My Gawd, boy! Run an' call th' boys below,—all hands! He's right on top of us an' he'll cut us in two before they're awake. Run quick as Gawd almighty'll let yer!"

The blood ran cold in my veins as I listened to the captain giving these orders in one breath and running to the forecastle I shoved both slides back at once and shouted: "All hands on deck, ahoy! Tumble out quick! A steamer is running us down!" Then I ran back to the captain's side, as the oncoming steamer loomed up out of the darkness with her red and green lights away above us and scarcely two seas away. Down, she buried her bow, parting the sea and plunging through, seeming to shake her head like a mad bull charging directly for us.

"Ring th' ship's bell, loud as ye c'n," the captain shouted, still waving the torch in hope of attracting the steamer's attention.

I kept ringing the bell as loudly as possible, while Bill and the cook appeared in their underclothes. Everything was in confusion and I was too inexperienced and frightened to remember the many orders given by the captain at this particular time. Neither do I remember just how we were able to keep clear of the steamer's side. But I remember seeing her green light shining down upon us and disappearing along our side and hearing the captain say: "Thank Gawd! we're aout of that mess. It's th' closest call I evah had in all my life." Wiping his face with his bandana handkerchief and heaving a deep sigh of relief that everything was well, our troubles started in afresh. The big black side of the steamer to windward had taken the wind from our sails and we were blanketed. I saw our jib-boom pointed dangerously close to the steamer's stern and coming out from under her lee, the gale caught us on the other tack with all our sheets to windward. We were in a precarious position, for the wind blowing directly across our beam, the schooner was thrown over to starboard with lee rail going under water.

"Let go the jib-sheet! Come aft and help me with the fo's'l," shouted the captain, jumping off the forecastle and holding to the weather rail as he made his way aft.

I jumped for the jib-sheet and threw the coil off the pin, intending to slack away handsomely but didn't count on the strength of the wind and before I knew it there was a slat of the old reefed-jib and the sheet got entirely beyond my control—off the pin and everything to leeward. A couple of flaps and the whip unrove. Rip-bang-slat, flapped the jib and in an instant the sail was split from head to foot while the big club at the foot was being threshed about the topgallant forecastle-deck one minute and the next, against the foremast, as the schooner came into the wind.

Swinging into the wind our bow raised over a mighty wave and I felt the vessel go down by the head while high above me came a huge green sea. Before I could get to a place of safety the sea broke over the bow. I braced my feet to withstand the shock but the on-rushing sea swept me off my feet and carried me across the deck directly towards the foremast. Putting out my hands to avoid being knocked senseless, the force of the water was so great that I was pinned against the mast as if I had been nailed there. Instinctively I caught the first rope I came in contact with which proved to be the tack of the gaff-topsail. The water surging around the mast swept me under the fore-boom where I was entangled among the ropes but still retained my hold on the tack. Then I felt the schooner shiver and tremble as she shook herself free. It was a mighty sea that swept her fore and aft.

Dragging myself from under the ropes, somewhat bruised, I stood by the foremast. The noise was deafening; the jib flapping in the wind was whipping the club across the deck against the stock of the anchor and over the bitts, resembling the old-fashioned flail, while beating the deck of the topgallant forecastle; and the shrieking of the wind through the rigging played a good accompaniment. Realizing that if I stayed there much longer there was great danger of being knocked out by the club, or sheet-block, should they carry away, I ran to the weather fore-rigging as a safer place. No sooner did I get a firm grasp on the rigging, than I heard the voice of the mate calling me. He was coming forward with Bill and the cook.

"Here I am, sir," I shouted, making my way along the rail towards him.

"Good Gawd, boy! Why in hell don't ye answer when yer called? We all thought ye were overboard with that sea. I've been a-callin' of ye fer ten minutes."

"I didn't hear"—

"Haul daown th' jib!" broke in the mate who for the first time saw the condition of the sail. "Git up thar', damn lively, or we won't have no jib!" whereupon he ran to leeward to let go the halliards while Bill and I ran forward to haul it down. The end of the downhaul was made fast at the knight-heads, directly under the jib, and to reach it we must pass the club that was sweeping the whole topgallant forecastle-deck.

Bill, seeing the situation, wouldn't go on the forecastle-head, but I had been watching the jib for some time and waiting my chance for a wave to knock the bow over to leeward I ran up the weather cat-tail and on to the knight-heads and started to pull the sail down. The mate, in the meantime, had secured the club of the jib by throwing a running-bow-line around it, hauling it taut to the pinrail to leeward.

Bill then came up, but pull as hard as we could we were unable to get the sail down for the jib had blown itself into a fringe at the head and around the halliard-block, hanks and stay above, so tightly that they refused to slip.

The mate coming to our assistance, we put every ounce of strength on the new downhaul (which luckily we had rove off in Sandy Hook), without fear of parting it, and the fouled hanks gradually gave way to our purchase, slipping down the wire stay sufficiently to enable us to get a gasket around the old jib, which we furled after a fashion. Had the stay been of hemp, rigged like most of the schooners at that time, I doubt if we could have hauled the jib down at all and it would have been a total loss.

We were now riding under reefed foresail alone and shipping very little water. Bill was allowed to go below and I put on a change of dry clothing and kept the lookout till eight bells (4 A.M.) as the mate said it needed an experienced man at the wheel during the night; but he would give me the wheel in the morning watch from 8 A.M. to 10 A.M.

After breakfast I took the wheel. The wind was moderating and hauling back to the southwest. At two bells (9 A.M.) we set the flying-jib with orders to keep her "full and by" (as near the wind as she would hold without the sails flapping).

The *Floyd* had a travelling wheel, *i.e.*, the wheel and barrel were fastened in a frame on top of a massive square wooden tiller, which was shipped into the rudder-head on the *forward* side. A single block, with the sheave parallel to the deck, was hooked into an eye-bolt on the side and at the end of this tiller. The tye of the tiller-rope was spliced into the ring of the single block and led across the deck to a single block in the rail, just above the waterways; reeving from aft, forward, through this block and back to the single block in the tiller, then aft, and under a sheave fastened in a cleat on the side of the tiller; then up and over the barrel three times, where it was made fast through a staple in the barrel.

There were two tackles of this kind; one to starboard, the other to port, so that, in throwing the wheel over, the tiller-ropes wound up on one side and unwound on the other, while the tiller travelled across the deck beside the man at the wheel, who gave way, or followed the tiller as the barrel turned.

Being a novice at the wheel I nearly walked my legs off, trying to keep the schooner straight; but the mate was there to see that I didn't get into trouble and by the time I had steered my trick I was master of the situation.

At four bells (10 A.M.) we shook the reef out of the foresail, set the mainsail and jib-topsail, holding our course with the wind abeam. The sea having gone down with the change of wind she showed her ability to sail by passing everything in sight and living up to her reputation although our jib was furled.

We rounded Cape May Wednesday evening and came to an anchor for the night. In the morning the wind backed around to the southward again; but we hove up anchor and with a moderate breeze sailed up the Delaware. In the afternoon it began to rain and at 6 P.M. we dropped our starboard anchor off the mouth of the Schuylkill River and furled all the sails. The glass was very low which, the captain said, "was a sure sign for th' line-gale" (the Equinox).

That evening it was my anchor watch from 8 P.M. to 12 (midnight). The wind was blowing strong from the southeast and while below we could feel the schooner swinging and surging on the chain cable. I dressed for a wet night and going on deck all was still except the constant flap of the throat-halliards against the mast and the whistling of the wind through the shrouds—a dismal sound. The canal-boats, from the river above, were being blown from their moorings and about four bells (10 P.M.), several drifted by although it didn't occur to me that they were actually adrift until I saw two in collision off our starboard bow. I could hear voices above the roar of the wind, which grew louder as they approached, and there was the sound of chafing timbers, the cursing of men and the cries of horses or mules, as if in pain, as they drifted by within one hundred feet of us. It was a wild night with the wind increasing all the time. I was alarmed at the drifting canal-boats and in the darkness of the night I took as a landmark, a light on the shore which soon proved conclusively that we were also drifting. Calling the mate he came forward and let out about thirty fathoms more of cable; but we still drifted and waiting for the schooner to swing to port, he let go the port anchor and bending a two-inch line to the kedge anchor, with the assistance of Bill, who had also been called, we dropped it over the bow, paying out all the chain we had. The two additional anchors were sufficient to hold the schooner from further drifting and we rode out the gale nicely while two other large schooners drifted by and went ashore astern of us.

Sailing vessels of to-day generally carry two anchors at the bow, of the same weight, because the windlass is operated by steam instead of hand power. In early days, the port, or left bower, as it was called, was the lighter anchor and was always operated under ordinary conditions. The starboard, or right bower, being heavier, was only used in severe weather, as was the case on the *Floyd*, at the mouth of the Schuylkill River.

Attached to each anchor is a chain cable, 120 fathoms (720 feet) long, made up of eight shots or lengths shackled together. Each shot is fifteen fathoms in length. In anchoring with fifteen or thirty fathoms of chain out, the shackle appears just inside of the hawsepipe, where it is handy to unshackle. In early days, before harbors were dredged, large ships were obliged to anchor outside and discharge cargo in lighters, which were towed in over the bar. If, in the process of discharging, a gale should arise, it was often necessary to slip (unshackle) the cable and sail away from the land until the gale was over. The cable being marked by a buoy, was picked up when the ship returned and reshackled to the chain. A good account of slipping the cable may be found in Dana's *Two Years Before the Mast*.

If lying with the port anchor out, it becomes necessary to drop the starboard, instead of dropping the anchor directly behind and in line with the anchor already out, where it is liable to foul the cables as the vessel is constantly swinging from port to starboard by the force of the wind, when the vessel swings as far to starboard as possible, the starboard anchor is dropped. Enough chain is then slacked away until the vessel drifts back and the chains are stretched out in the form of the letter V. If the vessel will not swing far enough to starboard, a little headsail is raised, a staysail or a jib— just enough to swing the bow away. The third anchor is usually the kedge anchor, which is a light anchor and is not attached to a chain. It is a spare anchor to which any heavy rope, according to the strain necessary, may be bent or tied and dropped to the bottom between the two bowers. In this position there is not much chance of the vessel drifting, when the strain on all three becomes equal.

The *Floyd* was anchored as well as could be and we were indeed fortunate that some of the drifting canal-boats or schooners didn't foul us as they drifted past. Had they done so we would have gone ashore with the rest. In the morning, as far as the eye could reach, the shore was piled up with wreckage of all sorts of craft. Rowboats, canal-boats, house-boats, steamers, launches and schooners. A tidal-wave couldn't have made the scene worse. The two schooners, directly astern, were surrounded with logs, roots of trees and stumps of all sizes. It looked more like a barnyard in the wilderness than a civilized seaport. If a tidal-wave can destroy any more property I certainly don't want to be shipmates with one.

On account of the wreckage we were unable to get a towboat for two days. Everything that had power was busily engaged, both up and down the river.

CHAPTER IV

HOMEWARD BOUND ON A COASTER

ON SATURDAY, October 6, 1875, we were towed up to Pier 11, at Port Richmond, where we took in a load of hard coal for Georgetown, Maryland, and on the eleventh, sailed down the Delaware, passing everything in sight. I enjoyed my trick at the wheel for there was no sea to bother me. One after another of the big fleet of colliers was overtaken and passed and if you have never sailed on a schooner under similar conditions you have missed one of the most exciting races. It is true, the International Yacht Races take the lead in this sport and the Cape Ann fishermen have their races; but if you think that the colliers, racing from port to port, are anything like an ice-wagon, you have only to engage passage on one for a trip and on reaching home you will sing the praise of the Atlantic colliers as you have never done before, unless it be that you were seasick the whole voyage.

No wonder Captain Winslow was proud of his schooner. He had a right to be for we took the lead through the Capes and passed Cape Charles on the twelfth, but on account of light winds didn't reach the mouth of the Potomac till Sunday, and Georgetown, till Thursday, the eighteenth, where we were docked at a wharf under the canal bridge and took on a load of soft coal for Newport, Rhode Island. We were then towed down to Alexandria where we anchored for the night.

As we tripped our anchor the following morning, the schooner *Abner Daley*, a sister ship to the *Floyd*, over which there was much discussion regarding the relative sailing qualities of the two schooners, passed us under full sail. We were waiting for a negro pilot who soon came off in a new lapstreak boat. It was his sole possession and cost him thirty-five dollars which, in those days, was a small fortune to a negro pilot. It probably took two years' earnings to purchase the boat. It was painted white, outside, with pale green thwarts and a lavender-colored bottom. As he came alongside he put over a couple of fenders as though it had been James Gordon Bennett's steam-launch.

"Good mawn'n', Cap'n," said the pilot. "I'se been watch'n' fo' yo' signal all de mawn'n', asho'e dar."

"You lazy, black rascal! I've had my flag flyin' since daylight. I've a good notion to sail without ye. Git under way at wunst, Mr. Cardiff," said the captain; then turning to the pilot he said, "What are ye goin' t' charge me to take me down the rivvah?"

"Five samoleons, Cap'n," answered the pilot. "It's ah berry long road to de Cape."

"Git aout! I nevvah paid mor'n a dolla' for any pilot and ef ye want the job fer that, git aboard," said the captain.

"Fo' de lub ob God, maan! Whatsha talkin' 'bout? Dar ain't nobody what'l take de job fo' dat. Now I doan want t' pesticate you, Cap'n, wi've a globerashun ob words, so I ask yo' calmly t' twistify dat statement, fo' yo' know it can't be did at so 'dickilus a price," rambled the pilot.

The captain took a look at the *Abner Daley* which was fast leaving a gap between us and as impatient as he was he held on to the pilot as we gathered headway. He, no doubt, knew his man for he still held to his price, one dollar or nothing.

"Now, see heah, Cap'n," said the pilot. "What's de use ob argufyin'? You know dat dis nigger got t' buy shoes fo' de ol' woman and six lil' pickaninnies an I sho' can't a-ford t' go away down dis ribbah fo' less dan two dolla's. Yo' see I'se gwine t' come down a little, but de good Lawd heah me, I can't go below two dolla's. No, sir-ee! Be reasonable, Cap'n! I pray yo' be reasonable! Yo' can't go widout dis nigger fo' yo' sho'e run aground ober dese flats."

I was sent to the wheel, when we filled away, and as she gathered headway and listed to port, the pilot's boat began to jump up and down from the wash of the waves and chafe against the side of the schooner. The pilot scrambled aboard to save his boat and running aft with the painter in his hands, made it fast at our stern where there was no danger of marring the sides, giving the boat about thirty feet of rope. As was the custom in those days we were loaded clear to the scuppers and thirty feet looked a good deal too much; but she was far enough astern to be out of the way. I saw the captain smile to himself as the pilot came aft and he was still smiling when the pilot made his boat fast and after this was done he turned to the captain and seeing the smile on his face, said:

"What fo' yo' grin like dat, Cap'n? Do yo' tink I'se gwine t' take dis hear schoonah down de ribbah fo' one dolla'? Ef yo' do I might as well go asho'e. Dis nigger wants t' passify yo', Cap'n, but I tole yo' all de time dat it can't be did. No sir! It can't be did!"

"All right," said the captain, "jump into yer boat and pull ashore."

At this remark the pilot grew alarmed and his face wore a puzzled look. He glanced at his boat, towing astern, and then at the captain. He seemed to be between the devil and the deep blue sea. But he got no comfort from the captain's face, as he slowly paced back and forth, and going aft he began to pull his boat up under the stern. In the meantime the captain let him alone. When she was under the stern the pilot took a turn with the painter and looked into his boat and then at the captain. He was still undecided what to do and all this time was rapidly being taken away from home. In a disgusted frame of mind he again made the boat fast and turning to the captain, said:

"Now, wh'ts de use ob getting mad, Cap'n? I hope I hasn't 'fended yo' conscious. I'd be de las' man fo' t' do so an' I wish yo'ld calm yo'self an' lissen t' me. I'se de bes' pilot on dis ribbah an' yo' schoonah am jes' as safe in my hands as yo's. Now, what yo' all try fo' t' beat down my price? I jes' can't a-ford t' jep-o-dize my credenshuls an' take away my good name, so I ask yo' calmly an' 'libertly fo' de las' time, will yo' gib me two dolla's?"

"No! ye black rascal," said the captain.

"Den I'se sho' in a deep quand'ry," said the pilot. "I'se gwine t' be away two days. I got t' eat an' sleep, an' how d' debble can I on one shribbled dolla'? No, sir! No, sir-ee, Cap'n, it can't be did!"

At this the pilot took a fresh chew of tobacco and rolling it back in his cheek, looked into his boat and then at the shore, in the distance, threw off the turn of the painter and held it in his hands.

The breeze was strengthening, as the morning advanced, and it was all he could do to hold her for we were sailing through the water at a lively clip. A dip into the wave drew the painter through his hands and he was obliged to take a turn around the cleat to hold the boat. Again he made her fast, taking a good deal of time; he was loath to give up and finally addressed the captain.

"Ah say, Cap'n! Ef yo' gib me mah dinna an' suppa aboa'd, I'se heah t' say dat I take yo' all down fo' $1.35 and considda all ob de 'gotiashuns closed."

The captain well knew he must have a pilot and he also knew he must feed him and the further away he got the more difficult the chance of getting another. The *Abner Daley* had dipped her colors in passing us and was in the lead, about a mile, which was entirely too much to suit Captain Winslow. His patience was about exhausted and, weighing the matter carefully, he said:

"Waal, pilot! I hate t' give you so much, but I've got t' ketch that schoonah ahead and ef ye can put the *Floyd* on the shortest course, I'll hire ye."

"Good Lawd, Cap'n! Dar's plenty ob water heah an' all yo' got t' do is sail. Gib her de canvas." So saying, the pilot gave his boat all the rope as before and took his position on top of the cabin.

The captain then turned to me and said: "Fred, there's a good many people that thinks the *Abner Daley* can outsail the *Floyd*. I know we can beat her an' et's your trick at the wheel. I want ye t' steer as ye nevvah steered afore. Keep her straight an' don't give her too much wheel. Damn him! I'll show him up afore we reach th' Chesapeake, ef I do have a weak topmast."

"All right, sir!" I answered. "I'll handle her all right in this water, I think."

Both schooners were loaded to the scuppers and were as much alike as two peas, with the exception that we didn't have our jib-topsail set, owing to our weak topmast, while the *Daley* had all canvas spread.

It was a beautiful sail down the river and to think we were racing in earnest! I was determined to show Captain Winslow that he could rely on me. He paced to-and-fro on the weather side of the quarter-deck, watching the weather and gauging the distance from time to time.

With the increasing wind the *Floyd* was picking up. I watched the schooner like a hawk and soon the captain came aft, rubbing his hands and smiling and said: "Fred, we're gainin'! We're gainin' an' ovahaulin' of him. Ef this wind keeps increasin' I've got him whar th' hair's short. It won't be long afore he's got t' take in his topsail an' then I've got him."

With each puff of wind the *Floyd* heeled over, parting the waves, and I held the wheel in a viselike grip as she strove to point her bow higher to windward. The captain, glancing at me, thundered out,

"Mind yer eye, boy, an' keep her straight."

This was a warning and I redoubled my efforts to steer a straight course. We were slightly to leeward, but the captain said, "As long as we are gainin', keep her as she is." The distance was being reduced each hour and the old saying, "A stern chase is a long one," was brought vividly to my mind as we sailed in this race; but we gradually crept up on him and at four bells (10 o'clock) the *Daley* was off our weather beam and I was relieved of the wheel, walking forward with a cocky air, pleased to think that I had steered the schooner in a race that would be the talk of the waterfront when we reached Newport. The captain had complimented me as I was relieved and the cook shook hands with me on going forward, slapping me on the back and asking "How she steered," etc.

"Your name will be in the 'Newport Mercury' when we git in. Just watch th' Cap'n. He's as tickled as a boy with a new sled. He won't do a thing but talk this race all th' time he's in Newport. We've got all th' breeze we c'n stand an' I don't see why the *Daley* don't take in his jib-tops'l. It's some glory t' pass a schoonah of her caliber, t' lu'ard; but I wish't th' Cap'n had gone t' wind'ard an' took th' wind out'n his sails. Believe me! Th' air would be blue on board th' *Daley*, an' I guess ef any should ast ye, it's blue thar naow." Our conversation was broken by a cry from the captain.

"Take in th' tops'ls, Mr. Cardiff. It's no use t' spring a mast. Thar ain't airy one of th' colliers, 'cept th' *Daley*, got 'em up an' I b'lieve we c'n beat him without 'em."

As we took them in the *Daley* followed suit and still we continued to gain in the race and by the time they were furled we were quite a distance ahead, the wind increasing all the while. It was not long before the captain gave orders to take in the foresail. By that time the *Floyd's* rail was clear to the water's edge and she flew through the waves, which were rising as the wind increased, leaving a pretty seething streak of white foam far astern.

The captain still kept on his course and wouldn't luff enough to spill the wind from the sail; consequently it bellied out like a large balloon. Pull as hard as we could, there was no such thing as smothering it. What little motion from the waves the schooner had, was enough to tear the sail loose from our grasp and it stood against the lee backstays like the side of a big white barn. Finally I ducked under the boom, climbed up the lee shrouds and grasping a couple of reef-points in my hands, jumped on the sail. My weight was enough and we came down to the deck nicely; but as the schooner rolled, the wind blew under the sail and I was lifted bodily up in the air again with it—seemingly twenty feet. There was a flap and a slat of the sail as I hung grimly to the reef-points. My hands were now in much better condition than when we were in New York or I certainly would have been flung into the Potomac. As it was, instead of going overboard, I hung on. I felt my feet going up with the flap of the sail and the next thing I knew I was descending rapidly. I must have been whipped over my head for I landed, feet first, in the companionway of the galley, still retaining my hold on the reef-points. Whether the captain put her into the wind or not, I am unable to say; but the wind was out of the sail and we soon had the stops around it.

When we pulled the boom amidships, the mate exclaimed, "My Gawd, boy! ye'll be a sailor yet."

Two compliments in one day, and the first I had received since coming aboard, gave me the satisfying feeling that I was at last making good. Eight bells soon rang and I went to dinner with a good appetite.

It was my wheel from 2 P.M to 4 P.M. and when I took hold of the spokes we were well down the Potomac and the waves were very high—enough to make the *Floyd* pitch a good deal. The pilot's boat still towed astern, with too much rope, yawing and surging back and forth over the waves, with each swing, shipping more or less water. I motioned to the pilot to come aft and look after his boat, which he did, immediately pulling in all of the extra rope and making her fast as short as possible. There was quite a lot of water in her causing her to roll from side to side quite heavily. He had no sooner taken his position on top of the house again than there was a report over the stern like the sound of a rifle. I turned just in time to see the boat fill and capsize, rolling bottom-side up. An extra large wave, raising our stern high in the air, had jerked the boat up with us, and being half-full of water had parted the painter and she was a derelict in the middle of the Potomac with a high sea running.

The pilot ran to the cabin door, calling, "Oh Cap'n! Cap'n! My boat done broke her paintah! Fo' de lub o' God, sah! please t' hurry up on de deck an put de schoonah about an' try fo' t' git ma los' boat, fo' it's all dat dis nigga hab got in dis wide, wide wo'ld."

The captain was not long in getting on deck and looking at the boat astern and then at the waves, turned to the pilot and said:

"Yer don't think for an instant that I'm goin' t' put th' schoonah abaout for yer boat, dew yer? Not I! Not I! We're bound for New York an I won't be delayed in this breeze for eny rowboat."

The pilot wrung his hands in misery and pleaded with tears that actually rolled down his cheeks.

"Oh, Cap'n! Doan yo' go fo' t' say dat. Yo' all take de berry bread out'n dis nigga's mouf. Please lowah de longboat an' try t' bring heah back t' me. Dat's all I'se got an' how is dis nigga gwine t' git back home ef he ain't got no boat. Tell me dat."

"Haow d'ya' think we c'n put a boat ovah in this sea," said the captain. "Besides, who undah God's heavens would volunteer to risk their lives even ef we got her ovaboard?"

The look on the pilot's face was more than I could stand. He was surely an object of pity, so I spoke up, "Captain, I'll go, for one."

The captain looked astern, at the *Daley*, and took a survey of surroundings in general, and then asked if I was willing to risk my life in an attempt to pick up the pilot's boat and on my assuring him that I would go, he went forward, reluctantly, keeping his eye on the *Daley* all the while. Evidently he decided to try it for he brought back Bill and the mate. After talking the matter over with the mate they decided to come about and sail to the capsized boat, heave to, and lower the longboat hanging from the stern davits, row to the wreck, roll her over, right side up, bail out the water and tow her back.

Taking the lashings from the longboat we put in the oars, a bailer and a spare rope for towing. At that time sailing vessels were not equipped with spare boats, fully provisioned, or provided with releasing tackles, as they are now. When our schooner ran into the wind, to windward of the pilot's boat, we (the mate, Bill and myself) climbed into our boat hanging at the davit falls. Ours were the old-time, dumb-sheave blocks, with a clumsy hook, one of which was hooked into a ring at the stem and the other in the stern and in lowering a boat into the water with the waves as high as they were running at that time, both blocks must necessarily be simultaneously unhooked or there was great danger of being thrown into the sea when the waves receded, should one block, only, be unhooked, then the other end of the boat would hang in the air. The mate took his seat in the stern, Bill was amidships and I sat in the bow.

The captain and cook were stationed on the port quarter, holding the fall of the stern davit tackle, while the pilot took the starboard side holding the fall to our bow. I was given positive instructions to unhook the block just as soon as we should strike the water and Bill was told to stand by with an oar to keep us from being caught under the stern of the schooner. The tackles must be watched, when unhooked, that they didn't catch under the thwarts or gunwale. We must watch ourselves and be quick with our oars, etc. These instructions were repeated time and again by the captain as he held us suspended from the davits. When all was ready, the captain, watching the waves for the right time to lower, sang out, "Lower away, all!" We began to descend and swing with the roll of the schooner. A mighty wave, coming up from under the schooner's stern, was our resting place. We were not lowered so very far when my block became slack and giving it a good shake and a pull on the tackle it was released nicely from the ring. There was no trouble with the mate at the stern and I thought we were clear of the schooner, but the next rising wave swept us under the stern, scraping the transom, and we were nearly swamped. When the wave receded I managed to put out my oar and swing the bow off a little and we were soon clear of the schooner.

The mate, in the stern-sheets, used an oar as a steering-oar over the stern and soon had us pointed for the capsized boat some hundred yards away to leeward. On came the waves, raising our bow almost perpendicular, when it seemed that the waves would surely break over the stern and fill the boat; but we would clear them and the next moment the bow would settle while the stern would keep on rising until one would think it would come end-over-end and throw us all into the sea.

Bill was not much of an oarsman for we were no sooner clear from the schooner than he "caught a crab," *i.e.*, he couldn't keep his oar free from the water, and the mate sang out: "Here! Here! Don't try any of that stuff ag'in or ye'll be makin' a swim fer the pilot's boat. Watch yerself!"

It was no easy matter to pull an oar under those conditions. I had been in a dory off Cottage City, Martha's Vineyard, when it was all I could do to keep my seat in the ocean swell; but there was no wind blowing against the current such as we were now battling with and this was an experience I shall never forget. We were getting along, quite well, when a sudden choppy wave arose, as we were pulling, lifting Bill's oar and oarlock free from the gunwale. It came so quickly that he lost his balance as he braced himself for a pull and he fell backwards, over the thwart, into the bottom of the boat. His feet were higher than his head and he floundered about before he recovered himself, losing hold of the oar, which was twisted from his grasp. The mate pulled in his oar and tried to catch the floating oar as I pulled at the bow. The wave balanced the boat just right for a spin around with the result that we headed for the trough of the sea. The oar eluded his grasp and he nearly fell overboard while the wind carried us farther away. Before Bill had regained his seat we were in the trough and had shipped a tubful of water over the rail, which nearly swamped us. Here, the mate gave utterance to his feelings in very impressive language, of which Bill was the recipient. Grabbing him by his coat collar, in no gentle manner, he pulled him from the seat and flung him into the stern-sheets of the boat as if he had been a bundle of canvas or merely a wet dog and told him to sit there until he was wanted.

Taking Bill's place with the steering oar, it was some time

before we could turn the boat and a much longer time before we succeeded in picking up the oar. After regaining it,
the mate and Bill exchanged seats again and once more we
headed for the derelict. The wind in our favor helped amaz-
ingly, but at times we could do nothing save hold on to the
thwarts or slip off. Upon reaching the capsized boat we encountered more difficulties for it was impossible to get near
enough to work to advantage. We couldn't get alongside for
there was nothing to hold to except the keel, which was bottom up, and there was too much beam to hold on with our
hands, consequently we must work at the stern of the boat,
pitching up and down. After a good half-hour of hard work
we succeeded in rolling the boat right side up, but the next
wave completely rolled her over again and holding on in an
effort to keep her right side up we were nearly swamped and
were obliged to abandon our work.

The mate, not in the best of humor, for we were now wet
through to the skin, from the splash of the waves, finally
said:

"To hell with th' boat! There's no such thing as right'n'
her in this sea an' ef we keep on we'll all be overboard next.
Let's see ef we c'n tow her."

Whereupon we bent the spare line to the painter of the
pilot's boat, making it fast in the stern of our boat, and put
out our oars. The *Floyd* was quite a distance to windward.
It was a hard pull and no sooner did we pick up the slack of
the towrope than Bill threw up, in a fit of seasickness, and
vomited all over the boat. He was a sight and absolutely of
no account. Again the mate threw him into the stern-sheets,
in a heap, and the poor fellow simply lay where he was
thrown, rolling from side to side as we continued to bob
around with the waves. The mate took Bill's oar and with
clinched teeth, heaped curses on Bill, the pilot and everybody. Bending his back, as his oar dipped, this mighty Sam-
son of a man expected me to keep up with him. He didn't
have long to pull before the wind caught the bow, in his
favor, and pull as hard as I could there was no such thing

as pointing up again and I was at his mercy and like Bill, my work was all in vain, and it was as much as we could do to keep clear of the capsized boat, let alone trying to tow it. He then turned on me with his adjectives, exclaiming in part:

"Now what in hell is the matter with you? Can't ye keep her straight? or are ye like Bill, too sick t' row? Why didja tell th' cap'n ye wanted t' lower th' boat an' go with another man? Another man! M-A-N! (spelling the word). Do ye git it? A fine specimen of a man you are an' ye drug me into et with ye. Why in hell I came with ye is more'n I know; an' all fer a nigger pilot! Ef et was a white man's boat I wouldn't keer, but t' lower a boat fer a nigger, in a sea like this, takes th' cake, with a couple of sick pills that calls themselves men. This is th' worst voyage I ever was on and ef Gawd almighty'll spare me till I git home, one thing's certain, I'll quit the sea fer good!"

And so he ranted, cursing his luck, abusing first Bill and then me. I pulled away at my oar in silence until my arms were so tired that I could scarcely lift it free from the water. On the crest of each wave he would glance over his shoulder, in the direction of the *Floyd*, to see if we were making any progress with our tow. It was plain to be seen that we were not and it finally dawned on the mate that we were pulling in vain. At last he stopped rowing.

"Et's no use, boy," he said. "We haven't gained a foot an' ye may as well take et easy till th' cap'n sees we ain't doin' nothin'. Why in hell he hasn't seen that we haven't been makin' any headway with th' tow, is more'n I know, an' he might of known we couldn't tow her."

After this speech I could have gotten down on my knees to him, for it was impossible for me to last much longer and my hands were in a cramp from holding the oar so tightly, consequently I was relieved both mentally and physically.

It was probably a quarter of an hour before the captain became aware that we were simply riding the waves, but at last he gave the *Floyd* a weather helm and off before it she came, going to leeward of us in a big circle before he jibed, and with sheets eased off headed for us evidently intending to pick us up as he sailed by.

The cook stood just abaft of the fore-rigging, on the starboard side, brandishing a heaving-line over his head most frantically to show his intention of throwing it as they sailed by. The heaving-line was not the regulation size but was a spare rope or jigger-tackle fall and entirely too heavy to throw very far, consequently, when the schooner came up as close as she could, the distance was too great and it was a sorry throw for he missed us by twenty feet. The schooner went into the wind, but she had so much headway that the captain again wore ship to make a second trial, which was much better, but the *Floyd* had more headway than he reckoned and when the cook threw the rope it went over my shoulders and I only managed to catch the end with hardly enough rope to make fast. However, I succeeded in passing a turn under the forward thwart, as the line became taut, and I was forced to hold on for all I had in me, for the cook had already made the other end fast to the pinrail and there was no time to slack away as the schooner forged ahead. Both ends being fast, our boat took up the strain and, sailing at right angles to us, I expected the rope to part before the mate could turn our boat.

We were handicapped inasmuch as the pilot's boat was towing astern, and rising on top of a huge wave our bow went completely under, but I held the turn determined not to give any slack. We went through the crest of the wave, shipping much water, and going over the wave headed directly for the schooner's side like a meteor. The stern of the schooner rose above the water and I looked under her counter, which seemed like a death trap for us. If we should shoot under and the schooner came down upon us, our boat would certainly be stove to pieces. Meanwhile, the mate was exerting all his strength to pull the stern around and I held the bare end of the rope in my hands determined to hold on to the last. There was no time to wonder what one should do under such conditions. One thing was certain, we were going to hit the schooner, good and hard, and I braced myself for the shock.

The schooner's stern, which a moment before seemed so high, suddenly settled in the waves and rolled towards us. The bow, of course, was lifted in the air and jerking our bow partly around we struck the schooner a glancing blow that stove in our port gunwale at the bow. The crash was so great that I was thrown out of the boat against the schooner's side. I released my hold, as it was evident that the bow of our boat was completely smashed in. There was no time to think of the mate and Bill and as I hit the side of the schooner, my arm encircled a stanchion in the taffrail around the quarter and as the wave receded it left me high in the air as the schooner rolled away to port.

The captain and cook had evidently expected an accident for they were both standing by and before I actually knew what had happened they had pulled me over the rail.

I tried to explain that I couldn't account for dropping the rope and leaving the mate and Bill in a wrecked boat, but the captain remarked,

"Et was a good thing ye let go when ye did or there would be no boat."

The longboat, it seemed, was not damaged as much as I had thought, for she was riding the waves apparently all right. We could see poor Bill's white face as he tried to hold his head up and bail out the water while the mate, with an oar, was keeping clear of the pilot's boat. No doubt the mate was cursing me for deserting him in this hour of trial, but I was too far away to hear him. To say the least it was not an enviable position for anyone to be placed in.

In the meantime, the captain had again wore ship and we were circling around the disabled boats. This time he decided to come from their lee, alongside, or to windward, and drift back to them. He timed her to a nicety so that when we had lost headway we were alongside all right. Another rope was thrown them which was made fast to the bow in the longboat. The mate then called for another for the capsized boat, saying that he would bend it to the davit tackle and we could hoist the bow enough to spill the water, which we did and she was soon floating right side up again. The longboat was not damaged much below the water-line and while she showed a badly splintered bow Bill had no trouble in keeping her clear from water. We soon had the longboat hanging from the davits again and I, for one, was mighty glad that all were safe aboard the *Floyd* again.

The negro pilot was very jubilant and profuse in his thanks to us all for getting his boat back. Every action showed a marked degree of happiness and a broad smile, exposing a double row of white teeth, transformed his face. I watched this happy negro from the wheel, as he walked to-and-fro on the deck of the house, a great deal more, I am afraid, than I watched the compass. So happy was he that I could hear him singing and whistling to himself, now and again rubbing his hands and slapping his thighs, while at every turn his feet apparently got beyond his control, shuffling a jig-step or two, not unlike a child with Saint Vitus's dance.

Finally he broke out into a tune, marking time with his step and a swag of his shoulders, swaying his body and swinging his arms and hands, acting a pantomime, as it seemed, for my special benefit. Now and then I would catch a smile which always broadened into a grin culminating in a nervous laugh.

After the sun went down the wind gradually decreased and the waves, which an hour ago were so high, assumed a more usual motion. The pilot finally abandoned his walk on the house and coming aft, paced the deck in front of the wheel, still singing as he walked. He was certainly very amusing and as he sang he kept up his pantomimical actions in a song that made a lasting impression as the words were as comical as his gestures.

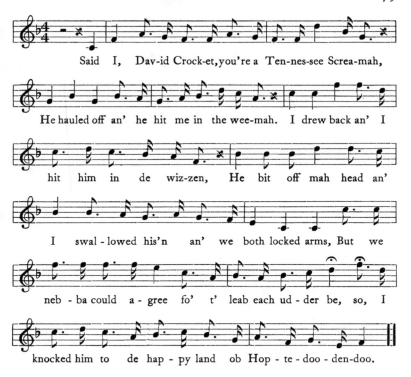

Said I, Dav-id Crock-et, you're a Ten-nes-see Screa-mah,

He hauled off an' he hit me in the wee-mah. I drew back an' I

hit him in de wiz-zen, He bit off mah head an'

I swal-lowed his'n an' we both locked arms, But we

neb-ba could a-gree fo' t' leab each ud-der be, so, I

knocked him to de hap-py land ob Hop-te-doo-den-doo.

The pilot turned to me, as he finished, with a wicked look in his eye and doubling up his fist, feinting at an imaginary object, exclaimed:

"I'se a bad niggah, I am! Bettah go hide yo' face, Mr. Crocket, an' doan yo' 'proach dis niggah too neah." Biff!— If Mr. Crocket had been within reach of his fist he certainly would have been counted out.

As soon as the waves permitted he took his leave, thanking us all for the assistance rendered, as he pulled away in his boat.

Having been delayed about three hours on his account, the captain decided to come to an anchor at the mouth of the Potomac, as he was uncertain of the way over the shoals of the Chesapeake at night. Our mainsail was left standing and at 2 A.M. the next morning we hove up anchor and got under way for an early start. Sailing down the Chesapeake with no further incident, we passed Cape Charles on Wednesday, at 2 A.M. where we took a fine breeze up the coast, overhauling sail after sail, there being nothing in the fleet that could catch us. We passed in at Sandy Hook, about noon, October 25, and hailed a towboat which proved to be the *E. H. Coffin*, the same tug that towed us out.

We gave her our line, for the wind was fast dying out, but before we reached East River, the captain of the *Coffin* hailed us saying that he was short of water and unless the wind picked up again he would be unable to tow us through Hell Gate. Captain Winslow didn't want to be delayed and so asked him to "Hold all" for he was certain we would have plenty of wind in the river which would carry us through and after leaving Corlear's Hook we did pick up a little breeze that filled our sails and lasted till we were well into the East Channel and nearly beyond Blackwell's Island. Here we struck a head tide and the captain of the towboat again called to us saying that he would be unable to tow us through.

Standing at the knight-heads, with his speaking trumpet, Captain Winslow called out lustily: "Hold on! Ye c'n make it all right. Ye're gainin' all th' time. Don't give up naow. Ye'll soon be through. Hold on a little longer," etc.

Our little "cat's paw" of a breeze finally died out and the towboat merely kept a strain on our line, not exerting herself in the least, while we drifted back, with the tide, nearly a mile or so, the captain all the while calling to the towboat not to give up for the evening breeze would be sure to come.

After drifting back nearly to the penitentiary we finally caught the evening breeze which came in light puffs at first but gradually grew into a steady wind. Our sails began to fill and the *Floyd* gathering headway sailed abreast of the towboat. Here, Captain Winslow entreated the *Coffin* not to give up, but to try once more, with the result that the slack of our line was taken up and going ahead again and holding

the breeze the towboat finally pulled us through Hell Gate
and around Lawrence Point, before letting go.

Before the evening passed the barometer began to fall and
the wind hauling to northeast the captain decided to run for
Huntington Harbor, Long Island, where we arrived about
midnight and anchored, remaining there till Saturday afternoon when we got under way again and arrived at Newport,
Sunday, November 3, 1875.

The next day I was paid off at the rate of ten dollars per
month, the captain explaining that he had promised my
father that I would not receive any favoritism at his hands
and that was the reason he was so gruff with me at first. He
had kept his word, but if I was thinking of going to sea
again he would like to have me go with him and he promised to give me a mate's berth the following year. All this I
declined with thanks, for I wanted to make a voyage in a
"deep-water" ship, and taking my leave of him was more
impressed with the idea than ever before that a voyage in a
square-rigger would be my next.

CHAPTER V

ABOARD THE SHIP *AKBAR*

AFTER remaining at home for a week I wrote to my uncle Frederick Pease, for whom I was named, at that time superintendent of the East Boston Sugar Refinery, where vessels unloaded both from Cuba and the East Indies, asking if he would interest himself in my behalf, and the latter part of November received a reply that through Mr. Peabody of the Australian Line, he had secured a position for me as ordinary seaman in the ship *Akbar,* then loading at Lewis Wharf, Boston, with general cargo, for Melbourne and Sydney. I was to report at once.

On looking up the shipping news in the "Boston Evening Journal," I found where the *Akbar* was advertised, as follows:

PEABODY'S AUSTRALIAN LINE.

FOR MELBOURNE AND SYDNEY.

The A1 clipper ship

AKBAR,

Capt. Lamson, succeeding ship MYSTIC BELLE, will have quick despatch. Loading berth, Lewis Wharf.

For freight or passage apply to HENRY W. PEABODY & CO., 118½ Milk Street, corner Batterymarch street. Messrs. Newell & Co., Consignees at Melbourne.

Advances made on approved consignments.

Oct. 14.

It didn't take long to pack my chest and sailor's bag and as the weather was cold I had a good outfit for the winter and bidding good-bye to father and mother, I took the morning train for Boston.

The next day my uncle went over to Mr. Peabody's office

View of the New York Quarantine, Staten Island. From a colored aquatint (1833) in the Macpherson Collection.

Ship "Akbar," 906 Tons, Built in 1863, at East Boston. From a photograph of a model built by Frederick Pease Harlow.

with me and I was introduced to him. We were advised to go to the ship and meet the captain and on reaching Lewis Wharf we walked around the head of the dock to get a good look at the *Akbar** before going aboard. She was a ship of about 1,000 tons with three royal yards, hemp rigged and with a bell-shaped bow that showed she would be a comfortable, dry ship. She was nearly loaded and we both commented that she was a fine-looking vessel.

Going on board we were just too late to meet Captain Lamson, but the mate, Mr. Burris, of Weymouth, met us as we walked aft and told us that the captain had left word that he was expecting us for Mr. Peabody had told him the day before to be on the lookout for his friend's boy. My uncle told the mate that I was the new hand and said that I

---

* The name "Akbar" had brought up quite a discussion at home, as to where it originated and the meaning of the word, and the encyclopaedia supplied the following account:

"AKBAR. Born at Amarkote, Sind, India, Oct. 14, 1542; died at Agra, India, Oct. 13, 1605. A great Mogul Emperor in India, 1556-1605. He was born during the exile of his father, Humayun. After 12 years, Humayun recovered the throne of Delhi, but died within a year, when, in 1556, Akbar succeeded him, ruling at first under the regency of Bairam Khan. In his eighteenth year he threw off this yoke. By war and policy he consolidated his power over the greater part of India.

"He put an end to the conflict between Afghan and Mogul and sought to reconcile Hindu and Mohammedan. He interested himself in various religions: Brahmanism, Buddhism, Mazdaism, and Christianity and even sought to establish a religion of his own.

"He sought to better his subjects by measures of toleration and improved social laws. He permitted the use of wine, but punished intoxication; tried to stop widow burning; permitted the marriage of Hindu widows; forbad the marriage of boys before sixteen and of girls before fourteen; to gratify his Hindu subjects prohibited the slaughter of cows; had his lands accurately surveyed and statistics taken; constructed roads; established a uniform system of weights and measures; and introduced a vigorous police.

"He was sometimes harsh and cruel and is charged with poisoning his enemies. The rebellion of his son Selim, later known as Jahangir, was a Mohammedan uprising against Akbar's apostasy. The rebellion was suppressed and Akbar returned to the faith. He was probably poisoned at the instigation of Jahangir. "

had just returned from Philadelphia, in the schooner *David G. Floyd*, etc.

"What's your name?" asked Mr. Burris. "Ever been to sea in a square-rigger?"

On telling him my name and that I had never been to sea, except in the schooner, he made no comment, but was very agreeable to my uncle.

Mr. Burris wore a light, tan-colored overcoat which he buttoned up closely about his neck. He was small of stature —about five feet six inches tall—of light complexion and wore chin whiskers of a reddish hue. He was not the broad-shouldered man one would pick for a mate on a deep-water ship, in fact, he was quite effeminate in appearance and if it were not for his whiskers, he would be the last man to pick out for a sailor, although he was very busy about the deck, coiling up the ropes along the rail to a uniformity. Looking aloft at the main-yard, from which the cargo was being loaded on board in slings, he suddenly discovered something wrong with the gin-block and leaving us abruptly, he hurried forward, clumping along the companionway, showing that he was lame. His ankles were very stiff and hobbling down the ladder to the main-deck below, he accosted the man at the guy of the slings in no friendly manner. Turning his face towards us so that we could get the full benefit of the conversation, we heard him say:

"I told you yesterday to watch the parceling around the main-yard. Now look at it. Damn you! You don't heave in another sling till you go aloft and fix that gin-block properly. If I hadn't seen it you would have let it stay there till you had a furrow in that yard as deep as a Jumbo plow path on a Down-East farm. You fellows are the limit here in Boston. You don't care for the owner's interest at all and if I had my way there would be no stevedores. I'd work the cargo with the crew and pay them in their monthly pay." So saying he hobbled back to us mumbling to himself as he walked.

Upon reaching us my uncle asked if he had met with an accident, as he saw he was very lame.

"Yes," said the mate, "I met with an accident that nearly cost me my life. We were lying at anchor in Bombay, waiting for cargo, and had all the hatches off airing the ship. Not this ship. I've only been aboard here a week. It was the ship *Oliver Cromwell*, an old-time ship with stern-windows. With stern-windows and cabin doors open, we could get a breeze that would suck out all the foul air in no time. One night I stepped on the combings of the booby-hatch, when my foot slipped and I fell to the bottom of the ship. I must have turned a complete somersault, striking the keelson and breaking both ankles. They picked me up unconscious and rushed me to the hospital. The bones were set all right, I guess, but I didn't stay there long enough. When our ship was loaded, the doctor told me if I left the hospital at that time I might lose both legs, should I go to sea and attempt to perform my duties as mate. When they asked me if I was able to go or not, I said I was and so sailed with the ship; but I've got two stiff ankles to show for my ambition. I guess they'll never be any better now but they are a great deal better than no legs, as the doctor would have me believe. I've got to be very careful about these icy decks, where water has been thrown and allowed to freeze, for I can't catch myself as easily as I once could." Then turning to me, he asked,

"When are you coming aboard?"

"When do you want me?" I asked.

"Well! if you want to begin to-morrow you can go up to the shipping office sometime to-day and sign articles and be on hand bright and early, for I can keep you busy clearing up the decks. She ought to finish loading to-morrow or next day."

The mate didn't ask if we cared to see the ship's cabin or the forecastle and so we went ashore, my uncle to his office and I to the shipping office, where I signed articles.

The next morning, December 2, 1875, found me aboard, bag and baggage. The mate and I were the only two belonging to the ship. He kept me busy stowing away wood, dunnage, clearing the decks, etc., and as there was no cook aboard we went ashore and bought our own dinners.

The next day, the boy, Alonzo Gould, from Lowell, came aboard with Captain Lamson and not long after the captain came forward and introduced Alonzo as the son of a friend. He said that Mr. Peabody had spoken to him about me and there was no reason why Alonzo and I shouldn't get along together as we were to occupy the carpenter's room. He had decided not to carry a carpenter on this voyage, saying that what little carpenter work there was to be done he would find a way of doing, either by himself or by us two boys.

Captain Lamson was a man about sixty-four years of age. He had been a man-of-war officer during the Civil War and was great for discipline. Everything had to be just so—a place for everything and everything in its place. He was a medium-sized man and like the mate wore chin whiskers, which were quite gray, but he always kept them neatly brushed. He stood very erect, but was quite nervous, standing first on one foot and then on the other as he talked. His eyes were a deep blue and his nose rather on the Roman order. He wore a gray mustache, stained in front from tobacco chewing, for without exception he chewed more tobacco than any man I ever knew. He would chew away, with his mouth full of tobacco juice, never expectorating until he wished to say something and then he would run to the rail and empty his mouth into the sea ker-plump.

Alonzo was about my age but heavier in build. While I was of light complexion he was the opposite, with black hair, bright rosy cheeks and a very pleasant face.

The mate put us to work sweeping the decks. When we had finished I asked, "What next, Mr. Burris?"

"Well! you might as well begin all over again. Keep sweeping until we finish loading."

We took in the last piece of cargo about four o'clock and thought we were through with the brooms but Mr. Burris told us to begin all over again.

"See how clean you boys can sweep and don't forget to

reach under the spare spars. The last ship I was in I cut the handles off every broom so that you had to bend over. If a man sweeps with a long-handled broom he never stoops to see under a spar, but with a short handle he can see because he is always stooped over. Now this is a warning to you. If you can sweep clean there is no use in cutting the handles, but just as sure as I find a bunch of dirt under a spar or in a corner, I'll cut the handles off every broom in the ship."

Alonzo and I both laughed as he said it, but the mate turned on us, saying,

"You may think I am joking, but you'll find I am not, before the voyage ends."

Alonzo replied, "Then it stands us in hand to always be on the stoop—door stoop!" and we both laughed again.

"It'll be a long time before you get a chance to sit on your mother's stoop, I can tell you," said the mate, as he walked off.

This tickled Alonzo and we began to count on our fingers just how many times we had swept the decks during the day. I counted eight but Alonzo swore it was thirteen times. He kept us sweeping until six o'clock before he told us to put our brooms away and while we were washing our faces and hands, before going ashore for supper, he walked forward and told us to hurry back from supper.

"There is no going ashore to-night, boys. I want you both aboard as soon as you eat your supper," said he.

Now I was counting on spending the last night at my uncle's house, for he had made special arrangements with my cousins to give me an evening of music. My cousins played the piano and violin very nicely and a friend, who sang very well, was going to be there. They had planned to give me a good send-off on my last night ashore, so I told the mate they were expecting me.

"Now, look here, young fellow! You've signed aboard this ship and aboard this ship you'll stay and if you go home to-night you and I will have a falling out."

He turned on his heel and left us, going into the cabin.

"What are you going to do, Fred?" asked Alonzo.

"There's nothing left for me to do except stay aboard," I replied, and he no doubt saw my disappointment, for he said:

"I don't believe he can make you stay here and if I were you I'd go anyway. I can't go home and get back again to-night, so I'll stay and see that no one steals one of our anchors. The mate, no doubt, is figuring on going ashore himself. We'll come back after supper and if we see him going ashore, you skin out. He won't be back again before midnight and by that time you will be here and fast asleep when he arrives."

His advice struck me as being all right and we went ashore together, taking our time before returning to the ship. The mate was watching for us at the head of the gangplank, as we came aboard, and without saying anything he watched us go into our room and not long after we heard him clumping down the gangplank and up the dock.

Watching my time I soon followed and though late in getting to my uncle's house was repaid by one of the pleasantest evenings of music I had ever had. I got back to the ship just as the cabin clock chimed eight bells (midnight) and had no difficulty in getting aboard and stealing forward without awakening anybody and no one was any the wiser, except Alonzo, that I had been away from the ship.

We were called by the mate at six o'clock the next morning and while dressing Alonzo said: "Well! I guess you can take your brooms and sweep the decks. Mind! you bend your backs and see that all the dirt is swept from under the spars or I'll cut your broom handles off before we leave the dock," and going on deck he shuffled his feet with a stiff ankle, imitating the mate to perfection. Sure enough, on going aft, Mr. Burris greeted us with the very words we were looking for and consequently we were not disappointed.

At eight o'clock we went ashore for our breakfast for the last time, for the crew came aboard about eleven o'clock. They were in very good condition, for while the most of them were feeling the effects of their last drink ashore, there were none unable to attend to orders given. The second mate, an Irishman, who went by the name of Mr. Sanborn,

was a typical second mate on the bulldog order. His head
had a port list, growing abruptly from his shoulders, which
were unusually broad, showing him to be a powerful and
strongly built man. Coming aboard with the crew, his first
orders were:

"You, men! Get into your working clothes as soon as possible. We expect the towboat here at any moment and I want
everything ready to let go as soon as she is alongside." This
was not said in any female voice. Far from it! It was an
order that one heard and it couldn't be mistaken. The man
issued the order authoritatively and when I said to Alonzo,
"Gee! I hope I don't get in his watch," he replied: "I don't
know! I think I had rather have him for a boss than the
mate. I think the mate is a regular grandmother and would
keep a boy sweeping the decks until we reached Melbourne
and that's all he would know about sailorizing. I'll take my
chance with the second mate for I want to know something
about a ship before we get back."

"Believe me, Alonzo! You'll know more about a ship
before you reach Melbourne," said I; and so we commented
while the crew were changing their clothes. Before they came
on deck the towboat *Elsie* came alongside to tow us to sea.
It was a beautiful day; quite warm, but with very little
wind. There was no attempt made to loose the sails and as
the men appeared we were told to take in the fenders and
extra moorings. I stood on the topgallant forecastle, holding the turn of the bow line as the *Elsie* backed us out. My
cousins were on the dock giving me a hearty "Good-bye,
Fred," as we were clear from the dock.

Here we had to stop, for there was a big, new ship entering the other side of Lewis Wharf. Her spars were all
scraped and oiled and the new manila rope against the black,
fresh-tarred hemp shrouds, stood out in great contrast. She
was a ship that one would stop and look over for her fine
qualities as a sailer. The name *Samar* stood out in gilded
letters on her bow, as she passed us. A main-skysail-yard
ship hailing from Bath, Maine, and many were the comments from the sailors regarding her good qualities as we

were being towed down the harbor. On arriving at the roads, about noon, we dropped anchor in a calm and the captain went ashore in the *Elsie*.*

After dinner we were all assembled at the main hatch where Mr. Burris gave us a little talk concerning the voyage we were just entering on.

"I called you men here," said the mate, "because we are about to sail on a long voyage. There are two parts to this ship—forward and aft. The officers live aft and I distinctly want it understood that we both live in our respective places. I don't mean that we expect to make this ship a "hell ship" by any means. You'll find that this ship is a comfortable ship. We don't propose to ask anything unreasonable of you men, but do expect, when an order is given, that you will act promptly and quickly with the working of the ship.

"This ship, like all others, must be manned by the men and you are called here to be selected in your respective watches. As mate of the port watch I will choose the first man and Mr. Sanborn, second mate, will have the next choice for the starboard watch and we will choose alternately till the last man is selected."

So saying he looked over the men before him and finally said:

"I choose you," pointing his finger to a fine specimen of manhood. "What's your name?"

"Hans, sir," he replied.

"Let me have your knife," requested the mate, who stood on top of the main-hatch, with a hammer in his hand, which he was all the while turning and twisting. Upon receiving the sheath-knife, which is as much a part of a sailor's uniform as his overalls and is always carried in a sheath or scabbard, hanging from a strap about the waist and back of the hips, where it is handy for cutting a rope, for a sailor is not dressed without his knife, the mate put the point of the knife across the iron band on top of the combings of the

* My cousin Ed Pease was mate of her at that time and later her captain.

hatch and struck a sharp blow with the hammer, breaking off the point.

"You probably didn't have the mate, in your last ship, break the point off your knife," said Mr. Burris. "But I always keep a ship sweet and clean by seeing that every knife aboard the ship has no point. This is for your own protection. If you get into a fight with a shipmate you know you can't stick him with your knife or he, you. Knowing this you both will fight like men and use your fists, the weapons God has given you to fight with."

Returning the knife to Hans, he was told to stand over to the port rail and I marvelled at the broad shoulders and big hands and arms of this Norwegian as he turned and walked away to the rail.

The second mate then chose Jim Dunn, a fine specimen of Irish manhood. His knife was broken in the same manner and he was told to stand over to the starboard rail. With each alternate choice the crew was divided into port and starboard watches. There were seven of us in each watch. I was chosen by the mate and Alonzo was taken by the second mate.

Here the mate addressed us: "Boys! Just a word before you go. First, we will start this voyage, watch and watch (four hours work and four hours sleep, through the day). I propose to make this ship an easy ship for you and you are the ones to say whether you want it or not. If you do your part as sailors should, all will be well with me. But just as sure as you fellows don't appreciate a good ship there will be no watch and watch and I'll see that every damned man earns his passage to Melbourne."

He then turned to the second mate, saying, "Do you wish to address the men, Mr. Sanborn?"

"No, sir," said the second mate, "I think you have said all that is necessary, except that while we lay here at anchor the men will have all night in, but we will keep an anchor watch."

After giving us our instructions the mates went aft together, leaving us to ourselves. Going forward I followed the men into the forecastle. A big Irishman by the name of

O'Rourke, was much put out by having his knife point broken and was saying as I entered, "I don't know phat ye's fellers tink about it, an' I haven't been to sea for ten years, but fifteen years ago I sailed in the ships *Live Yankee** and the *Phantom* and if ships of that caliber can make a viage widout breakin' our knives, why in the bloody hell does an' old tub like this wan want to do it? It don't look good t' me, at all! at all! an' I miss moy guess ef we don't have troubles wid th' bloody mate before we git t' Melbourne." There were a number who voiced the same opinion. I had been in the forecastle about fifteen minutes when I heard the mate calling me.

"Here I am, sir," I replied, going on deck. He was standing by the main-hatch, talking to Alonzo, and asking him what was wanted he broke out, saying:

"Look here, young fellow! Don't ever let me catch you in that fo'c'sle again. I've given you a room by yourself, away from those old sailors, and you and Alonzo are to have nothing to do with them whatever. I don't want you to get your head filled with old sailor's notions and tricks and if you are counting on following the sea, the less you have to do with them the better. I'd find you there I thought and that is the reason I am here to tell you. You'll never amount to anything if you hang around the fo'c'sle all the time. You'll get into their lazy habits and the first thing you know you won't be worth a tinker's damn and I warn you—stay away from 'em!"

"What's a tinker's damn, Mr. Burris?" asked Alonzo.

"It's a wim-wam for a goose's bridle, damn you! and don't you put your head in it," said the mate.

He left us abruptly, going aft to his room.

* The *Live Yankee* was an extreme clipper ship, of 1,637 tons, built in 1853, by Horace Merriman, at Rockland, Maine. She was sold by her builders to Geo. W. Brown and others of New York, and soon after to Foster & Nickerson of New York. On her first voyage to San Francisco, she logged 18 knots and in one day made 327 miles, under command of Capt. E. A. Thorndike. She loaded at Liverpool for Kurachee, India, sailed June 26, 1861, and was wrecked on the coast of Galacia. The chief officer and six of the crew were drowned.

LEWIS WHARF, BOSTON. From a photograph made about 1880, now in the possession of the Society for the Preservation of New England Antiquities.

CLIPPER SHIP "LIVE YANKEE," 1,637 TONS, BUILT IN 1853, AT ROCKLAND, MAINE. From a painting by Hingqua, Hongkong, showing the ship off Cape Horn in 1854.

"I rather got his goat, didn't I?" said Alonzo.

"I think you did," said I. "But I'd be careful and not get him down on you or he'll make life miserable for you when we are outside."

"What can he do with me? I'm not in his watch. I'll be asleep when he's on deck. He won't dare to haze me for he knows I stand close to the captain and I don't believe the captain will stand for any hazing from him," reasoned Alonzo.

"Well! I can see that he makes you sweep the deck with a short-handled broom," said I, and we both laughed at the idea.

The next day being Sunday, there was no work for the crew except that we were called at six in the morning and pumped the ship before breakfast. While the pumps were working, Alonzo and I were busy with our brooms giving the decks an extra Sunday sweep. After breakfast we put in our time learning the different ropes leading to the belaying-pins along the rail, etc. Here we saw a small brig coming in from sea, with all sail set, and while we watched her clew up the royal and topgallant sails, as she approached, we laughed at the pocket-handkerchief sails compared with ours. Running past us she went into the wind and dropped her anchor just ahead of us and I read the name on the stern *Lizzie J. Bigelow* of Provincetown.*

"Well, I declare!" said I to Alonzo, "That brig used to be a whaler, but I see she has a deck-load of Southern pine and no doubt she is in the merchant service now. She was a 'hell ship' on her maiden voyage. My brother Wiley shipped on her and was unable to get his discharge. He joined her on her first voyage with a 210th lay. The yarns he told regarding the hardships the crew were subjected to would turn

---

* The *Lizzie J. Bigelow*, 176 tons, was built in Pembroke, Massachusetts, in 1868, and floated through a channel in the marshes to deep water. She was fitted out at Provincetown, Massachusetts, in July, 1869, and was commanded by Capt. Josiah Cook of Provincetown. She went ashore at Point Allerton, Hull, Massachusetts, at the southern entrance to Boston Harbor, February 12, 1885, where she pounded to pieces. Charles E. and Benjamin Fabens, of Salem, Massachusetts, were her last owners.

your stomach. When once aboard there was no such thing
as getting ashore again. The meat was poor and rotten and
the hard-tack full of skippers. She sailed the Southern seas
and when short of water called at islands where the men
couldn't get away. They were given no money with which
they might buy fruit on such trips, consequently there was
more or less scurvy aboard. The second year things were so
bad that the men refused to report whales from the masthead and many a whale was allowed to pass unmolested that
might have been caught. During the two years he was on her
he ran away six times only to be caught and brought back to
the ship.

"He ran away from the ship upon arriving at the Isle of
Grande, below Rio de Janeiro, where he lived among the
Portuguese for a few days, only to be sold back by them to
the captain when the vessel was ready for sea again. Then
they cruised the South Atlantic as far south as the Falkland
Islands and north again to St. Helena, where he again took
French leave. Making his way up the mountain, he lived on
berries, hiding in the shrubbery over night, but was caught
the next day and taken aboard the ship. Then there was a
long cruise from St. Helena to Cape of Good Hope and up
the west coast of Africa to the Cape Verde Islands. Scurvy
broke out among the men and here the crew went aft in a
body demanding better grub. The captain heard their complaint and said, 'In future, you men will have the same kind
of food that the officers and I have,' and in less than a half-
hour he gave orders to square away for Barbados. Running
to the westward for two weeks, without a change of food,
they made Barbados and anchored off Bridgetown. Here ten
sick men left the vessel and strange to say the captain made
no effort to bring them back but reported to the United
States Consul that these men had deserted. Shipping a new
crew the brig left the island and the captain no doubt was
glad to be rid of the men who were in a sick and disabled
condition.

"My brother was one of the ten and coming down with
the scurvy he reported to the American Consul, who con-

ferred with the head physician of the Marine Hospital, where he was taken care of for three weeks. On getting his release from the hospital he again went to the consul for aid in securing passage to the United States. Being without money and none too well dressed the American Consul would have nothing to do with him, classifying him as a deserter.

"Thrown on his own resources and half starved, he managed to get enough work to live on the island for nearly three months and finally got away by shipping aboard the bark *Elora*, a lime-juicer, of Liverpool, England, bound for St. Thomas, Virgin Islands, for orders. It was a heavenly home for him after the hardships encountered on the whaler. Arriving at St. Thomas, they took orders for Ponce de Leon, Porto Rico, where they loaded sugar for St. John, New Brunswick. From there he shipped in a big fore-and-after, the *Helen G. King*, for Calais, Maine, where they loaded lumber for New York, and that is how he managed to get home after being away three years.

"You never know from the looks of a vessel how they will treat you when a member of the crew. She is a beautiful model, but I am glad that I'll get my supper aboard the *Akbar* and that we are not outward bound to cruise for whales."

Sunday evening the wind hauled to the northeast, with snow and rain, and the mate gave the ship thirty fathoms of chain.

A word here will not be amiss concerning our windlass, which was the common type of that day. It was made from a solid oak tree and was turned out similar to any round piece of timber from the turning lathe. Instead of a lathe, the timber was turned on a frame, by four men. This frame, or skid, was well greased, enabling the heavy stick to be turned as the hewer requested and after being shaped it was fitted with iron bands and angle irons where the cable came over.

There were four turns of the cable around the windlass, for each anchor. If the port anchor was being hove in, the starboard cable was slackened over the windlass and thrown over an iron bar above the windlass which ran through the carrick-bitts, one for each end and about a foot or more above the windlass. Being raised above, it slipped around as the windlass turned.

On Monday morning all hands were called at five o'clock to heave in the thirty fathoms of chain that we had let out the night before. Our chain was much heavier than the one used on the *David G. Floyd* and while one man could take care of the chain, behind the windlass, on the *Floyd*, it took three of us to pull the cable back and coil, or flake it, on the chain-rack, which was made of two-inch plank and was about ten by five feet square and raised from the deck just enough to allow the water to run freely underneath.

There were two racks, one for each chain, placed on each side of the fore-hatch, while the anchors were hanging at the bow. When a vessel goes to sea the chain is unshackled and stowed in the chain-locker, beneath the deck, while the anchors are brought inboard and lashed on top of the top-gallant forecastle.

Andy, Alonzo and I were employed in pulling the chain back from the windlass as it came in. The first layer on the chain-rack runs fore and aft and the next goes across, or athwartship, starting aft and working forward, so that when the anchor is dropped the chain runs out smoothly. The third layer is like the first and the fourth like the second and in this manner the chain is bound at every layer without fear of falling down. The links are pulled back by means of a chain-hook, to insure one's hands from being bruised, but although my hands were hardened and calloused, the work was very severe on them. Poor Alonzo's hands were soon blistered and bleeding, the cold, chilly morning adding to his discomfort. We were both glad when the mate sang out "Avast heaving."

I gave my prescription for blistered hands to Alonzo, which was the same that the cook of the *Floyd* told me to use, *i.e.*, stick them into salt brine. He tried it, but only with one hand, preferring to wrap them up with linen rags.

We were still at anchor on Tuesday and the crew were employed in the rigging. The next day the men were called at five o'clock in the morning to give the ship thirty fathoms of chain. A good deal of snow had fallen during the night and the decks were very slippery. A strong northeast wind was blowing almost a gale.

The ship was surging and swinging at her chain and a couple of turns were raised from the windlass to allow the chain to run freely. (The *Akbar* was an old-time ship with hand-brakes heaving up and down and not connected with the capstan. Nor had we a donkey-engine like most of the modern ships.) Snow and ice were in the chain and it started with a run, going over the windlass as though it had been greased. It didn't take long to run off the chain from the rack and the mate called for a fender to jam against the windlass. Pat, a fine, large Irishman, jumped on top of the chain, in an effort to hold it, but his feet were knocked from under him and falling on the running cable he was carried to the windlass where his leg was caught, breaking the bone and tearing the limb completely off below the knee. So great was the force that he was carried clear over the top of the windlass against the heel of the bowsprit. His sufferings were something awful. I turned my face away from the scene while the men rushed to his assistance.

I saw big Hans running forward with a spar-fender, to stop the cable, in answer to the mate's order, but how they succeeded in stopping the running cable I didn't look to see. Poor Pat's groans were a little more than I could stand at that moment and I didn't fully recover until the cable was secure. In the meantime Pat was carried to the cabin by four sailors, where a tourniquet was placed around his leg to stop the flow of blood. We all went aft, in a body, only to be told to keep out and go forward. Here the second mate discovered two extra men among us who were stowaways. They were from the North Street Boarding House and had come on board with the sailors, intending to hide below in the cargo until we were out to sea; but the cries of Pat got the best of their curiosity and brought them from their hiding.

The mate upon hearing there were two stowaways on board, called to the second mate: "Give those stowaways something to do. Make them sweep down, fore and aft. I'll have no one aboard who doesn't earn his passage."

"Better cut the handles, Mr. Burris," said Alonzo. "My broom was too long."

"A good idea! Suppose you cut it," said the mate; whereupon Alonzo gave me the wink and going forward soon returned with a broom from which he had sawed off two-thirds of the handle.

"Here's your broom, Mr. Burris," said Alonzo.

"Fine! I'll see how they sweep and if they don't do better than you, I'll give it to the one that needs it," said the mate, and without further comment he took the broom into his room while the stowaways began sweeping and were kept busy till breakfast time.

While we were at breakfast the *Elsie* came alongside with supplies for the cook and we were immediately called to give a hand with the meat and groceries while Pat was being removed from the cabin, for the mates decided to send him to the hospital. We lowered him in a canvas sling to the deck of the towboat, where he was taken below.

The rolling of the *Elsie* gave him much pain, while he was being steadied before he was finally landed, and he kept calling out, "For God's sake handle me easy. Can't ye see ye're hurting me! Let go! I tell ye! Let go o' me leg!" etc.

The accident cast a gloom over the ship and as the weather was cold and disagreeable the men were excused from further work for the remainder of the day.

After supper we were called to point the yards, as the wind showed no signs of going down. This gives the minimum resistance to the wind against the yards and the vessel has less chance of dragging her anchors. It is done by bracing the fore and mizzen yards hard in to starboard and the main yards to port. Thus, the main yards are thrown against the fore, on the starboard side, and against the mizzen, to port. The yardarms, nearly touching, are then in the position of a zig-zag rail fence. This was the first time I had actually

seen the yards swing and I entered into the work with a
great deal of energy; the sound of the patent-sheave blocks
on the lower yards, swinging from the pendants, was music
to my soul.

"That's well, the fore! Belay! Belay!" etc., shouted the
mate, and in turn the topsail and topgallant and royal yards
were swung, to the "Yo-ho-ho-boys" of real "deep-water"
sailors. So easily were the yards swung that I was sorry when
it was over and we were told to clear up the decks. The ropes,
or braces, were then coiled up and thrown over the pins
against the rail, which was a relief to Alonzo and me for we
fully expected the mate to take us away from the braces and
set us to work with our brooms; but the stowaways came to
our relief and after the last brace was hung from the pin and
we were through for the evening, Alonzo said,

"Thank God! we have at last graduated from the
brooms," no doubt thinking he had seen the last of them;
but he was doomed to disappointment.

The night was cold with a regular northeast snowstorm
setting in. We had no stove, either in the forecastle or our
room, and the only warmth we got was from a kerosene lamp
that we burned without a chimney. Turning up the wick for
light as well as heat, our room was soon filled with small
particles of soot emitted from the wick and we were forced
to open the door in order to breathe. Our room being in the
after part of the forward house, the snow didn't bother us
much but we were obliged to "turn in" in order to keep
warm using all the coats we possessed thrown over our
blankets. Ships in those days didn't furnish blankets to the
crew and very few sailing vessels equipped the forecastle
with a stove or dishes for the men to eat from. Each sailor
provided for himself a tin pan for a plate, a tin dish for a
soup-plate and a quart pot for his tea or coffee, which was
made by the cook in the galley, in a ten-quart pot, sweetened
with molasses which was allowed to boil in the pot while the
coffee was being made. If poor Jack was rich enough he
bought himself a knife and fork and tablespoon. If not, he
used his sheath-knife and drank his soup from his tin dish

or coffee pot. There was no table in the forecastle from which to eat, but there were always two benches for the men to sit on. The food was brought from the galley and placed in the middle of the floor, in large dish-pans, where the sailors helped themselves, filling their tin pans and holding them between their knees. If the ship was in a heavy sea, sometimes Jack would spend the greater part of his dinner-hour, balancing his coffee in one hand and holding his plate in the other, before he could get a chance to feed himself and many a time the situation would become so ridiculous that no one could eat from laughter and with each roll some old salt would say, "Who wouldn't sell a farm and go to sea!" bringing forth another round of laughter. I sigh when I think of the good old days never to return again.

Thursday morning we were called at five o'clock to shovel from the deck the snow that had fallen through the night. The wind having gone down the weather was much warmer and after breakfast we got the deck-pump out for a wash-down. The second mate held the hose while three men abreast, with kaya brooms (made of a kind of willow), scrubbed the deck from snow and ice, while the second mate washed it away with the hose. These men took their position abreast, going down the deck slowly as they scrubbed in unison, first to the right and then to the left, like one man, while Alonzo, the two stowaways and I, followed with our cornbrooms, drying off the deck. Here Alonzo got into trouble. The mate, as usual, going about the deck looking for dirt, found a rope-yarn frozen to the deck under a spare spar where Alonzo had been sweeping and walking back to him said:

"Alonzo, in my room behind the door you will find a broom. Go and get it for me."

"Aye, aye, sir!" said Alonzo, going to the room but returning without it and with a smile said,

"I don't see any broom in your room, sir."

"The hell, you don't," said the mate as he saw Alonzo's smile. "Now come off of your high perch! If the broom was hanging from the maintruck you'd have no trouble in seeing it, but the trouble with you is you never look down. Now go aft again and keep your eyes on the deck and you'll see a broom about this long (measuring with his hands about two feet). A *small* broom, made for *small* boys—especially made for *small* work aboard a *small* ship. When you bend your *small* back and cast your *small* optics on the deck you'll see what I want. That broom is the one you cut last night. Now go and bring it to me damn quick and I'll tell you what I want with it."

Alonzo's smile vanished as he turned to do the mate's bidding. He had no trouble this time in locating the broom, for he returned immediately with it in his hand. The mate took him to the place where the rope-yarn stuck under the spar.

"Do you see it?" asked the mate, pointing to the rope-yarn.

Alonzo, standing erect, made no effort to see it and answered, "No, sir! I don't see anything out of the way."

"Damn it!" said the mate. "Bend your back until you *do* see it."

Alonzo, who was treating the matter as a joke, saw he had gone about as far as he could and taking the mate's advice he looked under the spar. "Oh, yes," said he. "There's a rope-yarn; but I couldn't see it standing up."

"Then go after it and see that you get it," said the mate. "I'm going to make you a present of that little broom, all for yourself, and you are to use it every time you sweep. You'll find it will aid your eyesight and when it's worn out —well! We'll see whether you have earned another."

Alonzo reached for the rope-yarn but couldn't sweep it clear from the deck. He stood there sweeping in one spot while the mate was talking and making no further effort to get it clear. By this time the mate had exhausted all his patience and his true nature began to show. He had carried himself, up to this time, befitting a first officer's position. I had heard men swear before, but this man had a system of his own that I have never heard since. He took great delight in running off in one breath all the oaths that were ever heard, joining them together with an est —est —est, where possible; all the dirtiest, vulgar, foul-mouthed epithets until he was actually black in the face; and here he gave us all an example of his wit, if it could be called such.

"Get down on your hands and knees and reach for it! Of all the stupidest, damnedest, provokenest, —est, —est, etc. You take the cake!" Here he paused for breath and looked us over to see whether any of us laughed or not. I stood with my mouth wide open and, catching his gaze, broke into a laugh whereupon he reprimanded me.

"What the hell are *you* laughing at? Get busy with your broom."

Then turning to Alonzo, who had pulled the rope-yarn from the ice in the meantime, he exclaimed,

"Now sweep under every spar, fore and aft, both port and starboard sides, and mind you sweep clean."

Alonzo was a sorrowful-looking boy, going about the deck with his short-handled broom while the sailors cast a quiet smile as he passed them, and being the recipient of his own little joke he felt it exceedingly, for he was a boy who took great pleasure in passing a joke to others; but it was a different story when the laugh was on him.

After washing down we hove in the extra chain and squared the yards and the men were kept at work in the rigging for the balance of the day.

CHAPTER VI

GETTING UNDER WAY

FRIDAY is a Jonah for most ships, but the next morning, although cloudy, brought a northwest wind. We were called, as usual, at five o'clock and the mate greeted us at the door giving Alonzo his short-handled broom and starting us in the usual manner. There was a great deal of joshing from members of the crew as Alonzo bent his back, much to his chagrin.

About ten o'clock the captain came off in the *Elsie*. He had taken advantage of the past three days of bad weather and stayed at home; but he brought another sailor, Dave, who hailed from Hobart Town, Tasmania, to take the place of Pat, who was in the hospital. Coming alongside he called,

"Man the windlass, Mr. Burris, and get under way at once."

"Aye, aye, sir! Man the windlass," called the mate. The men at work at their respective jobs were not loath to quit and hurried to the forecastle-head with a glad, "Man the windlass, sir!"

The brakes were shipped and the men in a cheerful mood at the thought of getting under way and out to sea, went to work with a will, while Andy, Alonzo and I took care of the cable as it came over the windlass, as before. The music of the pawls dropping—clank, clank, clank—was broken by Jerry, starting a chantey, the first one sung aboard the ship. Up and down worked the windlass brakes in time to his solo and before the last word of the solo was fairly sung, the crew, in their eagerness, broke in on the chorus with a rousing, "Heave away, my Johnnies!" showing what frame of mind they were really in. Jerry had a fine voice and started the chantey in a clear tone which rang out in his crescendoes beyond comparison.

HEAVE AWAY MY JOHNNIES

We're all bound for Liv-er-pool, I heard the Cap-tain

say; Heave a - way my John-nies, heave a - way. . . . .

Oh! there we'll have a bul-ly time with Nel-lie and Ju-lia and May;

Heave a - way my John-ny boys, We're all bound to go.

Solo	As I was walking out one day, down by the Clarence Dock;
Chorus	Heave away, my Johnnies, heave away.
Solo	I overheard an emigrant, conversing with Tapscott;
Chorus	Heave away, my Johnny boys, we're all bound to go.

"Good morning, Mr. Tapscott!" "Good morning, sir!" said he,
"Oh! have you got any packet-ship, to carry me over the sea?"

"Oh, yes, indeed! I've got packet-ships; they sail in a day or two;
I've got the *Josie Walker*, besides the *Kangaroo*.

"The *Josie Walker* sails Friday; her hatches all ready to seal;
With all, four hundred emigrants and a thousand bags o' mail."

"You'll not sail me on the *Walker* ship, I'll not climb over the rail;
To hell with you and your packet-ship and your thousand bags o' mail."

Some say we're bound for Liverpool; some say we're bound for France;
But now we're bound for Melbourne town to give the girls a chance.

The clouds are floating steady; the wind is blowing free;
We'll heave her short and be ready for the towboat to take us to sea.

As a matter of note Tapscott, in the foregoing chantey, in the early fifties was one of the wealthy shipowners of Liverpool. His vessels were noted for strict discipline, as well as cruelty to the crew. His *Josie Walker* was an emigrant ship trading between Liverpool and New York and her voyages, to and from the Continent, were marked by unheard-of cruelties, the stories of which spread along the water front and the ship was known to all sailors as "Tapscott's Josie Walker." The mention of this "hell ship" stopped many a good sailor from shipping in her and being unable to secure good men was the cause no doubt of the many perversities to a green crew.

Tapscott's name being associated with the ship, gave food to the chanteyman for his verses and this chantey was seldom sung without the "Good morning, Mr. Tapscott!" It was exceptionally adapted to the heaving up and down of the windlass-brakes which, in old ships, worked like an old-fashioned fire engine, except that they were never worked from the extreme height to the bottom, in one stroke, but on the contrary were pulled down to the halfway point where it was necessary, on account of the heavy strain from the cable, to change the position of the arms in order to shove the brake to the bottom, while the men at the other end were doing the opposite.

Windlass chanties are in 2/4 and 6/8 time or two beats to the measure, the accent falling nicely as the brakes are pumped, making "Heave away, my Johnnies" one of the best chanties written for this kind of work.

There are several different sets of verses to this chantey but sailor Jack is privileged to use any old words to help out the song and so with Jerry who sang until the cable was short (up and down), when the mate, who watched proceedings from over the bow, sang out, "Avast heaving!" and going to the break of the t'gallant-fo'c'sle, raised his hands to his mouth for a speaking trumpet and shouted to the captain, "Anchor's short, sir!"

"Very well, sir!" answered the captain. "Send a couple of

men aloft to loose the courses and topsails and heave away your anchor."

"Aye, aye, sir!" answered the mate and in the same breath he ordered,

"Heave away, the windlass!" This was answered by the men,

"Heave away, the windlass, sir!"

"Send a couple of men aloft, Mr. Sanborn," he then called to the second mate.

"Aye, aye, sir!" answered the second mate. "Jump aloft, a couple of you fellows and take the gaskets off the sails."

"Aye, aye, sir!" they answered and two men for each mast, scrambled up the rigging like so many monkeys. "One of you go aft and take the wheel!" called the second mate.

"Take the wheel, sir!" answered another, before the order was fairly given, for the foxy sailor knows that if he can get to the wheel while the sails are being set, he is out of a lot of hard work. If there is anything he can do to be a little further aft than the rest, he will be where he can drop his work and hasten to the wheel.

Clank, clank, clank, dropped the pawls, as the windlass revolved; the heaving became harder and harder as the anchor refused to let go and the men gave all their strength as they hove away at windlass brakes, giving utterance to expressions, "Heave! Oh, heave! Heave and bust her! Heave and let go!" etc., till finally, with the aid of the towboat alongside, the ship forged ahead and the anchor yielded from its clutch below, while the heaving became easier as the anchor was on its way to the surface of the water. Then the mate called again to the captain, "Anchor's aweigh, sir!" while the men kept on heaving.

The gong in the engine-room of the *Elsie* rang out above the clank of the windlass and we heard her propeller churning the water white; now forging ahead and then backing to swing the ship's head from the northwest wind, for the bow must necessarily be turned to the north and east for an open course to the Atlantic.

We were anchored in Nantasket Roads where all "outward-bounders," awaiting a fair wind, were accustomed to lay. Ships, barks, brigs and schooners of all sizes were anchored there, as Nantasket Roads is for Boston the favorite grounds for anchoring, as Sandy Hook is for New York. The common herd of sailors, who knew no different, used to speak of this anchorage as "Boston Roads."

Nantasket Roads is between Gallop's and George's islands, to the north, Windmill Point and Nantasket Hill to the southeast, and Paddock's Island, to the south. George's Island, about a quarter of a mile to the nor'ard and east'ard, sheltered us from the northeast gale, but now with a nor'-west wind, we had a fair wind to sea, as our course was nearly due east to clear Cape Cod, forty-five miles away.

The *Elsie*, churning away as our bow swung to the north, the pilot called to the man at the wheel:

"Port your helm! Hard aport!"

This worthy gentleman, who up to this time had had nothing to do but watch the men on the foot-ropes of the main-yard, with head well back and chewing a mouthful of tobacco from which the saliva in his throat was near to running over, quickly turned his head, upon hearing the order, and emitting the juicy weed and the contents of his throat into the box placed for that purpose on top of the wheel-box, directly behind him, with a sputtering reply called out lustily,

"H-a-r-d aport, sir!"

Over and over he whirled the spokes of the wheel until the helm was hard-down. Then wiping his mouth with the back of his hand he dove into his pants pocket and brought up a piece of navy plug for a fresh chew. Looking it over for a clean spot to bite he jammed the plug into his mouth, sinking his eye-tooth into one corner and with a jerk of the head and a twist with his hand he severed the connection and surveyed what was left. If there were any ragged edges they were promptly bitten off before slipping the plug back into his pocket. He was now set and ready for the pilot to tell him, "Keep her as she heads," as the ship swung in a circle going forward all the while.

Soon the pilot called to the captain,

"Give her the jibs, sir!"

The captain, walking the deck on top of the cabin, immediately called to the mate,

"Set the jibs, Mr. Burris!"

"Set the jibs, sir!" he at once replied. "Jib-halliards, a couple of you. Up with flying-jib and jib-topsail, also!"

The stops and gaskets had already been taken from the jibs and these sails quickly filled to the breeze aiding materially in swinging the ship on her course. Here the towboat cast off her lines at our side and running under the bow took our hawser for the tow to sea.

Then heaving away again on our anchor we hove it up to the hawsepipe but didn't bring it to the cat-head, simply hooking the fish-tackle pendant in the ring and taking a strain on the tackle preparatory to catting the anchor.

The fish-tackle is suspended from the fore topmast-head. The wire pendant runs over an iron pulley on the forward side of the cat-head and is long enough to hook into the ring of the anchor at the hawsepipes. This big pendant and fish-hook to correspond was not much like the one on the *David G. Floyd*, where one man could handle it with ease. Here, it took several men, for the blocks and pendant were very heavy. The fish-tackle on the *Floyd* was a double purchase, while the *Akbar's* was triple.

In early days the cat-head was fitted with three sheaves and a cat-block below for a tackle in catting the anchor. Our cat-head still carried the sheaves, but they were never used. At the present time one seldom sees an anchor swinging from the cat-head. The modern stockless anchors heave clear into the hawsepipes and in a few more years the cat-head will be a thing of the past.

Our port "mud-hook" was different from the old straight anchor where the arms and shank were in one piece of iron with a fixed wooden stock. Our anchor was self-controlling and was made of forged iron. A projection in the center of the arms worked in a recess at the hub of the shank and no matter how the anchor landed, the flukes would turn, pointing down when the strain was on the cable. A Frenchman by the name of Martin is credited with this patent. The anchor in its improved form is very common to-day, but in the early '70's it was not much used. With us it was something of a curiosity with the crew, not many having been "shipmates" with it, and in Australia the pilot was very wary in trusting to it off Williamstown, where we anchored for the night in squally weather. Our anchor was fitted with a wooden stock, for they took no chances in those days and instead of the flukes being in one piece each revolved around a pinion at the end of the shank. A shoulder on top brought up against the shank, keeping the arm of the fluke rigid.

Our starboard or right-bower was an improved Trotman's anchor. The arms, instead of being solidly connected with the shank, were movable. Pivoting about a bolt passing through the crown-piece at the end of the shank, the upper arm turned forward until the flukes rested on the shank, giving more holding power with less danger of fouling the cable than the old standard anchors.

It was no easy matter to fish those anchors and still more difficult when the ship was rolling; therefore we took advantage of the smooth water, at that time, preparatory to catting before getting outside.

While we were busy with the anchor the lower topsails had been sheeted home. There is no hoist to the lower topsails. The yards are trussed to the cap at the lower masthead, while under the truss there is an iron supporter or standard which leads from the center band about the yard down in front of the heel of the topmast to the top below.

The *Akbar* carried lower topsail-lifts which, instead of running from the yardarm, were shackled to a band around the yard about ten feet inside the topsail-sheet sheave and a little abaft the center of the yard on top.

These lifts were about ten feet long, taking a whip leading to the masthead above and enabling the yard to be canted or squared by the lifts. Not much good was derived from them, for not only did the topsails chafe from slatting across the lifts, but the upper topsail yard, in being lowered, was always hindered by riding the lift or catching on the block before the yard was down. We carried no topsail downhauls. The weight of the yard was generally sufficient; otherwise it was necessary for a man to run aloft with a slush bucket to slush the parral or mast where needed. Ships of to-day all carry downhauls.

The tacks and sheets of the lower topsail were of chain leading out to the yardarm below, through a sheave and under the yard back to the slings, through a block and down in front of the lowermast to an iron pin in the bitts. In furling the sail, the clews were clewed up to a quarter-block under the yard and not out to the yardarms, as ships of to-day are rigged. In the '70's, very few shipmasters were looking after the welfare of the sailors. They took pride in having everything shipshape. A harbor-furl on a square-sail was not complete without tapering nicely from the bunt out to the yardarm and it made no difference to them how much work it took to furl a sail so long as it looked well.

The upper topsail sheets were shackled to the lower topsail yardarms and were not clewed up for furling. The man aloft had just let go the bunt gasket as we were hustled aft to assist with the main upper topsail. This was a long and heavy hoist requiring all the men available.

A chain tye, leading from the slings of the yard through a sheave fore-and-aft in the mast, just above the band of the futtock shrouds, was shackled to a block, abaft the mast, taking a chain runner. The port end shackled to a chain-plate in the channels between the fifth and sixth shroud and led up through the block and down the starboard side to which a double-purchase hooked into the chain-plate in the starboard channels, corresponding to the port side. The fore topsail, also the mizzen topsail to port, the main topsail to starboard.

The old chain pendants are now a thing of the past. Wire rigging has supplanted chain and hemp where possible. Not only do wire pendants render through a block more easily but there is no chipping of iron rust and painting in order to preserve them.

The fall of the topsail halliards was then taken to a snatch-block hooked into an eye-bolt in the deck for that purpose and with four men at the hoist and the rest of us stringing across the deck, we hauled away to the cry from "Handsome Charlie," with his "Yo—ho! Rise him a-hoy!"

Charlie, on account of his clear complexion and clean face, devoid of whiskers, with pink cheeks, was always dressed well in clean clothes of navy blue, taking pride in his general appearance and seeming to be of better standing than the rest of the crew. He was always good-natured and a likable fellow and on account of his clear complexion was dubbed "Handsome Charlie." This name stuck to him for the entire voyage. He started his cry, or sing-out, in a low, soft tone, but as the work became harder he increased the tone in proportion to the work. This Norwegian had an exceptionally musical sing-out and always took the lead in our watch. It is surprising what a difference it makes to the pull. If the chanteyman has a true voice the work is entered into more vigorously. If his voice is not quite up to standard, the men pull in a listless manner.

Stringing across the deck with our feet braced and pulling most energetically, I was just behind Jerry on the pull when Alonzo came up looking for a place. He tried to squeeze in ahead of Jerry and asked this worthy sailor to move back far enough to make a place for him.

Jerry, seeing that it was the boy, gruffly brushed him aside exclaiming: "See here, boy! Learn your place and don't ever put yer bloody self in front of me again. I'll have no joskin of a boy taking my place aboard this ship. Git to hell out'n here! Surge! Tail on behind!"

The stowaways had a great laugh at his expense which brought the blood to Alonzo's face. He stood back from the rope chagrined and was forced to take his place behind, but from his looks I judged he had no kindly feeling for the stowaways.

The patent-sheave blocks of the topsail halliards kept up a lively accompaniment to "Handsome Charlie's" cry, as the yard was being mastheaded. There is, indeed, a merry tone to the click of the ball-bearing rollers in the sheave; a feeling that the big blocks above are doing their utmost to help poor Jack lighten his work and one can almost hear them say:

"Go it, old boy! I'm with you!"

Those heavy topsails must have been a source of worry to the sailors before the double topsails came in. Originally they were one big sail for each mast, having three reef-bands. But on account of the heavy work in setting and reefing these sails, some Christian man devised a scheme whereby the lives of the sailors were prolonged and in many an instance saved. It is said that an American shipmaster by the name of Howe first proposed to change the rig into two separate sails calling them the upper and lower topsails. This met the favor of practical shipmasters with the result that we now have not only the double topsails but the double topgallant sails as well.

In stormy weather it was as much as one's life was worth to lay out on the yard of a single topsail. This sail, being very long in hoist, when clewed up for furling left an enormous bunt at the slings of the yard giving the wind more opportunity to raise the bunt and throw the sail over the yard and the heads of the men standing on the foot-ropes. If the men were not knocked off the yard by the flap of the sail in their faces, a loose buntline or leachline might whip under the sheath-knife of poor Jack, when the sail blew back again, and twist him off the yard into Davy Jones's locker below.

With "Handsome Charlie" at the hoist it will not be out of place to give his peculiar sing-out which is still fresh in my mind.

He kept this up until out of breath, when Jerry came to his rescue by starting "Whiskey," the chantey I so much wanted to hear. This chantey was generally sung upon getting under way at the topsail halliards and I would certainly have been a disappointed boy had they started some other chantey. Every deep-water sailor knew it as a child knows his A-B-C's and while I knew the song I had never sung it pulling on the end of a topsail halliard.

The ship was beginning to feel the motion of the long swell. We had passed George's Island and the broad Atlantic was ahead of us. The wind on our quarter, with only the lower topsails and jibs set and the towboat ahead to help us along, put us all in a happy mood which was shown by the manner in which the men joined in on the chorus. As for me, I wouldn't have changed places with the President of the United States. I was bound for Melbourne and now a true sailor.

WHISKEY

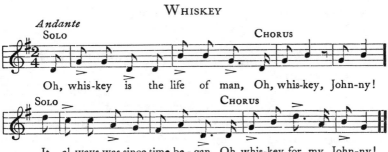

A whiskey ship and a whiskey crew,
When whiskey goes, then I'll go too.

Oh, whiskey made me wear old clothes,
And whiskey gave me a broken nose.

Oh, whiskey caused me much abuse,
And whiskey put me in the calaboose.

Oh, whiskey killed my poor old dad,
And whiskey drove my mother mad.

Oh, whiskey here and whiskey there
And whiskey almost everywhere.

If whiskey comes too near my nose,
I tip her up and down she goes.

I drink it hot and I drink it cold,
I drink it new and drink it old.

Oh, whiskey straight and whiskey strong,
We'll raise the yard to this old song.

Oh, whiskey made the bos'un call,
"Pull all together! One and all!"

I think I heard the "Old Man" say,
"We'll splice the main brace here today."

Oh, bring a drink to the chanteyman,
In a glass, or cup, or an old tin can.

Here comes the cook with the whiskey can
And a glass of grog for every man.

A glass of grog for every man,
And a bottle full for the chanteyman.

And so we sang until the mate called out, "Belay! Belay! the main topsail!"

This chantey is one of the best for a drag chantey. The pull comes nicely on the accented notes. With the mastheading of the main upper topsail, we hoisted the fore and mizzen upper topsails and the *Akbar* heeled over nicely under

the stretch of canvas. Then we went back to the fo'c'sle-head
to cat and fish the anchor.

The fish-tackle fall was taken to the capstan, while I held
the turn. Heaving away, the anchor was brought up to the
cat-head, while the cable was slacked away through the
hawsepipe, giving chain enough to reach the cat-head. Not
only must the anchor be raised, but there is also the weight
of the cable, which is quite a tension on the fish-tackle.

Holding the turn was new work to me and I got into
trouble in a very short time for although the *Floyd* carried
a capstan I had never held the turn. We had no such heavy
anchors to hoist and the work being light I always took the
capstan-bar while the mate held the turn.

As the men walked around the capstan, stepping over the
ropes of the fall, with each revolution the rope kept working
down the barrel of the capstan, which is tapered out at the
bottom. Holding the fall with a strong arm and allowing no
slack, there was finally a sudden jump of the rope, slipping
up the barrel, that shook the whole foremast and for a moment I thought we had lost our anchor as the pendant
slipped back over the cat-head. This brought a curse from
the mate.

"Damn it! Why in hell don't you surge that fall? Do you
want to take a leg off of some one? Mind your eye and surge
before you do."

Of course I knew that it was necessary to surge (slipping
the fall easily and keeping it in the middle of the barrel),
but this comes from experience and getting used to the
weight of the hoist; also, the turns around the capstan.
Three turns are usually enough and if the rope slips with
three, a fourth is taken, which may be more than enough, in
which case it is necessary sometimes to ease the fall with
one's hands.

After the mate's curse I watched the turn and soon found
that it wasn't necessary to hold the fall as tightly as I had
been doing and the anchor was finally "two blocks" (the
ring, as far as it could go) under the cat-head. Passing a
chain-stopper through the ring we secured it to the cat-head.

Then fishing the flukes we hove them up over the rail and with the shank-painter made her fast.

The bunt gasket of the foresail having been let go, this big sail hung in heavy festoons above our heads only waiting for the clew-garnets and buntlines to be released. Here the mate sang out, "Fore tack down!" and releasing the weather clew-garnet, the port fore tack brought the clew of the foresail down to a flat, convex, iron hook about three inches wide, through which it rendered while being boarded. The hook was like an elongated *S*, the smaller end hooking into a ring-bolt on top of the cat-head. With a lazy-tackle, the rope-tack was relieved and a chain, clipped into the clew-iron, took its place and was taken to the capstan where it was made fast. When the clew is brought down sufficiently, the mate calls, "Make fast the tack!" and the next order is, "Haul aft the fore-sheet!"

"Haul aft the fore-scoot, sir!" is answered by the men and a couple rush aft to lend a hand. The sheet is loosely hanging from the lee clew and a lot of slack rope must necessarily come in. If the cook is properly on to his job he will be watching from the galley for the order as our cook did. This is the only rope he is supposed to help with in making sail or tacking ship and if he is not "Johnny on the spot" he is liable to get his curses the same as any old sailor.

Our cook, Brainard, was a middle-aged man and knew his duty, for he shot out of the galley door when the order to "Haul aft the fore-sheet" was given and throwing the coil from the belaying-pin, in true sailor style, braced his foot against the spare spar and with his hands close up to the sheave in the rail, flung the loose rope behind him as he pulled hand-over-hand as fast as he could, entering into the spirit as a fox terrier might shake a rat and by his run-away yell he brought in the slack as follows:

A - way - a - a - ah - hey - a - a - hey, etc.

Instead of running along the deck with the rope, which was customary and often done with the braces, the man hauling in the sheet took his position close up to the sheave in the bulwarks, where the rope came through from the outside, and with one foot braced against the spare spar, which rested in a chock on top of the waterways and was lashed to the bulwarks, he could pull and sing out to his heart's content.

The standing part of the sheet was hooked into an eyebolt in the hull of the ship, just abaft the fore channels, with clip-hooks and seized to insure them from unhooking; then leading up through a single block in the clew of the foresail and back, outside the rail, to a sheave in the bulwarks, which was about ten or fifteen feet abaft the channels, it came inboard and forward to a pin in the rail.

The foot of the courses was longer than the width, or beam of the ship, and the sails spread out and around the shrouds. If the vessel was close-hauled (as near the wind as possible), the clew of the sail was brought around the shrouds and hauled aft. The foot of the sail often would saw or chafe against the shrouds, in sheeting home, and to prevent undue chafing the foot of the sail was fitted with leather, while the swifters were covered with chafing gear and the backstays with wooden or bamboo battens.

By the time our cook had pulled in most of the slack of the sheet there were enough hands to help sheet home the sail.

With the singing of "Whiskey," at the main upper topsail, the crew were in an exceptionally happy mood and the hard work of setting sail was somewhat eased by a couple of bottles of whiskey that had been concealed in the forecastle, that I was not wise to; but the sailors knew where to go and made frequent trips through the door, coming out in a short time with a fresh chew of tobacco, as if that were what they went after. No sailor was permitted to spit on the deck, but the lee scuppers were sometimes pretty black with tobacco juice before it was washed off. Expectorating over the rail perhaps led me to believe there was whiskey among the men, for each man, with a huge quid rolled up in his cheek, would have a merry twinkle in his eye as he wiped his mouth with the back of his hand, as he shuffled along the deck in an earnest manner, as only a sailor can, and it didn't require much thought to find out that he was feeling better than usual. The hearty sing-out and the energy behind it was an inevitable telltale.

The second mate was wise to the situation for he went into the forecastle and made a thorough search, raising mattresses in the bunks, turning over the sea-boots, etc., and was finally rewarded by bringing out a bottle, half-filled with whiskey, which he took into the cabin. Whether he shared with the mate or locked it up with the ship's stores we never found out, but it is only fair to say it didn't go back to the fo'c'sle.

With the setting of the foresail we next dropped the mainsail. The tack brings the weather clew of the sail, when on the wind, down almost to the rail, by a two-inch rope which renders under an S hook, like the fore, except that it is fitted with leather or pigskin and is hooked into a ring-bolt in the waterways. The tack leads from aft, forward, up to an iron pin in the rail. But with the wind on the quarter, as we were sailing, the weather clew is raised to allow the wind to fill the foresail, while the sheet trims aft to a sheave in the bulwarks near the break of the poop, coming inboard and forward, about fifteen feet, to a pin in the rail, giving room for six or eight men to grasp the sheet in sheeting home this big sail, which is the largest sail on the ship.

As we neared Boston Light and were about two miles to the southward, the pilot's boat was pulled up under our lee quarter preparatory to his leaving the ship. Soon after the captain called: "Mr. Sanborn, send those stowaways aft. We'll send them ashore with the pilot."

"Aye-aye, sir!" answered the second mate and going forward where they were working he marched them aft. As they passed Alonzo he couldn't resist giving them a "send off."

"You dirty curs!" said Alonzo. "You thought you were going to have a fine time with me on this voyage, didn't you? You didn't know that it was *I* that got your goat, did you? If anybody should ask you, I am the one you can thank for not completing this voyage," and pointing to himself with one hand he raised his cap and bared his head, bowing most gracefully as they passed.

"Oh, to hell wid you! Let me tell you one thing and put it in your pipe and smoke it. I'll be standing on the pier-head wid a belayin'-pin in me hand; an' damn me, I'll bust that fat face o' your'n wide open, so help me God!" answered one who went by the name of Mike and who was a son of the keeper of a noted North Street Sailor's Lodging House, whose reputation was indeed shady. No doubt he thought he would have a good opportunity of making good his threat as I was told later that he had been in the habit of meeting inbound ships as a runner for his father.

If the lodging house was in keeping with Mike's appearance it certainly must have been a filthy hole. I only knew of one man who was filthier and that was Bidley Soule of Duxbury, Massachusetts. This man was never known to take a bath, summer or winter, and he only made two shifts of clothing during the year. In the spring he took his heavier garments off for lighter ones and in the fall he exchanged them for heavier ones.

Bidley could never have gotten by with it in this age of sanitation and fumigation and how under the sun he was permitted to roam about the streets in his condition of filth and vermin I don't know, with ladies crossing the streets to get from under his lee or making sail into a neighbor's front yard until he passed, for he always had the right of way whether on the port tack or running before it. Everybody either hove-to or gave him plenty of sea room, keeping well to wind'ard of him. His appearance was enough and for one who didn't seek your company he had the widest acquaintance of anybody; yet I could never quite understand why he was allowed to run wild in that condition. To-day, he would be called upon by a waiting committee or dumped off the Mill bridge.

The stowaways went over the side, followed by the pilot, taking leave of us about 11 A.M., when they pulled away for the *Elsie,* to leeward, she having given us our hawser, which we pulled in over the bow and coiled on top of the forward house between the spare boats, to dry. Picking up the pilot and whistling three long whistles as a parting salute to us, she steamed away for Boston while we proceeded to set all sail, steering east by south.

Our crew by this time were all feeling the effects of the whiskey and were in the right mood for anything. On the whole they were most jubilant and with the order to set the main topgallant-sail, which is a long hoist, but not as heavy as the topsails, these gypsies of the deep, with muscles of steel, laid hold of the halliards, running their hands up the rope high above their heads, now swaying to the right and again to the left, as they pulled in unison, using their strength of arm as well as their bodies, the merry click of the patent blocks playing an interlude before the sing-out and soon brought forth the cry, "Oh, masthead her, ahoy!"

Jerry, who was exceptionally jubilant, having imbibed quite freely from the bottle in the fo'c'sle, and just in the mood for another chantey, started the "Drunken Sailor," giving all a chance to sing with him. This chantey is usually sung with a solo and chorus, but the condition of the men determines entirely how it shall be sung and there is nothing out of the way if all sing in unison. It was fifty-fifty with us and I doubt if they could have been headed off with a club, so earnest were they in their desire to be heard.

The drunken doctor, mentioned in this chantey, doesn't refer to a doctor of medicine. The cook of the vessel is dubbed "Doctor," but whether the name was given him on account of his mixing qualities, in concocting palatable dishes for the crew from the salt beef and briny pork with wormy sea biscuits, or in rationing out lime juice, in hot climates, as a preventive of yellow fever, I am unable to say. Be it as it is, all used the term and it was as natural for a sailor to address him as "Doctor," as it was to call the mate "Mister" or the carpenter "Chips"—a little matter of sailor etiquette understood by the whole crew.

Tug Boat "Elsie" of Boston. From a photograph made about 1890. Courtesy of Edward Upton Gleason.

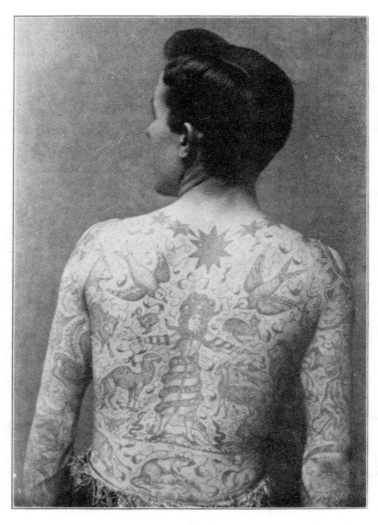

THE TATTOOED BACK OF A SAILOR

From a photograph by courtesy of E. W. Liberty

The Drunken Sailor, or, Up She Rises

What shall we do with a drunken sailor?
Chuck him in the longboat till he gets sober.

What shall we do with a drunken skipper?
Lock him in his stateroom till he gets sober.

What shall we do with a drunken chief mate?
Put him in the lazeret till he gets sober.

What shall we do with a drunken steward?
Lock him in the galley till he gets sober.

What shall we do with a drunken doctor?
Put him in the coal locker till he gets sober.

What shall we do with a drunken boy?
Hoist him to the royal yard till he gets sober.

With the setting of the topgallant-sails and royals the *Akbar* began to pick up headway with her easy roll and I looked about for Alonzo to see how he was making it as a sailor. I was just in time to see his pale face (for his pink cheeks had lost their color) coming from behind the house on the run bound for the lee rail to feed the fishes. He lost his breakfast and hung over the rail like a wet rag. The mate also saw his condition and hurried to his side as I supposed to help him. Not so, the mate.

"What in hell are you trying to do?" said he. "Trying to paint the side of the ship without a paint brush? If I catch you slobbering up the paint work you'll get that short-handled broom in damned quick order."

Alonzo turned and staggered towards his room, with the mate at his side, who told him in short order what to do for seasickness.

"Go to the Doctor and ask him for a piece of salt pork. Tie a rope-yarn to it and hold it in your hand. Stand by for a rush of guts to the head and when you feel it surge, swallow the pork, but hold on to the lanyard. The pork will drive it back and with everything quiet below pull the pork back with the lanyard."

At this, Alonzo lost all control as he reached his door and sitting on the sill, not caring whether he was in or out, he gave relief to his holdings right on the deck.

The mate at once grabbed him by the collar and stood him on his feet in no gentle manner. There he stood like a drunken man; knees, feet and hands, all limp; and shoving him roughly across the deck the mate made him get a bucket and the short broom. Trailing the broom behind with a bucket half-full of water and the mate prodding him along, Alonzo could only go as far as the main hatch where he set the bucket down between his knees and sitting on the comb-ings with his elbows on his knees and holding his head with his hands, the spasmodic contraction of the diaphragm was anything but hiccoughs.

"Get up, damn you, and get to work!" said the mate. I don't know how much further he would have gone had not the captain interfered. He had evidently been watching proceedings from the top of the cabin for he called to the mate:

"Mr. Burris, I think you had better send that boy below. He is in no condition to work. Set the main topmast-staysail."

"Set the main topmast-staysail, sir," replied the mate. In the next breath, he called, "A couple of you at the main topmast-staysail-halliards." I saw a look of disgust on the face of the second mate as the mate left Alonzo and couldn't help thinking what Alonzo said when we first came aboard, that he "would rather be in the second mate's watch than in the mate's." It showed that although Mr. Sanborn was gruff and severe yet he had a heart and that is more than the mate had shown during the past half-hour. Although the men were feeling pretty good from the effects of the whiskey, O'Rourke showed his disapproval of the mate's actions by saying in an undertone, unheard by the mate, while hoisting the main topmast-staysail:

"This bloody mate will git us all in trouble b'fore the viage ends, I'm a-tellin' ye's. Phat in the bloody hell does he git out o' ridin' a mere b'y loik thet? Ef he gits by wid it he'll soon be a-tryin' it on wan o' us an' I'm here t' tell ye's thet he'd better brail in his spanker an' not run against me luff or damn me, some dark night th' ship'll be need'n' another mate. That's phat it will!" Then to me, "Take a turn," for the sail was getting the breeze and was much harder to hoist.

Taking a turn under the belaying-pin, O'Rourke and "Handsome Charlie" began swaying off. The halliards led down to the starboard side of the fife-rail around the mainmast. Bracing their feet below and grasping the halliards above their heads these two men swayed away from the bitts, throwing their bodies backward for all the weight they had. This brought the halliards down until their bodies stood at right angles from the fife-rail; then bending their knees and holding all they had gained, they rendered the rope under the pin while I pulled in the slack ready for another pull.

The sing-out for this kind of work varies in call from

"Yo-ho, *he-oh!*" or "A-hoy, *boys!*" with the pull coming on the last word, to a semi-chantey. "Handsome Charlie" broke out in the latter,—one of negro origin.

Oh Ma-ry! Come down with your bunch of ro-ses! Come down when I call, Oh, Ma-ry! Oh, Ma-ry, come down!

Here, the pull for the sway-off comes on the accented notes. In the same measure a hold or pause is necessary while the rope is being rendered under the belaying-pin, giving time for the men to regain their feet and secure a fresh hold on the halliards above.

Mary and Julia are favorite names aboard ship, with the sailors, particularly in the sway-off, and the cry of "Oh-ho, Julia!" denotes a heavy pull all together, on *Julia.*

With the setting of the sail we next ran up the main topgallant-staysail and the mizzen topmast and topgallant-staysail followed. The ship was now under full sail and doing her best. At eight bells (noon) the second mate's watch went below for dinner while the rest of us were busy with the ropes, clearing the decks from the tangled mess. Fathoms of rope from the halliards, sheets and braces were coiled separately and neatly, at uniform length, from their individual pins along the rail and by the time we were called for dinner everything was in shipshape order.

Our dinner consisted of mutton stew, potatoes, boiled salt pork, soft-tack (white bread), ginger bread and coffee sweetened with molasses. I was as hungry as a bear and wasted no time in starting in. When I brought it into our room, Alonzo couldn't stand the smell of the stew and crawling out of his bunk again made for the lee rail where he remained for sometime, but came back before I had finished and rolled up in his blankets, turning his back to me. I asked him if he had rather I should go on deck and he replied in a feeble voice: "I don't think so. I guess I can stand it." His tone of voice told me plainly that he couldn't, so I took the safer side and picking up my tin plate of mutton and pot of coffee, finished my dinner on the main hatch in the cold.

Steering east by south from Boston Light, to clear Cape Cod some forty miles distant, we sighted the Cape about 3 P.M. At 4 P.M. everything was snug aboard the ship and the second mate's watch went below in the first dogwatch, all hands having been kept on deck during the day, busy with the sails, etc. There was no work in the dogwatch except to sweep up for the night and I was glad when the mate told me to put away my broom for I had been working pretty hard during the day.

Dave, the Tasmanian, who was in our watch, singled me out to talk to as we walked the decks together. There is no sitting down aboard ship while on deck during the day, except in the dogwatch, and sailors are permitted to do about as they please, but must be handy for a call at a moment's warning. Unless they are unusually tired, however, one seldom sees a sailor sitting. He walks for a rest and the habit remains with him through life.

It was about half-past five and just at dusk when Dave said to me: "Well, Fred! Take your last look at America. She'll soon be out of sight and it will be a hell of a long day before you see her again. Were you ever in Australia?"

"No, Dave," said I, "this is my first voyage to a foreign country."

"Is that so!" said he. "Well! you are bound for God's country, me boy! Melbourne is a fine city. Clean streets with water from the mountains running on both sides of the street to carry away the rubbish. The Royal Parks and Public Gardens are filled with pretty girls and it's no trick at all to sail alongside a fair damsel and enjoy yourself of a Sunday afternoon. America is too cold for me. I was told that Boston Common was a swell place for pretty girls, but damn it! I didn't see anything but ice. Wait till I git you in Melbourne.

I'll show you a town worth seeing. And when you've been with me an afternoon, I'll bet a sovereign you won't want to return to the States."

Twilight was fast approaching and the steward came out of the lamp-room with the side-lights and put them up in the fore-rigging, after which he walked aft with the binnacle-lights, two small brass lamps that lock into the binnacle, one on each side, throwing the rays of light on the compass for the benefit of the man at the wheel.

Kruse, an old Russian Finn, took the lookout on top of the t'gallant fo'c'sle deck. He wore his pea-jacket collar turned up around his ears and walked from port to starboard sucking a short-stemmed pipe from which the smoke curled from under his cap, drawn tightly over his forehead, resembling a miniature galley stove-pipe on the move. One would have thought the old man was there for the night instead of only a half-hour.

The *Akbar*, racing onward with a fine nor'west wind on the quarter, plunged into the waves ahead scattering a bright phosphorescent light about her bow as if to brighten her course. A cold, clammy feeling came over me in the silence about the ship for there was nothing to be heard except the squeaking of yards above where the jaws clung to the mast holding them in place as the vessel rolled to leeward. The mate was walking the weather side of the poop, alone, while the captain and second mate were below at supper. Big Hans was at the wheel and "Handsome Charlie," O'Rourke, Dave and I stood on the spare spar, to windward, watching the last rays of light on the land to westward. With the disappearance of the land, Cape Cod Light, a white light of unusual brightness, shone over the water off our quarter, a beacon, indeed, to warn approaching mariners of the danger ahead and to keep well to the nor'ard in entering Massachusetts Bay.

"Fred," said Charlie, "that's Highland Light and a mighty good one. You seldom see a brighter one and I'll tell you she looked mighty good ven ve sailed into Boston Roads last month."

"That's a good light, all right," said Dave, "but not half as bright as 'I'land Light below New York."

"A-h, phat th' bloody hell yer givin' us anyway!" said O'Rourke. "Dis Highland Light is de brightest light on d' coast or why d'ye call et Highland Light?"

"Bli' me! You don't know what you're talking about," said Dave. " 'I'land Light is the brightest on the Atlantic coast. It stands away up on a bluff and they nicknamed it 'Never Sink Light,' because it shines so far out to sea that vessels always have time to come about and fill away on another tack before grounding and that's why there are no wrecks around New York. They never go ashore and they never sink."

"A-h, phat do yous know about it! Where d'ye git th' informary?" said O'Rourke.

"Well, that's what they told me in New York," said Dave.

"Noo Yorick, be damned!" replied O'Rourke, "Phat d' they know about Cape Cod Light in Noo Yorick? That's phat I'd loik t' know, be dad!"

"Mr. O'Rourke," said I.

"Mister, be damned!" interrupted O'Rourke. "Dare's nobody but th' high-brows aft thet ye'll be after a-callin' Mister. Moi name's O'Rourke. Call me O'Rourke."

"I was going to say," said I, "that I think Dave is right about the brightness of the two lights."

"An' I'd loik t' know phat th' bloody hell yous know about et? Did ye ever see et?"

"Sure, I've seen it," I replied. "But to settle the argument, I've got a list of lights on the coast in my room—a small book published by the Government. That will settle the question."

They all followed me to my room where I read from the "Light List" of the Department of Commerce at Washington:

Cape Cod Light on the north-east side of Cape Cod, lat. 42° 02' 23″ N. long. 70° 03' 40″ W. Stands 195 feet above the water; is a white light of 1st order with 9,000 candlepower.

Navesink Light, on the easternmost spur of Navesink Highlands, N. J., lat. 40° 23′ 46″ N. long. 73° 59′ 09″ W. Stands 248 feet above the water, having two fixed white lights of 1st order with 9,000 candlepower each.*

"There you are," said Dave, "I thought I was right."

"An' so did I," replied O'Rourke. "Yous didn't know no more about et 'an I, an' phat th' bloody hell do th' book know about candlepower? Any —— —— could print thet in a book."

Dave and O'Rourke went on with their argument until the light disappeared in the distance astern. Finally Charlie brought up a new subject, saying,

"Who takes the veel at eight bells?"

"Faith! I tink ye's better be after lavin' thet job t' me, for it's been a long toime since I've had th' spokes of a weel in me mitts an' I' don't waant t' be chasin' th' bloody compass from hell t' breakfast in th' middle o' th' noight, half asleep," said O'Rourke.

"No!" said Charlie, "I've got it mapped out this vay. Let Dave take it and Fred can follow from ten to twelve. In the mornin' vatch I'll take the veel from four to six, and you can have it from six to eight, ven it is light."

"But Fred has never steered a square-rigger. Why not let him have the wheel from six to eight in the morning?" replied Dave.

I objected, explaining that if I could steer a schooner at night I could steer the *Akbar* and unless she was awfully hard to handle I would like the chance of standing my trick at the wheel with the rest. And so we decided to take it as outlined by Charlie.

Four bells were struck. The starboard watch came on deck relieving the wheel and lookout and before getting my sup-

* Both of these lights have since been replaced by better and different lights. Cape Cod Light now stands 183 feet above the water and can be seen twenty miles, having a candlepower of 580,000 and flashing white at intervals of five seconds, while Navesink stands 246 feet above water and can be seen twenty-two miles. Like Cape Cod, it flashes white every five seconds, but has a candlepower of 710,000.

per from the galley I waited for Hans as the mate sang out, "That'l do the watch."

I met Hans coming down the poop-deck ladder, upon being relieved at the wheel, and asked how she steered, walking the lee side to the galley with him.

"She bane a easy wessel to handle an' stheers youst like a ya'at," said he. This information satisfied me that I should have no trouble during my trick at the wheel from ten to twelve in the next watch and leaving him I went to my room for my tin pans to get my supper from the galley.

Alonzo was covered up in his blankets, a very sick boy, and wanted nothing in the way of supper. Even beefsteak and hot biscuits didn't tempt him and so I ate in silence. The smoky lamp still continued to do its part and was too disagreeable to permit the door being closed. Alonzo wanted only air and after finishing eating, I doused the glim and talked with him in the dark till eight bells, with the door wide open. It is needless to say I did most of the talking.

I put on all the surplus clothing I owned, dressing as warmly as I could for the evening watch, and went on deck, with the calling of the watch, so bundled up that "Handsome Charlie" laughed at me.

"Anyone vould think that you vere in the region of the North Pole. You don't call this cold, do you?" said he. "You should have been vith me last month in the *Cleopatra* in about this latitude. Talk about cold vedder; ve had it good and strong. De ship was loaded vith nitrates from Walparaiso, down to the scuppers. It come on to blow about sundown. The bob-stays, knight-heads and fore riggin' vas so covered vith ice that she vas down by the head. You couldn't valk for the ice on the decks. Life lines vere stretched fore-and-aft to hold on to. After eight bells had gone all hands vere called to shorten sail. Holy mackerel! How it blowed! Ven up aloft she shipped a sea nearly throwin' her on her beam-ends. The lashings to the spare topmast vas all frozen and snapped off joust like paper and the topmast vas adrift on the decks. It didn't take more than a couple of seas, after she had righted, to carry avay the lee bulvarks and the bloody topmast vent on the run by the board. Ven ve got down from aloft the mate vas missin' and ve think he vent overboard vith the topmast and drowned. If he didn't drown he froze to death a-hangin' to the spar. There vas hardly a man vot didn't have his hands or feet frosted. There vas ice a-hangin' to the riggin' ven ve arrived in Boston and some of the newspapers had a fortegraph of us taken. Didn't you see it?"

I did remember seeing the account of it and told him so. Here Andy came past us and Charlie stopped him, catching him by the arm in good-natured way, saying:

"Vot are you doin' out here? Ain't you in this starboard vatch?"

"No," said Andy, "I'm in the mate's vatch."

"Vare vere you in the dogvatch? I didn't see you," said Charlie.

"Oh, I vas in the fo'c'sle, out of sight," said Andy. "I am not goin' t' show meself to dis mate any more than I can bloody vell help. He takes me for the poy an' joust so soon as he sees me, up aloft he sends me to pick Irish pennants out of the riggin'. Joust because I'm the littlest man aboard, I ain't a poy. I'm now five years as able seaman. Dis bloody mate makes me tired." And spitting a mouthful of tobacco juice down the mouth of the bilge pumps he showed his disgust by kicking a coil of rope hanging from the fife-rail, no doubt as he would like to kick the mate.

"This gives us another man at the veel that I forgot," said Charlie. "Now it's better and easier to keep run of because the man on lookout to-night will have the same hours at the veel day after to-morrow."

"How do you figure that way?" I asked.

"Vell, the *Cleopatra* had seven men in a vatch and that is the vay vith this ship. Seven men joust makes right. See!" said Charlie.

"Hold on, Andy!" said he. "Ve arranged in the dogvatch not countin' you in. It's better you go and relieve O'Rourke on the lookout now. Then you follow Kruse at the veel. This makes you come on at the veel to-morrow from four bells to eight bells in the afternoon."

Andy scratched his head, to think for a while, and said,

"Vell, if I don't steer till then, mox nix ouse vid me." So saying he went forward and Charlie explained that Andy being the last man and following Kruse he, of course, would be the last man in our watch to take his trick at the wheel.

O'Rourke wasted no time in getting down from the fo'-c'sle-head and joining us said, "That was a bloody good turn you done me, Charlie."

We continued to walk the decks while Charlie talked to me about his conquests in a North Street dance house where he spent all his earnings from the last voyage quicker than he thought he could have done; but being drunk most of the time, he concluded it must have been all right because he had nothing to show how he spent his money. He remembered on two occasions of inviting the whole house to drink with him and on several occasions of awakening from a drunken slumber with his shoes and stockings on. The boarding-house keeper took care of his money dealing it out in small sums as he wanted it, but never as much as he asked for. He didn't mistrust the keeper for he was always giving advice—how he should be very careful and not drink too much while at the dance houses and particularly warned him against the maids who would not hesitate to pick his pocket if an opportunity presented itself. His tale of awakening with no money left, when he thought he had plenty with the keeper, sounded like the stories we read of the poor unfortunate sailor ashore. It was awfully good of the house to find him a ship like the *Akbar*, bound for Australia, where times were good and no trouble at all for sailors to get a job ashore at twice the wages paid A B's in America; and by drawing a month's advance when he shipped, he was able to pay off his indebtedness. The boarding-house keeper had bills for everything he had spent, therefore he considered himself fortunate in being an inmate of so honest a house that could give an accurate account of the money he had spent while in a state of intoxication when other houses would simply steal him blind. So interesting was his account of his conquests ashore that four bells struck before I knew it.

"Four bells, Fred," said Charlie. "Your veel."

The mate walked the weather side of the quarter-deck as I made my way up the lee companionway ladder and on to the wheel.

"Southe-east by southe," called Dave, as I took the wheel.

"Southe-east by southe," I answered, while Dave walked forward thrashing his hands about his body in an effort to keep warm and was soon on the main-deck. I had a firm grasp on the spokes for there was a good breeze and quite a sea running and was surprised to see how easily the ship steered, but was brought to my senses by the mate calling:

"Who in hell sent you here at this time of the night? What do you know about steering? Here!—Dave! Dave! Come back here and take the wheel. What in hell are you all trying to do by sending this man to the wheel without standing by?" And hobbling to leeward he ran to the break of the poop, shouting as he ran.

I found that the diamond screw shaft of the wheel was a great improvement over the old tiller ropes of the *Floyd* which were often so slacked that at times the kicking of the wheel, from the action of the waves against the rudder, made it almost impossible to hold. With the *Akbar* there was very little kicking and I had no difficulty in keeping her straight. I was helmsman enough not to wear myself out by running the wheel hard up or hard down, as the compass swung from starboard to port across the lubber's-mark, and while Dave was returning I thought of the words of Captain Winslow, off Point Judith, "If she begins to swing too far, meet her with a spoke or two."

I had my eye on the mark and the ship was on her course when the mate and Dave returned. The mate stuck his head in front of me to see how she headed, while I looked aloft to catch a star, on the luff of the topgallant sail, to help me in my steering.

"Take the wheel, Dave, till I can get another man," said the mate.

"Hold on, Mr. Burris," said I. "I can steer this ship. She's on her course now and when I can't keep her straight you can send me for'ard. Let Dave stand by till you are satisfied. I have steered a schooner in a worse sea than this and I will have no trouble now."

He evidently soon thought so for he told Dave to stand by. After watching me for about five minutes Dave ventured to suggest that I was doing all right and asked if he couldn't go forward.

"I'll tell you when to go for'ard. You're doing well as you are," said the mate, without turning his head, which was thrown back on his shoulders while he watched the luff of the topgallant sail against the sky above, picking out a star near the sail that might tell the instant the ship would swing away from her course. I knew he was watching the star very closely and I determined to keep the ship on her course at all hazards. He looked neither to the right nor to the left and didn't speak a word till I rang five bells; then coming to the binnacle he took a look at the compass and then at Dave.

"What do you think, Dave?" asked the mate. "Do you think he can steer without your assistance?"

"Sure he can! I 'aven't given him any assistance all the time I 'ave been standin' here," said Dave, in an impatient manner, for he was cold and anxious to get down from the quarter-deck away from the wind to the main-deck which is more sheltered.

"You seem to think I don't know what I'm doing. I don't want any grouchiness from you and I want you to distinctly understand that you are here to obey orders. If I want you to stay here all the watch, you'll stay and stay pleasantly, do you understand?" questioned the mate.

"I understand, sir," said Dave, for there was nothing he could say to please the mate by telling him what he thought of the situation.

"I've a good notion to keep you here as it is," said the mate, "but I'll let you off this time. You can go for'ard and stand by for a call. We don't want the ship to broach to."

"You'll not see her broach to," said I.

"Shut your damned trap while you're at the wheel. I'll do all the talking aboard this ship when it's necessary," quickly replied the mate.

Dave went forward and the mate, walking the weather gangway, took turns in watching the compass and the star against the luff of the topgallant sail, while I was left to do the heavy thinking in silence. With a big sea raising the stern of the ship the bow would bury itself in the waves ahead as she rolled; then, with the wave amidships and a list to port, the *Akbar* would take a slant to starboard, while I stood with my feet braced on the grating, pulling up on the spoke with my right hand and shoving the spoke on top of the wheel with my left with all my weight. I held her in a grip that was indeed pleasing. Spoke by spoke as she needed it and with the raising of the bow again, the bob-stays and back-ropes dripping with water,—down would settle the stern with a splash on the sea under her counter that was to send her head again into a pillow of white spray as she raced over the waves; then giving a spoke or two, to ease her, and again holding with all my strength, I steered on enjoying every minute till eight bells.

Mr. Burris had no occasion, during this time, to sing out "Mind your helm" or even to complain that I was not on the course I was steering, for I was determined to show him that I was equal to the task of keeping her straight although the cold wind was chilling me through and through.

On a cold winter's night there is not much enjoyment in standing one's trick at the wheel; but cold as it was, it was a great satisfaction that I was able to keep the ship on her course. I looked forward with pleasure, however, as the clock in the cabin pointed near eight bells, and with the striking of the clock I jerked the lanyard of the small bell with a defiant air, giving a distinct pause between the two quick bells in succession, thus: Ding-ding! . . . Ding-ding! . . . Ding-ding! . . . Ding-ding! "Can you do any better?" thought I.

The mate was evidently as cold as I and before the last bell rang he was at the break of the poop calling, "Eight bells, there! Call the watch!"

I heard the reply, "Call the watch, sir!" but it seemed a long time before Jim Dunn came aft to relieve me. Giving him the course I glanced at the cabin clock, on my way to leeward, and was surprised to find not quite five minutes had elapsed since I rang eight bells and when you consider that Jim had to dress extra warm, after being routed out of a sound sleep, five minutes is none too long, on a cold winter's night, for a change of watches; in fact, it is about as quick as it can be made.

The day had been a strenuous one for me and I was pretty tired and glad of the opportunity to quit the deck and tumble into my "donkey's breakfast." Alonzo was apparently sleeping and on reaching the room I crawled into my bunk as noiselessly as possible, wrapping the blankets around my feet and legs and with my overcoat thrown over them, to give all the warmth possible where needed and was soon fast asleep and dreaming of steering the *Akbar* against the schooner *David G. Floyd,* in a race in which the *Floyd* had the weather berth and was gaining all the while.

I was awakened from a troubled sleep by a sailor calling, "Tumble out of there, Fred, eight bells are gone!"

Jumping out of my berth and lighting the lamp to dress by, Alonzo said:

"Gee whiz, Fred! You kept me awake all this watch with your twisting and turning. Are you sick?"

I answered by biting into a sea-biscuit, as I dressed.

"What made you groan so?" he asked.

"It was a bad case of nightmare," said I. "I'll tell you about it when the wheel has been relieved, and I left abruptly for the watch was assembling about the main hatch.

There was no sweating up of the halliards nor pulling on the braces and I was soon back talking with Alonzo.

The customary manner of calling the watch at night was much as follows: At eight bells the officer of the deck called to the men, "Call the watch." This was answered by one of them, "Call the watch, sir," and on his way to the forecastle he would take a belaying-pin from the rail and on reaching the door and sliding it back, he would beat a tattoo, making as much noise as possible and at the same time lustily calling out:

Hay - a - ay you sleep -ers! Port watch on deck   a - hoy!

In his natural voice he would then call: "Tumble out of there, you port watchers. Eight bells!"

The starboard watch was often called by members of the crew, "Star-bollins." These names didn't always apply for often names were given to the watch that couldn't be found in the dictionary and were not mentioned in prayer meetings. But whatever you were called there was no mistaking the idea that you were wanted on deck with all speed possible. The last man out or the last man at a pull on the braces, if the habit continued, was usually reminded of the fact in no gentle tones. Consequently we all had a certain pride in our work and adopted the motto, "Be the first to answer a call and see that you get there."

This spirit has long since died out and I blush for the sailor of to-day. In the '90's, I stood on the dock at Seattle, watching and admiring the ship *Spartan,* an old-time three-skysail-yarder, taking in coal from the bunkers. It was necessary to move the chute. The fore yard was at cockbill and the braces fouled the top of the chute as it was moved aft. The mate called to one of the crew to jump up and clear it. There was no hearty response of an "Aye, aye, sir!", but instead, the sailor looked at the mate, as much as to say, "How do you expect me to get up there?" and then looking aloft he surveyed the situation, without a reply, and took his good old time in clearing the brace. I walked away in disgust, glad that I had given up the sea as a means of living.

Some years later I had occasion to instruct a building contractor in the correct way to reeve a tackle for the hoist of an elevator. He was reeving the rope backhanded. Landlubber that he was he persisted, saying, "What's the difference? It will hoist, won't it?"

I explained that by reeving the rope as one would coil it from left to right, it would keep the lay of the rope in its place and give it a longer life. The man still argued that it made no difference; whereupon I told him that as a boy my first lesson aboard ship was to coil a rope and reeve a tackle correctly and I bet with him the drinks that any ship in the harbor would substantiate my argument. There he could see for himself that all tackles were rove in the same manner. So he agreed to go with me to the nearest ship, which was only a short distance from us. She was not a square-rigger, but the steamer *Valencia*, which I said would answer the question just as well.

On reaching her we found six lifeboats, swung inboard from the davits, and I was amazed to find that out of the six boats, on the side, there were only two tackles rove correctly. Two, out of twelve. Think of it!

Oh, you sailors of to-day! There is no incentive for you to improve in your work. No goal to reach. The same is true with the apprentices in most of the trades. You learn your trade by skimping through—pay your dollar dues and are called skilled workmen before your eyeteeth are cut. Put it to yourself! How does the journeyman of to-day compare with the journeyman of forty years ago? There is no comparison! And the same can be said of the sailors.

It is needless to say that the contractor had the laugh on me and as I agreed to go by what we found on the steamer I had to set 'em up; but we rove the elevator fall according to my way of thinking.

The following year, the *Valencia*, bound from San Francisco to Seattle, on January 25, 1906, overran herself, in thick heavy weather, off Cape Flattery, and piled up on the rocky coast of Vancouver Island, near Cape Beale, in the middle of the night, when 115 souls perished in one of the worst disasters on the Northwest coast.

In the course of the investigation I remember reading that the crew were all of the best and there was no question as to their seamanship. Now this crew had nothing to do with the ship the year previous, but one of the boats, filled with passengers, while being lowered from the davits, cockbilled, throwing the occupants into the raging waves below where they were drowned like rats. One of the falls either parted or got beyond control, smashing the boat against the side of the ship and one end came down with a run while the other hung in mid-air. This, probably had nothing to do with the correct way of reeving the davit falls, but no one could explain just how the accident occurred. Suffice to say, there was an accident for which we cannot account and one too appalling for words.

CHAPTER VII

SALT HORSE AND DISCIPLINE

IN THE afternoon watch of the second day we got our anchors on the forecastle-head and stowed the cable below. The wind had moderated to a gentle breeze, but there was quite a heavy swell. In unshipping the stock of the port anchor, which was of iron, it got beyond control and fell across the shins of O'Rourke, nearly breaking his legs. He wouldn't go below, although he was unable to be of any assistance about the deck, and spent the rest of his watch sitting on the bitts and rubbing his shins.

The morning of the third day we had little or no wind and what little there was came from the southeast and being still on the starboard tack we sailed close-hauled all day. In the evening the wind increased and at eight-thirty all hands were called to tack ship in a disagreeable rain.

Each man has his particular place and work to do in coming about. The mate stationed me at the lee cross-jack brace, which leads down abaft the mainmast to the fife-rail, together with the mizzen lower and upper topsail braces, to their separate pins, all abaft the mainmast. The coils of the lee braces were all taken from the pins and laid carefully down on the deck. The end of the brace at the bottom of the coil was hitched to its respective pin, so it would not unreeve when the yards swung round. The cross-jack brace lay well over on the midship plank while the mizzen lower and upper topsail braces lay next, in front of their respective pins.

The braces leading to the rail were flaked carefully along the deck, as in an endless scroll, care being taken that there were no kinks or bights that might foul while running through the blocks, for when the yards begin to swing all the braces uncoil and simply whiz through the blocks while the men on the other side of the vessel are pulling in the slack as quickly as possible.

In getting the ship ready for coming about, the mizzen

lower and upper topsail braces were taken from their pins to leeward and carried to the pin of the cross-jack brace where I was told to hold a turn and await the cry from the "Old Man" of "Mainsail, haul!" when I should let them all go by the run and jump to windward to pull down the mizzen-topsail brace, while Andy stood next to me to take care of the cross-jack brace.

When everything was ready for coming about the mate called to the captain, "All ready, sir!"

The captain, who was watching proceedings on deck from the poop, called to the man at the wheel, "Give her a good full," which he answered in the usual style.

The ship, falling off to a good full, gathered headway, throwing the spray over the bow, and when sailing at her best possible speed the "Old Man" sang out, "Ready about!"

This was a warning for us to be ready for the next command when he called to the helmsman, "Hard-a-lee!"

"Hard-a-lee, sir!" he answered, and stepping off the grating where he could get a better purchase on the spokes of the wheel he pulled down one after the other in rapid succession, until she was hard down. The ship answered the rudder quickly for the jib-sheets had been eased up and there was nothing ahead to hold her bow. On she flew into the wind, meeting the waves at every plunge and sending the spray high over the knight-heads. The ship was then "in stays" and on an even keel. The sails and blocks, flapping and slatting back and forth, were making a deafening noise, yet the captain's voice was heard above the din in his next command, "Tacks and sheets!"

Here the men in charge slackened away while those at the clew garnets, with their mournful cry, raised the corner of the courses towards the slings of the yard. This added more noise from those large sails which slatted back and forth; now, against the mast and then, with a slap, in the wind. With the wind dead ahead I heard the order I was waiting for.

"Main topsail haul!" cried the "Old Man," and I let the

braces go by the run. The yards on being released from leeward swung around in a lively manner and I ran in front of
Andy to help with the starboard braces of the mizzen lower
topsail. He stepped back to make room for me to pass and in
doing so stepped into the coil of the cross-jack brace which
was uncoiling at a rapid pace. A turn about his leg fastened
itself into a jam-hitch under his heel and lifted him off his
feet and with a cry he shot up above my head into the fair-
leader, which carried away from the force with which he
struck it some fifteen feet above my head.

"Hold on! Hold on!" he cried. "Don't pull on that
brace!"

This was meant for me, but in the next breath he came
down with a run, all in a heap, amid the flying braces, striking on his head and shoulders and rolling under the fife-rail,
half stunned, but soon picking himself up to pull in the rest
of the cross-jack brace that was left dangling a moment
before. All this happened so swiftly that I didn't know but
this part of the play was in the regular routine of tacking
ship. Everything was in confusion and everywhere each man
had his individual runaway yell. The mate was swearing a
blue streak and the captain was calling in an excited manner
at something I was unable to fathom. The sails at the fore
were all aback and the jib sheets to windward. With all this
headsail swinging the bow rapidly off the captain sang out,
"Let go and haul!"

This is generally the last order from the captain, but that
night things were different. The jib-sheets were let go to
windward while the fore yard began to swing. The heavy
yards were pointed to the wind and the sails catching the
wind, everything came around on the other side with a bang.
My sleeves were wet to the elbow from the rain standing
on the braces which oozed through my fingers and down my
wrist and forearm as I pulled down on the mizzen-topsail
braces.

In a drizzling rain there is nothing quite so uncomfortable
as to feel the cold water run down your shirt sleeve every
time you close your fingers around a rope. I didn't look aloft

any oftener than I had to, on account of the rain, and being a novice aboard a square-rigger I was unwise as to what had happened aloft while we were boarding the tacks and sheeting home the courses, at the same time obeying an order to "Take in the main royal and topgallant sails."

All this happened so quickly, while the men were hurrying back and forth, cursing at every breath, "A hell of a note," etc., that I asked Andy, my side partner, who was delegated with me to clear up the decks, if anything unusual had happened.

"Anything out of the vay? Ya-ah! Ve carried away the main t'gallant yard. The bloody mate didn't let go the brace an' she's hangin' in two pieces up there," said he.

Just then old Kruse came forward with a tale of woe.

"Waht d' ye tink happens for'ard? Nottings but the fore r'yal beckstay carried away," asking and answering the question at the same time. "Ye mark my vords, ve have one hell 'ev a time yet in dis ships," he continued. "Verst, Pat he looze a leg an' ees sent ashore. Den ve sail oon Friday. Holy Ghost! dat's bad! Now, ve tack ship de verst time an' de t'galland jard, he carries avay an' de fore r'yal beckstay ees busted. Vare vill ve be before ve gits t' Melbourne? It looks wery bad." All this was said in an undertone while we were straightening out the tangled ropes.

Kruse, a Russian Finn, from on the Gulf of Bothnia, spoke Pigeon-English, Swedish and German equally well. He was very superstitious and worried himself sick because of the signs that came and went while on the voyage. He was always asking me about dates, because he knew I kept a journal of the voyage and more than once he woke me in the middle of our watch below to substantiate some theory, and after a time he became a regular nuisance.

The fore yard bringing up against the royal backstay seemed to him as much of a calamity as the carrying away of the main topgallant yard. The topgallant yard was secured to the topgallant mast, by the men aloft, but it was five bells before we were sent below and I had a chance to get into a dry shift of clothing. There was only an hour and a half left in our watch, but I tumbled into my bunk as soon as I could for the little sleep that I was entitled to.

The following Monday came in with a drizzling rain and light and variable winds which finally settled in the north-west and blew stronger. In the latter part of the watch there was a call from the mate, "Stand by the royal halliards," and the wind coming in puffs it was soon followed by, "Let go and clew up."

After the sails were clewed up he called, "Jump aloft and take 'em in." I jumped into the mizzen rigging with a "Take it in, sir!" when he sang out: "What do you know about furling a square-s'l? Better come down out of there and let a man do it."

I was already above the sheer-pole with a good start and answered,

"I'm man enough for this job," and ran up the shrouds as quickly as possible for I was afraid he would insist on my coming down.

No fear of it! Not he! And I was soon over the top, in her roll to leeward, and halfway up the topmast rigging before I stopped.

From the topmast cross-trees I had to shin to the royal yard. The sail flapped above me, shaking the mast, and standing on the foot-rope, nearly out of breath, I paused to survey the situation, with one hand grasping the grommet and the other on the jack-stay. There was a good easy swell, but the ship listed under the stress of wind which was all she could hold and the deck seemed so small below, looking altogether different from this bird's-eye view than when on deck and entirely different from the view I had on the royal yard my brother and I had set up in the attic, and I smiled with a feeling of pride that I had mastered the art of furling a royal at home.

A puff of wind caused the ship to roll to leeward and a pitch into the next sea brought me to my senses; that I must take in the sail before the situation was any worse; and dig-ging my fingers into the canvas and bracing my knees under the yard, I pulled the canvas to windward, on top of the yard, holding under my stomach the sail gathered in until I had reached the foot, where I put a temporary turn around the yard with the end of the gasket until I had rolled up the sail. Then to leeward I went, pulling the sail towards the bunt until everything was rolled up nicely. Passing the gasket and going back to windward I finished with a regular harbor furl.

On regaining the deck the mate asked, "Where did you learn to furl a royal?" for he had watched my work aloft and thinking he was finding fault I asked,

"What's wrong with it, sir?"

"Nothing's wrong with it," said he. "But I don't see how you can learn to furl a sail that way in a schooner."

"I shipped as ordinary seaman," said I, "and an ordinary seaman is supposed to reef, hand and steer. If I couldn't do this, I'd still be a boy, sir," and without further explanation I walked forward with a cocky air, glad to hear that I had at last done something that the mate had not found fault with.

I had no sooner joined the other members of the watch than he called, "Stand by the t'gallant halliards."

Here, old Kruse came by cursing a blue streak. "Damn the luck! Deese is th' thurdeenth of th' month. I know'd sunthin' 'ud happen," said he. "What did I tole ye?"

"Let go and clew up!" shouted the mate. "A couple of hands jump up and take 'em in."

The flying-jib was also taken in and on reaching the deck, after furling the topgallant sails, the mate sang out, "Call all hands to reef the mainsail!"

The wind was now blowing a gale from the northwest, with the wind on our quarter and this big sail required all hands to handle it. The starboard watch came on deck with a rush and a cry at the clew-garnets and raised the clews while the tack and sheet were eased off. With the help of the buntlines, leech-lines and spilling-lines, some of the wind was smothered from the sail but there was a flapping of canvas about the mainstay that shook the whole ship in a tremor. The reef-tackles hauled the reef-band of the sail well out to the yardarm and then there was a race up the rigging by the sailors to see who should be first to straddle the weather yardarm, to pass and pull away on the earing and lash the cringle in the reef-band to the yardarm. Then, picking up the sail until the reef-points were reached, we waited the cry "Haul out to wind'ard," when every inch obtainable was stretched to windward and the weather earing was made fast. In the same manner the sail was then stretched to leeward with the "Haul out to lu'ard!" and likewise made fast. The men then knotted the reef-points around and on top of the yard and when all was secure and the main tack down, the sail was sheeted home and the ship put on her course again.

In the afternoon, with the weather moderating, the fore topgallant yard was sent down and crossed on the main, while the broken yard was sent down until we could make another. At five o'clock on the morning of the next day, the wind increasing, we took in the jibs and upper topsails and furled the reefed mainsail. It was my first experience and a queer sensation.

The men strung out along the yard, standing on the foot-rope, threw their heels high in the air and bending over the yard, with heads downward, reached with their hands as far down as possible in order to pick up the sail and roll it on top of the yard. At first I thought I was being thrown over the yard, head first; but I soon found that my knees, braced against the yard, held me quite secure and it was astonishing how quickly I got used to the situation and was able to use both hands without the thought of falling. With heels high in the air and a cry "Yo-ho, high-o!" our feet swung down as suddenly as they went up while I hung on for dear life expecting to be thrown backward. No such ill luck, for I had a handful of No. 1 duck canvas that I had dug my finger nails into. My fingers were bleeding at the nails because the sail refused to slacken enough for me to grasp it and so I fought and pounded to make a dent that I could hold on to. We all did it and the most of us fought and cursed the sail and everybody else until the air was actually blue from blaspheming.

That afternoon, with a high sea running and decks awash, while going aft to take the wheel, I watched my chance to run from the weather main rigging to the gangway at the break of the poop and got a good start, but before I could reach the corner of the cabin the ship lurched to leeward while I jumped for the corner. My hands caught the side of the cabin, but the corner, being rounded off, my fingers slipped as a sea slopped over the quarter rail, wetting my hands, and I lost my hold. The decks were wet and slimy and my feet slipped from under and down I fell, flat on my stomach and was thrown around sliding head-first across the deck. I tried to catch the spar on the waterways, as I slid, but failed and my hands went under the spar and my head struck the place where my hands should have been. My forehead was badly bruised and I came out of the water wet through, but not seriously hurt. Standing knee-deep in the scuppers I shook myself, very much as a water spaniel might have done, furnishing no little amusement for the rest of the watch while going up the lee gangway.

The weather continued unsettled for several days, during which we set and took in our upper sails every day.

Ten days out Alonzo came on deck for the first time since leaving Boston. We celebrated his appearance by sending down the fore topgallant yard that had been in use on the main, putting it back at the fore, where we had had no sail, and crossing the new main topgallant yard and bending the sails as before. He was unable to stay to see the job finished and had to turn in again. It was during this watch that I saw my first school of flying-fish. They were about the size of a smelt, having long pectoral wings. Jumping from the crest of a wave they are able to fly to windward from 500 to 1,000 feet or more, depending on the moisture of their wings. When they become dry they are obliged to dive back into the water. I have seen a dolphin chasing a flying-fish, breaking out of a wave just behind the flying-fish, which seemed to fly to avoid being caught. The dolphin kept just under the flying-fish waiting for it to alight, just as a trout watches a grasshopper flying into a brook. The flying-fish seemed to know that it was being watched and flew to a distant wave where it dipped its wings and darted off at a right angle, thus avoiding its pursuer. The dolphin is considered the swiftest fish that swims and the flying-fish must have a good start on the dolphin to avoid being caught. They usually fly at a height of about ten feet above the water and often strike against the sails at night. If the ship's cook is friendly, he will fry this little delicacy for the one fortunate enough to find it.

I found one that flew into the main-topmast staysail and Charlie was struck on the shoulder by another which he caught and gave to me. The "doctor" consenting to fry them for breakfast, I shared with Alonzo who said it was the finest eating of anything he had tasted since leaving Boston. It was really more than he could eat. The poor fellow didn't eat enough to feed a canary. His full face and rosy cheeks had vanished and he was beginning to show the effects of keeping in his bunk.

The cracker hash, which was our usual morning breakfast, was a mixture of broken pieces of hard-tack soaked in water until it became soft and then mixed with pieces of salt beef, pork and sliced onions to give it a flavor. This "lobscouse" was usually more than Alonzo could stand, but I was very fond of it when it was baked with a crisp top. The coffee, sweetened with sorghum molasses, now began to taste strong as the water was drawn from an iron tank and no doubt was quite rusty.

The cabin fare was the same as ours except that they had sugar for coffee and butter on their white bread (soft-tack) with a few delicacies thrown in. We had salt beef and pork, good of the kind, but the cabin was furnished with the choice cuts. The beef came in three-hundred-pound casks and was soaked in brine well saturated with saltpeter. When taken from the cask it was as red as a flannel shirt. It was put into a wooden oval cask, holding about forty gallons, larger at the bottom than the top to keep it from capsizing. The wood was usually scraped and oiled on the outside and bound with brass hoops, which were polished bright, and this piece of deck furniture, called a "harness-cask," was used exclusively for soaking out salt meat by covering it with salt water. The meat was allowed to soak for a day or so before it was fresh enough to cook.

It was customary at this time, when a cask of salt beef was opened, to let the steward first pick out the choice pieces, for the cabin, and leave the lean pieces for the crew. These were called by the sailors "old horse" and were thrown into the "harness-cask" only as the cook needed them. The name of "old horse" is ancient history. Richard H. Dana in his "Two Years before the Mast" says, "There is a story current among seamen that a beef-dealer was convicted, at Boston, of having sold an old horse for ship's stores, instead of beef, and had been sentenced to be confined in jail until he should eat the whole of it, and that he is now lying in Boston jail." He also quotes the rhyme all sailors knew in my time, "Old horse! Old horse! what brought you here?" This would seem to show that the name is purely American.

Another writer claims the words to be of Welsh extraction of years ago. The fact that Dana mentions the "harness-cask" would indicate that it was used years before he went to sea and he sailed from Boston, around the Horn to California in the brig *Pilgrim*, in the year 1834.

The "harness-cask" no doubt obtained its name from throwing the scraps of the old salt beef to be soaked out in a tub and it is easily understood how these scraps could have been called the horse's harness. Even in my day I have heard some old sailor with a grouch, when the evening meal was brought in, stab at a particularly uninviting dry piece of salt beef, with his fork or sheath-knife, in a vicious manner and with an oath that would arrest the attention of us all, hold it above the pan and reverently proceed to recite the well-known rhyme:

> Old horse! old horse! what brought you here?
> From Sacarap' to Portland pier
> I carted stone for many a year.
> I labored long and well, alack,

'Till I fell down and broke my back.
They picked me up with sore abuse
And salted me down for sailor's use.
The sailors they do me despise,
They pick me up and damn my eyes,
They eat my flesh and gnaw my bones
And throw the rest to Davy Jones.

On Wednesdays and Saturdays, we had soft-tack and duff. The cabin duff was seasoned with spice and plums or raisins and served with lemon or wine sauce. The crew's duff was steamed in a cloth sack and was seasoned with salt and dried apples and served with molasses. Too much spice and wine sauce is not good for sailors. It is liable to ruin one's appetite. The salt beef is not noted for its moisture and usually was as dry as a chip; but with salt pork, which we were allowed three times per week and is quite a delicacy, the beef was eatable. It takes a little time to get used to salt beef and at first it takes the skin off the roof of your mouth, but as with your hands in hauling ropes, your mouth soon becomes calloused and the sailor can digest anything he can swallow.

In rainy weather the "harness-cask" was scrubbed out and taken aft to catch the rain-water from the top of the cabin. A short piece of hose connected the down spout or scupper to the cask, from which the water was dipped from the top, by deck-buckets, and carried by the sailors to fill the empty water-casks on deck.

The water in the first cask was usually very brackish, but it could be used by the cook. One of the most disagreeable tasks aboard ship was to carry rain-water at night, in the rain, to fill an empty water-cask.

Although you may be wearing oilskins, more or less water slops from the bucket across your legs and over your feet while walking the deck of a rolling ship and on reaching the empty cask, where a funnel made of sheet copper is inserted in the bung-hole, on top of the bilge and about four feet from the deck, in raising the bucket over the funnel about half of the remaining contents is poured into the cask while the rest usually slops down your sleeves and about your stomach, as you lean against the cask, and by the time it is filled you are wet from head to foot.

In the daytime, unless it was raining very hard, the first catch, being brackish, was used for scrubbing paint work. While this work was also very disagreeable I preferred it to carrying water at night. While scrubbing we had a bucket of rain-water and a bucket half-full of beach sand, for two sailors. We also had a piece of old canvas to use as a cloth to wash the paint work about the bulwarks and this was not very soft so the rust stains and blotches of tar on the stanchions couldn't be removed as quickly as they would have been had the cloth been pliable. Dipping the canvas into the bucket of beach sand helped the work, but even this sometimes failed and then the mate in his generosity would throw a handful of lye into the water and this usually removed the stains, and the skin from your fingers as well.

A couple of hours' work in this solution would put a beautiful brown color under your finger nails and before you were through they would resemble shingles on a weather-beaten house in August.

On board ship we took pride in showing our flippers, stained and calloused, for delicate hands, before the mast, were a sign of effeminacy and meant shirking work. On shore it was different. A deep-water ship is rattled down, tarred, scrubbed and painted to look her finest just before reaching the home port. The sailor, also, on reaching shore takes pride in dressing his finest. But no matter how well dressed, his hands stand out in evidence of the hard work he has just been through and they look decidedly out of place when thrust through a pair of white grommets, called cuffs.

Upon reaching New York, after the voyage, I was entirely out of shore clothes and so bought a suit of clothes and a "biled shirt," etc., intending to go home properly dressed. I also decided that a pair of kid gloves might cover my ungainly hands and making my wants known to the clerk he asked, "What size do you wear?" I couldn't remember and he said he would take my measure. Not wishing to show him my horny hand, I extended it palm down while he passed a strap around, reeving the end through a buckle and cinched it up snugly.

"Now close your hand tightly," said he. I shut my hand, but in doing so the expansion of the muscles was too much for the slight strap and the buckle spread apart as if made of lead. The clerk looked in astonishment, but when I showed him the inside of my hands he laughingly suggested that I should be fitted with rubber gloves—something that would stretch. However, I bought a pair of kid gloves which I thought were as ungainly as my bare hands, and left the store conscious that everybody I passed threw his port eye at me in a knowing manner.

The night before Christmas came on with squally, rainy weather and I had the scare of my life in the evening watch. We were sailing under topsails with a strong northwest wind on our quarter. The night was dark and dreary and the lights in the binnacle were constantly going out. About 1.30 A.M. I was called again to light the starboard one. It had to be taken from the binnacle and carried to the lamp-room, opposite our room in the forward house, where there was no draft. Relighting the lamp I reached the companionway of the poop when suddenly I saw, standing in the darkness, the outlines of a big ship astern coming down upon us not one hundred yards away and carrying her topgallant sails as she ran before the wind. Not a light was showing on the ship and it seemed to me that my heart stopped beating as she towered above us with her huge yards spreading out like big arms ready to grasp and smother us. On, on she came and it seemed minutes before I could raise my voice to call the mate who stood on the weather side looking forward. The oncoming ship rolled heavily to starboard pointing her bow directly in our wake. It seemed to me that she was diving beneath the waves as her bow settled in the sea. My voice finally came to me and I yelled: "Look astern! Sail O! She's right on top of us!" while I raised the binnacle light as one might wave a flash light, running astern at the same time.

"Hard down your wheel!" shouted the mate and in the same breath, "Stand by the topsail halliards!"

Old Kruse, who was at the wheel, stepped off the grating facing the spokes and whirled the wheel down as fast as he could while I raised the lamp hoping that it might be seen. There was only one sea between us and the ship and while our stern was settling, up came the jib-boom of the strange ship directly above me. The splash from our stern sent the rays of phosphorescent light over the water and illuminated the bow, jibs and sails of the ship in a most uncanny manner. She was staggering under the stress of canvas that she bore and was overhauling us at a frightful gate. We both rolled to leeward at the same time, going down the waves together. If the *Akbar* felt the helm as our stern raised, I didn't see it. My eyes were riveted on that great bow astern whose jib-boom seemingly was playing over our quarter as though to see just how near it could come without striking or fouling our rigging. Our stern settled again while the strange ship threw her bow in the air until I could see clear under her fore foot. The jib-boom circled to port and like a whale breeching and leaping the ship fairly jumped out of the sea and buried herself so close to our lee quarter that one could almost step aboard.

In the splash that followed there was a dull, sickening sound of seething, foaming water. Her wash boiled over our stern in a mighty wave and I was thrown against the wheel box and into the lee wheel where I managed to hold on. The binnacle lamp that I held, flew over the wheel box striking Kruse in the face and cutting his cheek open in a gash two inches long. Whether the lamp struck him a blow hard enough to stun him, we couldn't figure, but he was washed away from the wheel, against the lazaret hatch where he sat in a dazed condition. I heard the rattling of blocks from the lowering of the topsails, but don't remember hearing the order to lower away or to let go. It seemed as if everything from aloft was coming down by the run and all was confusion. I was brought to my senses by the mate shouting: "Hard over your wheel, damn it! Hard over, I say!"

"Hard over, sir!" I answered, for the wheel, with no one to steady it, had been whirling back and forth and the ship was rounding to at a lively clip. Grasping the spokes and whirling them over she began to feel the rudder as she swung into the wind with everything flapping.

"Lee fore brace!" yelled the mate, running down the poop steps while the seas slopped over the bow. Just then both the captain and the second mate rushed up the companionway steps and on deck as I ran round to the weather side of the wheel.

"What's the matter here?" exclaimed the second mate. I pointed to Kruse, who was still clinging to the lazaret hatch, and to the vanishing ship in the darkness astern, for we were almost aback. He took in the situation at a glance and hurried to Kruse who was moaning in agony.

"What's the matter with you? Are you hurt?" asked Mr. Sanborn.

"Oh Got! Oh Got! I know'd it!" cried Kruse.

"What do you know? Where are you hurt?" asked the second mate, who rolled him over on his side, feeling the man from head to foot.

"Tell me where you're hurt?" said the second mate.

"I doan't know. It vas awful. I don't tink I live long. Aye, aye! Toot, Toot!" sighed Kruse.

"Get up on your feet. Let's see if you can walk," said Sanborn. And lifting him up and putting one arm around him, he walked him to the wheel box, where he stood, shaking from head to foot, as the second mate released his hold.

"Doan't leave me," pleaded Kruse, "I can't stand oop."

The second mate rubbed his legs and arms while Kruse held on to the wheel box. There was no cry of pain under the rubbing and pumping his arms up and down, whereupon Sanborn said:

"I guess you're not hurt much. Take care of yourself and don't fall overboard," and leaving him abruptly he went forward to assist in bracing the yards. The ship was beginning to get under way again and with the exception of a wet deck forward we were soon on our course. Meanwhile Kruse kept up a continuous moaning and talking to himself, half in Russian and half in broken English, laboring under an hal-

154 THE MAKING OF A SAILOR

lucination that he had seen the phantom ship *Flying Dutch-man.*

"I know'd it vas her, all de time. She bane after me, I know, fer to-day ees Friday. My Got! It's Friday! Tell me how dot ship could sail mit nopody at de veel an' nopody on deck? Tell me dot can jou?" he rambled. "I pet jou find somepody ees meessing. He come t' take somepody off dees ships. Did jou mind th' spun-jarn a-hangin' froom her cut-vater? Dot ees spun into manilla rope an' Got help th' man what runs afoul of et if et cooms aboard dees ships," said he.

The light from the cabin window shone on his face and I could see that the blood was dripping as he brushed it away with his handkerchief.

"Kruse," said I, "you'd better go to the captain and get something for that gash in your face. You'll have blood all over the poop and the mate will raise hell if he sees it."

Strange to say he didn't seem to notice that his cheek was cut so badly; he was so scared from the shaking up he had received that all he seemed to think of was the phantom ship that sailed by hunting for Russian-Finn sailors.

"Do jou tink dot de cap'n vill give me somethin' t' drink?" asked Kruse.

The idea of something to drink put new life into him and upon urging him to go he finally made his way on top of the cabin where the captain led him to the light of the skylight and seeing his condition took him below. I could see into his room from where I stood at the wheel and saw him washing the blood from Kruse's face, after which he put a couple of strips of sticking plaster across the wound, in the shape of a cross, to hold the skin in place, and then led him into the after cabin where I lost sight of him.

The mate didn't concern himself about my wet condition at the wheel and when the cabin clock chimed eight bells (for he kept me at the wheel all this time) I struck the bell without any delay, for I was cold and chilly. The topsails had been reset and I was relieved and the watch sent below. Upon going to my room I was surprised to see Alonzo sitting up in his bunk, after the shaking up we had had, for we were shipping a lot of water still.

"Gee! Isn't this grand?" said he, as I entered. "I like to feel the ship roll in this way and hear the spray against the house. It sounds like the rain on the shingles of our house at home in the attic."

This was adding insult to injury and I was in no mood to discuss the comparison. He was in a dry bed, comfortable and warm, while I was wet through, cold and chilly from the ducking I had received, and in pulling off my wet clothes, that clung to me so tightly, in my hurry to get into dryer ones, I lost all patience and exclaimed:

"You are a pretty one to sit there in your dry nest and tell how nice it is to hear the splash of water against the side of the house. You'd sing a different song if you had been on deck with me the last four hours. It may be nice to hear the splash inside your room, with your head buried under your blankets, but no sailor ever earned his salt by going to sea in this manner. Why don't you get up and stand your watch like a man? Do you think the rest of us are out in the wet for your amusement?"

"Did you expect to make a voyage without getting wet in weather like this?" retorted Alonzo.

"No," I replied, and taking up my wet shirt that I had just discarded, one hand on each shoulder to spread it out before him, I jumped in front of him and throwing it over his head and crossing the sleeves behind, brought them forward and tied them under his chin, squeezing out all the water that I could under the operation.

"If you like to hear the splash of water it's about time you felt it," said I, as I tied the sleeves.

This was more than he could stand and pulling the wet garment away from his face he jumped out of his bunk intending to strike me. I warned him that he'd better get back to bed before he got hurt, but that only made him more angry and we grappled, but I being the stronger held his arms down by his side. In the scuffle that followed, I pushed him against the door just as the ship rolled to leeward and it slid back, wide open, and we both pitched headlong over the sill and down on the wet deck together, sliding into the lee scuppers.

Aside from a bruised knee and a bump on Alonzo's head we weathered the gale. I helped him to his feet and picking him up in my arms carried him to the room where I tumbled him into his bunk.

"Now be a good dog and forget your troubles. I've got to get some sleep and I am sorry for what I have done," said I.

Alonzo saw the laughable side of the scuffle and we made up by shaking hands. Then he wanted to know what the trouble was when the watch was called, for he knew nothing of how near we came to being sent to Davy Jones's locker. I ran over the incident with him in a hurry and rolling up in my blankets was soon fast asleep, only to be awakened by old Kruse who was shaking me violently and calling, "Frade, Frade! It's better jou vake oop und go mit me to the poys in de fo'c'sle und tell me dot vas de *Flying Dutchman* vot sailed past our stern. Yes? Dey vill not pelieve me jet und I vant jou to splain youst how it happened."

I tried in vain to tell him that what he saw was a big ship and there was no such thing as the *Flying Dutchman*. The sea that washed over our stern should convince him that it was a reality and not a myth, but he stuck to his argument, which pleased Alonzo immensely.

"What did the *Flying Dutchman* look like?" he asked, laughingly.

"Vot jou mean how he look?" replied Kruse.

"I mean, how could you see something that doesn't exist or something you can't feel?" said Alonzo.

"I doan sabe exist, but I feel, feel plenty. Jou see my face all cut und blood, jet I see youst de same. Sure I see, und I seen de same ships off Cape o' Good Hope last jeer. Holy Got! but it blowed und ve seen big ball o' fire all over de bloody ships und she doan' cotch fire und on she comes mit no man at de veel I could see. Jes! She sail afore de vind und youmped right over us youst abaft de fo'must. She bane drag' in a hawser too vot fouled Christie, von o' de crews, und he vent overboard youst like a streak o' greased light'n'. Drug clean across de deck und over de side into de vater. My Got! how dot man hollered ven he vent over de side und into de vater und ven de ships rises on de sea jou could hear him avay oof in de dark, so terrible like, youst like he bane aboard."

"It gave you the weary Willies, didn't it? What did you do?" asked Alonzo.

"Do?" replied Kruse. "It vas so bad ve couldn't vork und ve all vent aft, de whole damn vorks, und told de captain he should put us all ashore at Cape Town or he could sail his dam' *Bismarck* home alone."

"Did he do it?" asked Alonzo.

"Ya-ah! Shore he did. He had to. But he tried t' fool us and run by, but ve all laid down und vould not pull a rope-jarn. Jou see ve had men vot knowed navigat'n' und ve fool *him*. Every time ve got a head vind ve could hear poor Christie groan so terrible-like avay t' vind'ard. He say: 'O-O-O! Save me! Save me!' Und ven ve hear it ve all go aft t' de Cap'n und say ve vill not vork."

"Did the Captain hear you groan?" asked Alonzo.

"I didn't groan," said Kruse. "It vas poor Christie all de time. Ya-ah! de Cap'n heard it joust like de rest of us, too, und ven he see dot he could not fool us he sayed, 'It's better I coom about.' So ve tacked ship und headed for Cape Town. As soon as de bloody ship vas headed for Cape Town, de vind came oop for t' blow und Holy Moses how it blowed! It vas tree veeks afore ve get back und ve hear Christie groanin' every bloody night. De Cap'n vas youst as skeered as us, und ven ve get in, all hands joumped over de side leavin' de bloody sails a-hangin' froom de jards. It's better ve stay down from aloft, for nopody vanted t' take any chances of falling. De foot-ropes might part ven ve vere aloft, so ve take no chances on de bloody hoodoo ships."

Old Kruse would have talked till morning had I not remonstrated and said that he was taking up too much time of my watch below and I needed the sleep. I emphatically told him to go forward—his yarn was a good one, but it would keep till the next watch. Finally he saw that I was in earnest and reluctantly closed the door and walked away.

"I wonder if the old man believed what he was giving us or did he think us a set of boobs that he could string us with such a yarn? What's he giving us anyway?" asked Alonzo.

"Search me," I replied. "You never know what a foreigner believes. He probably adds a little more to his yarn every time he tells it and now swears it's the Gospel truth, whether he believes it or not. Good night—I'm off for a sleep. We'll talk it over in the morning."

In the next watch old Kruse was very entertaining and while we tried to convince him there was no such thing as the *Flying Dutchman* he met our argument, in his simple manner, with facts that he knew were correct for he saw, with his own eyes, the ship in question and we, not seeing the ship that he saw, were not fit subjects to talk intelligently. He seemed quite annoyed that we did not agree with him.

While in the heat of the argument four bells struck. The wheel was relieved and big Hans coming from the wheel, stopped at the mainmast to light his pipe while going forward to the roundhouse.

It was our custom to wash down decks at daylight, after the wheel had been relieved. The mate's watchful eye saw Hans puffing away as he walked forward, whereupon he hurried off the poop swearing a blue streak and clumping along the deck until he reached the roundhouse.

"See here, damn you! I don't want you or any other old sailor smoking your pipe after the wheel has been relieved until I tell you whether or not there is any work to do. You know, damn well, that we wash down at this time and I won't have any man around the decks sucking a pipe when we are at work. If you do, I'll soon ram it down your throat and put a head on you," said the mate.

Hans was a good-natured Norwegian, ordinarily, but the sailors had been talking of the mate's tactics, so much of late, with his petty annoyances, that things were fast coming to a boiling point. Consequently Hans boiled over and ran out of the roundhouse and standing in front of the mate and slamming his cap to the deck, he jumped up and down brandishing his clinched fists in front of Mr. Burris' face and exclaimed:

"Jou put my head on, is it? Coom on! Coom on! Do jou tink jou can shoove my pipe by my troat down? It's better jou try it. Coom on I say! Ya-ah, I am vaitin' fer jou! Vy don't jou fight vid jour fists, ja? Jou fight all the time vid jour mouth. Damn it, man! I bane havin' all th' bloody talk from jou dot I vant. Jou never saw me smokin' ven dare vos vork t' do und I smoke joust so much as I bloody vell like so long as ve are not turned to. I bane vaitin' fer jou t' hit me. Vy don't jou hit me first? Dot's vot I stand by fer."

Here, Hans stuck his face close up to the mate's and begged the mate to strike him, saying:

"Vy don't jou hit me? I youst vant jou t' hit me von leetle slap und damn me, I swab oop th' decks vid jou in my hands youst like jou ver so year old" (measuring with his hands some three feet above the deck). "Jou don't vant t' fight, ja? Then vy don't jou be like th' second mate. He never bane havin' rows vid th' men in his vatch."

The mate had backed up against the rail while Hans talked, but both were very much excited. The mate, swearing all the time, had taken a belaying-pin from the rail which he waved in front of him taking good care not to hit Hans with it. It was a case of "One was afraid and the other dasn't." The mate, however, was in no hurry to hit Hans but we expected every moment that he would. He finally wound up the argument by saying:

"Oh, you make me tired! I thought by the way you came out of the roundhouse we were going to have a nice little mix up, but you are just the same as all Norwegians. A big streak of yellow! I've wasted too much time on you and it's time we were washing down," and calling to me: "You, Fred! Get the hose and attach it to the pump for washing down. Turn to, the watch."

With this order he walked aft carrying the belaying-pin and whirling it in his hand, but listening with his head slightly turned and on his guard that Hans might not slip up on him from behind and catch him unawares. When he was well aft, Hans became more excited and the farther away the mate got the more demonstrative he grew. Catching sight of his cap on the deck he kicked it about, swearing in Norwegian and broken English. He finally kicked it too high and the wind catching it, the cap sailed overboard. With the loss of his cap he was beside himself, jumping up and down and cursing the mate from hell to breakfast, beating his chest with his clinched fists and uttering oaths with each thump. Stalking forward along the deck, seemingly not knowing what he was doing, first into the forecastle, then under the forecastle-deck and back like a caged tiger, he finally picked up a broom and joined us in scrubbing the decks, which somewhat eased his excitement; but with every stroke of the broom he uttered an oath through his set teeth, sweeping the water to the right and left in no gentle manner.

When aft of the mainmast the mate took the hose and was none too careful with the water about our legs, which didn't add comfort to Hans and on reaching the grating in front of the cabin he turned the water under the grating with its full force directly under him. Whether it was intentionally done to wet Hans, I am unable to say, but the dirty water splashed up into his face and with a "Yeesus Christ," at the top of his voice, he swung his broom across the harness-cask, near where he was standing, with such force that the broom handle was broken short off. Then picking up the broken parts he violently threw them across the deck against the bulwarks to leeward. This so enraged the mate that he threw down the hose and ran into the cabin, shouting:

"I'll fix you, damn you! Mr. Sanborn! Tumble out and give me a hand! We're having mutiny aboard the ship! I want you to help me put this big Norwegian in irons before he takes the ship."

The second mate was soon on deck with a pair of hand-cuffs in his hands, followed by the captain who had heard the call for help, with a carbine at his side, dressed in his night clothes.

"What's the matter here?" he called, bringing the gun to bear on us as he stood in the doorway.

"That damned Norwegian is breaking up the ship's property. I've had more trouble with this man than anybody aboard the ship and if he is allowed to run loose he'll contaminate the whole crew. The best place for him is in the lazaret with a pair of iron bracelets on. Feed him on bread and water for a week or so and he'll damned soon come to his senses," said the mate.

"What did he do?" inquired the captain.

"He was smoking his pipe when I turned the men to and he defied me to make him stop, saying that he would smoke as often as he liked and be damned to me. Then to show his spleen he broke a new broom over the harness-cask and hove it across the deck against the bulwarks, scratching up the paint work," said the mate.

"If that is all he has done, why don't you charge him up with the loss of the broom?" replied the captain.

"But this isn't all," said the mate. "When I followed him forward with his pipe in his mouth and told him to quit smoking, he turned on me and struck me on the shoulder and if I hadn't ducked he would have knocked my head off."

"Jou are von domned liar," broke in Hans. "But I strike jou now."

Bareheaded, showing a disheveled head of hair, and with clinched fists, Hans looked like a wild man as he ran for the mate, who stepped behind Mr. Sanborn for protection. Now Hans was looking only for Mr. Burris to strike and did not count on the second mate to interfere. On he charged, swearing in Norwegian. In justice to the second mate who knew nothing of Hans' actions before he appeared on deck and who took it for granted that Hans was really in the wrong, from the evidence given, and could see that he was making for the mate with the purpose of striking him, there was only one thing to do and do it quickly. He let go a powerful right on Hans's jaw, as he passed around the second mate, which felled him like an ox. Jumping upon him as he fell, he had the handcuffs around Hans's wrists before he hardly knew what had happened. Then he and the mate dragged him into the cabin.

We could hear them scuffle as Hans was being securely fastened and the mate kept up his incessant swearing all the time. Not long after the mate appeared, greatly agitated, and addressed us, puffing and blowing, showing that he had really been exerting himself in the fray.

"You see—" said he (catching his breath), "what has happened—. This only goes to show—show what any one of you —may expect—. And, by God! I'll have you all there if there's any more insubordination."

Telling us to continue washing down he made his way up the weather gangway to the poop where he continued to pace the deck and work off his excitement.

We continued to scrub the decks in silence, for there was a damper on the watch and I was very much depressed. Finally O'Rourke broke out in an undertone:

"Phat t' bloody hell did Hans go an' fer t' do thet should put him in irons, a-tall, a-tall? Oi'm here fer t' tell yees ef anny more happining is t' be pulled off loik dis wan here, yees can count on me fer t' quit et. See! Put thet in yer poip and smoke et!"

This gave food for old Kruse who joined in with: "Und vot I tole jou. Didn't I tole jou dot dees ships vos a hoodoo? Und t'day is Friday, too. Mind vot I said before? Someting vill happen jet. Do jou knows t'morrow ees Christmas?"

"Holy Ghost," broke in O'Rourke. "A hell of a bloody Christmas we're in fer t' have. Thet bloody mate 'll hev us a-washin' down decks th' whole bloody day long–along. I hopes et rains so we carry water fer t' fill up th' empty water-casks instead."

And Andy was heard from, saying: "I see vere I spend my vatch aloft, a pickin' Irish pennants froom de riggin'. It's better I do it any vay. He von't be hazzin' me 'round de decks."

"I see jour finish," said "Handsome Charlie." "Jou and Hans are countrymen and he'll bloody well keep jou busy clear to Melbourne. Look out that he don't lock jou up vid Hans."

"Too much noise down there," sang out the mate from the poop. "If you fellows can't work without talking, I'll put you where you won't have anybody to talk with."

So saying, he came down the gangway and taking the hose threw the water about the deck and under our legs unmindful of where he turned the stream, preferring to splash us all rather than to wash the dirt across the deck. His presence had its effect by stopping any further talk from the men who were fast working themselves into a frenzy at the unjust treatment of Hans.

No doubt the mate surmised it was better to be among us, where we had no chance to talk, than to walk the quarterdeck alone. Accordingly we were all kept busy in a bunch together and when we had finished washing down, he had us swab the white paint work of the cabin and stanchions of the taffrail about the poop, for the remainder of the watch.

At breakfast time the news flew about the ship in an alarming manner but no one volunteered to go aft in Hans's behalf. Finally it was decided that Jim Dunn, who had sailed with the second mate on a previous voyage, should acquaint Mr. Sanborn with the full particulars and ask for a hearing before the captain, because, if one of our watch went aft with a complaint the mate would no doubt make life miserable for him during the rest of the voyage.

Jim was under the t'gallant fo'c'sle at this time, breaking out a barrel of beef for the cook, and "Handsome Charlie" said, "There is no time like the present," whereupon he left the forecastle and spoke to Jim who agreed to the proposition when an opportunity presented itself.

Before Charlie had a chance to get back, the second mate came forward, walking directly under the forecastle-head and Jim wasted no time in laying the matter before him. But Mr. Sanborn was loath to acknowledge a mistake had been made, whereupon Charlie requested him to go with him to the forecastle where the watch would substantiate the statement for further evidence. After talking it over with the men who were on deck at the time he could find no one that saw Hans strike the mate and asking if they were willing to testify to the captain to this effect and receiving word that they would, he went aft to talk with the captain.

Not long after we were all called aft and assembled in the forward cabin where Hans was handcuffed and tied in the revolving dining chair with his legs underneath and seized together behind the spindle in such a manner that he could do no injury should he attempt to kick.

The captain addressed us as follows:

"My men! I understand that there are conflicting statements made concerning this man in irons. We have made no mistake in handcuffing him, for I saw him when he tried to strike Mr. Burris, an officer of this ship. No sailor, no matter what the offense, is justified in striking an officer on the high seas—such an action is mutiny. I called you aft to acquaint you with the law. Mr. Sanborn tells me that none of you men saw this man strike Mr. Burris, before the watch was turned-to this morning, while the mate states positively that he did, and—"

"He's a bloody li-ar, sir!" broke in Hans. "I tole—"

"Never mind what you told him," interrupted the captain. "When I get through talking you can have a chance."

"Mr. Burris, did this man (pointing to Hans) strike you?"

"He did, sir!" replied Mr. Burris.

"Ag'in I say, it's a blood-y lie, sir!" broke in Hans.

"Keep quiet until I call on you," said the captain.

"Mr. Burris, where did this man hit you?"

"I don't hit-him, I told-jou, sir!" again came from Hans.

"Will you keep quiet? Mr. Burris, where did he hit you?"

"On the shoulder, sir," replied Mr. Burris.

"That will do, Mr. Burris," said the captain; and then addressing us in a body he asked,

"Did any of you men see this man strike Mr. Burris?"

"No, sir," we all replied in unison. The captain then turned to Hans, saying:

"Mr. Burris says you struck him. What have you to say in your defense?"

"I tole-you a tou-send times, I don't hit him, sir! But youst-you turn me a-drift und I fight-him vid-a hand behind my beck, sir. Ven-e cooms oop und shooks me und says, 'It's bet-ter I stop smokin' or jou und me falls out.' Ve vere not turned-to jet und I tole him youst-th' same. He bane ox-cited und I tole him det I vosn't 'fraid oof him, und ef-e vants-t' fight, youst hit-me wunst und I swabs-th' deck vidim oop, sir. He didn't dast-to, th' bloody pig, sir!"

"Well!" replied the captain, "Mr. Burris says that this man struck him and you all say he did not. It's his word against yours and nothing to prove. Had I not seen this man in an attempt to strike Mr. Burris, I might turn him loose; but I can't do it now and he must abide the consequences, serving his time in the pen for a week. At the end of that time if he still bears malice to Mr. Burris, he'll get more. That will do the watch."

So saying, the captain ended the kangaroo court and we left the cabin not any too well satisfied with the result of his findings.

The men upon going forward continued to growl, heaping curses on the mate and threatening to heave him overboard on the first opportunity; but as one after another turned in for needed sleep further demonstrations quieted down.

In the afternoon watch there was very little said, the mate taking good care to separate the men where no two could converse; but in the dogwatch both the port and starboard watches got together where free talk was cheap, for both mates staid aft out of ear-shot, and for a while I really thought that the mate's time had come so bitter were they in their denunciations. But while there was plenty of growling from the men it went no further and the night watches came and went as before.

CHAPTER VIII

CROSSING THE LINE

OUR Christmas was celebrated by having fine warm weather. We were in lat. 23° 0′ N. long. 35° 30′ W., and set the topgallant sails, spanker and main spencer. After clearing up the decks from the accustomed wash-down in the morning there was no further work for the day. Our Christmas dinner consisted of plain duff and turkey (Cape Cod)* which of course brought a big growl from the forecastle, with many comparisons with the Astor House, and this, with Hans in the lazaret, put the men in a state of unrest as they had nothing to do but growl. Strange to say the mate was on his good behavior. Alonzo sat up during the day feeling much better but awfully homesick.

Four days after Christmas we struck the northeast trade winds. On Friday, December 31, 1875, during the morning watch (2.30 A.M), Andy fell asleep while sitting on the spar under the weather main shrouds. The mate passing by and looking for happenings of this kind, grabbed him by the coat collar and jerked him to his feet with a curse.

"What in hell are you doing there asleep? Can't you get sleep enough below? I've cautioned you men before that I would allow no man to sit down in his watch on deck for just as sure as I permit it you would all want to bring your bed and blankets aft and ask permission to use the after cabin for a bed-room where it's nice and dry. Oh, you sailors! If I catch another man asleep after this, I'll keep you on the move all the watch and the first man to go to sleep I'll land him one right across the sconce with a belaying-pin that will make him think a cyclone has struck him. Now get a move on, you, before I kick the daylights out of you."

"Aye, aye, sir!" replied Andy, who really thought he meant what he said, for he walked briskly forward to get

* Salt fish.

away from the mate while the rest of us got busy throwing
down and recoiling some of the running rigging as if it
really needed it, with the men all the while growling in an
undertone. Old Kruse didn't hesitate to remind us that
Friday was an unlucky day on all hoodoo ships and that
"sometings" would happen before we reached Melbourne.

Every half-hour, till the end of the watch, the mate
would come to the end of the companionway and sing out,
"A small pull on the weather main brace," or "fore-topsail";
and after the ropes were coiled up again it would not be long
before he would order a small pull on the lee main braces—
anything, to be sure there would be no further dozing by the
watch. These orders were answered in no quiet manner and
usually the "Aye, aye, sir!" was preceded by a curse loud
enough for the mate to hear, for we were short-handed by
the absence of Hans; besides, the work was unnecessary and
we knew that we were being hazed.

New Year's Day came in with light winds, warm weather
and passing heavy showers. The variable winds kept us box-
hauling the yards in every conceivable way. We were truly
in the doldrums and outside of bracing the yards had no
work to do.

Hans was taken from the lazaret this morning and given
his liberty. Instead of being depressed at his confinement he
was quite jubilant, declaring that he had had a good rest and
was glad to be free from the drudgery of working ship. The
captain had provided a blanket and mattress for him to sleep
on and with three square meals each day, why worry? He
would just as soon stay aft longer with the high-brows.

A large shark that had been following the ship off and
on, showed himself again and the second mate got out the
shark-hook, a heavy iron hook about ⅜ of an inch in diameter, attached to a chain about three feet in length with a ring
at the end, to which he bent a piece of ratline stuff. Baiting
the hook with a large piece of salt pork he walked aft where
he trailed it astern. It wasn't long before the shark caught
sight of it and swimming on the surface of the water with
only his dorsal fin showing, turning swiftly on his side with

open mouth as he approached, he pounced upon the bait viciously and was hard and fast immediately.

Hauling him alongside, to leeward, by the help of three or four men, for everyone was only too anxious to lend a hand, we strapped a single-block to the fore swifter, about six feet above the sheer pole, through which we rove a line and making a running bowline around the shark-line, slipped it down and over the shark's head. A strain on the running bowline brought it snugly around his tail. Then heaving away on the whip-end, he was hoisted out of the water, hanging by his tail, and landed on deck where he jumped about thrashing his tail in a lively manner. Gasping and thrashing about we put him in a strait-jacket, *i.e.*, we took a turn with the shark-line around a belaying-pin and hauled taut on the tail rope. Then the second mate ran a hand-spike down his throat as far as he could reach, in no gentle manner, for a shark to a sailor is like a rattlesnake to a cowboy. Then rolling him over on his back and disemboweling him, we cut his tail off and gave him a passage (threw him overboard), which I understood was the custom with sailors for all sharks caught and landed on deck. Before cutting off his tail he measured twelve feet from tip to tip and we counted eight rows of teeth in his mouth,—one back of the other.

That afternoon we passed a French full-rigged brig, steering north, showing the loss of her fore topmast. She was too far away to make out her name. Alonzo was still confined to his bunk and no better. He wrote a letter to the captain asking permission to board aft, as he couldn't eat the fo'c'sle grub and offered to pay the difference upon arrival at Melbourne. Carrying it aft it was all he could do to reach the cabin, where he rested on the sill of the door before entering. His case was a mystery to us all and although he seemed to have a good appetite he could retain nothing in his stomach. The captain didn't commit himself but said he would see what could be done for him.

On January 7, the weather was extremely warm and I saw my first grampus, sometimes called a whale killer and also a cow fish. It is a mammal of the whale species with dorsal fin in the middle of its back. They can be heard often in a still night, blowing a short, sharp blow or puff, as they come to the surface of the water near the vessel. They grow to be fifteen to twenty feet long. Their color is gray with white streaks. Cannibalistic by nature they feed on porpoises and meat of their kind and often attack whales. It is said that three or four grampuses can kill a whale.

As we drew nearer the Equator we had less winds and very variable, causing us to box-haul the yards for every breath of air. The hot sun boiling down upon the decks melted the pitch which oozed from the seams in spots and was very annoying to us walking across the decks bare-footed, for our shoes had been put away for cold weather. The lazy roll of the ship and the slatting of the sails against the mast, breaking the stoppings of the buntlines, made life burdensome, for the eagle eye of the mate detected every-thing. He was always sure to send me aloft at a time when I couldn't jump into my leather pumps and must necessarily climb the rigging in bare feet. If you think it's fun to run aloft barefooted, with only a ratline to stand on (a ¾ inch tarred rope), just try it. After running up six or eight rat-lines you began to hunt for a soft place to stand on. Your feet, which have become parboiled from standing in water from the last heavy shower, are very tender. The ratlines are made fast with a clove-hitch around the shrouds and afford a better place than the middle of the rope and so you climb, using your hands to relieve your weight, with your knees pressing against the ratline above to help your hands and your toes at times against the clove-hitch on the shroud. It is vastly different from going up the back stairs at home in your stocking feet.

The mate watches you to see if it hurts and smiles at your discomfiture. You know he is watching and rather than have him "bawl you out" you grin and bear it until you reach the top. If the buntlines of the mainsail need stopping, you swing on to the yard where you can straddle the jack-stay with a foot on each side and release your teeth from your under lip which is nearly bitten in two from the pressure.

Here, you can take your good old time in overhauling the buntlines before passing the cotton string twice around and tying it with a square knot under the block, for buntlines are always stopped in this manner and plenty of slack is allowed, care being taken that they are not too tight to draw or chafe against the sail. When furling the sail, a sharp pull breaks the cotton string and the rope reeves through the block all right.

In these "horse latitudes" the rain comes and goes in streaks like the wind. The ship might be sailing in the bright sunshine, hot enough to start the tar from the seams in the deck, when a rain squall would spring up and pass within a few feet of the ship without a drop falling on board. It would be so clearly defined that the surface of the water would show the edge of the rain as it passed by the ship in a marked line; not in an Oregon mist, but a regular pouring rain storm. At times the ship might be in a dead calm and the same thing would happen, so light and variable were the winds.

When the squalls passed over the ship we caught enough water from the top of the cabin to fill our empty casks. Even the spare deck-buckets, on top of the cabin, were filled, and stopping up the lee scuppers in the deck, during the dog-watches, we caught enough water to wash all our clothes and blankets. It was an amusing sight to see the men, bare-armed, barefooted and with pants rolled up to their knees, sitting on the hatch combings, in the rain, with a deck-bucket between their knees, while they dipped a shirt or pair of stockings into the white soapsuds and scrubbed for dear life to get through their washing before the rest. Others spread their blankets on the deck and getting down on their hands and knees, soaped them and used a scrubbing-brush, if fortunate enough to possess one. A cocoanut husk, cut squarely off to the desired size, can be made into a very nice brush when used long enough to soften it. This is hard on one's clothes, but a tarry jumper or pair of pants sometimes takes more than ordinary rubbing with bare hands to start the dirt.

When the clothes are washed and hung in the rigging to

dry, I have seen men pull off what clothing they had on and wash their garments while standing entirely nude. Then soaping their bodies it was not an uncommon sight to see one sailor use a scrubbing-brush on another's back, to make a clean job of it, after which they would enjoy a refreshing bath in the water, knee-deep on the deck.

Waterspouts were common. While standing at the wheel one day I saw three, off different parts of the ship. I shall never forget that afternoon for we all had a good scare. Off our port beam and about five or ten miles distant, I saw what seemed to be two rain squalls coming together, head on. As the squalls came together on the surface of the water, the sea at that point was thrown up considerably, mixing in with the rain, while overhead a big black cloud, bellying down until the center of it tapered into a stem, dropped lower and lower until it met the sea where the squalls came together. I could see a splash and a twist upward of the waves while the cloud, bending down and away from the troubled waters, finally swooped around enveloping the rain and water in a twisting struggle in which all three took an active part as though to see which might conquer and be free.

The whirling cloud, like a huge octopus, with mighty twisting legs dangling down, wrapped around the rain and water, surging from side to side and gradually began to ascend, sucking up the water in a twisting, spiral, funnel-shaped mass, till finally the cloud above became blacker and blacker, spreading out as it approached us and looking like a mammoth balloon with the tapering end dragging in the water below and taking a course heading directly towards us while we were in a dead calm, helpless to move.

The captain, pacing the deck on top of the cabin, with a troubled face watched the development until about five miles away when he sang out to the mate,

"Let go your royals and t'gallant-s'ls, Mr. Burris, and stand by your tops'l halliards!"

"Aye, aye, sir!" he replied.

I watched the oncoming waterspout. The sky took on a peculiar hue as the cloud shaded the sun. The rattling of the blocks, as the yards slipped down the mast, didn't add to my comfort for it was a sickening sound and the gloom of the sky above was terrible to watch. Not a breath of air stirred and when the yards hung from their lifts all was deathly still, for there was not enough swell on the ocean to make the ship roll. The humidity of the air was depressing and all hands stood quietly at their stations awaiting orders and watching the twisting, surging waterspout which seemed certain to engulf us in a short time.

The tail of the big, black cloud, tugging away at another angle, finally altered the course and instead of coming to us in a straight line, the waterspout took an irregular, elliptical course, twisting at one time in a small circle from left to right and then picking up headway at a rapid rate it formed an arc, for a mile or so, only to be arrested temporarily, with renewed suction power, in another small circle, twisting and struggling, in which the wind joined forces and the whole mass came within a half mile of us before the spout finally parted.

We could plainly hear the roar and splash of water as it poured back into the ocean, while the big black cloud enveloped us in rain that came down in torrents. The wind, following, struck us abeam and with our topsails lowered we ran before it until able to keep on our course and then setting the topsails, followed by the topgallant sails, by the time we had the royals on her the sun came out as before, intensely hot, and the wind died out in an aggravating manner. The mate was soon hobbling about the decks whistling for a breeze and cursing our bad luck that we didn't have a ten-knot breeze on our quarter or at least enough to carry us out of the doldrums.

When relieved from the wheel Dave told me that old Kruse nearly died of fright when the waterspout broke. The day was Friday and he knew that his time had come and the ship would never reach Melbourne.

As we neared the Equator we were in company with vessels of all sizes and nationalities for it is conceded that there is more wind between the longitudes of 28° to 30° West, than at any other part on the Equator, consequently all sailing vessels try to cross the line in that vicinity. In the dogwatch I counted twenty-four sails in sight, making out one ship, thirteen barks, one barkentine, two full-rigged brigs, three brigantines, one schooner and three others too far away to be identified. We were all steering the same course.

In these light winds it was great sport to lay out on the jib-boom-end and fish for bonito, albacore and dolphin. These fish, all about the same size, weighing from five to ten pounds as a rule, played about the ship's cutwater.

The bonito and albacore are a species of the mackerel tribe. The bonito are the smaller of the two, averaging in length about three feet, and are beautiful fish with blue backs and black, oblique stripes and white bellies. Bonito is the Spanish for "Little Beauty" and it is rightly named. They feed almost entirely on flying-fish and leaping squid or cuttle fish and are very good eating. The meat resembles beef. The albacore are generally coarser and dryer but anything was more palatable than salt beef and pork. The dolphin are probably the fastest fish that swim and are known for their brilliancy in color. When dying they change from a silver white to all the colors in the rainbow.

By using a codline baited in the same manner as if trolling for bluefish, *i.e.*, by wrapping a piece of white cloth around the hook to resemble a small fish about the size of a flying-fish, and straddling the jib-boom-end, leaning against the fore-royal stay for support, one skips the hook at the end of the line on top of the water in front of the ship's stem, where these fish are wont to play, swimming back and forth across the ship's bow and just clear of the cutwater. They rise to the surface as a pickerel or trout after a fly.

These fish do not mix together but swim with their own. One day would be seen only dolphins and on the next, albacore, etc.

There are few objects more dazzling than the dolphin while leaping out of a rippling wave into the bright sunlight; and the beauty of the dying dolphin is wonderful to watch as it changes its color. As for me—I'd rather watch it dangling in the bright sunshine on the end of a trolling-line, struggling to be free as I pulled it hand-over-hand from under the ship's bow, singing out at the top of my voice:

"On deck! On deck! Bring out a gunny sack. I've caught a dolphin."

Keeping up this noise, as I pulled on the fish in my excitement, someone would soon rush to the knight-heads to see if I were overboard or not and by the time I had pulled the fish "short," with a turn around the fore-royal stay, and hugged it in my arms tight enough to squeeze the last breath out of it, the dolphin was deposited in the gunny sack and "rigged in" safely to the t'gallant fo'c'sle deck by the help of the other sailor. Blue-fishing and salmon-trolling is tame sport compared with trolling from the jib-boom-end.

After hurrying through breakfast one morning I ran forward to the knight-heads, looking for anything swimming under the bow. Several albacore were darting across the stem and without saying a word to anyone I went to my room for a trolling-line and was soon out on the jib-boom-end skipping the hook in front of the cutwater. It was not long before I hooked a fine fellow which must have weighed fully twenty pounds. Andy came running out with the gunny sack, in answer to my cry, swearing a blue streak when he saw who it was, exclaiming:

"Jou don't know how to ketch dees feesh und should not be allowed out here takin' jour bloody place vid a able seaman. I tole jou jesterday noot t' come out here und scare dees feesh avay."

And from his looks as he made his way out, throwing the sack first over the jib-boom and then over the flying-jib guys, in his haste to reach me, muttering to himself all the while, I couldn't tell whether he was after me or the albacore. We were both excited and after the fish was safely stowed in the gunny sack he wouldn't let me carry it for fear I should drop it. I was afraid that he might do the same thing and so followed him in. Between us both the fish was landed safely on deck. It was my first fish and I was very proud of my success as a fisherman. The albacore was a beauty, making supper enough for all hands. The boys congratulated me on catching such a large one, but Andy didn't hesitate to remind them that I would never have landed it had it not been for him. I think he was disappointed that my fish outweighed any caught by him the day before. He should have considered that I had beginner's luck.

After spending twelve days in the doldrums, box-hauling the yards in every conceivable way and with everyone out of sorts and ready to quarrel, on Sunday, January 16, we had a fine breeze from the southeast.

A ship and three barks that were off our lee bow the night before, were now astern, but an English ship overhauled us. Running up his ensign, we followed suit as he approached and when off our lee beam within speaking distance, the captain, standing at the weather quarter, hailed us through his speaking-trumpet.

"What ship's that?" he called.

"Ship *Akbar*, from Boston," answered Captain Lamson, who spoke through his speaking-trumpet from the lee quarter.

"Where are you bound?"

"Melbourne."

"How many days out?"

"Thirty-eight."

In turn, our captain then called:

"What ship's that?"

"*Queen of the Mersey*, from Liverpool."

"Where are you bound?"

"Singapore."

"How many days out?"

"Forty-two."

In the meantime, a blackboard about three by four feet, was got out on each ship and the latitude and longitude was marked in large white figures and the board hung up over the rail where it could be seen.

This was done in order to compare figures, after which our ensigns were dipped to the water's edge, in a salute of "good-bye," for the *Queen of the Mersey* was a smart steel ship and sailed away from us in no time.

I caught two more albacore that day, but the third fish bit off my hook which ended my fishing. When I took the fish to the "doctor" he was out of sorts and said:

"What th' bloody hell do you think I am? I've cooked all th' bloody fish I'm going to. Do you think that is all I've got to do, standing over a hot stove all day to fry fish for the crew?"

I stood in the galley door, a very disappointed boy, not knowing what to say. Finally he looked at me and seeing my dejected looks, said,

"Well! I'll cook these; but it will be the last time and if you bring any more to me I'll heave 'em overboard."

Thanking him for his trouble I went to my room to bend on another hook. This time I ganged the hook with a copper wire so that if the fish swallowed the hook he couldn't bite off the wire.

The breeze carried us down to the Equator which we crossed about 6.30 P.M. in longitude 30° West. Alonzo and I were sitting in our room about this time when we were told to get ready for Neptune who was expected to come aboard.

"Good heavens!" exclaimed Alonzo. "You don't think they are going to initiate us do you? By golly! I'm too sick to have any rough stuff pulled off on me and I'll tell 'em so"; but he said this to me after they had gone forward.

"Well! I hope for your sake, Alonzo, that they'll overlook it. Perhaps they are only trying to scare us for I haven't seen anyone getting ready for the occasion," said I.

It was not long after, however, that we heard a rattling of tin cans, forward, and the tramp of feet as the members of both watches marched to the cry of "Left! left! I had a good home and I left! left! I had a good home and I left!"

Presently they appeared, marching around the corner of the house and over the main hatch, beating time with a knife or spoon on the bottom of their pans as they stepped along the deck. Halting in front of our door, Jim Dunn acted as spokesman for the men and said,

"Fred, yous two are wanted for'ard." To which I replied,

"Speaking for myself, I haven't lost anything for'ard and prefer to stay where I am."

Alonzo then chimed in: "Boys! I've been up all the afternoon, and am tuckered out. I couldn't walk for'ard to see the fun and I've got to turn in now for I haven't strength to look at Neptune."

"Is that so?" said Jim. "Now we come here t' bring yous for'ard an' ef yous are too weak to walk there's enough men to wedge up an' lanch yous down the ways. So take my advice an' cast off an' git under way fer I'm here t' tell yous you'd better skin out while th' skinnin's good."

There was a look in his face that told me decidedly that he meant just what he said and while I didn't relish the idea of being made the goat in this old-time custom, I saw I was in for it and like it or not discretion was the greater part of valor for there were entirely too many men for us to cope with, consequently I stepped outside, but Alonzo was unwilling to come, muttering that it was a dirty Irish trick.

Jim was an Irishman and very sensitive on his nationality and so resented the way Alonzo talked.

"What d'ye mean, Irish trick?" he asked. "Have I done yous any dirt? An' d'ye mean t' say yer not comin'?"

"No! I'm not comin'!" replied Alonzo, imitating Jim's brogue, whereupon Jim picked him up in his strong arms, as though he were a baby, and carried him to the fore hatch while Alonzo kicked and struggled to get away. Jim only laughed at his puny resistance and on reaching the hatch turned him over his knee and spanked him as he would an unruly child, saying:

"Now, sonny, be keerful or papa'll spank. Be a good little boy now and don't run away."

The laughing and jeering from the crew was too much for Alonzo to bear and taking an iron belaying-pin from the bitts, he exclaimed:

"I'll brain the first man that touches me. You're a set of cowards to pick on a sick man like me and I won't stand it."

The words were hardly out of his mouth before one of the crew caught him from behind and took the pin away from him before he had a chance to use it.

"Now, I warn you Alonzo," said Jim, "there's t' be no rough stuff on yer part or ye'll git a damned sight more than yer thinkin', an' I'm here t' tell yous that. Yer here t' meet Father Neptune an' he's liable t' come aboard any minit an' he'll be a-lookin' fer yous when wunst he gits aboard." Then signalling the crew they again beat a tattoo on their pans and presently we were hailed by a voice over the bow, in a drawling tone, when the music ceased:

"S-h-i-p, a-h-o-y! S-h-i-p, a-h-o-y! Back your main top-s'l and take me a-b-o-a-r-d."

Then there was a sound as if someone was whacking the bob-stay and back-ropes with a hand-spike (no doubt to give us the impression that the ship had struck something). This noise gradually ascended to the t'gallant rail where Father Neptune crawled over the knight-heads dripping wet.

The crew heralded his approach by a clamor of tin pans, pots and cans and he walked to the break of the fo'c'sle deck where he stopped, giving us time to thoroughly look him over before he uttered a word.

A navy blue blanket for a robe, thrown over his head and fastened under the chin, draped over his shoulders and trailed behind. Its edges were trimmed with gulf-weed, and bunches of rope-yarn, painted green to give it the effect of eelgrass right from the bottom of the sea, were sewn on for the occasion. He wore a crown which was painted red and a canvas mask which had two holes cut for the eyes, and another for the nose, which protruded and was also painted red, while around his mouth and over his chin was a fringe of rope-yarn, for whiskers, the ends of which were picked out, blossoming into bunches of oakum over which he frequently squirted tobacco juice. In his right hand he carried a five-pronged grains-iron fitted with a pole, for a trident, from which dangled pieces of rope-yarn to give the effect of green seaweed and in his left hand was a speaking-trumpet. His big sea boots were much too large, but were in keeping with the rest of his costume.

Raising his speaking-trumpet to his mouth, he called:

"You Sons o' Neptune, this is a helluf a way t' meet yer King! Why in the bloody hell didn't you lower a boat ven I hailed you? There must be someone aboard this ship who has not yet joined the Order of the Sons o' Neptune or you would have done as I commanded. If there are any such they must pay th' price and I vant their names. Who are these suckers?"

No one answered his inquiry but I recognized "Handsome Charlie's" voice.

"Who in th' bloody hell are they? Don't keep me vaitin' all day," said he, impatiently striking his trident on the fo'-c'sle-deck.

"Fred and Alonzo are the only ones aboard thet have not yet crossed th' line, sir," said Jim.

"Are these suckers worthy and ready to join the Sons o' Neptune?"

"I think they are, sir," said Jim.

"If that's so, my Sons, show yer appreciashun an' all hands salute yer King."

"All hands salute th' King, sir," said Jim.

It was a laughable sight to see the crew bow and scrape their feet, with their ungainly hands and arms swinging about, for they were not trained in the art of grace and a more awkward set of men could hardly have been gotten together. The ludicrous sight was more than Alonzo could stand and he laughed aloud.

At this, Father Neptune raised his speaking-trumpet to his mouth and bellowed forth:

"Awast heavin' there, me lad! Yer duff-downhaul needs attenshun. Clap a stopper on it you Sons o' Neptune an' heave short an' belay. This sucker needs a strait-yacket. Put it on 'em both. I von't have this cer'mony interrupted."

"Aye, aye, sir! Put a strait-jacket on 'em," repeated the crew.

At this, a small piece of royal-canvas was thrown about our arms, around the waist, and we were secured with a piece of ratline-stuff so that we couldn't move our arms.

"Stand these suckers on the fore-hatch for inspecshun," ordered Neptune through his trumpet.

"Stand 'em on th' fore-hatch, sir!" repeated the crew, and we stood as directed.

Neptune then stalked down the fo'c'sle steps and marched majestically up before us. Prodding me in the arm with his trident, he asked,

"Are you clean and ready t' yoin th' Order of the Sons o' Neptune?"

"I am, sir!" I replied, whereupon he raised his trumpet to my ear and shouted:

"Liar! liar! You sucker, yer scales must come off an' I've got t' shave you before you can yoin this Order."

I couldn't raise my hands to my ears to shut out the sound of his voice which was made more unbearable by the clamor of tin pans, beaten close to my head, but I was determined to keep cool and not lose my temper.

By this time the mates, steward and cook had come for'ard and taken seats on the bitts and around the capstan, on top of the t'gallant fo'c'sle deck. Even the captain came as far as the fo'c'sle steps to see the fun that Alonzo and I were to furnish.

Leaving me for a minute, Father Neptune stepped in front of Alonzo and bellowed in his ear, as he had done with me:

"Vhat's th' matter vid you, anyvay? You must be sick! Are you?"

"Yes, I'm sick," said Alonzo.

"Liar! liar!" Neptune shouted. "You've done nothin' but soger ever since you come aboard and yer not a fit subject t' belong t' th' Order of th' Sons o' Neptune."

"I know I'm not and I don't want to be," said Alonzo.

"You refuse, do you?" shouted Neptune. "Whoever heard of a sucker not vanting t' yoin my family? Youst fer this I'll make you one. I don't vant th' sea filled vid sick suckers. I'll know where t' put you." So saying, he called:

"You Sons o' Neptune, you have heard vhat these suckers said. They must be blindfolded before they can enter my domain. Do yer duty!"

"Do yer duty, sir!" they replied in unison; whereupon handkerchiefs were tied tightly over our eyes and I was commanded to sit down.

I had seen nothing in the way of a bench that I could sit on and my arms being tied I was very wary where I sat; consequently I tried to feel around with my foot, but a rope had been thrown around my ankles and my feet were jerked from under me and I sat down on a board which had been placed across the top of a tub filled with water, which had been placed behind me while my eyes were being bandaged. Hearing the water under me, I tried to get up, but a hitch had been taken around my ankles and I was properly made fast.

Neptune again tried to break my eardrums by shouting: "Bring me my shavin' outfit. This sucker needs a shave!"

I knew what was coming for I could smell the Stockholm tar and had read in books that tar was the lather to be applied. There was no mistake. My head was held firmly and the tar was daubed across my cheeks in no gentle manner. I couldn't help myself and the only thing to do was to accept it gracefully. The next order from Neptune was:

"Bring me my keen-edged razor. Is it vell honed?"

"Well honed, sir!" someone replied. Then my face was scraped most unmercifully until it seemed as if the flesh had peeled off but I didn't utter a sound although I wanted to tell his Majesty what I thought of him. As the crew didn't get much of a kick from me, Father Neptune eased up and his next order was:

"Fred, I now pronounce you a true Son o' Neptune! Take him to my drawing-room."

"Take him to your drawing-room, sir!"

This was the keynote for my christening. They jerked the board, upon which I sat, from under me and I was drawn, not into a well-furnished room, but "ker-plunk" into a tub of water. My hands and feet being tied I was unable to get up and try as much as I could, I only made more fun for the crew. Finally with a roll to leeward, I lost my balance and capsized the tub which emptied itself and rolled off the hatch across the deck, while all hands roared with laughter. In the scuffle to regain my feet, the handkerchief slipped down from my eyes and I could see enough to show that I wouldn't be molested if I tried to free myself from the rope which bound my arms and feet; so I sat on the hatch and drew my feet up, with my knees under my chin, until I could reach the knot with my hands. It didn't take long before my feet were free and by squirming and working my arms I finally got the canvas over my head amidst congratulations from the crew.

Alonzo was not in sight for they had led him away where he couldn't hear what was going on. Jerry then handed me a looking-glass so I could see myself.

> O wad some pow'r the giftie gie us
> To see oursels as others see us!

My face was streaked with tar where Neptune's razor failed to scrape it clean and to the slush bucket I went and with a bunch of oakum greased my face thoroughly, wiping off what tar I could.

The next order on the program was to bring Alonzo for-'ard. He was still blindfolded and stood on the hatch where I had been.

"Alonzo," said Neptune, with his trumpet close to Alonzo's ear. "Are you now ready t' become a Son o' Neptune?"

"No! I'm not! I'm too sick, as I told you before," he answered.

"Neptune never changes his mind. I told you before that I vas goin' t' make you a Son o' Neptune so I must keep my vord," said Neptune.

"Set down on that bench," he commanded.

Alonzo was slow to obey, but his feet were soon jerked from under him and I saw how easily I had been made to sit on the board. Jim was behind to catch him should he fall.

"You're a dirty sucker an' I can't have any dirty ones in my family," said Neptune. "Your scales must come off an' I've got t' shave you. Bring my shaving outfit."

The shaving mug was nothing more than the tar pot with the brush in it and with it Alonzo's face was besmeared. With the first dab of the brush he cried out, "Oh, let up!" but there was no further outcry as Neptune thrust the brush into his mouth. Alonzo, who was helpless in their hands, choked, sputtered, spit and fumed at the treatment he received while the crew looked on and laughed. Jim held his head tightly from behind and Jerry kept a strain on the lanyard with which his feet were tied, keeping his feet just clear from the hatch and in this position he was as helpless as a child.

Then came the keen-edged razor. This was nothing but a piece of an iron hoop of a barrel with which Neptune scraped away as he had done with me. No wonder it hurt. After scraping Alonzo's face, Neptune called,

"Bring me a hot towel to steam this sucker's face."

"Hot towel, sir!" was answered, but instead of a hot towel a bunch of oakum was dipped into the tar and laid over Alonzo's face. Squeezing the oakum against his face and massaging it, the tar oozed out and down his neck it ran. His ears were not overlooked and really I pitied the poor fellow, because of his weakened condition, but Neptune only laughed with the crew, saying:

"Oh, you're not so sick as you think you are! A little more lather von't hurt you and it's good t' take ven vunst you git used t' it. Besides, it'll put hair on yer breast an' make you a deep-vater shell-back." Then he said to his assistant,

"It's better you now give him his face powder an' ve'll brush his hair an' set him adrift."

At this the "wet towel" was removed and one of the men threw a handful of the cook's flour in his face, at which the men again roared with laughter for it was, indeed, comical.

His hair was parted in the middle and carefully brushed straight down with a scrubbing brush and for hair oil, to keep it in place, the slush bucket was freely dipped into and smeared on his head and pasted down.

"Alonzo," said Neptune. "It gives me great pleasure to greet you as a Son o' Neptune. Take him to my drawing-room."

The board was jerked from under and Alonzo dropped into the bottom of the tub splashing the water in all directions. Jerry pulled a little too strong on the lanyard around his feet with the result that Alonzo was thrown backward, capsizing the tub and drenching him through. Unable to help himself he rolled over the hatch combings smearing the deck with tar wherever his face touched the planks.

The mate, who was watching proceedings from the fo'c'sle deck, seeing the tar stains on the planks lost all control of his tongue and jumping up, shouted:

"Of all the damnest, dirtiest, sloveniest, unshipiest, irresponsibilest, —est, —est, set of old sailors I ever saw, you men are the damnest. Where in hell and damnation do you think you are? Anyone would think you were all brought up on a farm, in a manure heap, instead of aboard an Australian packet! One of you men take the lashings from that boy and stand him on his feet where he can see! Get busy with those tar stains, one of you, and clean 'em off at once and don't let me see a spot on this deck! How in hell you fellows ever thought enough to put a piece of canvas over the tarpaulin, beats me, and someone will break out with brain fever for this display of grey matter or I miss my guess. Here! one of you bring a prayer-book* and be damned quick about it! Get down on your hands and knees and holystone that spot before it settles in!"

Rattling off a thousand different orders in rapid succession, interspersed with a fit of profanity, he broke up the ceremony without any more hilarity from the men who

* A "prayer book" is a small holystone used to scrub the deck while kneeling down.

sulked away to their quarters in disgust while I tried to console Alonzo in his misery.

"Here, Alonzo!" said Jerry, handing him the looking-glass. "Take a good look at yourself and see how one of Neptune's sons looks. That face of yours will admit you t' any Porti'gee man o' war in the world, providin' you keep it lookin' so. When you git through with th' glass, return it."

Alonzo took one good look and sat down on the hatch so mortified at his appearance that he nearly burst into tears.

"How am I ever going to get this mess off my face?" said he to me, viewing himself from all angles.

"Oh, a little slush will soon soften it," I replied.

"Slu-s-h! Ugh!" said he, with a shrug of his shoulders. "I can't bear the thought of it, let alone the smell. Ugh!"

"It's not as bad as you think it is," said I. "I'll bear a hand and help you."

Taking a bunch of oakum I dipped it into the slush bucket and set to work rubbing it well in on his face. The smell was entirely too much for his stomach and leaving me in a hurry he bolted for the roundhouse where he vomited what he had eaten during the day. Jim had no sympathy for him and said:

"What th' bloody hell is th' matter wid him anyway? Tar an' slush hurts no one and he'll come out from under wid his side-lights shinin' bright by and by. Too bad he wasn't stronger; I'd a raised pertic'lar hell wid 'im."

Alonzo came back and laid down full length on the hatch, moaning in his weakened condition. "I can't stand it any longer, I'm so sick. Let me alone, please! If I had strength enough to pull myself over the rail, I'd jump overboard and if I don't get any better soon, I'll do it, too," etc.

Wiping what tar I could from his face, I got a basin of hot water from the galley and a piece of toilet soap from his kit with which I washed the smell of slush away. This revived him somewhat and he was able to get to his room where he fell in a heap in his bunk. I took off his wet clothes, as well as my own, and just then Charlie came to our door to see how we were getting along.

"How's Alonzo?" he inquired with a smile. "I don't vant you boys t' think there was anything personal in my remarks for it vas only in fun ve acted. You fellers got off mighty light an' if Alonzo had been a vell man you vould both have got more. In th' *Cleopatra*, last voyage, ve had two boys crossing th' line, that made enough fun fer all hands an' th' cook fer two veeks, a-talkin' about it. You see, vone of th' boys vas mean an' kicked at everyting ve did. But ve fixed 'em plenty. Ve ran a vhip up t' th' main yard-arm, for th' cer'mony took place on the main hatch vhere Chips had made a throne for Neptune to set. I vas Neptune, too. Ve had four passengers an' th' cap'n gave th' bloody ship up t' us. So ve took th' lad that vas so mean, to a bos'un's chair vhere ve made him fast an' histed him two blocks t' th' yardarm. Ve didn't ask him if he vanted t' become a Son o' Neptune an' ven he hung by th' yardarm an' I spoke t' him vid my speaking-trumpet, I said, 'I now pronounce you a Son o' Neptune!' Then ve let him drop by th' run, sousing him clear under th' vater. Ve did this three times, an' believe me, ven ve took him aboard he vas a proper Son o' Neptune, for there vasn't much kick left in him for ve nearly drounded him."

At this, Alonzo said, "I wish you had done the same thing to me, without tying me in the bos'un's chair, for when I hit the water I would like to have slipped out of sight and gone to the bottom and ended it all."

"That'll do you!" said Charlie. "You're a long way from shark food and stood th' razz fine. Vhen you're homeward-bound next year you'll know vhat t' do vith th' next joskin a-crossin' th' line an' vill be able to bowse avay on th' vhip that sends him up t' the yardarm, an' vhen he flops into th' vater you can have your laugh an' say, 'You're gettin' it vorser than I did.'"

The steward came for'ard just then with a glass of wine for Alonzo, which he drank with a feeble smile, pronouncing it fine. From the smell, I thought so, too.

CHAPTER IX

THE DEEP-WATER SAILOR

THE morning after we "crossed the line," I saw several dolphins under the bow and immediately made my way out on the jib-boom, where I soon hooked a fine fellow and at once sang out for a sack to put him in. Andy heard my cry and came running out to where I held the flapping fish by the piece of copper wire that I had ganged on to the hook Sunday morning. Bending over the flying jib-boom he spread open the sack for me to lower the fish, saying, "That's a big fish."

It was, indeed, and it was all I could do to pull him in. Sitting astride the boom-end I couldn't raise the dolphin quite high enough to drop him into the sack, on account of his weight.

"It's better jou stand up on th' jib-boom-end. Then jou'll be high enough t' drop him in," said Andy.

Sliding one hand up the fore-royal stay and with the other holding the flapping fish below, I pulled myself up, standing one foot on the boom-end and the other on the flying-jib guy. Then swinging the dolphin over the top of the gunny sack, with one mighty flap of his tail he broke the copper wire and dropped between Andy's awaiting arms and the gunny sack into the blue water below.

I was a disappointed youth and Andy cursed the luck, blaspheming second only to the mate. By this time the second mate and two of his watch were standing in the knight-heads waiting to help us and when we came in he said,

"Never mind, Fred, there are plenty more under the bow and we'll rig the grains-iron and strike one before they leave."

The grains-iron is thrown into the fish as one would throw a harpoon. But the line, instead of being made fast to the pole, is hitched around the iron, close under the prongs, so that when the dolphin is struck he is brought up dangling on top of the grains-iron, while the pole hangs down perpendicularly beneath.

The grains-iron was fitted with the pole, just as Neptune had left it the night before, and the second mate was not long bending a piece of ratline-stuff to it and over the bow he jumped and stood on the martingale shrouds awaiting his chance as the dolphins swam back and forth across the bow. Almost instantly he struck one and was successful in landing it safely on the fo'c'sle deck. The second one he struck tore out of the iron and dropped back, staining the water with its blood. The rest turned upon him immediately, biting huge chunks from his side, literally eating him alive.

There were numerous arguments brought up by the crew in relation to the edible qualities of the dolphin when compared with the bonito and albacore. Some claimed they were poisonous and not fit to eat, while others said they were good eating and not poisonous. The cook swore that the dolphin wasn't fit to eat and should be thrown overboard. He even refused, point-blank, to have anything to do with it as he didn't propose to be blamed for poisoning all hands. Whether he meant it or not, I am unable to say, but I'm inclined to think he didn't want to bother with cleaning and cooking it. The second mate said he had eaten dolphin many a time. He had heard the same tale before and finally told the cook to clean it, after which, if he had any doubt, he could put a coin in the water with the fish and if it turned green it would indicate that the fish was poisonous; if it did not, he could go ahead and cook it for supper and he would take the responsibility of its poisoning anyone. The coin didn't change color and the dolphin was cooked for supper and I found it decidedly more palatable than the albacore.

With fine southeast trade winds we made about three degrees, south latitude, each day and the sails that were so numerous in north latitude all disappeared. Alonzo's initiation didn't seem to hurt him any for he came on deck in the afternoon as usual, but the only work he did was to finish scraping the tar from his face.

I was given charge of the tools in the carpenter's shop, as we had no regular carpenter, and began to be called "Chips." One day the second mate asked me to make him a fid (a wooden spike larger than a marlinspike and made of hard wood) and I turned out a beauty which pleased him so much that he showed it to the mate, telling him I had made it, whereupon the mate came to me and said:

"See here, Chips! What business have you to put your time in making a fid for the second mate? If he wants any carpenter's work done in future you're not to do anything until you see me. See! You belong in my watch and if he wants anything let someone in his watch do his work for him. Where did you get that piece of rosewood you made his fid from?" When I explained that there was another piece left he immediately told me to make one for him, which I did.

While running our parallels down to lat. 29° 22' S. long. 29° W., we struck a squall which compelled us to take in our kites and while clewing up the fore-topgallant sail, the lee starboard head-earing of the upper main topsail gave away, splitting the sail from head to foot. All hands were called to shorten sail and we snugged her down to lower topsails in a heavy head sea. The wind moderated in the morning and we unbent the torn topsail, replaced it with a new one, set the topsails and t'gallant sails and before the day was over gave her the royals and set the main spencer.

A night or two after this, Charlie was caught asleep on deck by the mate who, as usual, raised a rumpus of "hot air."

"Here, by God!" said he. "I'll have no more of this sleeping on deck and I've told you before that the first man I caught asleep I'd knock his block off."

"Vhen you git ready, just try it," said Charlie, doubling up his fists and showing a pair of well-proportioned arms, with the "Ship's Return" and the "Nation's Flags" tattooed on each forearm. From the remarks that the mate made I fully expected to see a fight, but he took one good look at Charlie and replied, "I'm not ready, now."

"No! damn you!" said Charlie. "You're not ready and you'll never be. You've threatened to lick all hands, time and again, an' you're no nearer t' it t'-night than you vere th' first time. You're a bloody bag o' vind an' dasn't hit nobody. That's vhat you are! It's better you take someone on purty soon or ve von't believe you much longer."

The mate evidently didn't like the looks of Charlie's dukes, for after sizing him up from head to foot he thought better of it and turned on his heel and went aft without uttering another word.

There was no more sleeping by the men and we kept awake by walking the deck, scheming in what way we could get even with the mate. No one wanted to commit murder, but they talked of dropping a marlinspike from aloft while he was walking under it and another suggested throwing him off the fo'c'sle-head and breaking his neck or anything that would keep him in his bunk until we reached Melbourne where all hands would jump and run. All swore that they were ready and willing to take a chance at the first opportunity and if eight bells hadn't been struck I was afraid they might have taken it upon themselves to run aft and heave him overboard before the watch terminated, so bitter were they in their denunciation against him. But when the watch was called and we were relieved of duty, not another word was heard and the men hurried to their quarters to sleep, perchance to dream of the offense they were about to commit.

The next morning, during my trick at the wheel, the captain came on deck, scanning the horizon for anything in sight. The mate, standing by, was watching for his first appearance and came hobbling along the gangway, drawing deep puffs from his pipe as he approached. He then rehearsed the incident with Charlie, in the evening watch, in which the captain took no part and I thought he seemed greatly bored while the mate blasphemed at the unpardonable sin of the watch sleeping while on deck. After a five-minute talk in which he finally "ran down" and stood awaiting a reply from the captain, he must have seen the captain's face as I saw it for he stammered:

"I-I don't know what I'm going to do with that lazy Swede. What would you advise, Cap'n?"

Captain Lamson stood shifting his weight, first on one foot and then the other, as he listened; a peculiar, nervous habit which kept him from standing in one position very long. Then, attempting to reply, he said,

"The next—" finding his mouth so full of tobacco juice that he couldn't finish the sentence, he ran to the taffrail, spitting the contents well to lu'ard and without losing his step returned, stroking his gray beard free from any drops of saliva, to finish what he was about to say.

"The next time you catch him asleep just take a rope's end and hit him with it. That will settle any more sleeping on his part."

He looked at the mate with a merry twinkle in his eye and a smile broke over his face as he spoke, no doubt knowing full well that the mate would never dare to hit a robust man like Charlie; then abruptly turning his back to the mate he walked up the cabin steps to the deck above.

Mr. Burris made no attempt to follow, but stood a little discomfited and replied: "All right, sir! I'll see to it."

The captain, evidently wishing to end the conversation, walked away without turning around and the mate stood watching him, knocking the ashes from his pipe against the cabin door. He, no doubt, saw how foolish he would look should he attempt to carry out the captain's instructions, for he wore a puzzled expression on his face and, being left alone, stalked forward along the companionway still knocking his pipe on the top of the cabin at every step, not any too well pleased.

As we got farther south there were many boobies, Cape hens and other strange birds flying about the ship. The booby, a species of the penguin or gannet, is rightly named. A booby will fly until nearly exhausted, when it will come aboard, lighting on the yardarm, spanker-boom or rail, and immediately go to sleep, often too lazy to tuck its head under its wing. While nodding in a sound sleep one can walk up to the bird and easily pick it off the rail, but as they are not good eating and are awfully lousy, there isn't much fun in making pets of them.

The Cape hen (giant fulmar) is a species of the albatross, but smaller, having a spread of wings of from seventy to eighty inches. The head, neck and lower parts are white, while the upper parts are a dusky brown color. The bill is light yellowish with very long nasal tubes, and there are sixteen feathers in the tail. This bird is known to whalers as the "Nellie Breakhous" or "stinker," from the habit it has, on being frightened or wounded, of vomiting the foul contents of its stomach to a distance of several feet. Like the albatross, it lays its dirty-white colored egg on the bare ground. It feeds on carrion and whale's blubber, when obtainable, and often eats so much that it is unable to fly and must await digestion, which takes a half-hour or more.

In no way can it be compared in beauty with the albatross, the largest bird that flies, which will soar about by the hour, scarcely moving a wing. Their color resembles the sea gull and they follow a ship as the sea gull follows a passenger steamer for scraps of food thrown overboard by the cook.

While the albatross is the most graceful bird that flies, it is also the most ungainly when it tries to stop suddenly to pick up floating scraps in its eagerness to get ahead of another bird. Its wings often measure fifteen feet from tip to tip, and they are long and narrow; not more than nine inches wide. With head extended horizontally, like a flying wild goose, the body is brought to a perpendicular position, the legs sticking out in front in a line with its head and neck; spreading its webfeet like a pair of boxing gloves, and bracing against the air, it tries to come to a standstill by backing water with its enormously long wings. The impetus of the body seems too great for its wings, which are kept working like the pistons of a locomotive, and as it comes to a stop, it falls all over itself as it plunges into the water. If it has not judged the distance correctly, there is a wild scramble through the water, its long wings trailing behind, beating the surface at one instant and above its head the next. In fact—

head, neck, wings, body and legs are doing their utmost to reach the coveted spot. It is a laughable sight.

After devouring the scraps it spreads its wings again on the crest of a wave and as it recedes the bird is left in the air where it can maneuver without getting tangled up in the water. In a calm, the albatross has great difficulty in arising because it doesn't have room enough to flap its wings, as their tips are submerged. Although its wings spread from ten to fifteen feet, yet the weight of the body rarely exceeds eighteen pounds.

The Cape pigeon or Cape petrel is another bird in this southern sea that is very beautiful. It gets its name from a resemblance to the tame pigeon. It is from ten to fifteen inches long, with black head, white back spotted with black and under part pure white. It is swift on the wing, flying low like a duck, and is seen more often in stormy weather than in a calm. It does not follow the ship for days, as does the albatross, but flies about its wake where it suddenly drops into the water, diving beneath for scraps and bits of food. Like the Cape hen it ejects an offensive odor when caught or frightened.

One must not forget the stormy petrel or Mother Carey's chicken, sometimes called "Little Peter," because it appears to walk on the water as the Apostle Peter is said to have done. This is the smallest webfooted bird that flies and measures not over three inches long. There are over one hundred different species but their color is generally a sooty black, ranging from a blue black to a gray of various tints. Although small, its power of flight almost equals that of the albatross and like the Cape pigeon it is seen more often in stormy weather. It lays but one egg, which is white to a pale blue, and nests in holes in cliffs where it guards its eggs while setting and dies rather than fly from the nest, if preyed upon. These birds never fly ashore, except for nesting.

There is a superstition among sailors that the petrels carry the departed spirits of sailors lost at sea or otherwise, and should anyone attempt to harm them bad luck will follow the sailor, as well as the ship on which he sails.

In our last gale a flock of these little petrels came along-side, under our lee, extending their tiny slender legs below and fairly danced on the water while picking up the crumbs we threw them. Raising their little wings they showed a white spot on top of their backs, their little black, round heads turning from side to side as if asking us to throw more crumbs to "us little fellows," so far out at sea and away from home. We were all of the same opinion and nearly emptied the bread-barge. Hopping up and down they came so near that they actually stuck out their little feet to ward off the side of the ship as it rolled towards them. I tied a piece of black thread to a stick with which I thought I might catch one, by snaring, but, going to the rail, old Kruse surmised what I was about to do and rushed up exclaiming: "Noo! noo! Fread! Fer Got sake put dot away afore dees ships gits more bad lucks." The other members of the watch voiced the same opinion and my snare was snatched out of my hands and thrown overboard. Suffice to say I didn't catch a Mother Carey's chicken.

The reason so many birds were flying about was because the Islands of Tristan de Cunha were not far off, where they nest and feed. As the weather was thick and stormy we sailed to the south'ard of these islands, which was a disappointment to me. They are generally picked up by Australian packets, for a new departure, and are said to be very beautiful. Tristan de Cunha, the principal of this group of three islands, is midway between Cape of Good Hope and the coast of South America. It is nearly circular in shape and about seven miles in diameter. The mountains rise abruptly from the ocean to a height of about 8,300 feet and can be seen a hundred miles away. There is a volcanic cone in the center which is filled with fresh water and has never been known to freeze over. The cliffs, about 1,000 to 2,000 feet high, are very precipitous on all sides, except on the northeast where there are irregular fertile plains, one hundred feet above the sea. The climate is mild and adapted to fruit and vegetables, seed having been brought from the United States by Jonathan Lambert of Salem, Massachusetts, who took formal possession of the island in 1814. He issued a proclamation setting forth his rights to the soil and invited navigators of all nations, whose route might lie near the island, to touch at his settlement for supplies needed; trading vegetables, fruit and meat for anything that might be most convenient for visitors to part with, useful for him and his associates in their solitary abode.

Lambert had things well started for a colony, but after living there over two years he was drowned while visiting one of the other islands. His associates, disheartened at his death, shortly afterwards left on one of the ships touching there.

The islands and the birds were the chief topics of discussion in our night watches, for the old stories had been repeated so often that we knew just what the other fellow was going to say the moment he opened his mouth.

At the wheel I continually compared the brightness of the Southern Cross with the Big Dipper, but there really was no comparison. The Southern Cross is formed by four principal stars in a rough cross, but they are not of the same magnitude.

I was also much disappointed in the Magellan clouds, of which I had heard so much. These constellations are called, in astronomy, Nubecular Major and Minor, from their cloud-like appearance and are two small, oval masses of light, near the South Pole, seen at night by the naked eye and described by Herschel as consisting of swarms of stars, clusters and nebulae of every description. They are named after Ferdinand Magellan and resemble the stars of the Milky Way, though entirely detached. While the Clouds and the Cross are objects of admiration they are not to be compared with our northern constellations.

About the middle of February our potatoes began to feel the effects of the damp, chilly weather. Having been wet with salt water they began to sweat and decay and grew so strong and sour that we couldn't eat them. At last the men went in a body to the cook and told him if any more sour spuds were cooked for the fo'c'sle they would send them back; also, that he must "lay off" the duff he had been sending for they were tired of it and wanted a change.

The cook was getting so lazy that he hadn't been baking bread for the crew, as it was much easier for him to throw a mess of flour into a sack and boil it, so we had been getting duff instead of soft-tack. The talk had its effect and we were given fresh bread for supper.

Alonzo continued no better and stayed in his bunk instead of being up and around. One day the captain came to our room and told him he wanted to see him about the deck more, where he could get some fresh air and take a little exercise by walking. He took the tape measure and we measured from the front of the cabin to our room, a distance of thirty-five feet, and after figuring with his pencil the captain said:

"By walking this distance 151 times you will have walked just one mile. Now I want you to walk this distance every day. Try to get a little strength before you get so weak that you will be unable to navigate, for I don't want to roll you up in your tarpaulin jacket and heave you overboard."

"But I am unable to stand walking any length of time, Captain," said Alonzo.

"Well!" replied the captain. "Do as much as you can at first and when you are tired, take a rest for a spell and go at it again, for I want you to walk your mile every day. You've got to take exercise."

So Alonzo turned to and started on his hike, but he made bad weather of it and had to go below after the second lap. The ship being on the wind, pitched a good deal, and it was more than he could stand. It was fully a week before he logged off his mile.

When we were about four hundred miles west of the Cape of Good Hope the wind increased to a gale and began to blow great guns. We furled the fore, main and mizzen upper topsails and the flying-jib and jib. All hands were on deck and we clewed up the mainsail to take it in and raced up the rigging, running out on the yard to hand it. Time after time we had the sail almost under control when the gale would blow it from our grasp. The heavy, wet canvas was very severe on our hands. Digging away with our fingers' ends against the sail it refused to yield enough to allow us to pinch a seam, with our bleeding nails, for a hold. With the rise of the bow over a sea, during which the wind would spill more or less from the sail, we gradually picked up, inch by inch and foot by foot, this big sail, holding it under our stomachs, where we were at a disadvantage, to roll the sail upon the yard. Dave and I were in the quarter of the yard, where he told me to sit on the foot-rope and see if I could pass the gasket under the yard and over the sail to him for a temporary stop to keep the sail from blowing out again.

Releasing my hold on the sail, I sat down on the foot-rope, as in a swing, with one arm around the stirrup that supports the foot-rope from the jack-stay, holding the bight of the gasket in my other hand. After several attempts he finally caught the rope and passing it to me, behind the yard below, he pulling up on the gasket above and I pulling down, we held the sail well up against the yard and a couple more turns held it securely.

Then came the task of rolling the sail on top of the yard with the toss of the bunt. All sailors have been well educated in the art of swearing and on the *Akbar* they were all proficient and not backward in blaspheming as they tried, in vain, to raise the heavy, wet sail, cursing the luck that made them sailors, with expressions, "Who wouldn't sell a farm and go to sea!" "Oh, why did I leave my happy home!" etc., all of which was taken good-naturedly in spite of the blue air from the foul mouths with which they damned the ship, the ship carpenters for building her, the captain and officers for sailing her, and themselves for being found aboard her. It made no difference who they cursed. They were there to swear and they certainly did it. Finally, "Handsome Charlie," who was in the slings of the yard, sang out,

"Give her 'Paddy Doyle,' Jerry."

This is a chantey for tossing the bunt and is never heard anywhere else. Although there is not much music in it, it produces results. The words would indicate that Paddy Doyle must have been a fat man who couldn't bend over far enough, on account of his belly, to pull on his sea boots. The same was true with us, on the yard, where we were holding with our stomachs, chests and elbows, all of the sail we had gathered in and were loath to let go our hands for a fresh hold, farther down, for fear we should lose what we had already gained. But with Jerry starting, "To me way-a-hey," our feet were thrown high in the air, regardless, while our heads went down, with bodies hanging over the yard, as we reached below in another attempt; and with the pause "O," drawled out, everybody on the yard began the chorus in unison, holding all he had, knowing full well that it required a long pull, a strong pull and a pull all together, as we sang, "Paddy can't dive for his *boots!*"

On the word *boots*, down came our feet under the yard, every man pulling as one, and up rolled the sail, little by little, with the help of the song. Cursing was forgotten and a broad smile broke over the faces of the shellbacks who, a moment before, hated themselves.

This is one of the many places on board ship where the chantey does more to accomplish results than all the swearing, driving, pulling and hauling could otherwise do. A little song does more to lighten the work than the average person can possibly conceive. It changes the disposition of the men like magic. A moment before they were fighting mad; each one puffing and fuming like a spirited animal, working beside a calm dray horse pulling a heavy load out of the mire. If the high-spirited animal would do less jumping and snorting and wait for the word from the driver, when both should pull at the same time, the team would pull the load much easier. We have all seen it ashore. And so with the sailors. There must be teamwork to accomplish any heavy undertaking and the chantey, wherever sung, marks the time where all willing arms must pull in unison.

With several lines of "Paddy Doyle" bordering on the obscene, the words that we sang cannot be given here. Strange to say, all those men knew what was coming for they

sang the lines as if they were reading from a book, so familiar were they with the chantey. One seldom hears more than
two verses of this song, however, to toss a bunt.

PADDY DOYLE AND HIS BOOTS

To me way - ay - a - a-yah! Oh, Paddy can't dive for his *boots!*

> To me way-a-a-yah!
> We'll pay Paddy Doyle for his boots!
>
> We'll roll up the sail as we sing, a-yah!
> And pay Paddy Doyle for his boots!
>
> We'll toss up the bunt with a fling, a-yah!
> And hang Paddy Doyle for his boots!
>
> We'll all drink whiskey and gin, a-yah!
> And hang Paddy Doyle for his boots!
>
> To me way-a-a-yah!
> We'll all sling soot at the cook!

This little chantey has many changes in the last line of the
verse, but it is usually started, as above, with "Paddy can't
dive for his boots." And after Paddy's boots have been paid
for and he is hung, etc., the chanteyman finds words for the
bo'sun and officers, generally ending with the cook, who is
looked upon as the scum of the earth.

The sail rolled up on top of the yard and the bunt-gasket
having been reached and made fast to the chain tye, the temporary gaskets were released and I again took my seat on the
foot-rope, holding to the topsail sheet above and throwing
the gasket to Dave as before, for the yard and sail were too
bulky for one man to reach around. He pounded the sail
firmly down with his fist with each turn of the gasket and in
this manner we worked our way along the foot-rope from

the quarter of the yard towards the slings, while the others were doing the same at other stations along the yard.

The sail securely fastened, there was a scramble to get down on deck and it was surprising what force the wind had against our clothing. With our oilskin jackets tied about our waists with a piece of rope-yarn, to keep from blowing over our heads, and the ship thrown over to an angle of 45 degrees, staggering and trembling from truck to keelson, from the force of the wind, we almost had to pull ourselves down, for we were blown so tightly against the shrouds that it was with difficulty that our feet reached the ratlines below. In such weather there is no danger of falling from the shrouds, for the wind keeps one jammed against the rigging as if glued there.

Coming down from aloft we immediately reefed the foresail and held the starboard tack all that day with no signs of the wind changing.

On the sixteenth of February, the captain decided to try the southern latitudes, as we were too far north. The sea was running mountains high and for the safety of all we wore ship rather than try to come about. Everything was ready for wearing ship when the mate got into trouble by going forward just at that time. The captain had been riding him hard for the past three days, much to our amusement, for several acts of poor seamanship displayed on his part, in the recent gales. Consequently the mate kept as far away as possible from the captain when he appeared on deck.

Standing on top of the cabin and running between the boats as far as possible, he called, impatiently:

"Mr. Burris! Mr. Burris! Where in hell has that mate hid to now? Why don't you come aft and attend to the after yards? Do you want to carry away another t'gallant yard? Oh! you thing of a mate!"

"Aye, aye, sir! I'm coming," he replied, showing himself under the lee of the forward house.

With the helm up we swung off with an easy roll, squaring in the after yards until the ship was racing full before it. Here, it looked several times as if the sea astern would surely break over the poop, but she arose majestically to the occasion and rode the sea like a duck. Then bracing the fore yard hard to starboard and the after yards following suit, as she swung, we wore ship handsomely on the other tack.

Steering full-and-by for the next two days we finally ran out of the stormy weather and were able to steer a course for the first time in almost two weeks. The good weather was hailed by all and even Alonzo came on deck to try his luck in walking his mile. Although weak at first he gradually gained strength and could walk his mile without resting. While doing his stunt the mate presented him with the old short-handled broom and told him to carry it as a sentry might carry a gun, for he had given up all hope of ever seeing him use it in any other way. Alonzo replied:

"You'd better keep it in your room where it can be found when wanted. I may be able to use it yet and give you a surprise."

Two days later the course was altered from south to south-southeast and the mate got in bad again with the captain the same day. In changing the old foresail for a new one, he sent up the mainsail and the head of the sail was fastened with the robands in the customary manner. Hauling out the head-earing, Charlie saw that the sail was much too long and he called out:

"On deck! On deck, sir!"

"Well, what do you want?" replied the mate.

"This sail is too long, sir!" said Charlie.

"Go ahead and make it fast! The wrinkles will come out when you pull out to lu'ard," said the mate, with his customary cursing.

We stretched the sail as ordered and cutting the stoppings the sail dropped down like a shirt on a broomstick. The captain, who had heard the conversation and the swearing of the mate, had his weather eye on the sail as it dropped.

"You've got the mainsail up there, Mr. Burris. Why don't you mark your sails so you can read them? Get it off as fast as you can, for I don't want to be caught like this in the eyes of some passing ship, to give us the laugh. I'd hate awfully to acknowledge that I had a mate that couldn't tell a foresail from a mainsail," stormed the captain.

There was no sail in sight, but the mate lost no time in clewing it up again when we made the exchange. In the meantime the captain walked the quarter-deck most impatiently, telling the mate what he thought of him at every stride, which was enjoyed immensely by the man at the wheel who didn't miss a word the captain said and stored it up for the evening watch, in which he rehearsed the words of the captain and the manner in which he walked back and forth on the poop.

During the next week we had cold, stormy, rainy weather. The salt spray flew over the ship and we were unable to catch fresh rain-water. The water in the casks on deck wasn't fit to drink, so we emptied what water was left and drew a fresh supply from the tank in between-decks, drawing off a caskful only, and were sparing of what we used, relying on the rain and good weather to fill the other casks.

Old man Kruse never hesitated to bore in when things went wrong and he still swore we never would reach Melbourne. The head winds that kept us back, off the Cape, convinced him that ours was an unlucky ship and it was beginning to have its effect on the crew, for each night they schemed how they would desert on arrival at Melbourne. Already they had been making heavy drags on the slop-chest and the last pound of tobacco was gone. All the men were heavy poker players and after cutting the tobacco into small squares used it to ante. They knew if they deserted they must leave the amount of wages due them, so each one was contriving to draw his limit from the slop-chest.

O'Rourke had already gone his limit and the report was that he had a full caddy stored away. In a game one night, Jerry was a heavy loser and on going to his cache for more made the discovery that someone had been there before him and robbed him of his holdings. O'Rourke also claimed he had been robbed. This set every man looking for his own and it soon developed that all of them were touched, more or less; for forty plugs were missing from the starboard watch and five from the port watch. Who was the thief? It was all a mystery.

At last running into cool weather, the captain wanted a change of food and decided to kill one of the four pigs. He picked out the best-looking one and asked the steward if he knew how to kill a pig.

"Sure! I can stick a pig," said the steward. Whereupon the captain told him to get ready for the killing Saturday so as to have fresh pork for Sunday dinner.

The steward brought three butcher knives to the carpenter's shop and I was selected to turn the grindstone. He kept me busy all the afternoon watch, grinding first one and then the other, feeling the edge from time to time until he was satisfied that he could do no better.

Saturday afternoon Hans pulled the pig out of the pen for the operation and all the time the pig kept up his squealing as if he knew that his time had come. Taking him to the starboard side of the main bitts, we laid him on his back, Hans holding a fore and hind leg on one side and I holding the other two on the opposite. The pig threw his head about from side to side, so the steward called for Andy to hold the pig's head. In this position there was no earthly show for the pig. The steward then knelt down on the deck and feeling up and down the pig's neck, for his windpipe, finally satisfied himself that he had located the vulnerable spot and plunged the knife straight into his neck. The blood spurted over the deck and the squealing increased with every kick.

"Let him up, boys! He's done for!" said the steward.

The moment we released our hold the pig jumped to his feet and scudded before it up the starboard side and over the fore-hatch with everybody in chase.

"Catch him! Catch him!" shouted the steward. But the pig was too nimble for us and started down the port side heading directly for the cabin. The door being open, he jumped over the sill, then under the dining table, around the mizzenmast and into the captain's cabin. It fell to Andy's lot to finally catch him, for we all made missing tackles; but Andy fell on the pig, in the corner of the room, as a football player might tackle a man with the ball and his hold was sure. Hugging the pig under him it was some time before he was willing to take a chance to make room for us to help. It was certainly a great scramble in the after cabin and the floor was covered with gore.

Andy and I carried the pig back to the place where he was first laid on the deck and holding him, as we did at first, the steward began operations again, plunging the knife, time and again, into the unfortunate pig's neck. With each stab, weaker and weaker grew the squealing until at last we let go our hold. A post mortem showed that the pig had actually been murdered by the steward. Six times the knife entered his throat and the back of the neck showed three distinct gaps where the knife went through into the deck planks.

All this time the captain stood beside the main-deck capstan patiently waiting until the pig breathed his last. Finally he called to the steward,

"Steward, have you succeeded in killing him?"

"Yes, sir," he replied.

"Then get a bucket of hot water and a swab, as quick as God'll let you, and get busy in the cabin. I want you to wash up all the blood, taking out every stain." Then turning to the mate, he said: "Mr. Burris, leave things just as they are and when the steward gets through in the cabin see that he turns to on the deck. He told me that he knew how to kill a pig, but I didn't expect to see one murdered. Any old sailor could do that well. If he couldn't, I'd heave him overboard. See that he cleans up the mess, fore and aft, alone. He'll think, twice the next time, before he says he's a butcher. Oh, I don't know what we're coming to! The older I get the more I see how inefficient sailors of to-day are. There are no more sailors! If this man had done this trick on some of the ships I've been in, he would have been strung up by the thumbs, lashed and keel-hauled."

"Yes! and some of the ships I've sailed on, too, Cap'n," said the mate. "Last voyage, on the *Oliver Cromwell* (you remember she had stern windows), we had the same experience in about this latitude. After sticking the pig the men let him up, but instead of running for'ard, he made for the cabin direct and didn't stop until he jumped through the window into the sea. A shark had been following the ship all that day and, believe me, he wasn't long finding the pig, for scarcely had the pig struck the water than he gobbled him up like a piece of cheese. The captain was so mad that he knocked the steward down and jumped on him. I thought every rib in his body was broken; but he was able to clean up the mess and get dinner."

"Served him right," said the captain.

While Captain Lamson was of the old school, he was not a Tartar; but he never hesitated to growl and fume over petty annoyances in seamanship that happen every day. Anyone guilty of committing such an offense was no better than an "old sailor."

An "old sailor" was the depth of degradation, in his estimation; a nonentity, and had no standing whatever. The word was significant of a mark of unseamanship. If a royal or topgallant sail was furled in a gale and time not spent in putting on a harbor furl, the men were no better than "old sailors." "Old sailors" knew better, but had rather furl in a slovenly way than otherwise.

An "old sailor" had no ambition or pride to become better than a common seaman. His station in life was at a rest. Pride gone, he couldn't live down the drunken debauchery that befell him on every trip ashore. Awakening from the revelry and filled with remorse at finding himself shanghaied on some outward-bound vessel, he lived to exist and that was all. He accepted blunt rebuke from an officer, as a matter of fact, not batting an eye to show that his pride had been hurt. Not having any pride, the insult rolled off like water on a duck's back and he went on with his work indifferently. All such characters, whether young or old, the captain called "old sailors." If a turn, hastily taken under a belaying-pin, led the wrong way, you could hear him shout:

"Oh! don't be an 'old sailor'! An 'old sailor' always takes a turn that way. He may know better, but his ambition is gone, and he don't care a damn. Be ambitious and don't be an 'old sailor.' "

Having given his instructions to the mate, the captain walked aft to his quarters while we surveyed surroundings, following the course of the pig around the forward house and back to where the knife prints showed in the deck planks. The steward, in the meantime, was busy with his cleaning in the cabin while we triced up the pig, by the hind legs, to the topgallant sheets, on the lee side of the mainmast, to bleed.

After making several trips to the galley, for hot water, the steward and cook came together in an altercation that looked for a time as if something exciting would really happen. The cook having been under the weather for several days was very irritable and finally burst out,

"This will be the last bucket of water you'll get from me; so don't bother me any more."

The steward, somewhat taken aback, raised his head in a cocky manner and answered:

"See here, Doctor! You'll give me all the hot water I ask for, when I want it."

"Not on your bloody life!" retorted the cook. "I've got my supper to get and you or anybody else can't rob me of my hot water. So put that in your pipe and smoke it!"

"I'm not robbing you and even if I were, it's your place to do as I tell you. I am the steward of this packet and *you* get your orders from me. See!" said the steward, slapping his breast with each word to emphasize the meaning.

"Oh, who th' hell are *you*, anyway?" replied the cook. "Do you call yourself a steward? A fine looking steward *you* are! Where did'sha learn your trade? Sticking pigs in a Chicago slaughterhouse? Git t' hell out of here and skin aft where you belong."

That was too much for the steward's dignity and he let fly his right, catching the cook full in the face and flooring him. The cook was on his feet in an instant and snatching up a butcher knife he jumped out of the galley and was on top of the steward in one leap. With both hands, the steward caught the cook's uplifted hand, in which he held the knife, and both men fell sprawling on the deck.

There was murder in the cook's eye and the steward knew it. To make sure of his hold, he brought the cook's arm down between his knees and the knife cut an ugly gash through his pants and into the calf of his leg, from which the blood flowed profusely. Big Hans and Charlie rushed into the *mélée* to separate them, the mate shouting:

"Let the damn fools fight it out to a finish! If they don't, there'll be no living with them! Go back to your work and don't interfere!"

But Hans wrapped his big arms around the cook and raising him from the deck, like a child, grabbed the fist in which he held the knife and bent his hand back until the knife was released and fell to the deck. In the meantime Charlie held the steward in like manner, both of them puffing and blowing like porpoises and cursing each other unmercifully.

The steward was so enraged that he did not notice the cut in his leg until Charlie backed him away from the cook. Walking with difficulty, he looked down to ascertain the cause and seeing the cut in his pants and the blood-stained stocking, he realized for the first time that he was wounded.

"Oh, my God! I'm murdered!" he cried.

We rolled up his pants leg and found a gash four inches long on the inside of his leg. I brought the bucket of hot water, left standing on the deck, and started to wash the blood from his leg, but the mate called out:

"You, Fred! Get t' hell out of there! This isn't your funeral! If there's any washing to be done let him do it himself. The rest of you turn to on your work. I'll handle this man."

But the mate paid no attention to him at all. The captain, however, saw the scuffle and came to the steward's relief, dressing the wound and taking him to the cabin, where he was laid up for two weeks, I was called to fill the vacancy in the cabin and lived on the fat of the land. During this time, whenever old Kruse had an opportunity, he took particular pains to tell how the "Flying Dutchman" had put his mark on the *Akbar,* calling attention to the way in which the pig was killed and the fight that followed—a boding of ill luck to us all. Standing half bent over to one side, as he talked, and shaking the index finger of his hand in my face, slowly accenting each word, he said:

"Vot did I tole you? Mark my vords, Frade! Dees ships vill never reach Melbourne after such tings a happenin'."

Although I was glad of the opportunity to help the steward with his work while he was laid up, I longed to get back on deck. Washing dishes and running about the cabin with a wet swab, to wipe the dust from the top of the cabin doors, mouldings, etc., didn't appeal to me, and to stand back of the captain and mates, at meal times, with a white apron on, was work I despised. Although I had "all night" in, yet I had rather stand my watch on deck with the men and longed for that day to come again.

During my stay in the cabin, however, I was able to pass out a piece of pie or a dish of pudding to Alonzo—"come backs" from the table, which he seemed greatly pleased to get while he was doing his daily stunt of walking the decks. He improved in strength and on Tuesday, February 29, went aloft for the first time since leaving Boston, but only reached the lower topsail yard. Finding his strength leaving him he took a safer course and returned to deck, all in from the exertion.

On Sunday, March 5, I caught two albatross, by trailing a fishline astern, baited with fat pork. There isn't the sport in catching these birds that there is in trailing for dolphin, but anything out of the ordinary work was exciting.

After these birds land on deck they are unable to fly. Spreading their wings above them and standing as high as possible on their slender legs, which seem entirely too small for their bodies, their wings beating the deck as they hopped for a push off, they would fall all over themselves, so to speak, and being balanced from their wings' ends and pushing up from behind with their feet, it was a clumsy hop-step-and-jump across the deck, getting them nowhere but affording much laughter to the lookers-on, among whom was Captain Lamson who seemed to enjoy the sight as much as the rest of us. One must keep at a safe distance from their long beaks, during these struggles for liberty, for they bite and hold on like a bull-dog.

Although these birds are very beautiful, no one cares to keep them as pets for they are literally covered with vermin. They also have a strong, fishy odor which is quite obnoxious and they are quite unfit for eating.

The sailors clamor for the wings, head and plumage of the breast to carry home to their sweethearts, for, when properly renovated and cured, the breast and wings are very beautiful. The bones of the legs, being slim and hollow, Old Jack spends his time in the dogwatches scraping and fitting them for stems to his pipes, claiming they make better and sweeter stems than any other.

On Wednesday, March 8, we were ninety days out. Steering full and by, we ran down the forty-fourth and forty-fifth parallels for the next week, during which time I was busy making a gangplank, while the sailors were making "drunk nets" for the requirements at Melbourne. A rope net is hung under the gangplank, and one over the side, amidships, to catch anything slipping from the slings in unloading. Poor Jack is often saved a wetting from this precaution, should he fall when coming aboard "half seas over."

During that week of head winds, everyone was out of sorts. The molasses had been strong and rusty for some time and the sailors decided they had had enough of dirty treacle, for Andy found a clot of iron rust in his coffee and said something must be done at once before all hands were poisoned. The cook had been complaining of indigestion and the second mate was troubled with neuralgia in his head, so they decided the molasses was the prime cause of the sickness and all hands went aft to interview the captain.

Captain Lamson heard their complaint and replied he was sorry but could do no better; the molasses was all he had for the fo'c'sle and if the men couldn't use it they would have to go without. This brought on a growl which was finally quieted by the captain promising to supply "Golden Syrup," the same that was furnished the cabin. This pleased the men who returned well satisfied with the interview. For supper that night there was a pitcher of syrup for tea and no growl from the men, but the following morning at breakfast, there was a growl that the coffee didn't taste natural and the day following it was worse and they were not slow in calling the syrup "Baby-food," "Angel-dressing," etc., and not fit to feed sailors, for it was a poor substitute for molasses to sweeten coffee.

March 13 came in with a gale from the north, with heavy showers. The weather main-topgallant sheet parted in one of the squalls and we took in the sail. The gale increasing we took in the mainsail and lowered the upper topsails, furling everything on the mizzen, while we ran before it under lower topsails, foresail, fore-topmast staysail and main spencer until morning, when the wind moderated and we set the topsails with the help of the starboard watch, who were kept up from their watch below.

While clearing up the decks, Mr. Burris asked Mr. Sanborn if he would go aloft and bring down the end of the topgallant sheet that had parted in the sheave block the day before, as there were a couple of patent links fitted to the chain that he wanted. Although it was his watch below, Mr. Sanborn went as requested. I went to the carpenter shop to work on the gangplank and was followed by the mate, who gave me instructions as to how it should be made. We had not been there long before Mr. Sanborn appeared at the door with the piece of chain. Balancing himself with the roll of the ship, he said:

"Here's your chain, sir! What will you have done with it?"

The mate, who appeared very busy with his instructions, either didn't hear the second mate or else did not want to and Mr. Sanborn asked again,

"What do you want done with this chain, sir?"

"I don't give a damn what you do with it! Heave it overboard," replied the mate.

"Heave it overboard, sir!" said he, and overboard he threw it without asking why.

"Christ Almighty! You didn't heave that chain overboard, did you? That's all the patent links we've got in the ship," said the mate, alarmed at the second mate's behavior.

The second mate stood, with a stern look in his eye, and quietly but emphatically said:

"When you give me an order you may depend on me to carry it out, for I was ten years in Uncle Sam's navy and was taught to obey orders whether right or wrong. A *good* sailor always obeys orders."

Without another word he turned on his heel and walked aft, while the mate bit his lips, chagrined at the turn of affairs. The topgallant sheet was none too long and with the broken end thrown overboard, it worried him not a little. Before the day ended the wind moderated and we repaired the topgallant sheet and set the sail as well as the royals and staysails.

The wind working to W.S.W., it later increased to a gale and the same work of shortening sail followed. Light sails were taken in; we reefed the mainsail and also took in the upper mizzen topsails. During the night we shipped much water and the next morning we scrubbed her down with sand and our coir brooms to cut the slime from the decks, which were becoming very slippery from the seas slopping over. The second mate, who hardly ever went below in his first hour, took the hose as we scrubbed. Passing the pigpen he threw the stream into the pen hoping to clear the scupper-holes which had become stopped up during the night; but the water was so deep he couldn't force it. I was scrubbing near the pen when he called:

"You, Fred! Drop your broom and jump into the pen and clear those scupper-holes."

"Aye, aye, sir!" I replied. I had admired him the day before in his reply to the mate that "a good sailor always obeys orders," so I jumped into the pigpen without a moment's thought. The foul water was knee-deep on the lee side and with the roll to windward, the wash hit the side with a splash, spattering me from head to foot. There wasn't room for me to stand erect and groping my way in search of the clogged scupper-holes, the next roll threw the water to leeward where it was impossible for me to see, so I asked the second mate for a belaying-pin to punch out the dirt.

"Belaying-pin be damned!" he exclaimed. "Take your finger and punch it out. A little clean dung won't hurt you."

"I was a good sailor," and rolling up my shirtsleeves, above the elbow, I went after it. There was little sense in rolling up my sleeves, for my arm went clear to the shoulder in the dirty water, and before the scupper-holes were cleared my dungaree overalls were as much wet as my shirtsleeves and on getting out of the pigpen it was necessary for me to make a complete change of clothing.

The second mate laughed good-naturedly when he saw my condition and I couldn't help laughing at his appearance, for he was almost as wet as I from the sloppy waves and slipping about the wet, slimy decks in his bare feet. It was a circumstance that we couldn't avoid and we made the best of it.

Mr. Sanborn seemed to take delight in washing down decks in his bare feet, with pants rolled up above his knees, displaying a pair of white legs, highly tattooed. There was no mistaking him for a man-of-war's man, for his left leg was tattooed with a big green snake, its head extending down the top of his foot to the junction of his great toe, while its body encircled the ankle and twined about the calf of his leg twice, extending over the knee and about his thigh above. On the calf of his right leg a beautiful nude woman was tattooed, with her hair twisted in a knot, showing a very pretty face and bust, with her legs extending down on each side of his leg. Truly a masterpiece of art.

He seemed to take delight in showing these masterpieces when the occasion demanded, but other parts of his body were not often seen. He afterwards explained, "I was a damned fool for having it done, but being drunk at the time I was in such a condition that anything suggested was all right with me."

His breast showed a full-rigged ship with studded link chains running from the hawsepipes over each shoulder and down his spine to the coccyx. His forearms both showed work that only a man-of-war's man could do. On his left was the "Sailor's Return," while the right displayed the "Flags of all Nations." His hands were a sight! Bracelets on each wrist; nude women on his hands, the thumb and fore-fingers outlining their legs; and bands of rings around his fingers. In fact, there was hardly a place left on his body for any more tattooing. Such was the work of man-of-war's men and whalers of that day.

While I was changing my clothing he dropped the hose, complaining of a severe headache and passed my door holding his head in both hands. At dinner time he was suffering so much that he didn't appear for dinner. He was no better in the evening and the captain stood his watch; and the next day the second mate was confined to his bed, the captain taking me in his watch until the second mate was able to resume his duties.

I welcomed the change and although that night we had one of the worst gales and were kept up from our watch below, from midnight till 3 A.M. shortening sail, I did a sailor's work instead of chasing errands on deck at the beck and call of the mate. He began by ordering me in his accustomed manner:

"Fred, run forward and get that watch tackle under the t'gallant fo'c'sle. When you get back, get a couple of slings from the booby hatch. Here! coil up those ropes in the gangway and get 'em from under foot."

Here, the captain interfered, saying: "You've given that man enough orders. Let up on him! Coil up some of those ropes yourself and send him aloft where he is needed."

"All right, sir! Skin up aloft and lend a hand with the mizzen topsail," said the mate, and I lost no time in getting under way.

After snugging her down under fore-topmast staysail and lower main topsail, we hove to for the rest of the night.

We sighted King Island at noon, April 1, 1876, off the

starboard bow. The second mate was still very sick and the cook was not able to do his work and had turned in for the day—another sick man. With the sight of land, Alonzo brightened up and reported for work. The steward acted as cook and Alonzo did what he could in the cabin. At ten o'clock in the evening, the next day, we hove to waiting for daylight to sail up Bass Strait. At 5.30 A.M. we squared away again and later the wind hauled to W.N.W. and we were obliged to tack ship on our way to Port Phillip Heads.

At noon Hans relieved me at the wheel. There was a large steamer from Melbourne passing out, her decks lined with passengers who waved their handkerchiefs as they passed us to leeward, about half a mile away.

"Full and by," I gave him the course in the customary manner, but instead of answering, "Full and by," he exclaimed:

"My God, Frred! There's a vimin! There's a vimin!" rubbing his hands and slapping his thigh exultantly. The ladies certainly looked nice in their summer dresses of bright colors; a great contrast to our crew of sunburned men in faded dungarees.

At 2.30 P.M. a pilot, from the pilot boat *Rip*, came aboard, the boat no doubt named from the tide rip that forms outside of Port Phillip Heads, known as "the Rip." The tide from Port Phillip recedes through a narrow channel at the Heads, which are two abrupt cliffs on each side, and while rushing out to sea forms a clearly defined rip, kicking up a nasty sea in a head wind. As the pilot boat cruises back and forth across "the Rip," for vessels bound in, the name is very fitting.

Tacking back and forth, during the afternoon, we finally passed in at 4.30 P.M. in a fine, light wind, when we backed our main yard and awaited the health officers to come aboard. We were all assembled aft and after they had examined our papers and called the roll, to which we individually answered to our names, and satisfied themselves that Mr. Sanborn and the cook had no contagious disease, we were allowed to proceed. Filling away we passed Mud Island and steered a straight course up Port Phillip for Melbourne, some thirty miles to the north.

During the dogwatches, Dave was very busy with the men, teaching them an old-time chantey, "South Australia." As it would be too late to dock at Sandridge (now South Melbourne) he declared we would have to anchor at either Williamstown or Sandridge before docking; and to give the ship a good send-off before leaving (for they were all determined to make a "pier-head jump"), the chantey would be very appropriate while heaving up anchor for the last time.

True to his predictions, when the sun went down, a northerly wind came off the land with indications of rain and a blow. It was 10.30 P.M. before we reached the head of the bay and the wind being squally we sailed under topsails as we approached Williamstown, where the pilot gave orders to clear the port anchor. When he went forward and saw the oscillating flukes, he exclaimed:

"Bli' me eyes! w'at kind of a bloomin' mud-'ook his this, sir? From all hindications hit looks like a blow t'-night. Are you sure this hanchor will 'old?"

"You bet your life it will hold," replied the mate.

"Really! Hi'd much prefer the other," said he, surveying the starboard anchor and returning with a troubled look.

"You'll have no cause for worry on account of this one. What kind of bottom have you got here?" asked the mate.

"We've got good mud and clay, but Hi don't care t' take the blame hif we 'appen t' drift an' foul hother ships in the 'arbor. Really! Hi'm not at all acquainted with the 'oldin' qualities of this queer lookin' thing. The starboard hanchor is quite sufficient, don't you know, sir!"

"Don't worry! Don't worry!" reiterated the mate. "I'll take all the blame. This is just the anchor for mud and clay."

"Very good, sir! Hit's quite satisfactory with me so long as you take the blame. You Hamericans 'ave queer patents, don't you know! Every year you 'ave somethin' different and quite puzzling t' understand," said the pilot, shrugging his shoulders and shaking his head as he walked aft, not yet quite satisfied. At six bells he threw her into the wind and as we lost headway he gave the order,

"Let go your hanchor."

"Let go the anchor, sir!" replied the mate, as he knocked the catch of the ring-stopper loose with a top maul, and with a splash our anchor dropped amid a clamor of chain flying over the windlass below that shook the ship from stem to stern; gradually growing fainter as the cable ran out until all was still after 117 days of unrest, 115 of which we were out of sight of land. Notwithstanding old Kruse's prognostication that we would never reach Melbourne, we were there to watch the twinkling of lights ashore, off Williamstown to the westward, with Sandridge to the northeast. They sparkled like diamonds as we furled the sails and cleared up the decks for the night and were good to look at, for we all longed for a chance to get ashore. It was my first foreign shore and I looked forward with pleasure for an opportunity to stretch my legs for a walk on solid ground.

Turning in for the night I could hear the wind whistle through the rigging and the patter of rain on the house above. Rolling my blanket high above my ears, to shut out the sound, I smiled and hugged my pillow with a satisfying feeling and could not help shouting: "Blow, damn you, blow! It's my time now. I've got all night in and you'll have to blow harder than this to get me out of this dry bunk." I slept a contented sleep until called at 5.30 A.M., when we hove in thirty fathoms of slack chain, in a drizzling rain, the wind having abated.

Dave called my attention to the old English convict ship *Success*, about a thousand yards away, which was being used at that time as a reformatory ship. Anchored fore and aft, a row of piling was driven around her, some fifty yards away, not unlike the piling of a ferry slip. Near the top of the piling was a walk for the guards or sentinels, who paced back and forth with loaded rifles. They were there to shoot should any break for liberty be attempted aboard the ship.

This ship afterwards came to America, having sailed from Glasson Dock, near Lancaster, England, in 1912, to Boston,

The Convict Ship "Success". Built in 1790 of Burmese teak and still afloat.

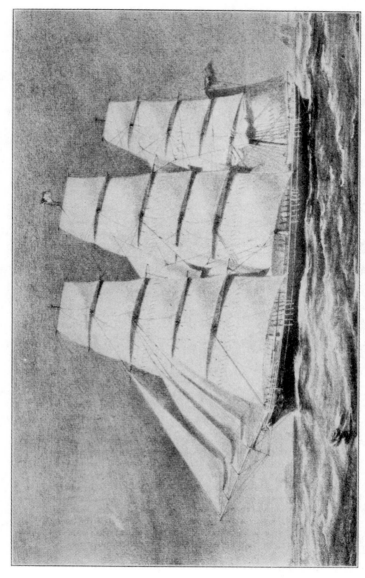

Clipper Ship "Thermopylae," Built in 1868, at Aberdeen, Scotland. From a lithograph in the Macpherson Collection.

without any consort, an unheard-of achievement for a ship one hundred and twenty years old.

The *Success* was built in 1790, at Moulmein, of Burmese teak (as well as her spars) and her original mainmast was still standing. Her length was 135 feet, beam 30 feet and her midship timbers, 2 feet 6 inches thick, with keelsons in proportion; tonnage 1,100. She was built for the East India trade but, unlike the China clippers of the '60's, had a very bluff bow with a figurehead of the Queen Elizabeth type, running far out under the bowsprit, which was raised to an angle of almost 45 degrees. The high poop and square stern carried the usual stereotyped gilded scroll of that day, while her quarter galleries were docorated with elaborate carving.

In 1802 she was chartered by the English Government to transport convicts from England to Australia, making many a voyage with untold hardships. Her three decks were fitted with staterooms and cells, and with a domineering overseer the life aboard this ship was anything but pleasant. In 1851 she was permanently stationed at Melbourne as a receiving prison. Here, for six years, the prisoners were subjected to unheard-of cruelties, knowledge of which finally leaked out, when it was decided to abandon the hulk system and use her as a reformatory ship. This was done some time after and she was used until the order was given that all prison ships were to be broken up and sold for junk. Through an oversight this condition didn't appear on the contract of the *Success* and she escaped destruction.

In 1885 she sank in Sydney harbor, remaining at the bottom, off Fort Jackson, for five years, when she was raised and fitted out as an exhibition ship. All the antique prison implements of torture that could be obtained were gathered, together with ancient guns, pistols, swords and anything of interest connected with early prison life, as well as charts and ancient documents. In the lower hold life-size wax figures of bushrangers and noted criminals were placed in the different cells, making the exhibition well worth seeing.

After exhibiting the *Success* in every port in Australia, Tasmania and New Zealand, she sailed for England and was on exhibition until 1912, when she came to America. After a short stay at Atlantic ports, she was brought through the Panama Canal to San Francisco, for the Panama Pacific Exposition of 1915, and later went to Portland and Seattle. She then went east, through the Panama Canal, finally bringing up in the Great Lakes.

No other vessel can boast of such a career and it is to be regretted that public interest couldn't have been aroused to save from the "bone yard" some of the old clipper ships built by the peerless Donald McKay and keep them afloat as a monument to his memory. The *Glory of the Seas*, built in 1869, was the last ship afloat of his great work. She was dismantled and used as a barge between Seattle and Ketchikan, Alaska, for several years, when it was finally decided to burn her for junk. A movement was started to tow her to Boston and preserve her, but the cost of towing around was more than could be raised at that time and the project was abandoned. She was hauled ashore at Endolyne, Seattle, and burned May 14, 1923.

The steamer *Resolute*, of Melbourne, came alongside as we were finishing breakfast and we were called to heave up anchor. Dave, who had been telling me of the different places of amusement in Melbourne, was quite jubilant at the thought of once more getting ashore and as we turned to said that he would take pleasure in showing me the sights as soon after supper as we could get ashore.

Shipping the windlass brakes, he could hardly wait for the order to "Heave away," before he started the home chantey that he had prepared and taught the other members of the crew the day before. His voice could not be compared with Jerry's, but he was a good chanteyman, outside of a decided nasal twang; he also had the happy faculty of making up rhymes to fit the occasion as he chanteyed, which was immensely enjoyed by all. With the order "Heave away," he broke out as follows:

SOUTH AUSTRALIA

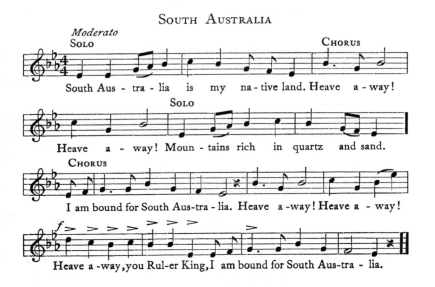

South Aus - tra - lia is my na - tive land. Heave a - way!
Heave a - way! Moun - tains rich in quartz and sand.
I am bound for South Aus - tra - lia. Heave a -way! Heave a - way!
Heave a -way, you Rul - er King, I am bound for South Aus-tra - lia.

Gold and wool, brings ships to our shore,
And our coal will load many more.

Here's a packet anchored off the pier,
There's a bar ashore with foaming beer.

Heave! Oh heave! and we'll all go ashore,
Where we will drink with girls galore.

Glasses filled, we'll touch with a clink,
Heave! bullies, heave! the girls want a drink.

I see Julia, standing on the quay,
With a dame for you and me.

At the head of Sandridge Railroad pier,
Straight to Mother Shilling's we'll steer.

Julia slings the sheoak at the bar
And welcomes sailors from afar.

In the dance hall there you'll pick your girl
With golden hair and teeth of pearl.

She will drink you blind while at the bar,
And call you, "Dear, my own Jack Tar."

She'll waltz you round in a dizzy dance,
While you're half drunk and in a trance.

Then we'll drink to Mother Shilling's name,
And drink again to the lovely dame.

In the arms of girls we'll dance and sing,
For sheoak will be Ruler King.

Drunk! For sheoak's gone to our head,
The girls can put us all to bed.

Sheoak is the name of a high-proof, keg beer made in southern Australia. A few drinks is generally sufficient to "put a man under the table."

Chanteying in the cable, we soon had the mud-hook off the bottom, when we were towed up to Old Pier, Sandridge, and dropped anchor again awaiting a berth at the dock. The *Resolute* took the captain ashore immediately after.

The next morning the *Resolute* again made her appearance at six o'clock and we were called to man the windlass, heaving in forty fathoms of chain and chanteying "South Australia," which the men seemed to enjoy singing. Dave, who had made a voyage from Melbourne, in the clipper ship *Thermopylae*, to Woosung, where she loaded tea for England and left Woosung, July 15, 1874, arriving at Deal, October 27, making 104 days between ports, said they never hove up anchor without singing this song. She was a very fast ship and Captain Kemball hung on to the last before shortening sail. She was a brute and Dave left her, paying his way to Boston and finally shipping for home in the *Akbar*.

Upon arriving at the dock we made her fast, fore and aft, and got our sheoak nets under the gangplanks. It was ten o'clock before we got our breakfast. The usual work of getting ready for the stevedores kept us busy until three o'clock, when we knocked off work for the day.

CHAPTER X

MOTHER SHILLING'S DANCE HALL

TRUE to his word Dave hurried me ashore soon after supper to show me the sights and get ahead of the others. While walking up the dock everything looked bright overhead, because there were no heavy yards and hemp rigging above, but I began to stumble and Dave shook me saying:

"You stagger like a drunk! Come out of it! If we're going to see the sights you'd better 'urry."

At the head of the dock he pointed to a sign, at the left, on which read, MOTHER SHILLING'S INN, and over the door at the corner, BAR. "Let's go across and get a drink," said he, and I followed. Going into the saloon I found it was none too well kept and decidedly dirty. A high, wooden bar extended across the room, with an "L" at the end, behind which were no mirror or glasses to be seen, while in front of the bar there was no furniture except two wooden benches in a corner. Sawdust was sprinkled over the floor, where one could spit tobacco juice at will. A couple of half-drunken sailors sprawled over one of the benches immediately got up and staggered to the bar as we approached.

" 'Elloa, shipmates!" said one of them. "I shay! Going t' set 'em up?"

"Wot'll you 'ave, gents?" broke in the bartender, coming forward.

"Give me a Tasmanian cocktail," said Dave, with a smile. At this, the bartender looked at him and exclaimed: "For the love of God! Dave Price! Ware in th' bloody hell did ye's come from? Shake, old pard, shake! I ain't seen ye's since ye's shipped in the *Thermopylae,* for Sydney, over a year ago."

Dave began giving an account of himself and his voyage to England, but was interrupted from time to time by the drunks who kept up an incessant conversation while they lounged over the bar, unable to stand alone, and calling: "Hi shay, shipmate! What'd'-ye-shay you're going t' 'ave? When-d'-we git that drink," etc. Finally Dave could stand it no longer and throwing a shilling down on the bar, he impatiently said:

"For God's sake! Give these fellows a sheoak and stop their bloody gab!"

The drinks coming forward, Dave asked: "How's Mother Shilling? Is Julia with her yet?"

"Oh-I," he replied. "Wait till I call her," and going to the door opening into the dance hall, he called: "Come 'ere Mother! Guess who's 'ere!"

A portly, middle-aged woman made her appearance followed by a slender, light-haired girl. Both stood in the doorway for a moment when the elder exclaimed, "Well, if it isn't Dave Price!" while the younger rushed past her into Dave's arms, who hugged and kissed her repeatedly, saying:

"Julia, my sweetheart! How glad I am t' see you! How 'ave you been all th' time I've been away," etc.

Both women seemed truly glad to see him and after I was introduced Mother Shilling invited us both inside. Going through the door we were ushered into the dance hall where several sailors with their girls were drinking beer at different tables. Drawing up chairs for four, at one of the tables in the corner, she bade us be seated and immediately left for a bottle of wine. Dave and Julia kept up a lively conversation while I surveyed surroundings.

At our end of the hall there was an old square piano, badly scratched and showing stains of beer over the corners. The legs looked as though they had never been dusted. The chairs and tables were not much better, but the floor, about 15 x 50 feet, was waxed for dancing and was very good. Mother Shilling was not absent long, and opening the bottle poured us each a glass of sherry.

As we sat there sipping the wine she asked if this was my first voyage to a foreign country and upon learning that we had just come from the ship and that Dave was going to show me the sights in Melbourne, she said:

"Dave, you're not going fer t' leave this place until you've 'ad a dance with Julia; and Fred, I'll git you a nice girl an' you might as well enjoy yourself 'ere. You'll not find eny nicer girls up in the City than right 'ere. It won't be long before th' music starts. Wait 'ere a bit," said she hurriedly, for fear we both would leave.

In vain I protested, saying I didn't dance, when Julia came to her assistance, saying: "Oh, you're not thinking o' leaving us this early, are you? Go get Kitty, Mother. She'd be tickled t' death t' learn you t' dance, Fred, an' besides, she's a pretty girl. I know you'll like her," and taking hold of both my hands she pulled me back into the chair from which I had risen and deliberately sat in my lap, so I was forced to stay while Dave looked on and laughed at my discomfiture.

Mother Shilling was not long in bringing Kitty back with her. She was a wiry, little English dame, with black hair and blue eyes, and as plump as a chicken. Julia was right in saying she was a pretty girl. She was more. She was handsome. Coming to the table she saw that we had emptied the bottle of sherry and remarked:

"I s'y, Julia! Mother Shilling told me that you wanted to see me. Did you want I should 'elp drink the sherry? Really, you know, I much prefer sheoak."

This was a laugh on us. After that Dave and I were introduced and I, of course, ordered sheoak for the crowd.

Taking a chair next to me, she looked me "full and by" in the face, for I was a bashful lad; yet I couldn't keep my eyes away from her as I answered her many questions about the voyage to Melbourne in which she seemed much interested. Sitting where she showed up to best advantage, she soon won me over and I was not anxious to leave at all; in fact, I rather enjoyed being in her company. But Mother Shilling was very anxious to have Kitty teach me to dance and on learning that I was a novice, she took both my hands and in her winning way urged me to permit her to show me.

Her touch was magnetic and holding her small, plump hands in my horny, calloused flippers, I never held a main brace with a firmer grip; in fact, I wanted to bowse away and take a turn and belay. She smiled as I squeezed her hands and with a nod of her head towards the floor (for she couldn't point with her hands), her gentle pleadings found me a willing lad.

"Really, you'll find the flawh not hawful bad," said she, tugging away till at last she succeeded, and bidding me put my arm around her she proceeded to show me the waltz step.

Counting one-two-three, first forward, then backward, with a bend of the knee, etc., I was surprised to find how easy I was getting along. Then, at the turn, this little dame threw herself into my arms—"head on." Another squeeze and my feet got mixed up with hers and we started all over again. Under her guidance with a whirl first to starboard and then to port—never complaining when I occasionally hit her foot as I misstayed, coming into the wind, she complimented me at almost every whirl.

It is surprising how hard one works when trying to learn and although I was loath to release my hold around her waist, a sense of politeness told me it was time to give her a rest for we both were perspiring freely. Taking her hand, which she permitted me to hold, I led her back to the table where Dave and Julia both complimented me at my showing.

Whether it was the beer or my confidence in Kitty's teaching, I was so elated, as I stood wiping the perspiration from my forehead, that I felt obliged to order another round of sheoak. In fact, I was willing to buy anything and drawing my chair close to Kitty, I noticed that Julia was sitting on Dave's lap. I saw no reason why Kitty shouldn't do the same with me and putting my arm around her she offered no resistance and so we sat sipping beer, while every remark seemed awfully humorous. I had forgotten all about Dave's showing me the sights in Melbourne, as he promised, and was content to remain in Kitty's company, for she was such a charming girl. Then the music started to play and Dave and Julia got up to dance. Looking around I was surprised to see the small hall filled with couples that were there unnoticed by me before, all of whom were in an extremely happy

frame of mind. Then Kitty got up and asked me to dance
with her, but I said that I was afraid of stepping on someone's toes in the crowded hall.

"Bally rot!" she cried. "You do quoit well and not hawlf
bad. Really, Fred, you dawnce better now than some."

I had had just enough sheoak to make me think she really
meant it and finishing what was left in my glass we got out
on the floor. With my arm around her again I held her
tightly while she steered me through the crowd in time to
the music, which consisted of a violin and piano. The piano
was badly out of tune and the violinist played anything but
well, but while holding Kitty in my arms any music was
heavenly. The dance was entirely too short, but as Dave and
Julia went back to the table, I asked if we shouldn't do the
same.

"That's quoit in horder," said she. Now, there was nothing in her reply that should make me think it was the fun-
niest thing she had yet said, but I laughed till the tears ran
down my cheeks. "Quite in order," I kept saying, as we
reached the table and then Dave said,

"I think we'd better 'ave another, eh, Fred?"

"Quite in order!" I replied, at which we all laughed and
laughed again. The glasses filled, we talked and laughed till
the music started again.

"Come on, Fred!" said Kitty, and she didn't have a
chance to ask a second time, for I was now sure that I could
dance as well as anyone in the room.

"Quite in order, Kitty, dear!" said I, arising from the
table. My eyes were riveted on the girl standing before me,
her large blue eyes sparkling with mirth at my reply and her
rosy lips half parted, displaying a set of pearly white teeth
that I had not particularly noticed before. All at once it
dawned on me that she was very beautiful and impulsively
I tried to kiss her. But she turned her head, saying:

"No! no, Fred! It cawn't be done 'ere!" pushing me
away.

This rather nettled me and for a moment I stood non-
plused. Was it possible that this girl was purer than the rest

of the dance hall girls here? I mused, looking searchingly into her beautiful eyes. She evidently guessed what was running through my brain for she stood erect with her head proudly thrown back displaying her snowy white neck, with her bosom rising and falling like waves of the ocean. A beautiful smile graced her lovely face and her eyes danced merrily at my predicament.

"Kitty, dear! You've got me coming and going! Why is it that a beautiful woman like you is in such company?" I asked.

"Aow! daon't bring up the pawst, please! Come on, let's dawnce!" said she impatiently and not wishing to press the matter further we got under way once more. By this time my head was whirling faster than my feet and consequently I held her tighter than I had previously done.

"Are you afryed of losing me?" she asked, laughingly looking into my eyes and I couldn't resist the desire to make a clove hitch around her waist, with my two arms, right there, when she gave a little scream and we bumped into a couple.

"I s'y! Square th' main yard, me 'earty, an' give 'er a good full!" the sailor laughingly said.

"Quite in order! A good full you have it!" I replied, wearing ship only to run foul of another couple.

Now this couple I had noticed before and the man, instead of being a sailor, was a white-faced, long-drawn-out pimp belonging to the house. He and Mrs. Shilling had occupied a table next to ours and I found out afterwards that he was very sweet on Kitty.

"See 'ere, me joskin! Wot in 'ell are you trying t' do? If I was you, I'd git t' 'ell out'n 'ere an' learn t' dawnce before you knock somebody's ribs in. Take my advice and skin out before somebody lands on you."

"Aoh, Pete! Restryne your tongue!" exclaimed Kitty. "Cawn't you overlook a jolly little matter like this? 'E didn't do it on purpose."

"The 'ell 'e didn't!" said he. "Wot business is it o' yours

anyway? You must like t' dawnce with a drunken bloke like 'im with 'is two harms around you."

Kitty's soft blue eyes changed in an instant to a cold steel gray, while a scowl came over her face and her eyelashes fairly snapped with rage as she bit her lips in restraint. Although a little woozy myself, I could see that she was trying to curb her tongue and I had sense enough to know that she was being insulted by a man who said I was drunk. I was not drunk, I reasoned, and being in company with a lady, I resented his slurring remarks. My first impulse was to knock him down, but as Kitty stood biting her lips in silence, I was too polite to make a disturbance in the hall before everyone, so answered quietly:

"See here, my man! You're entirely out of order. Isn't he Kitty?" turning to her sympathetically.

"Hindeed 'e his," said she.

"And you are no gentleman or you wouldn't address a perfectly respectable lady in this manner and as long as she is in my company I won't permit you to insult her," I added. It didn't dawn on me that I was among the toughest set of men and women that could be found on the water front. I was having such a pleasant time and the crowd seemed so happy, laughing and singing as they danced around the hall, that I saw nothing of the half-drunken sailors about me. But it was far from a church sociable, for when I said I wouldn't permit him to insult her, he turned upon me, exclaiming,

"That'll do, you!" and before I was aware what he was up to he hit me on the point of the chin, which jarred my whole head. This brought me quickly to my senses, or lack of sense, for in an instant I lost all politeness and saw neither sailors nor girls. The only thing vivid was the white face of the man before me who stood with a determined look and clinched fists ready to give me another blow. Not waiting for him to advance I jumped in front of him and at the same time dealt him an uppercut under the chin, with all my force, that doubled him up like a jackknife and completely knocked him off his feet. A moment before I was as docile as a lamb, but now I had all the furor of a wild beast within me and as soon as he was on his feet I struck him over the ear, which completely knocked him out. Rushing in and standing over him, I shouted,

"Get up, damn you, and take what's coming to you!"

The crowd rushed in with cries of "Take him out! He's killed! Call the police!" etc. Mother Shilling then appeared on the scene, crying:

"By's! By's! For God's sakes be quiet! You'll have the cops down upon us an' bag us all! I cawn't afford t' lose me license! Dave! Dave!" she called. "Tyke yer friend aout th' back door quick! The cops'll be 'ere awny minute!"

With everything in confusion, the girls screaming and the crowd surging back and forth, eager to get a look at Pete, who was being dragged to an open place where he could get air, a couple of sailors took me by the arms to rush me away against my will, for I didn't remember doing anything I was ashamed of.

With cries of "Keep quiet," etc., and with a dizzy brain, I was forcibly pushed through the back door just as I heard Mother Shilling say:

"Aoh! My God! 'ere they come! Get 'im aout quick!"

The door was shut in my face as I tried to get back. Everything was as dark as a pocket but the fresh air was a stimulant which acted quickly on my befuddled brain. "Come this way, Fred," I heard Dave say. "We'll get as far away as we can."

Then he walked me from one street to another, telling of incidents in the dance hall that I didn't remember. How I fell asleep and was carried upstairs to bed, all of which I denied happening, for I knew I had remained downstairs all the time; besides, the evening was yet young.

"Young, be damned!" said he. "What time do you think it is?" and he pointed to a clock that showed 2.30 A.M.

"Holy smoke! Is it that late?" I inquired. "Let's go back to the ship."

Dave was only too willing, for we were quite a distance from the dock and I had no idea in which direction it was. At length we brought up at the dock, when Dave proposed having another drink, but the mere thought of it nauseated me and I declined with thanks. He then went to Mother Shilling's and I to the ship, where I passed over the sheoak net in safety; and that was how I saw the sights of Melbourne on my first night ashore.

Filled with remorse I was no exception to the rule, "the day after the night before," when I was called in the morning. With an aching head, while on my way to the galley for the accustomed pot of coffee, before turning to, I stopped at the water-cask with an insatiable desire to drink it dry and appease my thirst; but the dark-brown taste was there and nothing tasted right. The coffee had lost its flavor and the sea-biscuits stuck in my throat and were hard to swallow. The watch was called entirely too soon to suit me—in fact, nothing was right at all and I shuffled out of the room hating myself and everyone else.

With the call of the watch, the mate could only round up Hans, Andy and Jim Dunn. All the other members of the crew had made a pier-head jump during the night. Alonzo, who was acting as both cook and steward, didn't count in the watch. Both Jim and Hans showed a night of dissipation ashore, for their eyes shone like a couple of burnt holes in a blanket; but the mate kept us washing down decks until breakfast time, which we did in silence and our only recognition of each other was a sickly smile occasionally as we passed. The mate must have been ashore also for he was finding fault and cursing a blue streak all the time for fear we wouldn't get through before the stevedores came. I was glad when we were finally knocked off for breakfast and I was left to myself. It was then that the stevedores opened the hatches and started to break out cargo.

The second mate and cook were still very sick and after dinner were taken to the hospital. Alonzo went along with them, ostensibly to carry their valises, but in reality to look for work in his line of trade. He came back in time for supper, very jubilant, saying that two engraving establishments were looking for a man and he was advised to stand by ready for a call. He was resolved to quit the sea and said he would never leave Melbourne in the *Akbar*, and was ready to become an Australian right then, for he was much impressed with the looks of the city, standing on its seven hills, with wide streets intersecting each other at right angles. He told of the running water from the mountains, flowing down the gutters on each side of the principal streets, carrying off all refuse; with wooden approaches or bridges over the gutters for pedestrians and on every other corner a comfort station. The massive stone buildings compared with anything in Boston. He was loaded down with a lot of literature on Melbourne which was very interesting reading for us and we planned on going to the parks and public gardens the following Sunday.

That evening we both went ashore with Hans. Kitty was standing at the head of the dock and greeted us smilingly. Hans proposed going to Mother Shilling's for a drink of sheoak and Kitty joined the crowd. She begged Alonzo and me to stay and have a dance, but we excused ourselves, much to her disappointment, as we were on our way to the city. I offered to take her with us, but she said she couldn't get away.

The tram cars were a novelty with their first-, second- and third-class passengers. We bought a second-class ticket and were locked in like criminals, the door being on the side with a running board beneath where the conductor took our ticket. The car made me think of a fo'c'sle with a table in the center and a bench on each side running athwartships.

On reaching Melbourne the door of our car was unlocked and we were permitted to get out. I found Melbourne all that Alonzo said it was and we walked up and down the streets until tired out, taking the last tram back to Sandridge.

Andy, the night watchman, had quite a yarn to spin the next morning, about old Tom, the cat, having a fight with a large wharf rat he had tackled but was unable to hold. They fought for nearly half an hour, when the rat caught Tom by the fore foot, holding on like a bulldog, while Tom scratched and cried with pain. After getting away from the rat he gave it up and ran into the cabin. Andy showed us the

rat which he had killed with a belaying-pin after Tom re-
treated. It was nearly as large as Tom; in fact, I never saw
a larger one.

On Saturday the cook came back from the hospital saying
the only reason he left was that he was being starved to
death and wanted to get back where he could get enough to
eat. The next day Alonzo and I went up to the hospital to
see Mr. Sanborn, taking with us for luncheon a few sea-
biscuits. The first question he asked was, "Did you fellows
bring anything to eat?"

We showed him our luncheon and he exclaimed, "For
God's sake let me have them quick!" His action spoke louder
than words, and made us think that they were trying to
starve their patients. He said it was the first thing he had
eaten except gruel, since he came there. His headache was
nearly gone and he said he would be back aboard the ship in
a few days. When we left him I asked him if there was anything he wanted that I could get him and he said: "No! But
don't come back without bringing me some grub."

We then toured the city and after spending a delightful
day in the parks we walked about the streets until late at
night and returned to Sandridge about midnight. When we
reached Mother Shilling's we saw an excited crowd in front
of the saloon. The police wagon was just leaving and we
learned that a drunken sailor had stabbed another, three
times in the side, and both were being taken to the lockup.
No one was permitted to enter the saloon and curiosity getting the best of us we remained with the mob outside. Presently I saw Dave near the entrance and elbowed my way to
his side. He said it was Hans. That he had stayed at the
saloon ever since we left, drinking sheoak with Kitty, and
when a couple of English sailors came in half-seas-over and
insulted Kitty, Hans got into a fight in which he got the
worst of the argument, for he was knocked down with a
chair. When he got on his feet he opened his jackknife,
before anyone could stop him, and with the clutch of a
giant he grasped the other sailor by the throat and stabbed
him in the side and shoulder before they could be separated.

The wound was painful, but not serious. He was tried the following Wednesday and sentenced to three months' hard work.

The American ship *Samar* arrived from Boston on Monday, April 10, 1876, in the remarkably short time of eighty-four days (seventy-five days from land to land), which was a record. She was the new ship that pulled into Lewis Wharf the day we left Boston. The *Mystic Bell* was lying at Long Pier, so there were three American ships in port. She had loaded ahead of us, at Lewis Wharf, but was a cranky ship and nearly capsized while off King Island and so was undergoing extensive repairs. The three American flags looked mighty good. The *Samar,* instead of coming to an anchor as we did, immediately docked on the other side of the wharf from us. Her bright spars and yards, together with her new rigging, stood out in bold relief and she certainly was good to look at.

Alonzo received word that morning to report for work at the engraving establishment. The captain gave his consent and he left the ship a mighty tickled boy. The captain told him he could work in Melbourne during the day, but if he cared to sleep aboard the ship he could do so; so while we were in port he got his dinner and breakfast aboard the ship.

Although short-handed, the mate, Jim, Andy and I, sent down the mizzen topgallant mast. The cap at the topmast-head was split (our caps were of the old wooden type with an iron band around them), being season-cracked, and had to be condemned and a new one made ashore.

Good Friday came on April 14 and was a general holiday for all vessels. Early in the morning Andy told us that old Tom's foot was so bad from the bite of the wharf rat that he went into a fit at five o'clock and after running about the deck spasmodically, finally jumped over the side and headed for Williamstown. He probably drowned. The boys from the *Samar* came aboard in the morning. There were two ordinary seamen and two boys. One of the boys came from Falmouth and the other from Salem, Massachusetts, and they seemed to be above the ordinary. I am ashamed to say I have

MELBOURNE FROM THE SOUTH, NEAR THE ST. KILDA ROAD. From a colored lithograph (1855) in the Macpherson Collection.

Ship "Samar" of Boston, 1,111 Tons, Built in 1875

forgotten their names. As it was a holiday we all decided to go up to Melbourne and make a gala day of it, and accordingly went to the station and bought our second-class tickets.

As the time for leaving approached so large a crowd gathered that it became necessary to provide extra coaches. Dan, an ordinary seaman from the *Samar*, was full of life and sailor-like was the first to take the lead. He suggested that when the train backed in on the switch, we make a run ahead of the crowd and jump on where we could secure seats by being first in the coaches. This we did and swinging onto the running board were soon comfortably stowed away in a compartment by ourselves, with congratulations that it was done so easy. The crowd rushed to the train, but occupied other coaches ahead of us and strange to say seemed to overlook the coach we were in, so that we commented how simple they were in rushing madly at other coaches when there was so much room in ours. Finally, the conductor arrived at our compartment and asked for the tickets, which were handed to him in a bunch. One look was sufficient.

"Heigh there, me boys!" he shouted. "Wot in hell are you doin' in this tram? Your tickets are all second clauss! Tumble out immediately. Where have you been that you cannot read a number so beastly clear on your tickets? Come now, get a move on yourselves! You caun't ride in a first-clauss tram on a second-clauss ticket, you knaow! Take the tram car ahead, for you haven't much time before we start."

"What's the bloody difference?" asked Dan. "If we get out there'll be no one left in this compartment," said he, trying to argue with the conductor.

"Bli me eyes! You caunt ride in this tram, don't you knaow! It's first clauss!" said he.

"First class, be damned!" said Dan. "Why, you haven't got a plush seat in the coach. You ought to see our coaches in America."

"You're not in America now. Neither can you ride in this tram and I'd advise you to hurry before the train starts or you'll get left," said he, excitedly.

We all tumbled out and ran to the coach ahead, but everything was filled to overflowing as we passed coach after coach. The head brakeman shouted, "All a-b-o-a-r-d!" and the bell began to ring on the engine and as there was no time to hunt further we bolted into the door of a third-class car where we were locked up like sheep and had to stand all the way to Melbourne. But we all enjoyed the fun of the thing, however, and laughed heartily at the peculiar ways of Australia. Arriving at the city we went immediately to the parks and showed the kangaroos and other animals to our new-found friends.

Dan was a comical genius and at dinner, in a café, he had the waitress so puzzled that she couldn't wait on us. Pretending that he couldn't read he asked her if she wouldn't read the menu.

"We have soup—consommé, barley and oxtail," said she.

"Oxtail!" said Dan, with a sober face. "What kind of soup is that? I never heard of oxtail soup in America. What kind of soup—what does it look like?"

"Oh, it's very nice! All cut up in small pieces and quite all right," she replied.

"Small pieces!" said Dan, in bewilderment. "Has it got the hair on it? Ough! I don't want any," said he, shrugging his shoulders as if disgusted. This was too much for us and we all burst out in laughter while the poor girl squared away for the back door in a hurry, trying to contain herself, for she then knew she was being kidded. Another girl had to come to her rescue, to take our order. Dan kept all hands in an uproar, all through the dinner, with his funny remarks and was the life of the party until we returned to the ship.

The second mate reported for duty on Saturday. Like the cook, he said he left the hospital in order to get something to eat.

Going ashore that evening, with the boys from the *Samar*, a runner from the Sailor's Mission met us at the head of the dock and said there would be a nice entertainment at the Mission, contributed by the sailors from the different ships in port, and invited us all to attend. We promised to be there by the time it started. At the appointed hour we appeared

and were ushered to the second seat in front. An English
apprentice opened the entertainment by trying to play the
"Maiden's Prayer," on the organ. He made bad weather of
it and finally stopped in the middle of the piece. Shaking his
head he remarked that his fingers were "too bloody stiff,"
but he would try it again. He got no further the second time.
Scratching his head in a bewildered way, he said:

"I caun't quite make it, you knaow! Before we left Liverpool I played it quite all right." This brought laughter from
the house, which ended with someone shouting, "Three
cheers for Old England!" which were given in a rousing
manner.

The entertainment consisted of songs, instrumental pieces,
recitations and temperance speeches, winding up by passing
around a Total Abstinence Pledge which our crew all signed.
Alas! The next night, I am sorry to say, all hands were
drunk except Falmouth and myself. The runner from the
Mission evidently knew of it for he was always watching for
us at the head of the dock, night after night, beseeching us
not to get lu'arded into Mother Shilling's saloon as we went
ashore.

The next Saturday night we all went ashore as usual and
the Mission runner soon hove in sight and invited us to
attend another entertainment. We all agreed to go with him,
but on the way, Dan saw some meat pies, in the window of a
bakeshop, that took his eye.

"Come on, boys!" said he. "I'll stand treat."

The runner begged to be excused, but Dan took him by
the lapel of his coat and looking him full in the face, said:

"See here, my friend! I agreed to go to your temperance
meeting and have invited you to come with us into this café.
Are you ashamed to be seen in our company? If so, we'll cut
you and your Mission right here."

"But really, you knaow! I've just been to supper and
caunt eat a beastly mouthful," said he.

"Well!" said Dan. "A little meat pie won't hurt you.
Come on in!" And taking him by the hand he was pulled

into the bakeshop, much against his will, and up to the counter where Dan ordered pies for us all.

I bit into mine, but the lard seemed rancid and the mutton smelled none too fresh so I looked at the others to see how they were getting along. The runner stood holding the pie in his hand, untouched, as Dan turned, evidently intending to question their freshness, but when he saw the chap holding the pie daintily between his thumb and forefinger, he said:

"What's the matter? Can't you eat it?"

"Oh, it's very nice you knaow! But, really, I'm not hungry."

"If it's nice, then eat it," commanded Dan. "You have come into this bakeshop with us Americans, at my request, and we'll feel insulted if you refuse. Won't we shipmates?"

We all saw the spirit of Dan's remarks and together we explained that it would never do for him to refuse to eat after having been invited, or he would incur the displeasure of us all, which would end with the result that we would all go to Mother Shilling's for the night, instead of to the Mission.

He stood like a frightened child, halting between two opinions, and finally decided to try it and took quite a big bite. We surrounded him watching his every move. He tried to chew it, but made a sorry attempt. Dan saw his predicament and slapped him energetically on the back, exclaiming:

"I knew you wouldn't disappoint us! Good man! Take another bite and show us your good will."

He stood with his mouth full, but the slap on his back caused him to swallow more than he intended, with the result that he was half choked; coughing and spitting into his handkerchief what was left in his mouth. I'm afraid we were none too polite while watching him.

"Good, isn't it?" said Dan.

"Y-e-s-s. But really, you knaow, I ate such a jolly good supper that I fear I'll not be equal to it," said he.

"Do you mean to say these pies are no good?" questioned Dan. "Come on and take another bite. We won't leave this place until you have eaten it all."

At this we began to nibble at our pies while Dan talked to the stripling until he had eaten all of his. I had a cast-iron stomach, but I must admit my pie was too much for me and I threw what was left into the street. How the runner ever managed to keep it down was a mystery, but he showed no signs of weakening while on the way to the Mission. Dan walked beside him and every now and then gave him a sharp slap on the shoulders, nearly doubling him up, with exclamations that he was so glad to see him behave like one of us, etc.

On April 24, 1876, we finished unloading and began stowing cargo for Sydney and a week later we finished loading. The Custom House officers came aboard, as usual, at five o'clock and sealed our hatches for the last time. It had been their custom ever since the hatches were opened, to seal them up with red tape every evening, putting the government seal on the sealing wax, which was not used sparingly.

One new sailor came aboard and the next day there were three more, all of whom shipped "by the run," *i.e.,* were paid two pounds ten for the trip to Sydney. The steamer *Hercules* came alongside at one o'clock and an hour later the pilot came aboard and we immediately hauled into the stream and anchored for the night. The balance of the crew came off May 4 and a passenger came at midnight. Our clearance papers were received in the morning.

On Saturday, the sixth, a fine breeze sprang up from the northwest and the pilot coming aboard we tripped our anchor and sailed past the *Samar,* which also lay in the stream. I jumped on top of the rail, by the main rigging, as we passed and waved my cap which was answered by someone; but before I could distinguish who it was the mate called out:

"Get to hell down off of that rail and get busy! When we left dock the other day I thought you were getting ready for a pier-head jump, the way you were waving and throwing kisses at that dame Kitty? Do you expect to see her aboard the *Samar?* I'll be damned if I see why you should wave to a mess of sailors! Oh, you make me sick! Go for'ard and get busy with the fish-tackle."

He looked around to see if he could raise a smile from some of the men, but most of them were shaking off a headache from the last night ashore and were far from being in a happy frame of mind, consequently his bright remarks fell flat.

With everything set except the main spencer, we steered a course for Port Phillip Heads and at seven o'clock passed Point Lonsdale, to the northwest, and Point Nepean, a bold sand spit, to the southeast, when the wind began to fail. At eight the pilot left us and soon after the passenger came on deck, for he had been keeping out of sight ever since he came on board. He was a man about fifty years of age with a light complexion and quite portly, and seemed delighted to be on deck, for he wore a broad smile. The captain addressed him as Mr. Butler, but whether that was his name or not, I never knew. There was a gentle laugh from both when the captain addressed him and, therefore, I was inclined to think there was some mystery about his being on board. The second mate was the only man aft I was chummy with, but he failed to give me any information.

With the appearance of Mr. Butler on deck the crew in a body went aft, whereupon he beat a hasty retreat below and the captain went to the break of the poop to meet us.

"What's up! What do you men want aft here?" demanded the captain.

One of the men answering to the name of "Liverpool," was spokesman for the crowd.

"Cap'n," said he, with head bared and cap in hand. "We're hal blaasted nigh done hup. Caun't you give us ha little wee bit hout ho' the black jug, you knaow, just t' start us hon the run hafresh? Most ho' us 'avn't 'ad ha bloody drink t' day, hand Hi saoy, sir, we needs it badly, daon't sher knaow, hand we're 'ere to saoy, we'll work the ship just loik we'd signed hon by th' month he'f you'll oblige us wid ha wee drop."

"Umph! I suppose if I give you fellows a drink to-night, you'll all come aft to-morrow night and *demand* it," replied the captain.

"So 'elp me God, sir! We honly want hit this wunst t' freshen us hup ha bit, sir," said "Liverpool."

"If you'll promise not to come back again, I'll see what I can do for you," replied the captain.

"So 'elp me God, sir! We honly wants hit to-night, sir!" With this, the captain called, "Steward, bring up a bottle of gin!"

"Thanks, sir!" said "Liverpool," bowing most graciously, swinging his cap in front of him and at the same time giving a nervous shuffle with his feet on the deck with a rat-a-tat-tat, for he was more than pleased with the result of his request in behalf of the men, and turning to us, smiling and winking in a "know it all" manner, he said,

"Come up you Johnny Tars, hand splice th' main brace!"

The steward brought up the bottle and a whiskey glass and proceeded to pour a small portion for each, when "Liverpool" objected, saying:

"My God, man! His this th' smallest glauss hin th' cabin? Caun't you dig hup ha bigger one? This his honly a teaser, daon't sher know!"

"You ought to be bloody well pleased to get this much," said the steward.

"Then fill 'er hup full! Look hout! Daon't spill eny hov th' precious stuff, fer you knaow hit's 'ard t' get," said "Liverpool."

With a shot to each of us, "Liverpool" came back for a second helping, but the steward had his number and refused to give him any more. During the argument that followed, Jim Dunn slipped around again and got a second drink followed by another member of the crew. Here, the steward got wise to the fact that if he stayed there much longer his bottle would be emptied, so pouring another glass he raised it above his head, saying:

"Well! Here's to you all, boys! Here's hoping!" and with a smile he threw the contents into his throat and downed it in one gulp. Clearing his throat with a little cough and a shrug of his shoulders, his face clearly showing that it burned all the way down, he turned to go into the cabin, when "Liverpool" caught him by the arm, saying:

"Hi saoy, hold chap! Daon't forget the bloody man hat th' weel."

"Oh, to hell with him! He doesn't need it," said the steward with a smile and walked into the cabin, much to our disgust.

Now the steward liked his toddy as much as any of the crew and at heart was a fine fellow; so, leaving us guessing, he simply walked through the cabin and up the after companionway, where he was seen doling out a drink to the man at the wheel, after which he tossed off another for himself and the crew went forward in much better spirits.

Sunday evening we were becalmed within a quarter of a mile from shore. There was a beautiful moonlight and three ships were in sight. A large English ship was so close we could distinctly hear the bells struck every half-hour and the lookout call, "Lights burning bright, and all is well, sir!"

It was the first time I had ever heard it on a merchant ship, though I understood it was the custom on most of the flash packets. It was a mournful sound, just audible, coming over the water and the slatting of our sails against the mast and the creaking of the yards, with the drip of water from our bow as we arose on the ocean swell, had a spooky effect. The bracing of yards on the near-by ship, to catch every cat's-paw of wind, and the minor key sing-out, by some member of the crew, all added to the picture of a hobgoblin rhapsody and I was glad when we at last caught a breeze that filled our sails and carried us on our way again.

A crew shipped "by the run" were not supposed to do any work except what was necessary with the elements of the weather, such as bracing the yards, shortening and making sail, washing down decks, etc., consequently our work was light.

On Sunday, May 14, we raised Port Jackson light and hove to for the night, about fourteen miles from shore. The pilot came aboard at eight o'clock the next morning and the steamer *Mystery* took our line soon after and we headed for

VIEW OF SYDNEY COVE, NEW SOUTH WALES. From a colored aquatint in the Macpherson Collection.

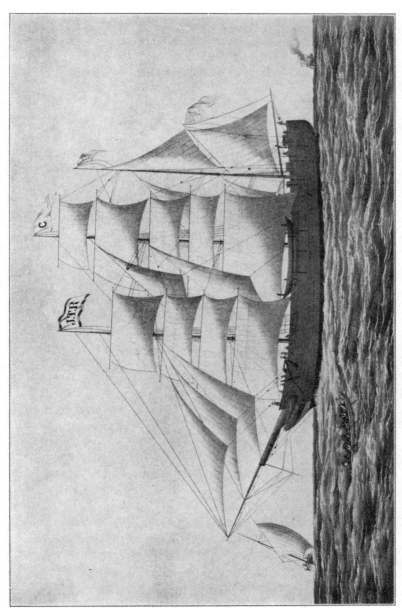

Whaling Bark "Catalpa" of New Bedford, 261 Tons, Built in 1844. From a lithograph, after a drawing by E. N. Russell, showing the rescue of Fenian prisoners in Australia, in 1876.

the rocky promontories that look from the sea as if there
was no entrance; but as we neared the land the entrance
opened up to the wonderful harbor of Port Jackson, or
Sydney, one of the finest harbors in the world. Its area,
including all its bays, is about fifteen square miles, with a
shoreline of one hundred and sixty-five miles and the water
is generally deep in all bays, with good anchorage. Sydney
lies on the southern shore about four miles from the Heads,
which are about three hundred feet high, and there is no
view of the basin from the sea.

We dropped anchor opposite Fort Dennison, where we
remained until the following morning when we were towed
up to Alger's Wharf. After dinner the men went ashore and
were paid off. Jim, Andy and I were the only ones of the
crew left except the steward.

The next morning the stevedores came alongside and
rigged their purchase, but didn't start to unload till Thursday on account of a heavy rain. They were just a week unloading and the last day gave us a hand till dark furling our
heavy sails, which had been dropped to air and dry from the
recent rains.

There was no work and a general holiday on May 24
because it was the Queen's birthday and the steward and I
went ashore together to take in the sights and especially a
military review before the Governor. There were no grand-
stand seats, but the field was large and the crowd was kept
back far enough for all to see and to give the soldiers ample
room for marching and maneuvering.

They presented a queer appearance with their red coats
and small caps, which were held in place by a black patent-
leather strap drawn tightly under the chin. I missed the blue
uniforms of the American soldiers, but the Australian red-
coats showed themselves to be thoroughly drilled in marching with their different formations and I have never seen
anything equal to their hollow square.

Squad after squad of men, marching in line, would back
and fill before the Governor, when all at once about 10,000
men, in a right-about-face, formed a hollow, oblong square,

two deep, coming to a halt and with "Present arms," the order was given to "Fire."

Beginning at the upper right corner, and in rapid succession, the guns pealed forth. Down the long line, across the bottom—up the other side and across the top, to the starting point, like a cyclone going away and returning in all its fury. It was well executed and brought forth great applause from the spectators present. This was the grand finale of the afternoon and we returned to the ship well satisfied with the review.

Owing to the congestion at Newcastle we were unable to get a cargo of coal for two weeks and so stayed a week in Sydney, making minor repairs. We had been chartered to take a load of coal to Sourabaya, Java.

Early in the afternoon of June 8, the steamer *Challenge* came alongside to tow us to Newcastle. After the runners came aboard we unmoored ship and hove up our anchor (vessels mooring at the dock were obliged to have an anchor in the stream as well) and early the next morning we dropped both anchors in Newcastle Bay. After breakfast we rigged in the jib-boom and unbent the sails. The runners left the ship after dinner and were paid off.

The next morning was Saturday and a gang of men came off to us to take out our ballast. A full-rigged brig, the *Lalla Rookh*, came alongside to receive it. Rigging a purchase, the man aloft on the main yardarm of the *Lalla Rookh* dropped his sling, which fell at my feet. The mate told me to take it up to him and with an "Aye, aye, sir!" I jumped into his main rigging which seemed no larger than ratline-stuff, and before I knew it I was up at the futtock shrouds. I smiled as I jumped on to the foot-rope, for his main yard seemed no larger than our royal. It seemed a cinch to furl such a pocket handkerchief and no chance for a "Paddy can't dive for his Boots" in tossing such a bunt.

While the "lumpers" were at work unloading our ballast, Jim and I painted the ship, outside. As the ballast was unloaded it was necessary to stiffen the ship, on account of heavy winds, and a lighter, with eighty tons of coal, came off and was unloaded the next day. It remained alongside all night and the next morning a gale sprang up, increasing in velocity until at last the moorings parted and before we could get a line to the lighter, it swung clear of the ship and went ashore.

On June 20, we finished unloading the ballast and took in sixty tons more of coal which was all that was required for stiffening, but with the weather unsettled we remained at anchor until the twenty-eighth, when a gang of men came off to get our anchors up and help dock the ship.

With the variable winds and tide the ship had swung until we counted twelve turns in the cable. These were taken out by putting a seizing around both cables, at the water's edge; then the port chain was unshackled at the hawsepipe and the end passed around the starboard chain until the cable was free; then the port chain was again shackled and the seizings cut at the water's edge. Heaving away, our anchors were finally tripped at eight in the evening after a hard afternoon's work. Two steamers towed us into King's Wharf, where we moored her fore and aft. This wharf or quay, was about seven hundred feet long, running parallel to the railroad tracks and accommodating vessels of twenty-two feet draft.

In rainy weather, on the morning of the twenty-ninth, we took in our first "wagon" of coal. Each wagon held ten tons and was lifted bodily from the trucks and swung over the hatch, where the bottom was tripped and the coal dumped at once into the ship. The first load was pretty severe on the ship, but after several cars had been dumped there was scarcely any jar. One bad feature in loading in this manner was the inability of the trimmers to shovel the coal fast enough between the hatches, and with eight or ten ships in the stream, waiting for a chance to dock, our coal was dumped in a hurry. Not enough time was given the coal trimmers, in the lower hold, with the result that our hatches were full and running over before the lower hold was full and they began on the between-decks entirely too soon. Consequently we received our complement with a well-filled between-deck and plenty of room in the lower hold.

On Sunday, Jim and I took a walk ashore but didn't find much of a town and so walked over the hill to the cliffs, then past the Bogey Hole, a natural swimming pool in the rocks, and around to the bathing beach and back. There wasn't anything going on that interested us and we went back to the ship content to stay aboard.

By way of celebrating the "Glorious Fourth," the second mate fired his revolver and ran up our colors to the monkey gaff-end. We received the balance of our 1,200 tons of coal that afternoon and with hatches overflowing and the decks generally full, we hauled out to the buoy to accommodate another ship.

While staying at King's Wharf, a bright lad of fourteen had made himself generally useful and won the good will of the mates. He wanted to make a voyage with us and the mate sent him home to get permission from his parents. As we left the dock without him we thought he was unable to secure the letter, but after dinner a boat pulled off from the shore and Billy climbed up the Jacob's ladder with his "dunnage," which consisted of an extra shirt and a pair of stockings. He said his parents were only too glad to get rid of him and as he had made his own living, selling papers, etc., since he was ten years old he claimed it was a waste of time to go home as he seldom stayed there. He was given a berth with me, the mate supplying a blanket from the slop-chest; but before we turned in I suggested that he take a bath, for his face and hands looked as though water was a stranger to him. He seemed in no hurry, however, so I got a pail of water from the cook, as hot as possible, and giving him a cake of soap I stood by and saw that he did a good job.

CHAPTER XI

WORKING THE SHIP IN ROUGH WEATHER

THE crew signed on Tuesday, but didn't come off till the following morning, which was rainy and cold and a very disagreeable day. All the crew were sober but one, but before the day was over all were drunk but two. The man that was drunk was dead drunk and was hoisted out of the runner's boat in a sling which was put under his stomach, while his head and feet met below as he was being hoisted aboard. Landing him on deck he was rolled in a heap against a water-cask where he was left until he should regain consciousness. He came to about two o'clock, crazy with delirium tremens, under the hallucination that the ship was on fire, staggering aft and crying in terror: "Fire! Fire! The ship's on fire! Lower the boats and save yourselves."

I was alarmed at first, but the quiet smiles of the others, who knew his condition, soon convinced me that his upper story was not what it should be. He stood by the gangway, shaking like one with palsy, and pointing with his finger to the forecastle, shouted:

"See! See! The house is on fire! Watch the flames come aft! For God's sake man the pumps quick or the whole ship will be on fire!"

Then putting one arm over his eyes, as if to shut out the sight, he turned and went up the steps as if to jump overboard. One of the sailors took him by the arm and the mate instructed him to take the man forward and lock him in the forecastle, which was done much against his will, for he couldn't be induced to pass the galley door for fear of being burned. After he was left alone it was pitiful to hear him pleading to be taken to a place of safety and begging us not to leave him. Shriek after shriek came from the fo'c'sle with sounds of blows against the door which he tried to batter down. At last wearing himself out he fell to the floor, moaning and crying as if his heart would break.

As the afternoon advanced the new crew got more noisy and one after another had to drop out of the gang, being too drunk to stand and of no earthly assistance. The foresail and mainsail were both bent under difficulties, for the men on the yard, as a whole, had all they could do to hang on to keep from falling.

While bending the jib, an ambitious sailor called "Dublin," who didn't know his own strength, stood on top of the jib-boom and while reaching down to light up the sail, missed his footing as he was about to stand on the guys and fell through the back-ropes into the water. Being a good swimmer he soon reached a buoy where he held on till we got a boat to him. A couple of us pulled him out of the water and he reached the ship a more sober man. Regaining the deck, in true sailor fashion he made his way out on the boom again as if nothing had happened. The jib being bent this ended the work on the sails and we knocked off early in the afternoon.

On account of a falling barometer and stormy rainy weather from the north, we remained at anchor till Thursday, July 11.

Strong winds and anti-cyclones in the northwestern part of Australia are called "Willy-Willies," while those in Victoria, in the southeastern part of Australia, are called "Brick Fielders," on account of the dust arising from the brick fields south of Melbourne. In Sydney these gales, arising from the hot, desert sands, are called "Southerly Busters." While off Sydney the wind may be blowing from the north for a day or more, when there is a short lull and then, very suddenly, when the line of lowest pressure has passed, a strong wind often sets in from the south, increasing at times to the velocity of a hurricane, blowing up the coast and doing great damage to shipping off and on shore. These winds are also called "Southerly Busters."

It was during one of these lulls, while we were lying at anchor with fine weather and a stiff breeze from the south'ard, that the steamer *Challenge* came alongside and we immediately got under way. While crossing the bar at the entrance we struck pretty hard and the ship trembled from truck to keelson. The yards creaked and groaned and the second mate shouted, "Stand from under the yards!" but listing to starboard, the next sea carried us over and we did not strike again. On sounding the pumps there was no apparent damage done and all hands seemed satisfied.

All the whiskey having been drunk before we sailed, Brooks, the man who had the D.T.'s, came out of it all right, but a nervous wreck. He claimed he had been shanghaied, but philosophically remarked that if it hadn't been this ship it might have been worse. He was glad it was an American ship for he might be bound to England. His home was in Brooklyn, New York, and he had been trying to get home for ten years. Three times he had been to Liverpool, only to be shanghaied in English bottoms, and the last time he found himself bound for Australia instead of New York. Now he was through with drinking and would stay by the ship until she reached Boston. He was a well-educated man and had been master of ships, but his appetite for whiskey was his downfall. Arriving in port he was always full, consequently the chances for shipping as mate were against him and becoming discouraged he continued to drown his sorrows in the flowing bowl. Money gone, the sailor's boarding house wouldn't carry him and the only way to get rid of him was to shanghai him. And so, there he was, happy in the thought that eventually he would bring up somewhere near Brooklyn.

The crew were hardly over their drunk and couldn't arouse themselves sufficiently to sing a chantey at the topsail halliards, and clearing the bar with our topsails set, the *Challenge* lost no time in casting off the towline, for we were fast overhauling her in the strong, southerly wind. By the time our royals were set, the *Akbar* had all she could carry and was a bit cranky on account of our heavy load of coal in between-decks.

With the decks continually awash, Billy couldn't stand the heavy rolling and gave up to seasickness. Strange to say, Mr. Burris sent him below after he had lost his dinner. The mate no doubt remembered his call-down from the captain in Alonzo's case.

At eight o'clock that evening we shipped a sea over the starboard main rigging which filled the cabin floor. Soon afterwards the wind went down and with light baffling winds we held our course till off Cape Byron on Saturday, July 15, when the wind freshened into a gale from the southeast, the ship laboring heavily with decks more or less filled with water. While under topgallant sails, the outer jib stay was carried away and we clewed up and furled the fore- and mizzen-topgallant sails and later the main-topgallant sail came in. The upper fore and mizzen topsails were furled and the mainsail reefed, after which we were called aft to "Splice the main brace" and the same steward, who had been with us from Melbourne, trotted out another black bottle and joined in with the rest, not forgetting the man at the wheel and again drinking to his success. That evening we furled the upper main topsail, mainsail, foresail and jib. We were shipping much water and she was leaking badly, so the men were constantly at the pumps.

Running before it the *Akbar* would settle to port, when a huge sea would come over the rail, filling the decks. The additional weight above would cause her to stagger and tremble all over. With the rise of the wave amidships she would shake like a thing of life, trying to clear herself of the weight on deck. The stern settling again, as the sea rushed forward, she righted herself and the heavy mass of water rushed to starboard and away she listed, unable to free herself. The next sea came in over the starboard rail and in like manner we wallowed through each sea, first to port and then to starboard, all through the night. At the pumps we were wet as drowned rats, trying to avoid the wash by leaving the hand-brakes and jumping on top of the main bitts, or anywhere handy with something to hold on to, otherwise our feet would be washed from under and we would find ourselves in the lee scuppers.

In this situation Brooks showed his mettle. While the others were growling and cursing their fate, he shook his head in answer and said: "Well, boys! You are all far better off than I and we have all been in this kind of weather before. But when this blows over we'll come about and have fair weather home. We're in for it, to-night, but let's forget the weather and try a chantey and heave away cheerily. 'Heave Away Cheerily' will be a good one to sing at the pumps," so saying, he led the men in our first chantey since leaving Newcastle.

Heave Away Cheerily

The wind is free and we're bound for sea. Heave a-way cheer-i-ly, ho - oh! The lass-ies are wav-ing to you and to me As off to the south'ard we go - o, As off to the south'ard we go - o. Sing, my lads, cheer-i - ly. Heave, my lads, cheer-i - ly. Heave a-way cheer-i - ly, ho - oh! For gold that we prize, and sun - ni - er skies, A - way to the south-'ard we go.

We want sailors bold, who can work for their gold,
And stand a good wetting without catching cold.

The sailor is true to his Sal or his Sue,
As long as he's able to keep them in view.

They're crying, "Come back my dear sailor in blue,
For no one can fill the place vacant by you."

They love us for money, whoever he be,
But when it's all gone, we are shanghaied to sea.

Then sing, "Good-bye Sally, your wonders I'll tell,
But when with another I'll wish you in hell."

This chantey, although a windlass chantey, was sung at the pumps that evening with words that would hardly look well in print. Brooks knew the crew and sang words for their pleasure, while the seas chased us away from our work from time to time.

Our pumps were of the old hand-brake style and like the windlass moved up and down, but without a halfway pause. The stroke was directly up and down with a quick motion. Only one pump worked at a time, which was the farthest from the handles. Chanteys in 2/4 or 6/8 time can be sung at the pumps where the accent falls on the down or up stroke. During the daytime we seldom started a chantey at the pumps; but during the night we sang one after another during the entire watch.

Brooks was a happy-go-lucky fellow and liked by all. He was a thorough sailor and knew his place, adapting himself to emergencies as he found them. In all our bad weather I never heard him complain, either at the pumps or on the yard, shortening sail. He carried on his conversation as an equal to the one with whom he was talking and being a college graduate he could use the finest language when necessary—or the vilest, if that pleased the one with whom he was in company. When with the sailors he forgot his education and used their dialect to the Queen's taste. At the pumps his vocabulary in pumping chanteys, which are of the vilest, was at his tongue's end and knowing this the sailors begged, night after night, for a chantey with some spice in it and he generally accommodated them with words from

A to Z. This had its effect and pleased the men, for it served to take their minds away from the bad weather and helped them to forget their surroundings, which otherwise might have led to mutiny with a disgruntled crew.

At three o'clock in the morning we furled the lower mizzen topsail while the seas ran mountains high. At seven we shipped a sea over the main rigging which swept the booby hatch, a 6′ x 6′ square house, off the combings, capsizing and breaking all the buckets in the rack.

Here was more excitement, for the booby hatch was swept across the deck with each roll, endangering the life of anyone attempting to secure it. Sliding across the deck and striking the combings of the mizzen hatch, it rolled over and over, bringing up against the spare spars lashed to the bulwarks with such force that had it struck the bulwarks no doubt they would have been carried away and the booby hatch gone overboard. As it was, both the spars and the booby hatch were badly scratched and splintered. Luckily no one was injured while it was sliding across the deck. Finally a rope was passed around it and secured to the rail and another rope led across the deck to the other side and by slacking away on the first rope and pulling taut on the other we let the ship do the rest and when in position we rolled it over the combings in place. It was badly splintered and sprung out of shape, but we secured it as best we could, temporarily, until the sea went down.

While we were making it fast the steward came out of the cabin on his way to the galley for the breakfast. He had hardly got to the mainmast before he was swept off his feet and carried into the lee scuppers with such force that we thought his leg was broken. He was unable to get from under the spare spar without help and couldn't stand alone and had to be carried to the cabin. His hard luck was my misfortune for I was again called to take his place, which I despised.

With the ship under fore-topmast staysail, lower fore and main topsails and reefed spanker, we were riding out the gale, which increased in velocity, with a heavy running sea, when we shipped a sea over the starboard bow which carried away the jib stay and back-ropes, stove in the starboard fo'-c'sle door and the starboard longboat on top of the fo'c'sle. The sea struck it with such force that one would think a man had battered in the bottom of the boat with a top maul. It swept over the forward house and against the pigpen, on the main hatch, staving it to pieces against the main bitts. The two pigs that were in it were swept overboard and drowned. The men were continually at the pumps, as the vessel was making six and seven inches an hour. In this big sea we sprung our foremast and the captain decided to wear ship and head for Sydney. It was a dangerous undertaking and we had our fears of pooping a sea, but during a lull and by watching the sea until the three seas* went by, he ordered the helm up and we wore handsomely and shaped our course for Sydney. Almost immediately the wind abated, but there was no indication of the sea going down and it kept up the whole of the next day, although we had fine weather and a southerly wind during which we repaired the jib stay and back-ropes and set the topsails.

The next day, July 19, there was fine weather with a breeze from the westward and we set the topgallant sails. This was followed by light winds and calms, with a heavy swell. The steward got on his feet again and I was relieved. We set the royals at one o'clock and took them in at six and before we got down from aloft the wind sprang up from the south'ard increasing to a gale, so that all hands were called to shorten sail. At seven-thirty, the upper mizzen topsail split from head to foot and was immediately furled and at eight we reefed the mainsail, and took it in altogether at midnight and hove to for the night under fore-topmast stay-sail, lower topsails and reefed spanker.

The next morning had all the earmarks of a pleasant day and the men, while setting the main topsail, were so elated over the prospects of finer weather that Brooks started a chantey when the halliards were thrown from the pin in the rail, and we lost no time in hooking the snatch-block into the

---

* Big seas run in sets of three.

eye-bolt in the deck, when we tailed on behind and across the deck. No one could help putting his entire strength into the pull of this chantey, for not only were the men's voices unusually good, but the chantey was sung with a jerk and a swing as only chanteys in 6/8 time can be sung. While the words were of negro extraction, yet it was a great favorite with us and sung nearly every time the topsails were hoisted.

HANGING JOHNNY

They call me "Hang-ing John-ny," A - way - I · oh!

They say I hang for mon- ey. So hang boys, hang!

Why did you hang your daddy,
And then your mother, laddie?

They say, I hung my mother,
And then I hung my brother.

I hung my sister Nancy,
Because I took a fancy.

A rope, a beam, a ladder,
I hung them all together.

They call me "Hanging Johnny,"
But I never hung nobody.

I'd hang a brutal mother,
The same as any other.

I'd hang a noted liar,
I'd hang a bloated Friar.

I'd hang a highway robber.
I'd hang a burglar jobber.

I'd hang all wrong and folly,
And hang to make things jolly.

A rope, a beam, a ladder.
I'd hang them all together.

Come hang and sway together
And hang for finer weather.

They call me "Hanging Johnny,"
But I never hung nobody.

The words "Hang boys, hang," are used in a topsail-halliard hoist, when sweating up the yard "two blocks," where, in swaying off, the whole weight of the body is used. The sing-out, from some old shellback, usually being words such as "Hang, heavy! Hang, buttocks! Hang, you sons of ———, Hang!"

After setting the topsails we gave her the main-topgallant sail, which was all she could carry in a heavy head-sea. The decks were awash all day.

At eleven o'clock at night the wind came up from the W.S.W., strong and squally, and at midnight we took in the topgallant sail. We were then pumping every half-hour. At eight o'clock the next morning we reefed the mainsail, after which the captain gave orders to "Splice the main brace!" This was hailed with joy by all for we had had a hard night of it, in very disagreeable weather, with heavy rain squalls, so that oil-skins seemed of little account.

On Saturday, July 22, the gale increased, with passing heavy rain squalls. The upper topsails were furled at four o'clock and we again wore ship in a heavy sea. The watch at one o'clock in the morning furled the foresail and mainsail and not long after we shipped a sea which stove in the port fo'c'sle door, carried away the port side-light in the rigging and stove in the bow of the port boat, over the fo'c'sle.

Having no extra red light we tore up an old ensign and wrapping the red bunting around a lantern hung it in the fore rigging, as a side-light, which answered the purpose pretty well. No sooner was it in the rigging, than we shipped another sea which stove in the port galley door, filled the galley floor and washed the pots, kettles and pans out of the racks in a more or less damaged condition. With the fo'c'sle doors both gone, the men had an unusually hard time, as their bedding and mattresses were wet through. Canvas was nailed over the openings and served to keep out the cold air and the men turned in, wrapped up in wet blankets, glad to get away from the wet decks and lost no time in catching what little sleep they could, for no one could say just what moment we would be called on deck to shorten sail. In this condition they were soon steaming away like planks in a steam box. When the watch was called they turned our fairly parboiled and assembled around the main hatch where the quick clank of the pumps greeted them.

With the orders, "Relieve the wheel!" and "That will do the watch!" we took our stations at the pumps as the old stage-saying broke out afresh, from those going below, as a parting salute, "Who wouldn't sell a farm and go to sea!" This was too much for the watch on deck and one could hear the curses heaped upon themselves for being caught in a leaky ship like this, etc. But Brooks, in his soothing manner, usually poured oil on the troubled waters and broke out in a chantey and so we sang and pumped through the watch, interrupted continually by heavy seas coming aboard. Not only were the gates kept open, but we also used an axe to cut through the bulwarks in the waist and between the ends of the spare spars, amidships, to allow the water to run off as quickly as possible.

The phosphorescent light from the whirling mass of water on deck, dashing against the spare spars, acted as footlights to the scene, illuminating the yellow oil-skins and the dripping faces of the men, washed by the rain squalls, in a ghastly manner. The trembling of the ship and the shrieking rigging, as she wallowed about, told the strain she was under; meeting the wind as she righted only to be buffeted and thrown back again, by the force of the gale, nearly on her beam-ends.

In the morning, the steward, who had been limping about,

either was afraid to go to the galley for the breakfast or was really unable and so he succeeded in having me do his work; but the day being Sunday there wasn't much to do.

At dinner time the second mate and I, eating together, were caught in a peculiar situation. Bringing in our soup and coffee I placed the soup and crackers on the swinging table rack, above the dining table, and went into the pantry to pour the coffee into cups. Returning with a cup in each hand, the second mate held his pan of soup in both hands, for the ship was rolling so hard that the swinging table would bring up with a jump and to keep it from spilling he was using both hands to keep it steady. Releasing one hand he took the cup while I reached for my pan of soup, now nearly empty, and sat opposite him with both hands full. It was impossible to put either the soup or the coffee down with safety. At one moment I would be above the second mate and far away from the table while he would be jammed against the side of the table, to leeward, with both arms on a level with his head and so vice versa. It was some time before I dared to raise my eyes from the soup and coffee which I was holding, and finally looking across the table to see how he was getting along our eyes met and he burst into laughter. I must have had a puzzled look on my face for he laughingly said,

"Why don't you eat your dinner?" at which we both laughed for he, like myself, could do nothing but hold the liquid to keep it from spilling. So we sat for some time until the coffee cooled sufficiently to drink when he jokingly remarked that it was "a hell of a dish for a hungry man to serve on a day like this."

It was one of the most trying situations it had been my fate to meet. There was no such thing as eating out of a plate, on the table, with a knife and fork, for, unless we held the plate in our hands, it would slide across the table with the roll of the ship. So we ate our dinner from the swinging rack, like the revolving table where you make your selection and grab your dish before it gets beyond your reach, for in rolling to leeward the rack brought "hard up" to windward where the second mate ate what he could before the ship started to roll back, and I waited patiently for the ship to roll the other way giving me the same opportunity. It was "catch as catch can" throughout the dinner, with many amusing incidents.

In the afternoon, just before setting the topsails, Mr. Burris told "Dublin" to put new rovings in the upper main topsail. Instead of taking out the old ones, "Dublin" filled the eye of the sail with the roving, cut off the end and hove what was left overboard. The mate, watching proceedings, shouted to "Dublin" to take out the old ones, but couldn't make himself heard, whereupon, in his usual way he began cursing and damning "Dublin" and everyone aboard ship for their ignorance, swearing by note, as it were, and generally making himself ridiculously disliked. "Dublin," not hearing the mate, went right on with his work and was soon down from aloft. The mate rushed up to him, as he swung from the sheer pole to the deck below, shouting and shaking his fist.

"Damn you! What do you mean by cutting those rovings? You deliberately defied me and kept right on cutting and slashing when you knew a damn sight better. I'll have you know that orders aboard this ship have got to be carried out," etc.

"Dublin," not knowing why he was accosted in this manner, stepped back as the mate advanced, giving him the impression that he was afraid of him and the mate, gaining confidence as he cursed, caught "Dublin" by the shirt collar and shouted, "I'll have you put in irons for insubordination!"—with his usual flow of adjectives.

The captain was standing at the break of the poop as "Dublin" was rushed aft.

"Cap'n," said the mate, "I've got to put this man in irons before he runs away with the ship."

"What's the matter now?" asked the captain, emptying his mouthful of tobacco in the wash at the bottom of the steps. He listened impatiently to the mate's complaint and with a sneer, said,

"I see no grounds for your flying into a passion like this

and if you would use less swearing and more thinking you'd do a damn sight better."

After giving "Dublin" a little advice, in which he was cautioned to be more particular and in future to do his work in a more seamanlike manner, he was told to go forward. The mate also came in for a reprimand from the captain, in which he was cautioned that scenes like that only served to bring discontent among other members of the crew besides filling their minds with mutinous intentions and in future he must watch his step. The mate stood by without answering a word and seemed in no hurry to get away. Finally, the captain told him it was time to get the topsails on her and he answered immediately:

"Aye, aye, sir! 'er—Set the main topsail!"

The men were in a dejected mood and didn't reply in the usual spirited manner, so that the topsails were hoisted with only a sing-out. By the time the fore topsail was set they had time to cool off and with the mizzen topsail, orders were given to set the main-topgallant sail and Brooks led the men in the hand-over-hand hoist, in the chantey "Tommy's Gone to Hilo."

TOMMY'S GONE TO HILO

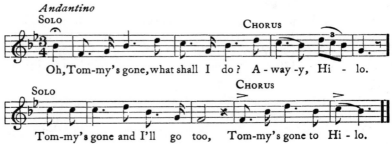

Oh, Tommy's gone, what shall I do? A-way-y, Hi-lo.

Tommy's gone and I'll go too, Tommy's gone to Hi-lo.

To Hilo town, we'll see her through,
For Tommy's gone with a ruling crew.

Oh, Tommy's gone from down below,
And up aloft this yard must go.

Oh, Tommy's gone, we'll ne'er say nay
Until the mate sings out, "Belay!"

I think I heard the old man say,
We'll get our grog three times a day.

Oh, one more pull and that will do,
So let her roll and wet us through.

She'll ship it green again to-day;
The mate is sore and hell's to pay.

Oh, Tommy's gone, what shall I do?
The mate is sore and so are you.

Oh, Tommy's gone and left us, too;
We like the mate—Like hell we do!

This brought a burst of laughter from us all which was
more than the mate could stand, for he ran across the deck
shouting in an excited manner and addressing his remarks to
Brooks:

"See here, by God! You're not going to make me the
laughing stock aboard this ship and if I hear any more such
words from you, you can stow this away in your head and
that is, you and I will simply fall out. So cheese it!"

His face was ashen white with rage and his little gray eyes
had a look that told us he was mean enough to work off any
hardship on Brooks, even to keelhauling him for a second
offense.

The chantey was abruptly brought to an end but Brooks
made no reply and went right on with the hoist giving the
regular sing-out just as though the chantey ended in a natural way and completely ignoring the mate who was still
cursing a blue streak.

We continued hoisting away until the yard was "two-
blocks," before he walked away, and seeing that we couldn't
hoist any further, he bellowed out, "Belay! belay the main
t'gallant! Lee upper main topsail brace!"

This took us all aft to leeward and out of ear-shot while
he slacked away to windward and it gave him an opportunity

to cool off. The watch was relieved and the old ship again carried all she could stagger under for the rest of the day.

In the dogwatch I made an important discovery which quite upset me for the time being. Billy was helping the steward in the cabin and I went to my room to mend a shirt. While stitching away I found myself continually scratching my head. My first thought was that I was breaking out with the itch; but I could see no indication between my fingers and so resorted to a fine-tooth comb which revealed the fact that my hair was inhabited. I found three of the prettiest little wingless, suctorial parasitic insects belonging to the tribe *Pediculina* and sometimes regarded as degraded *Hemiptera Pediculus Capitis,* in plain sailor language and better known as head lice. They were surely everything that was said of them in Webster's Dictionary.

I was provoked, to say the least, for after having Billy take a bath, prior to our sailing from Newcastle, as he was drying his hair in the doorway I noticed that he was scratching his head a good deal and when I asked him if he had a fine-tooth comb, he turned and indignantly said, "You don't think I'm lousy, do you?"

Really, I thought he was, from the way he was digging away in his hair; but he seemed so insulted at my inquiry that I didn't investigate further. But now I was the insulted one and immediately went to the pantry, where Billy was just finishing up the supper dishes. I led him forward by the hand in no gentle manner.

"What do you want with me?" he asked.

"Come into the room and I'll show you," said I.

After showing him the comb and telling him what I had found, in no gentle tones I told him to get a deck-bucket and take a seat on the main hatch, for I was going to see how many fish I could catch.

His hair, naturally curly, was long and matted and I was unable to run the comb through it, so I gave him a hair cut and being a novice I hacked away, cutting it as closely as possible. In those days clippers were not used in cutting men's hair and were practically unknown. The rolling and

pitching of the ship didn't help matters and my efforts were
a dismal failure, from a barber's point of view; but his hair
was cut as close as possible and I cared but little how it
looked so long as the hair was removed. With the first swipe
of the comb I nearly lost my supper and I hope I will never
again see another sight like it. It is hard to believe that anyone could carry so many lice without showing it, for the
comb was filled to overflowing. It made me sick at my stomach and unable to go on with the work; besides, there was
danger of all hands being contaminated if I combed out
promiscuously on the deck.

On the spur of the moment and without thought of the
consequences, I reasoned that kerosene oil might kill them
and so rushed into the lamp room and taking the gallon can
poured it over a bunch of oakum until it was well saturated.
With this I swabbed Billy's head, putting it on good and
thick, and while waiting to see what effect it had, I felt like
touching a match to it.

I didn't have long to wait for Billy's head was more or
less raw from his scratching and the biting of the lice and
the smarting must have been terrible. Suddenly he jumped
from the bucket and danced up and down shouting in agony:
"Oh, my God, Fred! Oh! Oh! I can't stand it!" and stepping on the side of the bucket, which rolled over, he lost his
balance, sliding off the hatch and across the deck where he
rolled and writhed about in great pain. Crying and sobbing
he pleaded for something to be placed on his head.

I was alarmed and fearful that I had made a mistake in
applying the kerosene, so ran to the water-cask and drew a
dipper full of water and poured the contents over his head.
Whether Billy had got used to the smarting or whether the
water washed off the kerosene, I am unable to say, but he was
soon out of his misery and could smile again. Telling him
to use the comb, when he was able to, and to stay out of our
room until he was free from the lice, I left him to work
out his own salvation.

Just before eight bells he came to me and reported there
were no signs of life left, that the kerosene had done its

work, and asked to be taken in again. Here, the watch was called and it was my lookout, so I left him; but at four bells, when I was relieved, I found him fast asleep in his bunk and I didn't have the heart to turn him out. It was just as well that I left him for I never saw any indications of lice afterwards; nor did Billy have any bad effects from the kerosene.

In the morning watch Brooks started a whistling chantey and jokingly remarked: "It's a good thing I am not superstitious or I'm afraid I'd never sing this chantey again. We are sure having our share of wind." This song did more to keep the crew good-natured than anything else.

While "Hanging Johnny" had its melancholy tune, the new chantey, "A fal-de-lal-day," was decidedly humorous. The word "fal-de-lal-day" fitting in at the most opportune time and usually kept us laughing because it was so ridiculously funny that when it was time for the first chorus, which was whistled by all, not half of the men could pucker sufficiently to whistle,—breaking up the song with loud bursts of laughter.

Picture hilarity in such a stage setting, with seas breaking over the rail! I was generally the "watchdog" for the men and stood on top of the pump-beam, treading up and down with my feet while I held the chain topsail sheets in both hands, with an eye to windward, watching for the huge gray seas to come aboard. If the crest was particularly thin and green, it was an indication that in meeting the ship's side more or less of the wave would slop over. The greener and higher the wave the more water we would get. The men at the brakes had their backs to the sea and were in no position to see what was coming, so it was left with me to judge whether it was time to leave the brakes or not. When an unusual sea ran high I would call, "Here she comes, boys!" and the song would cease and like so many monkeys we would scramble on top of the bitts out of reach of the tons of water pouring over the rail and across the deck. This was "Life on the Ocean Wave," and when one turns out of a nice steaming blanket and jumps into clammy, damp clothing to meet a situation like this, "Who wouldn't sell a farm and go to sea?"

It is not fitting here to give all the words sung by Brooks. Suffice to say the words in a way followed Thomas Heywood's noted "Rape of Lucrece." Some of the words are given in "I'll Go No More A-roving," another pumping chantey and by far the most musical of any. It was often sung at the windlass while heaving up anchor.

As we were continually pumping we repeated each line of the following, to make the chantey last the longer.

A Fal-de-lal-day

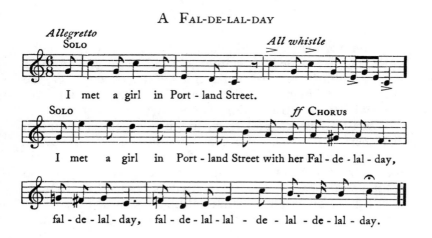

I met a girl in Portland Street,
The sweetest girl I chanced to meet.

Said I, "Young Miss, how do you do?"
Said she, "The worse for meeting you."

"Young Miss," said I, "I like your style."
Said she, "Young man, just wait awhile."

I took her hand and on we trod;
Said she, "Young man, you're rather odd."

And to her room, not far away,
She bade me call another day.

I put my arm around her waist;
Said she, "Young man, you show good taste."

I pulled her down upon my lap;
Said she, "You now deserve a slap."

Her ankle next, I placed my hand;
Said she, "For this I will not stand."

I pulled her dress above her knee;
Said she, "Young man, please let me be."

And why did I no further go?
Alas! her leg was cork, you know.

As on former occasions we sang throughout the watch while the seas slopped over the rail; but there was more or less grumbling from the men at times and between songs, the "Flying Dutchman" and phantom ships being the chief topic of conversation and on going below they passed it along to the starboard watch and they, in turn, began to complain that there was a cause for all the wind blowing from all points of the compass and for the leaky condition of the ship and they even went so far as to say that we should stop chanteying, meaning of course, that our whistling chantey should be dropped; that our condition was worse than ever before and we should try to help things along all we could.

The cook, a native of New Orleans and as black as the ace of spades, was a very superstitious fellow. He was a man about forty-five years of age and as I got my breakfast after the crew had been served, it was his custom to come to my room, while I was eating, and spin yarns about his bad luck.

He told me that his mother was a slave at one time and the mistress of a southern planter, who was his father. There was no indication of white blood in his veins, but he explained that God had placed the mark of an illegitimate child, not on his body, but in his mouth, for he was born with two rows of teeth which filled his mouth until they were so uneven that he was continually biting his tongue. By working the inner set with his fingers or with a skewer, while at sea, he had succeeded in digging out most of them and now he had a mouth that gave him little or no trouble in eating. He opened his mouth and showed me one of the most uneven sets of teeth I ever saw and I think he must have told the truth. On this particular morning he came to my door, complaining of our general bad luck, saying,

"Dis ship is an unlucky ship, yes!"

"Oh! I don't think the ship is unlucky; it's the way we are loaded," said I.

"What fo' you all sing dat whistlin' chantey in de night watch? Doan't yo' all know dat whistlin' brings up de wind?"

"I don't think it makes a particle of difference. It's an old sailor's superstition," said I. "I suppose some of the old sailors in the 'Flying Dutchman' would throw a fit if they were aboard of this ship and should hear us sing the whistling chantey; and if they knew that in Melbourne we had a cat that jumped overboard one night in a fit which was caused by his tackling a big wharf rat, in which the rat got the best of it for he nearly chewed up old Tom. He was bitten in the foot, which swelled twice its size, and getting no better, he finally went into a fit and jumped overboard and we never saw him afterwards. I suppose they would lay the chief cause of all this bad weather to the cat. Wouldn't they?" I asked.

There was a look of terror in his face as he exclaimed:

"Good God, maan! Do yo' mean to tell me dat yo' all had a cat in Melbourne what jumped overboard an' drownded? Why didn't yo' tell dis niggah ob dat befo' we left Newcastle? I shuh would nebbah have shipped in dis vessel. Dat goes fo' to explain all dis bad luck. We shuh am fated an' will nebbah see port agin. Yo' mark my words! Why? 'Case, fu'st de cat jump overboard. Second, yo' all sing dat whistlin' chantey, night after night, an' while yo' sing in de dark hours, de wind comes up an' sing through de riggin' an' byme-by de mate he sings out, 'Call de watch an' shorten sail.' After de secon' mate's watch comes on deck, dey doan't sing dat bloody whistlin' chantey. What am de consequences?

Why maan! De wind goes down an' we make sail agin an' sail along all right till de night time, den yo' watch begins to pump and whistle. What do it do, maan? Dat shuh brings de wind ebry time and all de wind dat bro' up north, turns 'round an' bro's right back agin. Why? 'Case yo' all whistle fo' it. Dat what yo' do. An' what do de wind do? I'll tell yo' what it do. De wind comes up gentle at fu'st an' den comes on fo' to bro' hardah and hardah. De big seas roll up an' peep obah de rail an' say, 'Watch out, maan! I'se comin' aboard!' But yo' all pay no 'tention an' byme-by we gits it obah de starboard bow—fo'c'sle doah stove in; two pigs drownded an' spare boat busted in. Dat's only a warnin' fo' yo' all not to sing dat chantey. Ain't dat 'nough warnin'? But yo' all don't seem to care. De ship roll an' groan an' shake all de time an' last night de wind follow yo' all 'round and byme-by, *biff!* We git it obah de port bow an' de port fo'c'sle doah am stove in an' de side-light am carried away, an' de big sea roll an' growl obah de top ob de galley an' says, 'Watch out niggah! Yo' next!' What did it do? I'm heah to tell yo' dat it did! Dat's all ob dat; but we ain't through yet. Dis ship am a-leakin' mo' an' mo' ebry day, an' yo' can't tell dis niggah dat de cat had nothin' to do with it, fo' he suah put his mark on dis ship, an' I know it. She's unlucky, an' fated. Dat means she'll go to de bottom befo' we git in!"

This last remark caused me to laugh outright and he jumped up, shaking his fist in my face, exclaiming:

"Laff! damn yo', laff! What do yo' all know 'bout de sea anyway, I'd like to know? I'm sixteen yeahs in deep-water ships, an' yo',—yo' all ain't dry behind de eahs yet, fo' dis am yo'ah fu'st voyage."

He was very much exercised and disgusted at me and left abruptly, with a sneer on his face, walking proudly to his galley with head high in the air as if I was completely beneath his notice.

CHAPTER XII

MANNING THE PUMPS

W E HAD fine weather for a day or two and all sails were set and the decks dried off nicely. At the same time we dried out our mattresses, blankets and clothing which were more or less wet with salt water. A man-of-war, on washday, had nothing on us, for everywhere the rigging was decorated with shirts, coats, etc. The pleasant weather didn't last very long, however, for the wind came up from the northeast and increased to a gale. It was another bad night and after getting down from the foresail we had a call to "splice the main brace."

Captain Lamson was not a "tight wad" and on almost every occasion when we reefed the foresail or mainsail, he trotted out the little black bottle and when the weather was unusually thick and disagreeable the second mate lightened our hearts with a cheerful word while clewing up: "Hurry aloft, boys! You're all entitled to 'splice the main brace' when you get down again." At once there would be a scramble up the rigging to see who would be first out on the weather yardarm.

After reefing the foresail we made our way aft while the ship labored hard, wallowing in the seas with decks awash and many a time the weight of the water to leeward, on deck, was enough to put the rail clear under, and thus we rolled like a water-logged vessel. Life lines were stretched fore and aft to keep the sailors from being washed overboard for it was a dangerous undertaking to go aft without them; while we at the pumps got our accustomed exercise of dodging the waves as they swept across the deck. There was no such thing as trying to come about on another tack and we wore ship at 8.30 that night without pooping a sea and steered an easterly course, the ship making about seven inches of water an hour.

After snugging her down we again started the pumps, when Brooks broke out in "A fal-de-lal-day" and "Dublin" tried to shut him off saying: "For God's sake, Brooks, lay off that chantey and give it a rest. I'm not superstitious, but damn it to hell, try somethin' else." Brooks only laughed and kept on with the song, but when it came to the whistling chorus he and I were about the only ones to whistle.

The phosphorescent light showed up the men's faces in a ghastly manner, as they stood in their oil-skins, moving up and down with the brake-beams. As the brake came up I watched the troubled look appear on their faces as they came to an upright position. There is nothing very hard in working the pump-brakes up and down, but to keep them moving, hour after hour, tires the most hardy and when dressed in oil-skins, with the rain and spray flying in one's face, there is more or less of a scowl that comes over a man; a determined wink of the eye or a sudden duck of the head to catch the flying spray on his sou'wester, which otherwise would run down his neck, and any troubled look, while singing a song under such circumstances, depicts a very sad scene and is more or less depressing, according to the dissatisfied condition of the men.

Brooks was not a man to irritate anyone and it didn't take long for him to see that the men were dissatisfied and troubled, so he wound up the chantey in quick order, switching to "Clear the Track, Let the Bulgine Run," in which he used words only befitting a pumping chantey and certainly not fit for publication.

It was a dismal night and I was glad when eight bells were struck giving me an opportunity to pull off my wet clothes and get into my bunk for a four hours' sleep, if lucky enough to get it. Wedging myself by bringing my knees up for a brace against the bunk-board, I slept while the ship was rolled and tossed by the wind and waves outside.

At eight bells, with the call of the watch, we tumbled out and the watch on deck remained to help set the topsails, for the wind was moderating and the sky was clearing and the sea going down. The starboard watch, after losing an hour's sleep, was sent below and we resumed our task at the pumps.

The next day was Friday and towards evening the gale shifted to southwest with a heavy cross-sea. Furling the fore-sail and mainsail resulted in another call to "splice the main brace." During my trick at the wheel, from ten o'clock to midnight, the captain was continually on deck. We were rolling unusually hard and finally a heavy sea threw us over until I thought the ship would never right again. She shook fore and aft, trembling like a thing of life, but finally cleared herself and righted.

"Take in the topsails, Mr. Burris!" shouted the captain and after they were lowered, Mr. Burris came aft, saying: "She's carried away the starboard light and the other galley door is stove in, sir! The sea is now washing clear through the galley, into one door and out the other. What will we do for a green light, sir? I don't think there is a spare side-light in the ship and what's more, there is no green bunting that we can tie around a lantern, the same as we fixed the port light, sir."

"You'll have to tear up a strip of blue from the old en-sign," replied the captain. "We've got to get up a starboard light of some kind and the blue bunting will be better than nothing, for we can't afford to take any chances out here of being run down by some passing ship or steamer. Better get it out at once."

The watch was called to shorten sail and I held the wheel until all was secure above. After being relieved and going down the lee poop steps, the men at the main bitts were taking in the slack of the topsail sheet to a sing-out I had never heard before and which ran as follows:

Corn broom, hick - o - ry broom, squil - gee, swab!

Swaying off on the pull the others came out strong on the word *swab*. The pull was a strong one and had its result be-sides giving a little sunshine—a smile drawn forth from the old set "Yo-hoy-boys"—and left the men in better spirits.

They needed a variety for in such weather we were all more or less tired out, grouchy and ill at ease.

The gale increased, with heavy passing showers, and the next morning at four o'clock we carried away the weather lower main topsail sheet and "goosewinged" the sail, *i.e.*, the weather side of the sail was furled, leaving the lee side intact, which gives the sail the appearance of a wing of a goose. After goosewinging the sail we took in the lower mizzen topsail and by nine o'clock we were making such bad weather of it that we were compelled to take in the lower fore-topsail and heave to under goosewinged main topsail, fore-topmast staysail and reefed spanker. We were shipping much water and the men were continually at the pumps. After furling the mizzen topsail all hands were ordered aft to "splice the main brace."

The next day was Sunday and in filling away, after setting the lower fore-topsail, we shipped a sea over the fo'c'sle that carried away the spare topgallant mast, the pole of which rested on top of the forward house and the heel of the mast, lashed to the gallows just in front of the booby hatch. The mate called all hands to secure the mast, but the ship was rolling so hard and such seas were coming aboard, with scuppers full of water, that we were unable to handle it.

Here, the second mate asserted his authority by shouting, "Give the damned spar a passage, boys, before one of you loses a leg," and with this he jumped in, leading the men. Picking up the heel of the mast, which was floating in the starboard lee scuppers, we raised it and rested it on the break of the poop. Then, running forward, we picked up the other end and with a "Way-hey-a-a-a," we launched it aft along the gangway. Then raising the heel on top of the taffrail and the stern of the ship settling down, we again launched it aft, over the rail. At the middle it overbalanced into the water just as the ship's stern began to rise again and the second mate called, "Give her hell, boys, in a hurry!" There wasn't much need of the order for the weight of the mast below was doing the work, but we helped it along, sousing it completely under water as the ship's stern reached its apex.

Here occurred an unforeseen situation. The mast went down at an angle of 45 degrees or more. Then, with the power of its buoyancy, we saw it coming up, pointed directly at us from below. Would the ship settle fast enough to clear it? was the question. There seemed to be a race as to which could travel the fastest. On came the spar and down settled the stern as the second mate sang out, "Lay aft here, men, and stand by to ward off the mast!"

The stern was first in the race, but on the rise again the topgallant mast overhauled us and before there was a chance to ward it off, the pole ran under the taffrail, ripping out about fifteen feet of the rail. We quickly breasted the mast over the quarter chock into the sea, where it remained rolling over and over in the wash astern.

The loss of a few feet of taffrail was nothing compared to a hole under the counter which would have happened had the spar rammed us a moment later; but it cheated the cook from saying, "I tol' you so." However, he managed to keep up a fire in his range, day and night, while the wash from the decks rolled through the galley, and he didn't miss a day in having coffee ready at 5.30 A.M. for the crew. He told me afterwards that he didn't want to go down in the ship with "a troubled consciousness."

The ship had been hove to almost continually since Friday and it wasn't until Monday, July 31, that we got a "shot" at the sun and found that we were about sixty miles southeast of Sydney.

With the gale blowing strong from the south'ard, we set the reefed foresail and reefed mainsail. While sheeting home the foresail the second mate led the men in "Haul away, Joe." There was not much music in his voice; but how he could pull when chanteying! He seemed to have the strength of three men and the watch doubled their efforts to keep up with him. Mr. Sanborn was similar to Brooks, in his vulgarity, but he put more life into the men and heavy work seemed easy when he condescended to jump in and lend a helping hand.

The ship felt the strain of the added canvas and buried

her nose in almost every sea. The foresail was some "kite" to handle in this gale and the scuppers were running deep with water, much more so than common, but the captain crowded on all sail that she could carry, for he was now determined to get back to Sydney at all hazards.

The men were strung out along the deck, knee-deep in water, where they held the sheet of the sail, and the second mate took his position close up to the sheave and standing on top of the spare spar, one hand free and swinging in the breeze he sang at the top of his voice so as to be heard above the gale by us all. There was a merry twinkle in his eyes that I will never forget as he looked over the shoulders of the men awaiting the last word, "Joe!" They all knew the song and knew what to expect and looked for words that are unfit to print.

Few people can understand what it means to sing in such weather. It was absolutely necessary to stretch the foot of the sail, all it would stand, and bring the clew as far down as possible. Having no steam it was up to us to do the work which could not be done on this ship without the short drag chantey. Here, the second mate, singing at the top of his voice as he neared the end, suddenly turned, grasping the sheet with both hands, while he crouched with bended knees, and on the word "Joe!" straightened out with one mighty pull, with the help of the others, that brought the rope whizzing through the sheave, while I held the turn around the pin and took in the slack as the men rendered it up to the pin.

HAUL AWAY, JOE

Saint Pat - rick was an I - rish-man, He came from Dub - lin Cit - y. A-way, haul a - way, Haul a - way, Joe!

He drove the snakes from Ireland, and then drank all the whiskey.
Away, haul away, haul away, Joe.

He built a church in Limerick, and on it put a steeple.
He held high mass for forty days, but couldn't fool the people.

Away, haul away, come haul away my Rosie.
Away, haul away, my Rosie she's a posy.

Oh, once I loved an Irish girl, but she was small and sassy,
And once I loved an English girl and she was stiff and flashy.

And then I loved a Spanish girl, but she was proud and haughty.
And then I loved a French girl. Oh, say, but she was naughty.

Oh, once in my life I married a wife and damn her, she was lazy,
And wouldn't stay at home of nights which damn near set me crazy.

She stayed out all night, Oh, hell! what a sight,
    And where do you think I found her?
Behind the pump, the story goes, with forty men around her.

I have often thought how easy it would be for a crew of
deep-water sailors to enter a tug-of-war contest, with every
man's son, flat on his back and with feet braced with the
stretch of the rope, pulling his utmost, then a nice little
chantey like "Haul away, Joe" would completely up-end
the men on the opposite side and bring home the bacon.

With the setting of the reefed mainsail we squared away,
steering north in a very heavy sea; but before getting fairly
under way an unusually high comber broke over the mizzen
quarter, carrying away the monkey-railing on both sides,
breaking the skylights and flooding the cabin floor. We were
surely in a dilapidated condition around the poop, with most
of the railing gone, to say nothing of the state of affairs
forward, and the ship, a proper "lame duck," wallowed in
the sea throughout the night.

At four in the morning the gale moderated and we attempted to set the upper topsails. With the order from aloft
to "H'ist away," we raised the main-topsail yard about four
feet, but couldn't hoist it any farther. It was raining hard
and our hands were softened and sore from pulling the wet

ropes, but pull as we could we were unable to raise the yard, when the mate sang out: "What the hell's the matter? H'ist away, damn it all!"

A turn was taken under the belaying-pin but the sway-off wouldn't raise it any farther.

"Take it to the capstan, if you are too weak to raise it!" shouted the mate and we did as ordered. Heaving around a couple of times we gradually came to a standstill and the mate sang out, "Heave away!"

"Heave away, sir!" was answered and heave we did.

"Heave, oh heave!" was the cry. "Heave, and bust her!"

The wet halliards were stretched to the utmost and the water oozed out from the lay of the rope to the deck below. There was a sudden jump of the capstan and the halliards went slack as down came the chain runner, which had parted on the port side, running through the block above, coming down by the run between "Dublin" and me, not two feet away. We both instinctively hugged the barrel of the capstan, for in the dark no one could see how the chain was falling. It was a sickening sound—a swish back and forth on the hard pine deck at our feet—and the suspense was awful. It seemed hours before the rattling of the chain ceased, while in reality it was only a few seconds.

There was nothing more to do with the main topsail and after setting the fore and mizzen topsails, we found that the tye of the upper main topsail had slipped over the sheave and jammed into the mast in such a way that a link in the chain was crossways on the fore part of the mast, acting as a toggle. The runner being the lighter of the two chains, it had to break.

On Tuesday, August 1, we had fine weather until night, when the wind freshened, and after taking in the topgallant sails and furling the mainsail, upper topsails and jibs, the watch was called at 11.30 A.M. to furl the foresail. At the ordinary call of the watch at eight bells—"All hands on deck, ahoy!"—the hands dress and await everybody being ready before going on deck, but "All hands on deck ahoy, to shorten sail!" implys instant action and the hands all know that it is necessary to move and move quickly and on hearing the order, they tumble out of their blankets, snatching clothing, oil-skins, boots, etc., which are always handy, and jumping into their trousers, with a hitch of the belt about their waists, many times they are on deck before the caller has had time to reach the main hatch.

The wind was piping in great gusts while the sea again took on that peculiar green color as it broke over the rail. With the order to "Lay aloft" and furl the sail, the men rushed up the rigging in a bunch at the futtock shrouds, where some ran over the top on their way to the lee yard-arm. I was one of the last up the rigging and while running along the deck to the weather fore swifter, I saw a huge green sea coming up directly in front of me. There was only one thing to do—grab a belaying-pin and duck my head close to the pinrail before it caught me. I hugged the pin with both hands as the sea broke over the rail, throwing the ship nearly on her beam-ends. Being close under the rail the sea swept over me hardly wetting my face, but striking the side of the fo'c'sle it dashed over the boats and swept along the rigging, for the ship was over to such an angle that the men in the foretop were drenched. Although the sea was a big one, scarcely any water remained on deck, the bulk of it dashing over the ship, far to leeward.

She was making more water than usual and we had trouble through the night with the starboard pump which was continually choked with coal, making it necessary for us to draw the boxes two or three times during the watch, until finally we were unable to get any water at all, although it showed eight inches in the hold. When morning came investigation revealed that constant pumping, the pump being choked with coal, had worn through the pump just below the upper box putting it entirely out of commission.

The gale having moderated, with the call of the watch at eight bells, we came about and stood on the starboard tack, dropping the foresail and hoisting the upper main topsail to another walk-away chantey. The sun was shining brightly and the spirits of the men revived when going aft to set the mizzen topsail. We had never sung a chantey on the poop knowing that the captain despised a chantey; but he had just "shot the sun" and was below figuring up our position and Brooks gave us the wink and we started—

STORM ALONG JOHN

Oh, Storm A - long John was a son of a gun, To me way - hey - a - Mis - ter Storm A - long. Storm - y's gone and I'll go too, To me way, oh, Storm A - long.

Stormy, he is dead and gone.
A good old man was Storm Along John.

They dug his grave with a silver spade;
His shroud of the finest silk was made.

They lowered him down with a golden chain,
Their eyes were dim with more than rain.

He was a sailor, bold and true;
A good old skipper to his crew.

He lies low in an earthen bed;
Our hearts are sore, our eyes are red.

He's moored at last and furled his sail;
No danger now from wreck and gale.

Old Stormy's heard an angel call,
So sing his dirge now, one and all.

The captain rushed on deck just as the mate sang out, "Belay the upper topsail!" He ran to lu'ard, emptying a mouthful of tobacco juice under the main brace, and quickly turning to the mate shouted: "Mr. Burris, relieve the man at the wheel and send the watch below! Rig the pumps and pump her out! Send a man aloft to look for land to wind'ard!" He plainly showed that he was displeased at something. No doubt it was on account of singing a chantey on the poop for he growled at every step as he paced back and forth almost in a run.

The wheel having been relieved we were sent below for breakfast and found that the cook was much concerned over the pumping. He had heard of the starboard pump giving out and while at breakfast he went into the fo'c'sle and re-iterated what he knew about hoodoo ships. He knew this ship was doomed and cited the many misfortunes we had encountered during the past twenty days and found willing ears from most of the men in the fo'c'sle. In fact, "Dublin," who had no use for the mate ever since he got the call-down when we first left Newcastle, was so bitter that he joined the cook in his tale of woe and they only had to point to the clank, clank, clank of the pumps to convince the others that it would never cease, for the starboard pump was played out and it was only a question of time when they would all be caught like rats in a trap, and a leaky one at that, and it was time to leave while the leaving was good.

It was finally agreed that in the mate's watch (12 to 4 A.M.) they would lower the captain's gig, which was the only boat left that would float, and make a get-away. The cook was to have a barrel of hardbread and a ten-gallon keg filled with fresh water, handy to lower into the boat and "Dublin" volunteered to either gag or throw the mate overboard, while Carlson agreed to rig a tackle from the cross-jack yard while "Dublin" was taking care of the mate, so the others could sling the boat and put it over the side while he was coming down from aloft.

It was a daring undertaking and I firmly believed those men wouldn't hesitate at even murder should anything thwart their plans. They were a disgruntled set and worked up to such an extent that they were willing to take a chance at anything rather than stay aboard the ship any longer. But fortunately there was a cry from aloft, "Land ho! to wind'ard," which the captain said was Bird's Island. We ran up the pilot's flag at the fore and not long after sighted a steamer coming to us. She proved to be the *Rapid*, from Newcastle, without coal enough to tow us to Sydney, but could take us to Newcastle. As much as the captain disliked to turn her down he explained that his interests lay in Sydney and that was where he was bound and nothing else would do, finally pursuading the captain of the *Rapid* to take a letter ashore. This he agreed to do and turned back to Newcastle while we kept on our course towards Sydney, much to the disgust of the cook and other members of the crew.

In a light wind we stood on our course and in the fore part of the afternoon the steamer *Challenge*, our old friend that towed us to sea from Newcastle, came alongside and took our hawser, when we immediately shortened sail, taking in everything except the fore-and-aft sails.

It was my wheel in the afternoon, the sun shining brightly and the air quite warm. The captain paced the weather side of the poop and his dog Wag followed him until he found a warm spot beside the wheel box where, after turning around several times, he coiled up and lay down for a quiet snooze. Knowing that a good steamer had our hawser at last, the men entered into their work with renewed life. Light sails were neatly furled with a harbor stow and in rolling up the mainsail, with a toss of the bunt, there rang out on the still air, "Away-y-hey, O-h, Paddy can't dive for his *boots!*"

Wag jumped up, startled, as if he had been shot, and pointing his nose high in the air let out a yelp and a cry that ended in a sharp bark. I couldn't help laughing and even the "Old Man" smiled, but quickly chased the smile away and with a growl said: "Hump! No wonder you bark! I'd bark myself if I was a dog. I wouldn't stop at a bark either! I'd bite some old sailor and put new life into him!"

It was a hard situation for me, at the wheel, for one is

not supposed to talk or even pay attention to another's conversation but to stand like a bump on a log and watch the compass. So I bit my lip and was forced to turn my head where I could smile without the captain seeing me. He, no doubt, was watching for he called, "Keep her straight, Fred!" and continued his walk as if nothing had occurred.

There was no watch-and-watch that afternoon all hands being employed getting ready for port. Chains were run out of the hawsepipes and shackled to the anchors ready to let go upon arrival at Sydney. Here, it leaked out that the cook, "Dublin" and the two Swedes had concocted a scheme for deserting the ship which so enraged the mate that he swore he would have them all arrested as soon as the ship arrived; and then he began hazing them, giving them the most disagreeable work he could find. Toilets were scrubbed, masts slushed from masthead down, Irish pennants cleared, buntlines stopped, signal halliards rove—in fact, they were running from truck to keelson for the rest of the day.

At 12.30 A.M. we sighted Sydney Heads light and at 2.30 A.M. the pilot came aboard and seeing our condition remarked that if there ever was a "lame duck" entering port, the *Akbar* certainly had a right to that name.

Everything went well until 3.30 A.M., when just inside the Heads we grounded and stuck fast while every swell lifted us up and we pounded the bottom in no gentle manner. There was the general cry from the mate, "Stand from under those yards!" which brought the cook on deck in his underclothes, very much excited, with teeth chattering and voice trembling, exclaiming: "Fo' de lub o' God! She's gwine t' break in two! Take dis niggah asho'e befo' she done bust wide open!" He was a general nuisance about the deck until the second mate took him in hand and told him to go below, saying he would call him in plenty of time before she broke up.

The pilot assured us that we were on sandy bottom and that as the tide was flooding we would soon be afloat, but we pounded away until 4.30 A.M. before getting off. There was no material increase of the water in the hold and we went on

our way and were towed up to our old anchorage off Fort
Dennison where we let go the port mud-hook and soon
afterwards were told to go below. It was a welcome sound
and all hands turned in pretty well used up.

At eight o'clock we turned to again and it was discovered
that the cook, "Dublin" and the two Swedes had made a
"pier-head jump," having stolen aboard the *Challenge* and
been taken ashore. These men had all drawn their month's
advance in Newcastle so there was nothing due them from
the ship and there wasn't as much as a "donkey's breakfast"
left to show they had belonged to the crew.

After breakfast the first thing was to pump her out. The
brakes were shipped and for the last chantey we pumped
her out to,

LEAVE HER JOHNNY, LEAVE HER

Oh, pump her out from down be-low, Oh, leave her John-ny,
leave her. Oh, pump her out and a-way we'll go,
For it's time for us to leave her.

Oh, the times are hard and the ship is old,
And the water's six feet in her hold.

The starboard pump is like the crew,
It's all worn out and will not do.

They made us pump all night and day,
And we half dead had naught to say.

The winds were foul, the sea was high;
We shipped them all and none went by.

She'd neither steer, nor stay or wear,
And so us sailors learned to swear.

We swore by note, for want of more,
But now we're through and will go ashore.

We'll pump her out, our best we'll try,
But we can never suck her dry.

The rats have gone and we, the crew,
It's time, by God, that we went too.

This so worked on the mind of little Billy that he wisely concluded he had seen all of the sea that he wanted and accordingly asked the mate for his release, which was granted. The captain gave him a pound note and Billy left the ship that afternoon in the butcher's boat, a very happy boy.

CHAPTER XIII

THE PLEASURES OF SHORE LEAVE

WE WERE employed during the day unbending the sails and stowing them below. On Saturday we sent down the upper fore-topsail and the topgallant and royal yards. We also sent down the fore-topgallant mast and unbent the foresail and mainsail and rigged in the jib-boom. During the following week the ship was stripped of all yards. Everything came off of her except the main yard.

As the foremast was sprung, we took all the rigging off the mast and all the yards were scraped and the seams filled with pitch and repainted, after which we crossed the maintopsail yards, cross-jack and mizzen-topsail yards. The lighter yards we kept on deck. The latter part of the week was very disagreeable, with chilly rains during which we chipped the rust from the chains and other iron work.

On Monday, August 21, the steamer *Mystery* came alongside at eight o'clock and we hove the anchor up immediately, without a chantey, strange to say. The men were tired of chipping iron rust and not in good humor.

After tripping the anchor we were towed up to Johnson's Bay, intending to load our coal into an old hulk before going into the dry-dock, but with our usual bad luck we grounded before reaching the hulk. Casting off the steamer's line we ran a line to the hulk and made fast through the night and the following morning warped alongside. The lumpers came off at noon and started to discharge our coal into the hulk and while getting ready for them, Locker, one of our crew, had some words with the second mate and finally drew his knife and shouted: "Damn you! I'll cut your heart out!"

The second mate picked up an iron belaying-pin, to protect himself, and both cursed and swore at each other as they walked around like two game cocks awaiting an opening to rush in. This lasted for five minutes before Locker put up his knife. The second mate threw down his belaying-pin and

Locker then called him a vile name. At this the second mate rushed in and struck him a blow with his fist that knocked Locker over the spars on deck and before he could get up the second mate had pummelled him unmercifully. Both of Locker's eyes were closed and his nose was bleeding profusely when he begged the second mate to let him up, pleading for mercy and promising to behave himself in future. With another sailor he went ashore that night and got drunk and was locked up. The next morning the captain saw him and paid him off.

It took the lumpers until August 29 before they finished discharging, leaving about one hundred tons for stiffening, but the dry dock being in use, we were unable to take possession until September 15.

On the thirteenth, the *Mystery* retowed us up to Cockatoo Island, at the mouth of the Parramatta River, where we shackled our chain to a buoy in front of the Fitzroy Dry Dock.

As early as 1857, Cockatoo Island was a penal establishment and the dock, 300 feet long by 59 feet wide and accommodating ships of twenty feet draft, was blasted out of a granite ledge by convict labor.

Previous to that, in 1806, the citizens of Sydney were called upon to help fill in at other docks and a notice was put up on the fill: "All persons loitering about this work will be put to work at hard labor for the balance of the day." It had a good effect, for "swagmen" (tramps) and "humping blueys" (bums) were too lazy to work and beat it to other parts of the country rather than shovel dirt with no pay.

After the *Akbar* was hauled into dry dock she was trued by the tape at stem and stern and the sliding chocks hauled under the bilge and the pumps started. It took eleven hours to pump her dry. Three days were spent stripping off the copper. She was then caulked and recoppered while we sent down all the yards and the fore-topmast, putting them on deck, and housed the main and mizzen topmasts ready for the riggers. They offered to rerig the ship in wire, buying the old hemp rigging and giving $500 to boot, so a cable was sent the owners, in Boston, who gave their consent and September 23 the riggers put up the shears for the foremast and bowsprit, most of the crew having left the ship.

The water was let into the dry dock the afternoon of September 24 and early the next morning the pilot came aboard and the steamer *Breadalbane* towed us down to Roundtree's dry dock, Darling Harbor, Sydney, where we made her fast. There the riggers took out the foremast and bowsprit and the next day caulkers began caulking the side of the ship. The bowsprit having been repaired, we put it in again and unhung the rudder, which was found to be defective, so we were obliged to have another made.

On October 4 they finished caulking the side and began on the decks, while we painted the side and worked in the main rigging. In cutting the topmast backstays, the riggers made a mistake of four feet, too short, and wanted to lengthen them with another piece, putting in a long splice which they claimed would never be noticed and be just as strong. Mr. Sanborn was confined to his room with his old trouble and Mr. Burris was unusually grouchy and refused to have it done, storming about the decks and picking rows with everyone he met. I counted five different rows he was in before the day was over.

In those days splicing wire rigging was not generally known and the riggers agreed to teach both the mate and second mate if they would permit them to turn in the splice in the backstays. After a good deal of talking they finally agreed. The riggers took the backstays in between-decks where the work was carried on secretly, no one but the mates being permitted to see the work done; but at night the second mate took a piece of wire to my room where he taught me all that he knew.

He and I began to be great pals, going ashore nights together to the different theaters. J. K. Emmitt, the Dutch comedian, with his great yodel, "Go to sleep my baby," was then drawing crowded houses all over Australia. We heard him in Melbourne, in "Fritz," and he was playing the same in Sydney. Just before knocking off work for the day Mr.

Sanborn said: "Fred, let's go to the theater to-night. I believe that it will do me good and drive away this headache." The mate was standing close by and overheard the conversation.

At four bells, when we quit work, I rushed to the galley for some hot water to give myself a harbor washdown. My head was all in a lather of soap when the mate came up, saying, "Are you intending to go ashore to-night?"

I replied that I was, whereupon he turned to me in a low voice and said: "I am thinking of going ashore myself and if I do, you can't go. See!"

This put a damper on my going and I quietly finished washing my face and hands and went to the galley for my dinner. I took my time in finishing and while sitting on my sea chest, in full view of the cabin, Mr. Sanborn came out all dressed up. Seeing that I was still eating my dinner, he came to the door and said: "Hurry up, Fred! We want to get to the theater in time to get a seat."

I told him of what the mate said to me and he exclaimed, "Oh, hell!" and saying nothing more walked to his room and took off his shore clothes.

Soon the mate appeared and stood on top of the rail at the companion ladder, looking first at me and then glancing at the cabin door waiting for Mr. Sanborn to come out. Finally he called, "Come on, Mr. Sanborn, if you are going ashore!" Whereupon the second mate, dressed in his old clothes, stuck his head out of the door.

"Why! I thought you were going ashore!" exclaimed the mate.

"Well, I was, but now I'm not," said Mr. Sanborn.

I could have beaten a tattoo on my tin pan, *ff*, but knowing the mate I knew he would pay me back, with interest, if he saw me in a cheerful mood, so I quietly turned my face while he slowly walked down the companion ladder to the dock below, and I could hear his stiff ankles scuffling over the rough planks as he made his way up the dock.

After the sound died away the second mate came to my room and asked if I had heard him answer the mate. He smiled to think the mate had to go ashore all alone. "Never mind, Fred!" said he. "We'll take it in some other night."

On account of rainy weather we didn't go to the theater until Saturday night and although it rained all day we concluded to go, regardless. The theater was packed to overflowing and was close and stuffy. A small baby, in its mother's arms, was nearly overcome with heat and cried incessantly after the curtain went down on the first act. Two or three other babies followed suit so that the ushers, selling candy and chewing gum, raised their voices in order to be heard. Standing-room was at a premium and the overflow crowded over halfway down the aisles where the ushers elbowed themselves through with great difficulty, shouting: "Lollies! Lollies! Who'll buy the next box o' fresh lollies," etc. The hum and buzz of the audience gradually grew louder, each trying to be heard above his neighbor, until the noise in the parquet became a perfect bedlam.

On raising the curtain for the second act, the buzz of the audience and the cry of "lollies" stopped but the babies kept right on. The actors tried to make themselves heard and finally the babies ceased, except the one that first began crying, and finally the Gallery Gods began shouting: "I say! take it aout!" "Subdue that child!" "Stiffle it!" etc. An overgrown youth, with a second mate's voice, shouted, "Sit on it!" The poor woman at last arose, amid the shouting, but as the aisles were filled with people standing, she couldn't get out. The show stopped until she finally reached the foyer where she fainted and there was a stampede to see if she had died with heart disease or not, but the men in attendance shouting, "Give her air," finally quieted the mob and the play went on.

After the theater we started down King Street, in the rain, elbowing ourselves through the crowd, and on reaching the corner of the street the second mate called, "Good night, Fred." I turned to see what he meant and caught a glimpse of a blonde dame becketing him by the "fore lift," and they scudded across the street, both under an umbrella. The second mate was as ungainly under an umbrella as a hobo in the

Queen's chariot. It rather took me aback, for I had not seen her making any overtures, neither had he let on that he'd made a mash on the woman. She evidently knew her man and took him in tow, leaving me aground on the corner, so I made my way back to the ship alone and turned in for the night.

I hadn't been asleep very long before I heard the second mate's voice—"Fred! Fred! wake up!" and like a good sailor, answered with a jump, "Aye, aye, sir!" landing on deck and reaching for my trousers, half-awake, for I thought I had a call to shorten sail. The second mate sat on my sea chest, laughing heartily.

"Turn in," said he, "It isn't your watch on deck." And he chuckled and laughed, holding his sides. "I want to tell you what happened. I had a hell of a time with that blonde dame I quit you for." And then he unfolded his yarn.

"She took me to her room, a couple of blocks away, and quietly locked the door. 'It'll cost you a sovereign to stay here,' she said, 'and I always ask for my money in advance.'

"I gave her the sovereign and she turned out the light, bidding me turn in. I soon found that I had picked up an hermaphrodite, so I got up and dressed, while she remonstrated and said if I left the room she would expose me. I found a match and lighted the kerosene lamp and demanded the key, but she refused to give it to me. I saw her pocketbook on the bureau and at the same time she jumped for it. I caught her arm and took it away from her, putting the sovereign in my pocket, whereupon she began screaming at the top of her voice: 'Murder! Murder! This man is taking advantage of me.' I tried to gag her but she fought like a tiger, all the time calling for help. I couldn't open the door and soon someone tried the door from outside, demanding what was going on. 'Help! Help!' she shouted.

"They began breaking in the door and I rushed to the back window, which was partly raised. About ten feet below was the roof of a shed. Just as the door gave way and two men rushed into the room, I threw up the window and jumped out on the wet roof below. Both feet slid out from under and I landed on my back, bouncing off the roof to the ground below in the alley, while she called: 'Murder! Murder! Catch that man!' etc.

"I hadn't hat or coat and luckily I wasn't hurt when I slid into the alley; regaining my feet I ran as fast as I could.

"I heard her yell, 'If I ever catch you on the street, I'll expose you, you ——— ——— ———.'

"With no hat or coat I didn't dare to go on the main street and coming to the first crossing, a policeman stopped me and asked where I was going and where I came from. I said I was just running across the street to dodge the raindrops; my wife was sick and I was going after medicine. The story worked and I got by with it and here I am.

"I'll have to watch my step when I go up town again, for if this woman ever sets eyes on me I'll have to tack ship in a hurry, for she's got a dirty tongue. If her language to-night is any criterion, believe me! I'll cut and run before laying to, to hear what she's got to say. I'll hope I never see her again for she's a dirty slut and not in my class."

We laughed together while he told of his adventure and he didn't go to his room until the wee small hours.

The riggers taking full charge, those of the crew who wanted to leave were paid off. Andy went with the others and Jim Dunn and Dick were the only men left in the fore-castle. The next night I went ashore and after walking around looking at the shop windows, went back to the ship pretty well tired out. Just as I reached the dock, Jim was going ashore.

"What are you going ashore for at this time of the night?" I asked.

"Come along with me and I'll show you and give you a good time."

I did not want to be steered into a travesty, like the second mate, and so refused to go.

"Oh, come along, Fred!" he said. "We'll go up Cumberland Street to the 'Sailors Return.' Little Andy was paid off with quite a bunch of money and the stingy cuss hasn't spent a cent. I'm going up and make him loosen up. We won't get drunk; let the others do that. We'll just have a little night-cap on Andy and come right back again."

On the promise that he would come right back, I agreed to go. We found the whole crew there. Brooks, who swore he was through with boozing, was stretched out on the floor in one corner of the saloon, blind drunk. Poor fellow! He probably was shanghaied again and God only knows if he ever reached Brooklyn again. Most of the boys were drunk —half-seas over—and after shaking hands with them, Jim proposed having a drink on him. But Mike, one of the crew, said:

"Your money's no good! Put it up and have one on me. We've all got money left and it's a poor shipmate that can't set 'em up while he has money." Everybody wanted to be a good fellow and they took us by the elbows and pushed us up to the bar.

Jim looked around and said: "Where's Andy? Oh, there he is! Come on Andy!" But Andy was nearly helpless and couldn't get out of his chair, so Jim lifted him up and walked him to the bar where Andy showed his appreciation by want-ing to shake hands with everyone.

A couple of rounds put the finishing touches on Andy and he was carried to a chair in the corner beside Brooks. Jim braced him in his chair, so he couldn't fall out, and asked the others if he had been a good scout, keeping up his end with the drinks. They all said that he hadn't, although he never refused to drink when asked.

"Then it's time he treated," said Jim. "Come on boys! Andy's got plenty of money, for he's been with the ship ever since we left Boston and I don't know of a single time when he's shouted. Let's go through his clothes and find it. It'll be a good lark."

Entering into the spirit of it, they felt in all his pockets. While taking off his coat and vest, Andy lost his balance and fell to the floor, where they rolled him over against Brooks. The inside pockets and lining of his coat and vest revealed nothing. Then Jim suggested taking off his shoes and they didn't stop at his shoes. Even his socks were taken off and turned wrong side out; but Andy had his money where it was safe from these wolves and they finally gave up in despair.

"Oh, well!" Jim said, "We've had a lot of fun with him anyway. Come on boys and have a drink on me and then I'll go aboard ship."

After the "nightcap" we bade them good-night. Under the next lamp post Jim put out his hand displaying two gold sovereigns.

"Pretty, ain't they?" said he. "Do you know where I got 'em? Mike took off one of Andy's shoes and I took off the other. When I pulled off his shoe, both sovereigns rolled into my hand and I slipped them into my pocket and kept right on searching for more without saying anything to the others." Jim laughed and chuckled to himself as he told how he had slipped it over the others.

"Of course you'll give them to Andy when he sobers up," said I.

Jim stopped and rolled up his eyelid, saying: "Look into me eye and see if you can see anything green there. What! Me give up these sovereigns? Not on your sweet life! When he sobers up he'll never know he had 'em. Yous don't know the ways of sailors. Besides, I'll be his banker and use the money to treat the others. He's sponged on us fellows long enough. The stingy pup!"

He reasoned that sailors only went to sea for a grand time at the end of the voyage. A day or two made no difference to them when it came to spending the money, for they were drunk from the first night ashore, spending money freely and keeping no account of the money spent. When it was gone, the sailor's boarding house would tell them in time to hunt for another ship and he might as well have the sovereigns as the sailor's boarding house.

The boss rigger said to me the next morning, "Fred, you must have a queer country in America."

"What do you mean?"

"Why, I was reading in a San Francisco paper last night, that a burglar entered the room of a man fast asleep, who had a gun under his pillow. Now, that's a queer way for a man to sleep, with a gun under his head. Not very comfortable, I should say. Why the bloody hell did he put it under his head when he could just as well stand it in the corner? The bloody burglar, it would seem, must of made a lot of noise, doan't sher knaow! Very bunglesome! For he woke up the man and the man shoved the gun right in his face and said, 'You git!' and the burglar said, 'You bet!' and quietly crawled back out of the window. Now, that's a queer way of talking, isn't it?"

I agreed with him that it was.

A young fellow named Joe McCarty, hailing from South Boston and about twenty-two years of age, signed articles a day or two later and brought his dunnage aboard. Upon learning that he was from Boston, we got to be quite chummy and asking my name, he said:

"Harlow? I used to know a sort of a city missionary, in South Boston, when I was a boy, by that name. He used to visit the sick in the poor district where I lived; but I guess he's no relation of yours."

I told him that that Harlow was my uncle, whereupon he shook hands warmly and said: "Your uncle was one of the best-hearted men I ever knew. Many a time he brought food to my poor old mother, who was up against it before she died, and also sent a doctor to care for her. I haven't forgot his kindness and one of these days I'm going to pay him back with interest for what he did."

Joe said that he had been going to sea ever since he was thirteen years old, mostly in fishermen; backing and filling from one schooner to another, without saving a cent, when he decided to try deep water. So he shipped in the *Golden Crown*, an English bark, for Teneriffe, Canary Islands. She was a "lime-juicer" of the old type—poor grub and worse treatment and upon arrival he jumped her and signed on the American bark *Catalpa*, a whaler, thinking he would be where he couldn't get ashore and where he could save money.

"*Catalpa*," I said. "I have heard of that ship but can't place her."

"If you have been in Australia any length of time, you probably saw where she rescued six Fenians, last April, at Fremantle, on the West Coast."

I then remembered that the Melbourne papers gave an account of the rescue.

"When I signed on in Teneriffe," continued Joe, "We cleared for La Platte but we kept on sailing for Australia and although a couple of whales had been taken, a lookout was kept at the masthead, continually, and although we raised whales time and again, no effort was made to get them. There were only three of us in the fo'c'sle that could talk English. There were Malays, Kanakas, Dagos and all sorts of men. The worst set of men I was ever with and I made up my mind that if ever I got ashore I'd desert the ship and upon arrival at Bunbury, when the captain and mate were ashore, us three that could talk English, lowered the boat and pulled for shore. The second mate on hearing the falls, as we lowered, ran to the side and called us back but we pulled for our lives for shore. He then ran up the police flag, which was seen ashore and the police were waiting for us as we landed. One big buck used me too rough and I hit him in the mouth with my fist, but he used his billy and I woke up in jail. The other two were taken back to the ship.

"When the bark cleared for Fremantle and the news became known that she had rescued the Fenians, I was considered a pretty good man for deserting such a ship and they gave me a light sentence of seven days for assault. On getting out of the cooler, I shipped in a coaster for Newcastle, *via* Adelaide, Melbourne and Sydney. Shipping was light at Adelaide and Melbourne, with American ships, for these were the only ones I wanted to get into and on our arrival in Sydney, the *Akbar* was the first ship I tried and here I am, tickled to death to be in a ship that will some day reach Boston."

One Sunday, Joe and I took a walk ashore and going down Macquarie street we came to a high, iron fence which enclosed a house, standing by itself in a park, beautifully laid out with well-kept lawns and shrubbery. A road of white powdered granite surrounded the house, which widened to a broad driveway to the street, some one hundred yards away, through a high arch in the iron fence. On either side of the driveway were arches for pedestrians and a sentry walked back and forth bearing a rifle at "shoulder arms."

"Let's go in, Joe, and see the grounds," said I; whereupon we both walked through the arch about fifty feet when we were quickly brought up with a "round turn," by the sentry who exclaimed:

"Hi, there, you fellows! Let's see your permit!"

Explaining that we were sailors ashore, sight-seeing, and had no permit, he said, "This is the Governor's House and I caun't allow you to pauss, you knaow, without a line of the pen." So we viewed the residence and surroundings through the iron fence and walked around to the Botanic Gardens, on the east side of Circular Quay, where in early days the convicts cooked their evening meal.

It was a beautiful, warm, sunny day and the people were out in crowds—women with their baby carriages and men wearing cork hats. Some of the boys wore straw hats. Both men and boys wore a kind of a linen sash, from under the brim of the hat, behind, that looked like the end of a hand towel, hemmed in red or embroidered silk with lace ends that fell over their shoulders. Whether this served to brush the mosquitoes away or whether it was a mark of dress, I didn't ask; but all well-dressed Australians wore the sash, both in Melbourne and Sydney, it being quite the fashion in those days.

In the evening, after supper, Joe and I took another walk over the hill to Upper Fort street and down George street on the west side. Passing the Seaman's Bethel, the evening services were just beginning. The windows were open and the strains of music increased in volume as we approached. But it was the words of the song that struck us full in the face, taking the wind out of our sails and setting us both aback. We both stood still, across the street from the Bethel, while they sang these words:

> Brightly beams our Father's mercy,
>   From his lighthouse ever more,
> But to us he gives the keeping,
>   Of the lights along the shore.

CHORUS

> Let the lower lights be burning!
>   Send a gleam across the wave!
> Some poor fainting, struggling seaman
>   You may rescue, you may save.

> Dark the night of sin has settled,
>   Loud the angry billows roar;
> Eager eyes are watching, longing,
>   For the lights along the shore.

(*Chorus*)

> Trim your feeble lamp, my brother:
>   Some poor sailor tempest-tost,
> Trying now to make the harbor,
>   In the darkness *may be lost*.

(*Chorus*)

I looked at Joe and he looked at me, saying: "That's mighty fine music, Fred. Let's stop and hear it."

"Let's go in," I said to him.

"All right!" and we squared away across the street but before we got across he said:

"Hold on, Fred! This is a Protestant institution and I am a Catholic."

Then the chorus broke out afresh: "Let the lower lights be burning. Send a gleam across the wave."

"Those are sailor words," said he. "Oh, all right! The priest won't know it; take the lead and I'll follow."

Going through the doors to the vestibule Joe asked where the holy water was kept for he did not see any. He was surprised to learn that Protestant churches didn't use it.

For Joe's benefit I led him upstairs to the balcony where we could overlook the congregation without being too conspicuous and we were lucky enough to find seats, for the Mission was crowded to overflowing soon after.

It was a special song service, with a fine pipe organ, which was well played. The minister in charge was full of pep and urged all to make a noise, whether they could sing or not. Giving out the hymn number he would sometimes say: "Now, everybody stand up and bear a hand. When you sing a chantey aboard ship, you come in on the chorus without being told. Make yourself think you're on the topsail halliards and bowse away on the chorus of this hymn."

This tickled Joe. Scanning the congregation we could see there were old men and young, interspersed with ladies dressed in bright colors. There were apprentices from the different English ships in port, in their bright uniforms, but Joe and I, in our flannel shirts, without white collars, took a back seat.

A swell-looking girl, with a good, strong voice, sitting next to Joe, shared her songbook with him, quickly finding the different hymns and taking particular pains to point out to him the page and the line being sung. There were familiar pieces such as "The Sweet By-and-By," "Hold the Fort," etc., and Joe finally found his voice and followed her with a fine tenor. No one could help singing under such conditions and the evening passed altogether too quickly.

After the service the young lady introduced herself as Miss Hopkins and seemed to take a great deal of interest in us on finding that we were from an American ship. Apologizing, that we were not dressed for church but simply ran in to hear the music, she shook hands with us warmly, saying: "A man is known by his deeds and not his clothes. I'm glad that you came in and I hope next Sunday I shall find you both here. I'll save these two seats for you for I want to hear your voices again. We make quite a trio and I enjoyed every song. Do come again," she entreated.

We both promised that we would come next Sunday and going to the ship, Joe commented on the services as the best time he ever had, saying if Miss Hopkins were to be there, next Sunday would find him close by her side. But alas!— next Sunday found us at anchor in the stream, with no liberty.

On Wednesday the steamer *Breadalbane* took us in tow from Roundtree's dock, over to Johnson's Bay, to the old hulk, where in very disagreeable weather and blowing a gale from the south'ard the lumpers reloaded our coal in six days. The riggers bent all our sails and November 1, Jim and I went ashore, with the captain, to sign the protest, at which time the crew signed articles but didn't come aboard until two days later when the mate again asserted himself by "rowing" with the different men, to show his authority and, as usual, fooled no one but himself.

The next day the *Mystery* took us in tow and with a falling barometer we dropped our port anchor again, off Fort Dennison. Here we remained at anchor until November 14, during which time all the chafing-gear was put on, the running rigging rove off and the paint-work scrubbed until the *Akbar* resembled a yacht, for cleanliness.

November 9 was the Prince of Wales's birthday and all ships in the harbor were decorated with flags and bunting. We ran up the Stars and Stripes and were given the afternoon off as a holiday, but not permitted to go ashore. I got busy with a hook and line, in the main channels, and caught enough small mackerel for all hands. No sooner did the hook strike the water than a fish fastened itself on the line. All the men who could raise a hook and line, were soon over the side in the same manner. The mackerel were a little larger than a good-sized smelt and it would have been great sport to catch them with a pole. As it was, we had no fault to find and enjoyed the afternoon immensely.

CHAPTER XIV

AMERICAN SHIPS AND ENGLISH SAILORS

THE *Mystery* came alongside at 2.30 P.M. on November 14; the pilot came aboard at three and the captain an hour later. The anchor having been "hove short" it was immediately tripped and we got under way and were outside at five-thirty, when the steamer left us and with a southwest wind we steered an east-northeast course, with all sail set, sailing full and by.

On account of the lateness of the year, in which light winds and calms abound in Torres Straits and about New Guinea and other islands inhabited by cannibals and pirates, the captain considered it unwise to attempt going through the Straits and took the southern route, south of Tasmania and up the west coast of Australia.

Not much happened of interest, outside of the regular routine aboard ship, except that we had our usual run of gales off the southern coast and while the *Akbar* was a much better sea boat than when leaving Newcastle, yet she shipped plenty of water, although recaulked and recoppered. While on the starboard tack we made three or four inches per hour and "rig the pumps" was not a strange sound. On the port tack she was not so bad. "Leaking just enough to keep her sweet," said the captain.

We got a very good crew in Sydney. Joe was in my watch and we continued to be great pals. Frank Stanwood, an ordinary seaman hailing from Gardiner, Maine, occupied the room with me. He sailed from Boston in the barkentine *Abdul-Kadir*, for Auckland, New Zealand, where he left and came to Sydney by steamer. He was in the second mate's watch and we grew to be great friends.

Besides Joe, there was a big, burly Englishman—Dick; and a well-educated American—Williams, who claimed he had been mate and master but, like Brooks, whiskey downed him every time he got ashore. He was also a big man and very conceited. Then there was a little Irishman—Dan; and a young fellow—"Cockney," who, without exception, was the most ignorant person I ever met. He wanted me to teach him his A, B, C's. Someone had taught him to write his name—Richard Dunn—and he did very well, but it took him more than five minutes to write it. When I asked him if he could spell, he replied: "Yes, some words; but what puzzles me is *God* and *Dog*. I know by spelling one of 'em backwards it's the other. But, damn me! I don't know how to start either of 'em." I spent a week, in the dogwatch, trying to teach him his letters and finally gave it up as hopeless.

In another ship he was in the sailors told of a floating island in China that was suspended in the air. He asked me if I had ever seen it and on telling him that I had not he began to enlighten me, telling of the queer persons aloft that did not dare to go near the edge without grabbing a grommet to hold on to. Not having any water to bathe in the dirt was caked on so thick that they couldn't be recognized. "Now how the bloody hell could anyone shin up there t' see?" he asked.

I couldn't enlighten him never having seen the island.

When we were off King George's Sound, a heavy squall struck us and carried away all three topgallant sails and parted the jib sheet. Before we got the jib down three breadths of canvas were whipped out. The squall lasted three hours. Two days later the wind increased to a gale and with a heavy sea running we shipped much water.

December 14 was cloudy with passing heavy rain showers, the wind from the northwest. We had two men at the wheel and at eight bells (midnight) she kicked so hard that the helm (an iron tiller four inches square at the rudder-head) was lashed and the wheel put in beckets. At two bells (1 A.M.) she kicked so hard that the tiller broke, six inches from the rudder-head, and we were forced to hold her by hand.

I was glad when four bells were struck, relieving us, for my arms and legs were sore, trying to hold the wheel. One minute she would kick down and the man on the opposite side would be lifted bodily off his feet and thrown half over the wheel and *vice versa*. It was the most disagreeable night I ever spent at the wheel.

On December 19 we were off Cape Leewin and held our own, in fine weather, until Christmas when we had a general holiday. The steward, a bright young fellow who joined the ship in Sydney, was a well-educated chap, claiming his ancestors were from the nobility, but hated himself and was ashamed to go home because he couldn't make good, being continually drunk while ashore. He became very chummy with Frank and me and on Sunday afternoons he would come to our room to "swap lies." On this Christmas he began telling us how the English, as a rule, dropped the h's, etc., but "You never hear me doing it," said he.

A few minutes later he told of the administrator dividing his father's estate among the different heirs, being particular to sound the *h*. I couldn't resist calling his attention to the pronunciation and smilingly asked him to repeat his last sentence.

He saw my drift and replied: "I know what I'm saying. Heirs! H-e-i-r-s," spelling the word and emphasizing each letter loudly.

Frank and I gave him a good-natured, merry, ha-ha! and I had to get the dictionary to convince him. He laughed it off by saying: "This doesn't prove anything. You've got an American dictionary. Why don't you get an English book? Get the Imperial Dictionary."

We joshed back and forth until Frank finally pushed him out of the room, when the steward said: "Come out and I'll show you the way we Briton's use our dukes. I'll give you some free lessons in the art of boxing."

"Not on your life," said Frank. "I don't know anything about boxing."

"Come on," said the steward. "It's time you learned and you can't begin any younger. I won't hurt you."

On the promise that the steward would not hit him too hard, Frank consented to be shown.

"I'll teach you the Marquis of Queensbury rules," said he. "Put your left foot forward until it touches my toe and with your left hand extended and your right in front of your chest, even with your left elbow—this is your first position. Now, then! What you want to do is to hit me on the nose."

The sentence was hardly ended before Frank launched out his left, quick as lightning, hitting the steward squarely on the nose; then turning around he ran with the steward after him. Frank jumped on the rail and ran up the main rigging with the steward at his heels. Reaching the futtock shrouds he didn't have time to go over the top so swung over to the main yard. The steward was not used to this performance and took his time in catching hold of the running rigging, for a swing, and by the time he was on the yard, Frank went to lu'ard and was on deck before the steward got off the yard. On regaining the deck the steward complained that his heart was beating excessively. He was troubled with heart complaint and shouldn't have tried to run up the rigging. If it had not been for his weak heart he never would have shipped as steward. He said he loved the sea and wanted to be a sailor and hoped some day that his heart would permit him to go aloft. He had never been higher than the top, where he had to lie down until his heart stopped beating so hard.

This ended the sport for the afternoon and we sailed lazily along until New Year's Day when, in cloudy and threatening weather, we raised Prince's Island and laid offshore until midnight; then squared away for the Straits of Sunda. We passed Cockatoo Island early in the morning and were off Angier Point at noon, dropping our port anchor in twelve fathoms of water between Maneater's and Horn islands, at five o'clock, on account of light head winds.

After supper Frank and I were watching the land, when the steward came up, saying: "Boys, do you know, this isn't a bad ship at all? I've always heard that an American ship one must steer clear of unless you want to be kicked about like a dog by the officers. I didn't remember signing on this ship and the next day I had my doubts about sailing in her and if we hadn't been anchored in the stream I would have jumped her. But I couldn't get ashore so I slept with a revolver under my pillow at night and carried it in my hip pocket all day, for a week, expecting at any minute to be knocked down by one of the mates; and I made up my mind that if any mate ever attempted a rough-house with me, I'd shoot. But so far I have not been molested. Why! this ship is a palace beside some of the ships I've been in and I don't believe all the tales told by the Britons are half true. I wish that some of the crews I've been with could look at the table set in this ship. Their mouths would water, sure."

It has always been a mystery with me why American ships are so shunned by the Britons. It is true, that in the '60's, some of the flash clipper ships had a hard name and, like their passages, made a record for brutality as well. But not any more so than the Scotchman, Dutch or even the English. I remember a second mate, named Bartlett, who made his boast that the last man out of the fo'c'sle was always a target for his boot and while in the *Black Hawk*, a Boston ship, he and the mate stood on each side of the gangplank when a new crew was shipped and when coming aboard they were initiated by a blow on the side of the head that knocked them down and they were told, "We want you fellows to understand that we are the officers aboard this ship!" Whether the man was drunk or sober (for all were served alike) he was left to wonder just how far he could go with the mates before getting another introduction. No doubt it had its merits with some, but that day has gone by.

I told Frank and the steward what Mr. Sanborn had told me, one night in Sydney, of a voyage when he was at Portland, Oregon, anchored in the Willamette River. In his words: "We had a crew of niggers. The smartest set of men I ever had. I had those fellows trained so that when an order was given they'd beat hell a mile to be the first at the tops'l brace or in the rigging.

"We were washing down decks one morning in the month of January and the ice in the river was drifting downstream. One big buck stood on the rail drawing water with a bucket, for the deck-pump was froze up. He had the lanyard fastened with a half-hitch in an eye-bolt in the rail. I told him to take another hitch before he lost the bucket.

" 'All right, sah! I'm a-watchin' it, sah,' said he, and he kept on drawing water. I noticed that with every dip the hitch loosened up, so I said:

" 'If you lose that bucket you'll jump overboard after it,' and we went on with the scrubbing. Soon after he shouted: 'Git me a boat-hook, quick! The bucket's done got away from me.'

"I sung out, 'Git t' hell over the side after it, damn quick!'

"Now I had no idea of his doing it, but he called, 'Aye, aye, sah!' and overboard he jumped into the icy water. He wasn't much of a swimmer and nearly drowned. I threw a rope to him which he caught and held on to but he was unable to swim much and swallowed half the water in the Willamette before we got a bowline under him and when we got him on deck he was so chilled that he had spasm after spasm and we had to send him to the hospital. Not long afterwards I was arrested for cruelty and the next morning the daily paper, the *Portland Oregon,* came out in big headlines: ANOTHER SEA-MONSTER CAPTURED! It cost the ship $500 to clear me and every nigger quit the ship and we had a hell of a time getting another crew. The *Akbar* was so well advertised that she was called 'a hell ship' and it was impossible to get a black or white man to come aboard in Portland so we towed down to Astoria where we finally got another crew after laying there a whole month."

It was a satisfaction to know that we could turn in for an all-night's sleep without being called at eight bells, but we were routed out at 5.30 A.M. to heave up anchor and got under way at 6.30 A.M., with all sail set, in a light breeze from the northwest.

"Cockney" took the wheel at eight o'clock, but soon got in bad with the "old man," for stargazing. I was coiling up the ropes on the poop when the captain called: "Fred, come and take the wheel! This man will have us ashore if he stays here much longer. He's made a half-dozen S's in as many minutes and with this wind I want someone that can keep her straight."

Taking the course from "Cockney"—"Full and by" the captain added: "Full and by, means keep her as near the wind as you can. Do you see that point of land off the lee bow? We've got to weather it on this tack. Now see what you can do."

"Aye, aye, sir!" I replied. "I'll watch her, sir!" and watch her I did, clearing the point nicely. Instead of being relieved again he let me steer the balance of "Cockney's" trick as well as my own, giving me an opportunity to view the Island of Java as we sailed past Batavia.

We passed Cheribon, Java, on January 4, 1877, and the next day wore ship off the Island of Madura, laying "off and on" until morning.

Having no pilot we furled jibs, topgallant sails and main-sails in squally, rainy weather, heaving the "dipsey-lead" (deep-sea lead) every four hours. This was done by bringing the ship into the wind with little or no headway. The line was coiled neatly in a tub placed abreast the main rigging. The end of the line was carried to windward, outside of everything, forward to the cat-head where it was bent to a 25-pound lead, conical in shape, with a cavity in the end filled with tallow or soap, so that when the lead struck the bottom the tallow picked up the kind of ground, whether mud, sand or rocks.

One man holds the lead, for heaving, with another in the fore channels and another in the main, each with a coil of the line in his hand, while one of the mates stands by to take the depth. When all is ready, he calls, "Stand by! Heave!" The man with the lead sings out, "Watch, oh! Watch!" and drops the lead and each man, in turn, as the line runs out, calls, "Watch, oh! Watch!" When the lead finally brings up at the bottom the mate in charge takes the depth as shown by the line. It is then put in a snatch block, hauled on board and coiled neatly in the tub again and the ship fills away again according to the depth shown by the lead-line. The length of a "dipsey-line" is usually one hundred fathoms.

The hand-lead, for depths of less than twenty fathoms, weighs about seven pounds and is bent to a line 25 to 35 fathoms long. Like the deep-sea lead it is conical in shape with a cavity in the end filled with tallow or soap. The hand-lead line is marked for showing the depth of water as follows:

> At 2 fathoms, a leather with two tails.
>   3 fathoms, a leather with three tails.
>   5 fathoms, a white rag.
>   7 fathoms, a red rag.
>   10 fathoms, a leather with a hole in it.
>   13 fathoms, a blue rag.
>   15 fathoms, a white rag.
>   17 fathoms, a red rag.
>   20 fathoms, a piece of cord with two knots in it.

There are *nine marks* on the hand-lead line. All other fathoms are called "deeps," *i.e.*, 1, 4, 6, 8, 9, 11, 12, 14, 16, 18 and 19 fathoms—11 in all.

In sounding with the hand-lead line, a man stands in the weather main channels and throws the lead forward, while the ship has headway on. If the lead strikes the bottom as the white rag touches the water, he sings out, "By the *mark, five!*" etc. If the water deepens on the next throw, he calls, "By the *deep, eight!*" etc., and if he judges the depth a quarter or a half more, on the next heave, he calls, "And a *quarter*," or, "And a *half, eight!*" etc., and if eight and three-quarters, he calls, "Quarter, *less nine!*" and so on, according to the depth of water.

HEAVING THE LEAD

Early Friday, January 5, we wore ship and headed for the land, steering south with everything set except the royals, but drifted to lu'ard of Pondy Island. We tacked ship every four hours, bringing up in the same spot and with variable westerly winds were unable to beat six miles to windward. But on Monday we got a light wind from west-northwest and ran through Sapuda Straits and came to an anchor in seven fathoms, opposite Pondy Island, furling the sails for the night.

As the night shut in the lights twinkled along the shore and we heard weird music—sounding cymbals and the monotonous tinkling of bells. The natives ashore were evidently having a jollification of some sort for they kept it up until midnight.

We got under way at seven, in fine weather, to beat up Madura Straits. Taking advantage of every cat's-paw we tacked and clubbed about several times during the watch. All went well until that evening when we ran into a rain squall. The main tack, having been taken direct to the pinrail, was forgotten and with the order to "Stand by the royal halliards" and "Let go!" the squall struck pretty hard, carrying away about ten feet of the pinrail on the port side. No other damage was done. The royals were taken in and the t'gallant s'ls were lowered until the squall passed, when we came about on the starboard tack.

It was my lookout from ten till midnight and in very light winds I raised a red light, off our lee bow, soon after six bells. There was no perceptible change in his course as I was relieved and on turning in was soon asleep. It wasn't long before I was awakened by a shock, forward, that sounded as if the anchor had been dropped; but there was a rattling of falling masts and I knew we had collided with some vessel. Instantly remembering the red light off the port bow, I rushed on deck just in time to see a topsail schooner drift into our main yard, which soon carried away his main topmast.

The schooner proved to be a Chinese merchantman and instead of giving way to us (for we had the right of way, being on the starboard tack) he was either asleep or not acquainted with maritime rules, for his jib-boom struck us just abaft the cat-head, running through our topgallant rail. The wind being light and neither of us hardly having steerageway, he was turned around as his jib-boom carried away and our fore yard took out his fore topmast, which was of bamboo. Then, drifting into our main yard, we took out his other mast.

By this time we were all on deck and the Chinese were shouting to one another, while Mr. Burris stood on the poop cursing them in the most blasphemous language he could command as they drifted astern.

I ran aft to see if I could be of any assistance, but we were not damaged and as I ran up the companion steps the captain sang out to the mate:

"What are you swearing about? That fellow is a Chinaman and don't know what you say and if he did he can't get back at you for he's a half-mile astern. Better save your breath and turn in."

The second mate stood beside me and gave me a poke in the ribs with a knowing wink, as much as to say, "You're a damn fool," pointing to the mate.

It took us till January 12 to beat up to Pasuruan, which is about forty miles from Sourabaya. We anchored there over night and the next morning sailed up the coast, in very hot weather, with only enough wind to fill the sails. The water was very shallow and we finally got stuck in the mud flats south of Madura and tried to kedge over the flats.

Lowering the longboat, the kedge was lowered in the stern of the boat with the stock resting on the gunwale and the arms and flukes over the stern. A line was bent to the kedge and we rowed ahead as far as we could, when the anchor was thrown over the stern. The other end of the line was taken to the capstan and after regaining the ship we began heaving away in the sweltering sun. The capstan-head was so hot that we couldn't bear our hands on it. The thermometer registered 115 degrees. All hands were barefooted and the decks were so hot that we had to raise one foot after the other, for the air to circulate underneath, in hopes of cooling off.

To lighten the work Joe started a chantey as we tramped around the capstan in an endless job. The kedge wasn't heavy enough to hold and was dragged home faster than the ship moved ahead for the mud was soft and mushy and with a good stiff breeze she would have sailed through without any trouble; but the wind was light and our only hope was to experiment with the kedge. As fast as it was warped in it was taken out again and so we worked all day long. It grew too hot, even to sing, and after a couple of chanteys we gave it up. The kedge didn't accomplish much and after a lot of extra work the captain gave orders to "tie her up for the night." The sails were furled and we dropped the port anchor and lay waiting for a pilot.

The next day was Sunday and we saw a small boat with a lateen sail approaching. It proved to be a coolie pilot. He was dressed in a kind of bright-colored wrapper which was tied loosely about his waist. He looked more like a woman than a man and was quite an interesting object to Frank and me for we had never seen anything like it before. Under the wrapper (a kavon) his legs were bare and his feet were slipped into a toe-split slipper or sandal, *i.e.*, instead of his toes being covered, a prong came up from the bamboo sandal, that fitted between the big toe and the second, and in these he scuffed across the deck. This sandal was worn by most of the working people, as well as the women ashore, in medium circumstances.

The pilot spoke in broken English and said that we were drawing too much water (twenty-two feet aft) to sail over the flats and that a steamer would have to tow us. When asked where a steamer could be obtained, he answered: "No sabe. No come day; come tomollow."

Not getting much satisfaction from him the captain went ashore to arrange for a steamer and was gone four days. The pilot came off each day with the same information: "No sabe. No come day; come tomollow."

During all this time the men were employed in the rigging and I finished the pinrail that had been carried away and spiked it to the rail. I also made a mast for the captain's boat and Williams made a cat-rigged sail, as we expected the captain would use it while at Sourabaya.

The captain came back on Thursday afternoon and we hoisted the jack for a pilot but it was late in the afternoon of the next day before he showed up. He was different from the first man and said, "Steambo't come tomollow."

True to his word a steamer came off and took both our hawsers and we were towed over the flats to Sourabaya where we let go the port anchor and gave her forty-five fathoms of chain. The next day we dropped the starboard anchor and unbent the sails, putting them below. The weather was very hot during the day but, as a rule, we had heavy rain showers at night which cooled off the decks nicely and we could get a good sleep.

We began unloading our coal with the help of nine coolies who worked on deck while we shovelled the coal into bamboo baskets holding less than a half-bushel. These baskets were made with a handle on each side of the rim and when filled were carried by the coolies across the deck to the rail where two coolies, standing on a staging, dumped the coal into a scow below. These men moved and acted more like apes than human beings. Their thigh bones were long, permitting them to sit down on the deck comfortably in an upright position and in moving from one spot to another they resembled monkeys.

The coolie's hat was made either from split bamboo or rice straw and had the shape of a shallow and wide funnel, starting from a sharp peak on top and widening out to about a foot in diameter over their shoulders, hiding their black hair, which was generally long and tied in a knot behind. When cut it was bushy, standing out in all directions.

The gang aboard the *Akbar* wore light dungaree jackets which were never buttoned, exposing their naked bodies to the waist, around which some wore the kain with the corners passed between the legs and fastened in a pajama effect.

Others wore light pants or overalls, but no more clothes than possible and all were barefooted.

They were excessive cigarette smokers, making and rolling their own cigarettes in corn-husk wrappers. When not smoking they chewed betel nut mixed with fine-cut tobacco. The betel nut, when chewed, was very red and the tobacco mixture was anything but good to look at and quite disgusting. After chewing the mixture to the right consistency, a quid about the size of a walnut was held outside the teeth, in the lower lip, which protruded like a shelf. The saliva oozing out had a tendency to run down the chin but the overflow was checked and drawn into the mouth at intervals with a sucking sound plainly to be heard. Naturally, both corners of the mouth were stained by this fluid.

It was quite the custom, with both men and women, to file off the teeth squarely and some of the women used a rat-tail file to hollow their teeth. A smile or a laugh would expose a mouth hideous to look at.

Our coolies came off in a large, open boat. If there was no wind they rowed; otherwise, they ran up a lateen sail which they handled with great dexterity. The natives of Java are second to none when it comes to sailing a boat. Their craft are long and narrow, like a canoe; but have an overhanging bow and stern carrying a lateen sail on a bamboo mast, besides rigging out to windward an outrigger of bamboo as long as their boat. If the wind is strong enough to raise the outrigger from the water, a man runs out on the brace or truss, to weight it down. Reaching the outrigger, if he is not heavy enough, a second or third man is sent out, and the strength of the wind is spoken of by the natives as a "one-man breeze," or "two-," or "three-man breeze."

It was a beautiful sight to see them race, for they fairly flew, and if one capsized no attention was given to the unfortunate by the others, for they are natural swimmers and hold on to the boat until someone picks them up.

Instead of a cabin, on the larger ones a matting was thrown over a bamboo raised in a crotch, acting as a ridgepole to a tent, to shed the water. It was not very high and to enter it one must get down on his hands and knees and crawl in.

As soon as we had finished our dinner Frank and I, from the rail above, watched the coolies while they finished theirs. After having cooked a kettle of rice in their boat, it was set on the deck where three coolies huddled around it, dipping their hands into the kettle for want of a spoon, and with thumb and two fingers they squeezed a bunch into a little ball which was carried to their mouths.

These men seemed to belong to the boat, for the others brought for their luncheon only a handful of rice wrapped in a fern leaf which was pinned with a bamboo peg and after they had eaten they came aboard and hung around the fo'-c'sle, awaiting for the crew to finish and give them what was left. Bread, potatoes and beef they ate with a relish, but being Mohammedans they were very superstitious about pork and couldn't be induced to eat or even look at it.

After the men in the boat had eaten they remained where they sat and each took from his pocket a comb and began combing another's head, over the kettle. The long black hair hanging over their shoulders, was carefully combed back from the head and laid apart. We couldn't understand the procedure until, all at once, we made the discovery that in parting the hair, like monkeys, they used their fingers to pick out the head lice which they quickly licked off with their tongues. Instead of the finder eating what he had found, however, it was given to the one on whose head it had grown.

Our curiosity was satisfied right there and we both jumped down from the rail so nauseated that we nearly lost our dinners.

CHAPTER XV

NATIVE GIRLS AND JAVA SUGAR

SOURABAYA, situated in the northeastern part of Java, stood next to Batavia in importance at that time and had a population of about 100,000. Cane sugar was the principal commodity, which was taken from the fields in the interior and floated down the Kali Mas, meaning "river of gold," in large, native, open boats with bamboo matting stretched over a ridge-pole (the same as the small boats) for shedding the rain. These lighters were called "prons" and held from 75 to 220 baskets of sugar.

In Cuba, sugar is handled in hogsheads and tierces, but in Java it was put into bamboo-matting baskets, holding from 400 to 800 pounds, cylindrical in shape and about five feet long.

As in most tropical countries the fruits in Java were delicious. The mangosteen, about the size of an apple and having a thick brown skin, contained a white, creamy, pulpy substance inside, tasting very much like strawberries and cream.

Alligator pears or custard apples were very palatable. The outer shell resembled that of an alligator—a hard, bristly shell of brown green, growing as large as four or five inches in diameter, but when opened containing a yellowish, cream-colored custard, with a few black seeds about the size of a hazel-nut meat. It was usually eaten with a spoon, but we sailors "got outside of it" without wasting any time.

After shovelling coal all the forenoon there was nothing quite so refreshing as the green cocoanut at noon when we came on deck. Boring a hole through the eye we drank the milk which resembled water more than milk and it quenched our thirst better than anything else. After drinking the milk we cut the nut in half and ate the inside with a spoon for the meat had not formed and was very cool and refreshing.

But of all the tropical fruit the little silver or sugar

bananas, which were about the size of one's fingers, when peeled, stayed by us better than anything else; perhaps on account of the cost, for with a gilder (about forty cents) we could buy a whole bunch. There was no trouble in getting fresh fruit daily, for the natives came off in bum-boats to sell almost anything that could be bought with money. One had to be an expert Jew to buy, for with plenty of time you could save half the price asked at first.

During our first noon at anchor the bum-boats loaded with fruit and tobacco and other wares to sell, swarmed about us knowing we were just in from sea and easy marks. We hadn't tasted anything fresh for so long that we spent most of our spare cash on fruit the first day.

There were all sorts of boats about the ship including a boat-load of maidens of ill repute who were licensed by the Government, under the supervision of a physician whose duty it was to see, under a rigid inspection, that no disease prevailed among them. There were six of these native girls in one boat which was rowed by a coolie directed by a matronly woman in the stern who was the chief spokesman for the girls.

All were dressed in different shades of bright colored kimonos. They were bare headed, showing their black hair plastered down flat on top of their heads with plenty of cocoanut oil and neatly combed back over their ears and tied in a twist behind. Bright colored parasols shaded their faces as they lounged about on cushions and pillows making themselves as comfortable as possible. Each one was smoking a cigarette.

Having been denied permission to come aboard these pretty girls, all dolled up in their finest, kept up a constant chatter, their musical pigeon English ringing out clearly above the voices of the bum-boat men who began pulling away to other vessels in the harbor because our attention was now centered on the girls in the boat under the bow as they looked up to us trying to make known their mission by introducing themselves.

"Me, Lucretia," said one; and "Me, Molly, bargoose

LANDING PLACE ON THE KALI MAS, SOURABAYA, JAVA. From a photograph in the Peabody Museum, Cambridge.

MALAY GIRL, SOURABAYA, JAVA
From a photograph in the Peabody Museum, Cambridge

girl," said another; bargoose being the Javanese word for
"good," as we understood it. All had English names which
no doubt had been given them by American and English
sailors. The matronly-looking woman in the stern kept looking from one of us to another and finally her eyes rested on
Williams, who no doubt looked good to her, for pointing
directly at him she said:

"Hi, you big sailor-boy! I like you! You like Molly?
Molly velly fine bargoose girl."

This brought a laugh from the rest of us that somewhat
nettled him for the girls in the boat seemed to enjoy his discomfiture as well. To show that he was not in the market
he replied:

"Oh, she's too young! Better send her home to her
mother."

Molly quickly resented the assertion for she stood
proudly erect, throwing back her head and exclaiming: "No!
No! big sailor-boy. You see!" And right before us all she
threw her kimono from her shoulders and it falling to her
knees she stood as naked as the day she was born, displaying
a well-developed form rivalling that of Venus and dis-
pelling any thoughts that she was a mere child. Then taking
her time she slowly pulled back the kimono and asked:

"What you tink now? Molly, bargoose girl!"

Here, the second mate rang two bells, calling us to work,
at which the girls sang out repeatedly: "Good-bye! Good-
bye! Come and see us," etc., while we waved our hands to
them as we left the fo'c'sle-head.

In this extremely hot weather we were compelled to keep
our shovels moving, regardless. We had been warned not to
drink too much water or we would all be sick and the captain
ordered two dippers of oatmeal stirred into a bucket full of
water of which we drank sparingly. This no doubt kept us in
good condition during the day and at night we were rationed
a half-cup of lime juice which had to be taken before
morning.

The oatmeal water was quite palatable and I found myself going to the bucket every little while, until the second

mate warned me that I was drinking too much and told me to put a small piece of coal in my mouth. My tongue rolling around the coal would cause the saliva to flow and I found that the roof of my mouth was not so dry nor did I require so much water.

Like the coolies we wore no more clothing than necessary, having on only overalls, while our bodies were bare. Our underclothes having been discarded, the coal dust stuck to our skin and on getting out of the hold we looked more like negroes than anything else and a bath in a bucket was necessary every night as the captain forbade us going in swimming on account of the sharks that infested the waters of the harbor.

About the third night Joe said: "Sharks, or no sharks! I can't stand this idea of taking a bath in a pint of water. I've got to have a dip in the bay." Accordingly he ran out on the bowsprit and slid down the martingale and stood on the martingale shrouds facing us, for we all stood on the fo'c'sle head to watch him. Looking on both sides of the cutwater for sharks, which failed to appear, he exclaimed, "Here I go, boys!" and dove into the water from which he quickly arose and swam to the cable where he scrambled out, saying:

"The sharks didn't catch me that time. Gee, that was fine!" Then, climbing up the back ropes, he said, "I'm going to try it again." He didn't stop at the second time and soon was swimming about with a piece of soap, washing himself until he had removed all the coal dust from his body. Then he called to us to come in as he said he didn't believe there were any sharks around or they would have appeared after he dove in the first time.

The swim was indeed refreshing and one after another followed Joe until it wasn't long before we were all swimming about the ship and the sharks were forgotten. Instead of taking our bath in a bucket after that we all went over the bow for a swim every night.

We finished unloading the between-decks on January 29 and reached the bottom of the hold two days later when one of the stagings gave way and four coolies were dumped into the coal below. They escaped unhurt but Archie, who was in the second mate's watch, was severely injured about the head and shoulders and knocked unconscious for a few moments. The blood was washed from his head and a piece of court-plaster put over the wound and after ten minutes he was ready for work again.

The next day we had made so much progress that it was necessary to place a couple of beef barrels, head up and about fifteen feet apart, on which we placed the baskets to relay out of the hold. We were working two gangs on each side of the keelson. Williams and "Cockney" shoveled the coal into baskets which I picked up and placed on a barrel. Joe carried them to the next barrel where they were taken by Dick and passed to the coolies on the staging who took them to the side-port and dumped into the scow.

The accumulation of coal dust on the barrels had to be brushed off every little while. We were all naked to the waist, except Dick, who was unusually grouchy. He weighed about 180 pounds and his undershirt and overalls were wringing wet with perspiration and he strutted back and forth puffing like a grampus.

In all sorts of work there are some who see the ludicrous side of a situation. While waiting for Joe to take my basket I brushed the dust away from the barrel. My hands being sweaty the dust stuck and as Joe turned to go, after taking my basket, I wiped my hands on his back. He smiled good-naturedly and upon returning paid me back with a handful thrown over my shoulders when my back was turned.

We played back and forth until Joe tried a handful on Dick and Dick reciprocated. On the next trip Joe pulled back his undershirt and threw a handful down his back. It was bad enough to feel the dust on your bare back but to have it stuck in an undershirt was a different matter and Dick dropped his basket and threw a handful at Joe, most spitefully, and a war of coal dust followed which soon increased to pebbles of no small size. The work stopped while we watched proceedings, bringing an oath from the mate who shouted:

"Here! Damn it all! If you fellows want to fight, get to hell out of the way and let the others work."

"All right," said Joe, "I'm willing."

"So am I," growled Dick.

Dick pulled off his shirt showing a white body with a black smirch down his back, standing out in great contrast to Joe's, which was as black as a negro.

"Are you ready?" asked Joe.

"Yes! Damn you!" said Dick, who rushed in only to be met with an upper cut from Joe's fist that brought the claret. Then Dick tried his fists but couldn't reach Joe, who was a better boxer, for he kept punching Dick at will.

Seeing that he was accomplishing nothing with his fists, Dick lowered his head and rushed in catching Joe around the body and being the heavier, pushed him half way up the coal where they both fell with Dick on top. Biff—bang! and Dick pounded Joe unmercifully about the head. He was taking an unfair advantage of Joe and I ran to his assistance, thinking to pull Dick off, but the mate stopped me, saying:

"No, you don't! I won't have anyone interfering with this fight! Get back to work!"

Others followed me, but the mate shouted: "You men get back to work and let these fellows fight. Let them kill each other or quit when they've had enough!"

We went back to our stations but all were interested in the outcome of the fight and we stood, like the mate, lookers-on, for Dick was shouting at the top of his voice, "You —— —— —— blankety,—blank,—blank!"

Joe turned his face to avoid punishment and rolling over on his stomach, caught Dick's leg with his arm and bracing his feet in the coal they rolled completely over with Joe on top.

Then Joe imitated Dick, showering blow after blow, with the same expressions,—"You blankety-blank-blank! You will, will you!" Biff—bang!

They were now at the bottom of the coal, on the floor, where Joe had command of the situation and Dick's head was pummeled almost to a jelly. His mouth was cut, his nose bleeding and his eyes were swollen shut for Joe's bare knuckles cut and ripped up the skin most unmercifully. It was the most brutal fight I had ever seen.

Dick's eyes being closed, he called:

"Let me hup! Let me hup, Joe! Hi caun't see any more! You've got me this time but Hi'll fight you again when Hi can see, hif you want to!"

Joe was not a brutal man and he could see that Dick was in no condition to carry on the fight, but before letting him up he asked,

"Have you got enough?"

"Yes, for Hi caun't see, you know," replied Dick.

Joe then got up and helped Dick to his feet, when he exclaimed:

"Taik your bloody 'ands haway! Hi want no assistance from you!" And shaking himself clear he staggered to the water bucket and after quenching his thirst began bathing his face in the oatmeal water.

"For God's sake get out of that water!" shouted the mate. "If you want to take a bath get some water from the cook, but see that you don't stay all day! We've lost too much time now on your account!"

Dick sulked away, a very much dejected and beaten man, while Joe rinsed out his mouth and wiped his face with his handkerchief. Outside of a couple of black eyes he came off better than I expected. Dick was a sight to behold, for he was almost unrecognizable, but he returned to work and it is needless to say there was no more dust throwing carried on in the ship.

We unloaded all but about one hundred tons of coal which was left for stiffening and then the sides and between-decks were swept clean for our cargo of sugar. The port watch then had twenty-four hours liberty ashore but they did not return until the morning of the following day when the starboard watch went ashore.

Our first two scows of sugar came off, one holding 210 baskets and the other 110, which was loaded in the lower hold. In order to keep the sugar from the skin of the ship, which was more or less damp, bamboo poles from twenty to thirty feet long and four or five inches in diameter were cut and placed against the side of the ship and held there by rolling the sugar against them. This gave a good circulation of air and kept the sugar dry.

These bamboo poles came off in rafts, ten or twelve feet wide and five or six feet deep, usually fastened by four bands of grass rope, one around each end and one at the quarters. Two men broke out the poles and passed them aboard. But when the bulk of the first raft was unloaded the poles began to separate and the tide soon carried them from under the lashings and they floated down stream and beyond reach. The second raft was handled differently for when it was made fast amidships the second mate called:

"Are any of you boys good swimmers? We've got to get a sling under this one."

"Aye, aye, sir! I'm your meat," sang out Joe, and with these words he jumped on the raft and proceeded to breast it away from the side of ship. Then taking the end of the sling over his arm he dropped into the water and swam under the raft to the other side. The end of the sling was then brought over the side and tucked through the bight where it was hooked to a whip from the main yard. A strain was kept on the sling, thereby squeezing the raft together as the poles came aboard and in this manner we didn't lose a pole. But it was dangerous business, not only because of sharks that usually lie under the bilge of the ship, but because of broken bamboo, sticking below to catch in one's clothing or the sling.

A plunge into the water was refreshing in that hot weather and we all stood by for a chance to be first in taking a sling under. It happened that I had the opportunity of going under twice. The first time, I must confess, gave me a chance to think of "home and mother" as I went into the water and a shark would have had to travel pretty fast to catch me, for instead of swimming I dropped under the raft and pulled myself across, catching hold of the bamboos and scrambling across to the other side as fast as I could make my hands move. I felt anything but safe and spit out a sigh of relief, with the water in my nose and mouth, on regaining the surface of the water on the other side. The hot sun quickly dried my clothes and I was cooled off for at least an hour.

As we had no donkey-engines, a purchase was rigged from the main yard in order to handle the sugar. The fall, leading through a snatch-block in the deck, was taken to the main-deck capstan where an awning was spread to keep off the sun. The pawls of the capstan were triced up and the capstan bars lashed in. The end of the fall was stopped around the barrel of the capstan so we wouldn't lose it in "letting go." Then, walking around the capstan, we hove the sugar up above the rail where a tackle from the mainstay was hooked into the sling and when "high" and ordered to "let go," we stepped aside letting go of the capstan bars which whizzed round as the fall unwound without restraint while the sugar swung over the main hatch, snubbed by the second mate who held the turn at the rail and lowered it into the hold where it was stowed away by the coolies.

We had now become somewhat acclimated and our hours for work were from 6 A.M. to 6 P.M., with an hour off at noon. To break up the monotonous work of walking around the capstan all day we sang many a chantey to lighten the work. Our first chantey was started by Archie. It was the "Banks of Sacramento," an old California packet-ship chantey in the '50's.

In order to make the chantey last throughout the hoist, the chanteyman usually repeated each line of the verse. It had a rousing chorus in which every man opened his mouth, singing his utmost. The song rolled across the water in the still air and was echoed back from a large Dutch ship off the starboard beam, which had her sails dropped for drying from the rain of the night before.

We had noticed a couple of ladies on the ship and to-day they shifted their chairs under the awning, evidently for a better position to hear the music. This gave new life to our

BANKS OF SACRAMENTO

Andantino

Oh, New York's race course is nine miles long. To me, hoo - dah! To me, hoo - dah! Oh, New York's race course is nine miles long. To me, hoo - dah! hoo - dah - day! Then it's blow, my bul - ly boys, blow, for Cal - i - for - ni - o, There's plen - ty of gold so I've been told on the banks of Sac - ra - men - to.

A bully ship and a bully crew,
A bully mate and a skipper too.

Oh, New York's race track, where we stood,
We bet on all they said was good.

Our watch, our shoes and every rag,
But lost our money on a bob-tail nag.

Our money all gone we shipped to go
Around Cape Horn, where strong winds blow.

We're bound for Cal-i-forn-i-o;
For gold and banks of Sacramento.

men and we did our best to please the ladies, selecting chanteys with a rousing chorus where all could be heard.

"Give 'em 'Rio Grande,' or 'Shenandoah,'" said Williams.

"'Rio Grande,'" we all clamored and Archie began the
chantey using words from the old Mother Goose melody
and branching off to words of the windlass chantey as given
below.

RIO GRANDE

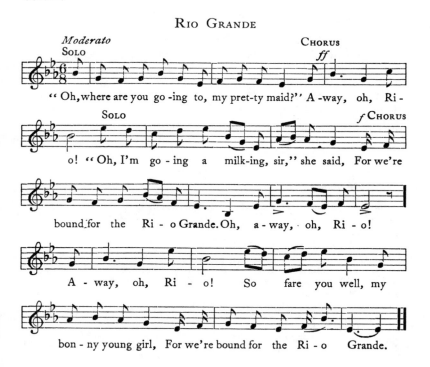

"Oh, where are you go-ing to, my pret-ty maid?" A-way, oh, Ri-
o! "Oh, I'm go-ing a milk-ing, sir," she said, For we're
bound for the Ri-o Grande. Oh, a-way, oh, Ri-o!
A-way, oh, Ri-o! So fare you well, my
bon-ny young girl, For we're bound for the Ri-o Grande.

"Oh, may I go with you my sweet pretty maid?"
"I'm sure you're quite welcome, sir," she said.

Oh, man the good capstan and run it around.
We'll heave in the sugar and then, homeward bound.

We'll sing to the maidens. Come sing as we heave;
You know at this parting how sadly we grieve.

Sing good-bye to Sally and good-bye to Sue,
And you who are listening, good-bye to you.

So heave up the sugar until it is high.
"Let go! Stand from under!" the mate, he doth cry.

Oh, heave with a will and heave steady and strong.
We'll sing a good chorus for 'tis a good song.

The ship she went sailing out over the bar;
They pointed her nose for the old Southern Star.

So good-bye, young ladies; we'll sing you no more.
But we'll drink to your health when we all go ashore.

Running around the slack for the next basket we took the strain and Archie started "Shenandoah" which is one of the most musical chanteys, I think, of all.

SHENANDOAH

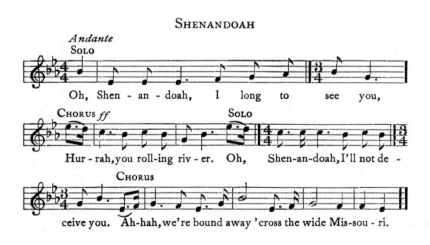

Oh, Shen - an - doah, I long to see you,
Hur - rah, you roll-ing riv - er. Oh, Shen-an-doah, I'll not de - ceive you. Ah-hah, we're bound away 'cross the wide Mis-sou - ri.

Oh, Shenandoah, I love your daughter,
I love the place across the water.

The ship sails free the wind is blowing,
The braces taut, the sheets a-flowing.

Missouri, she's a mighty river.
We'll brace her up till her topsails shiver.

Oh, Shenandoah, I'll leave you never.
Till the day I die, I'll love you ever.

Before the lower hold was finished we had a gang of coolies to caulk the deck which had dried out during the hot tropical weather. To every six or eight men there was a "serang" or boss, who chalked the deck into squares of from three to six feet, showing the work the different men were supposed to do during the day.

The coolies, instead of sitting in a caulker's chair, squatted down on their haunches, like so many monkeys and talked continually while at work, taking their own time in doing the work mapped out for them. Instead of bending over their work they kept their bodies erect and if it was necessary to reach a little farther they slid along the deck, in an upright position, to where they could work without bending. They were a comical set of workers, sitting about the deck sucking the saliva from the quid of betel nut which they held in their lower lips.

The mate was very much exercised over the number of idle coolies around the deck. Going up to one fellow, who was under the rail in the shade, he caught him by the collar and jerked him to his feet, exclaiming:

"What are you skulking around here for! Get up and go to work."

"Oh, me serang! No work!" said the man in much surprise.

Then he accosted every man in like manner but all claimed to be serangs, much to his disgust. It was really hard at times to tell who were serangs or who were supposed to work, for they were continually on the move. A tap here and a tap there and the mallet would be dropped while the coolie went in search of oakum or a drink of water.

But they were no worse than some of the men in the shipyards, during the World War, when Uncle Sam implored all to give their best to speed up work and get out the ships. Of all the "sogering" I ever saw among white men with intelligent brains, the shipyards were the worst. And the foremen were just as bad. I know of instances where good honest men wanted to work for their Country and were blacklisted because they were giving their all. And I record it with shame that the foreman made his boast that he didn't want men that "would make a record," under his charge.

There was something queer about the habits of the coolies. I never saw one of them touch his lips to our water dipper. They held it high above their heads pouring a small stream into their mouths, which was swallowed without discomfiture and without losing a drop. Frank and I tried it and nearly choked and we poured more down our shirt fronts than we got in our mouths.

One Thursday noon, when we had pork for dinner, the mate came forward while the coolies were lounging about the deck awaiting a "hand out" and told me to give him a slice of pork, which I did.

"Watch me, boys!" said he, "and I'll show you some fun."

With the slice of pork behind him he walked up to a coolie sitting on the deck in front of our room and catching him around the neck held him fast, saying:

"John, you sabe pork? Heap bargoose," bringing the pork in front of him where he could plainly see it.

"No, no, sabe pork! Me no like!" said the coolie, crying in terror.

"Heap bargoose, John!" repeated the mate, and then he proceeded to rub the pork all over the man's face. The coolie squirmed and struggled to get free, crying out most piteously, his cry reaching the ears of the other coolies who fled in terror on seeing what the mate was doing, for they did not want to be treated in the same manner and over the side they scrambled into their boat below.

The coolie finally got away from the mate and ran around the fo'c'sle while the mate followed, showing the pork in a menacing manner. The coolie's face plainly showed that he was a very much frightened coolie and he followed the others into the boat where they kept up an excited jabbering among themselves evidently considering that their souls would be eternally damned from that time on.

CHAPTER XVI

SHORE LEAVE AT SOURABAYA

AFTER supper on one of those hot, suffocating days, Frank and I sat on the bull-rail of the fo'c'sle deck with our feet over the side giving our feet and legs the benefit of any cooling breeze that might circulate. The Dutch ship was swinging with the tide, a thousand yards away, off the starboard beam. The ladies on the poop, dressed in bright colors, looked very comfortable under the awning and I remarked:

"Frank, I believe it is cooler over there than on this ship. I'll swim over there with you."

"All right," said he. "Let's keep our sheath-knives on for we might need them before we get back and it's a long swim." Without another word he pulled off his shirt and jumped overboard.

I had no idea that he would undertake to swim that distance, but he was a fine swimmer and a regular water dog. On evenings, when in swimming, he would dive from the back-ropes in one direction and be under the water so long that we were often alarmed for his safety. But he generally came up in the opposite direction, laughing to see the anxiety on our faces.

Having made the proposition to swim over to the ship there was nothing else to do but follow. So, in like manner, I jumped after him and we two foolish boys were on our way for a half-hour's swim.

As we neared the ship one after another of the crew came on top of the fo'c'sle-head to watch our progress and swimming to the ship's cable we hung on to rest. One of the crew could talk English and invited us aboard, but we explained that we were only out for a little swim, besides, we didn't want to appear before the ladies in our costume. He then threw us a bowline for each to sit in, which was much better than hanging on to the cable, and to comfort us while we rested, began:

"Ain't you boys afraid of sharks? I see dot you fellers go in every night, swimming. Our 'ole man' won't let us go in."

We explained that we also had the same orders from our "old man" but we had never seen any sharks about the ship and so concluded if there were any in the bay they were in another locality.

"Ya-h, dot's so," said he. "De ole man vent ashore last veek mit his dog und before he got ashore, beck, he hove for a swim his dog overboard. Soon a big shark gobbled him up and dere was noddings left but a streak of blood in de vater, yet. Ven he cooms aboard he say dot a coolie fishermans had his leg bidden off de same day, und by de same shark. Ya-h!"

It was the custom for the native fishermen to go out in two boats, spreading a seine between them in a semi-circle. Then all hands jumped overboard, shouting and splashing the water with their hands and feet, making as much noise as possible to frighten the fish into the seine. Then by drawing the two ends together the bottom of the seine was drawn up in the shape of a net and hauled into the boats. It was during one of these hauls that the coolie lost his leg.

We had seen them fishing in this way and reasoned that if they were in the habit of jumping overboard every day we could take the same risk. But, notwithstanding, the Dutchman's story of the shark biting off the coolie's leg set our brains to work and quickened the blood in our veins. To say the least it was not very comforting. Although they pressed us to stay longer we declined with thanks and were soon on our way back, Frank as usual in the lead.

The water was calm and glassy having a hue of gold from the afternoon sun. The mountains in the distance, in that peculiar haze of the same color, seemed in a dance from the rising heat, while the smoke from Mt. Smeroe, a volcano, staged a setting that can only be seen in the East Indies. We swam in silence but making better progress than when we started from the *Akbar*. Soon Frank swam into a bunch of loose sea-weed.

"Ugh!" he exclaimed. "I thought a shark was after me," and he turned, laughingly throwing the sea-weed off which was wrapped about his arms and body. Then we talked of sharks and what to do if we should see one. "I believe that we should stick together," said he. "Not that I'm afraid, but we are a long way from home."

It was comforting that he took this stand for he was a fine swimmer and I had to exert myself to keep up with him.

Suddenly, ahead of us, we saw what looked to be a cocoanut husk floating on the water; but instead of drifting with the tide there was a small ripple back of it and it was coming towards us. We both stopped swimming at the same instant.

"My God, Fred! It's a shark!" shouted Frank. "Get out your knife, quick!"

There was no need of his instructions for I already had mine in my hand. A cold shiver ran through my veins as I realized how helpless I was in attempting to combat such a foe and my disadvantage in not being an expert swimmer. But I grasped my knife tightly, saying:

"We'd better face him and keep side by side. If we can get him to come between us we'll have a better show for one of us to stick him."

The dorsal fin of the shark made a rapidly widening wake behind him in the smooth water looking as big as the wake of a ship under topgallant sails as he approached.

"He will turn on his side before he makes a strike at us," I said; and the shark came on evidently not in a hurry to strike, preferring to size up the situation before rushing in on us, which seemed hours to me. When about fifty feet away there was a sudden flurry with his tail and at the same moment Frank dived out of sight and I was left alone.

Reasoning that he would swim past me before making a plunge, I held my knife in readiness, determined to thrust it into his mouth should he turn on me. But before I had time to definitely decide there was a splash of water with his tail and I was struck in the side a terrific blow that carried me under the water. I had presence of mind, in rolling under, to still hold the knife and with both hands grasping it, as the shark swept by, I thrust the knife up where it took effect in his side, stuck fast, and was wrenched from my grasp.

It was several moments before I came to the surface and naturally my first thought was of the shark. But it was no-where to be seen. I don't know how long it was before I realized that Frank was calling, but I came to my senses when he caught me by the arm, exclaiming: "Are you hurt, Fred? Answer!" etc. I evidently had gone under a couple of times and there was an awful pain in my side and I was somewhat nauseated and dizzy. I remember answering that there was an awful pain in my side and the next thing—I found that I was in the ship's boat with a lot of faces bend-ing over me.

"Where's the shark!" I exclaimed.

"Never mind the shark, you're all right," said Joe, for it was he who had helped pull me into the boat.

I had been unconscious and Frank had held my head above water until the boys, who had been watching us, saw the shark, then Joe, Williams, Jim Dunn and Archie jumped into the captain's gig and rowed to our rescue. Frank had saved me from drowning and outside of a broken rib and a scolding from the mates for undertaking such a foolhardy thing, we reached the ship all right.

Frank, in diving, swam under the shark and drove his knife into the shark's belly. Feeling the cut it evidently swerved in its course and so knocked the breath out of me, otherwise I might be wearing a wooden leg to-day or have been food for the fishes in Sourabaya bay. It was a close call and one to be remembered. I was indebted to Frank and the others for saving my life but it was out of the question for me to reimburse them from my fat salary of $12.50 per month, the ordinary seaman's wages of that day. They were true sailors and quickly stopped any such suggestions on my part, saying, "It is no more than anyone else would do under similar circumstances."* Frank and I were close friends from that day on.

While in the water, in an unconscious condition, Frank said it was an easy thing to keep me afloat, for he pulled my arm over his shoulder where my head rested against his with no chance of the water reaching my mouth or nostrils. He was not alarmed for his safety for he had seen the boys from the *Akbar* rapidly pulling the boat towards us and he knew his ability as a swimmer to keep afloat until we were picked up. His only fear was that the shark might return before they reached him. The Dutch ship also sent a boat out for our rescue but it arrived too late to be of any assistance.

There was no indication of a broken rib but the pain was most severe to the touch and the captain prescribed liniment and I was told to massage my side thoroughly and "turn in" until he told me to report for work. There was a black and blue spot on my side as large as a hat and when the second mate carried me to my bunk and stripped off my wet overalls and rubbed in the liniment I begged him to quit for the pain was almost unbearable.

"Lay still and be quiet!" he ordered, "or I'll send you to the hospital to starve. It was bad enough for me in Melbourne but Sourabaya will be a damned sight worse and I'd hate to see you go. You probably cracked a slat instead of breaking a rib. Too bad we're not in Sydney! I'd send for that floosey that picked me up in front of the theater. She'd be a fine nurse for you."

In spite of the pain I couldn't help laughing at his ridiculous remark and begged him to be quiet. During the next two or three days, in which I kept to my bunk, the boys showered me with all kinds of tropical fruit. The swelling in my side gradually went down and at the end of two weeks I was able to do a day's work at the capstan bars.

We finished the last of the coal on February 27 and the next day a lighter with 218 baskets of sugar came off in the

---

* At that time the wages on board ship were about as follows: captain, per month, $100; first mate, $50; second mate, $35; cook and steward, $30; able seamen, $18; ordinary seamen, $12.50; boys, $8.

morning, which we had loaded by noon. Our force was doubled at the capstan each man having an additional coolie at his side who was supposed to run in the slack of the fall while we stood by to heave when the slack was taken up.

I got more enjoyment out of the coolies in watching their feet fly over the fall than anything else. While the pain was still in my side yet I could walk around the capstan, hugging the barrel, while the coolies would always take the end of the capstan bar and by walking as fast as I could they, being on the outer circle, had to run in order to keep up. It was a good deal like the disk-wheel (revolving inverted saucer) in the "Goofy-house" shown at fairs and expositions, where the people hang on only to be thrown off, one by one, as the wheel speeds up. And so with the capstan. One by one they let go—spinning across the deck and sometimes rolling completely over, being unable to keep their feet. They seemed never to know that by following me, close in to the barrel, they could keep up with me. One boy was hurt quite badly when he tripped over the fall, for he was thrown into the stanchion, under the gallows, nearly breaking his leg. That ended his work for the day.

By the help of the coolies we were now unloading the sugar in record time. Two lighters, one with eighty and the other with two hundred baskets, came off. We finished the second about three o'clock and started on a third, which brought out 115 baskets. About half past four another lighter was seen approaching. The mate, never appreciating what was done and having no tact, sang out:

"Hurry up with this lighter, boys. We'll soon have another alongside and we've got to unload it if it takes till eight bells."

We were then running in the sugar at a lively clip and I was feeling unusually well, always speeding up the coolies, so that the work couldn't possibly be improved on. There was a general grunt of dissatisfaction from the crew at what the mate said and Joe pulled off his cap and throwing it on the deck at his feet shouted,

"I'll be damned if I'll work after six o'clock for any damned mate!"

"What's that you say?" asked the mate, and Joe repeated his words in such a way that there was no mistaking what he said.

"I'll have you put in irons!" shouted the mate who at once jumped down from the rail and Joe jerked a belaying-pin from the fife-rail. Seeing that Joe was prepared for any fight the mate ran into his room and instantly returned with a revolver, exclaiming,

"You —— —— ——, I'll button-hole you!" pointing the revolver at Joe who still held the belaying-pin in a menacing manner. Joe defied him to shoot and pulling back his shirt, exposing his naked breast and slapping it with his right hand over his heart, he shouted:

"Shoot! damn you, shoot! You never had a better mark!"

Seeing that the mate was in no hurry to shoot, he said: "No, damn you! You dasn't shoot! I'm an American on an American ship and you dasn't shoot an American citizen. Are you going to shoot? If so, do it damn quick for I'm not afraid of that little barker."

I was standing close beside him when he implored the mate to shoot, and quickly got out of gun reach, followed by the others, for under the circumstances no one could tell just what Mr. Burris might do. Evidently he considered that the gun play wouldn't work on Joe and so he went to his room and brought out a pair of handcuffs which were slipped over Joe's wrists for he made no resistance whatever. It all happened so quickly and the principals were very much excited and worked up to such a degree that it was a wonder that someone was not hurt. By the time the handcuffs were slipped over Joe's wrists he cooled down enough to say:

"Well, I'm glad you are going to send me ashore, for it's the only way to get my discharge. I've had enough of this bloody bastard!"

The police flag (the ensign upside down) was run up to the monkey-gaff end after which the mate came to me saying in his sneering manner:

"You've got a nice friend, haven't you? I've told you all along not to have anything to do with those old sailors, so let this be a warning to you for if I catch you again among those fo'c'sle hands you and I will have a falling out! So put that in your pipe and smoke it!" Without another word he left me.

Joe was taken to the lazaret where he was kept until the captain came off and it was decided to send him ashore; but the police boat did not come off till morning. When he walked over the rail he turned to look at us boys at the capstan. I caught his eye and he called:

"Good-bye, old boy! I'll see you in Boston. Good-bye, Archie! Sorry you're not with me."

Although he was a man of quick, Irish temper, beneath it all he had a heart, sharing anything he owned with a shipmate. He was naturally of a pleasant disposition; quick, like his temper, and first at a brace or aloft; he knew no fear and was a good sailor. Pressed beyond a certain limit his good qualities vanished and he became a "he-man-devil." Although rated a desperate man he was not a bully and never picked a quarrel. I lost a good friend when he was taken ashore and I was sorry to see him leave the ship under a cloud.

There was no singing chanteys with the work that morning and consequently the sugar didn't come in as quickly for the men walked around the capstan in rather a dejected mood and strange to say the mate didn't urge us to hurry.

Taking advantage of the quietness, the coolies started a chantey which was not half bad. It was sung in their own language and I will not vouch for the correctness of the words but the music is given as they sang it. As near as I could tell the chantey was a tale about going from Sourabaya to Pasuruan.

They sang several chanteys during the morning but their songs were like the Chinese, the soloist beginning in a high, falsetto key, and as a rule they had no rhythm of music that we could comprehend.

Having once begun to sing the coolies inflicted their music

FROM SOURABAYA TO PASURUAN

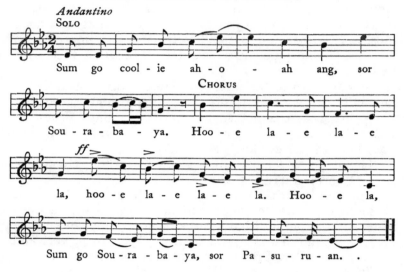

on us day after day. "Pasuruan" was a great favorite and we often joined in, but they would only sing it at intervals. Not appreciating their other songs some old shell-back would bring them up with a "round turn," with exclamations such as:

"Oh, give it a rest!" "For God's sake, start something else!" etc. In order to shut them off we were often compelled to drown them out by singing one of our chanteys.

The Sunday after Joe left us, Frank and I went ashore for the first time. We landed up the Kali Mas where the canal boats were anchored fore and aft, one alongside the other. While passing one of them, a native crawled from under his cabin and sat on the stern with his feet over the rail. He had evidently been in swimming for he was only half dressed and his long black hair was very wet which he proceeded to comb for anything that might turn up. His comb fell out of his hands into the water and sank and he uttered a cry. The troubled look on his countenance showed plainly how deeply he felt his loss. One after another on the

GOURA OR PONY CART, SOURABAYA, JAVA. From a photograph in the Peabody Museum, Cambridge.

DANCER AND STREET MUSICIANS, SOURABAYA, JAVA

From a photograph in the Peabody Museum, Cambridge

boat dived for the comb but were unable to find it. One would have thought they were diving for a gold watch instead of a brass comb.

Nearly every one of the canal boats gave us an example of the ways of the coolies in handling the fine-toothed comb, eating their findings like as many monkeys. It was not confined to the men; the women were just as bad. We turned away in disgust and struck out for the town back from the Kali Mas.

We found Sourabaya a beautiful place. The streets were very wide with overhanging trees. Many of the houses in the residential district had large lawns in front and the walks were shaded with palm trees. Most of the houses were only one story and covered a great deal of ground. The verandas, roofed with red tiles, stood out in bold relief when painted pure white and the background of palms and other tropical trees made one long to go in and lie in the shade away from the dusty macadamized streets.

The ordinary vehicle was called a "sado" and "goura" and was a sort of dog-cart, with two wheels, drawn by a small Timour or Sandlewood pony.

We walked a mile or so to the business district where every other store was a market place and where we bought the choicest fruit, cigars and tobacco for a song. After walking about for sometime we concluded to hire a "goura" and so hailed one that was approaching, whereupon the driver jerked the pony back on its haunches, stopping instantly in front of us. By making signs that we wanted to see the city and be brought back to the Kali Mas we gathered from his lingo that he would do it for one guilder (about 40 cents).

The pony was hitched to the "goura" in a pair of shafts with "signal halliard" stuff and reins of the same material. It had a single wide seat which was perched up high on a pair of springs. The driver faced the horse in front and Frank and I sat on the same seat, looking behind. With a short lash-whip he chirped and whipped the pony incessantly, trotting up one street and down the other in the hot boiling sun until the pony was covered with lather. While going around corners he never slowed down and the "goura" balanced on one wheel as he turned, we hanging on for fear of being slung to leeward.

His pony at last became exhausted and he drove to a large square where there seemed to be a livery stable, for there were a number of ponies hitched to "gouras," standing back to back in the middle of the square awaiting a call. He spoke a few words to the proprietor who ran into the stable and brought out another pony which they hitched to our trap, outside of the shafts, and whipping up the team we were off like a shot out of a gun, without much time being lost. The driver had no compassion whatever and the ponies were kept on a fast trot, regardless.

In this manner we saw the city of Sourabaya. The driver continually pointed to different houses and tried to tell us something, but our only Javanese word was "bargoose" and his breath was wasted on the hot air. However, we enjoyed the reckless driving and the beautiful homes as we passed by in a hurry.

Finally arriving at the outskirts, on the other side of the city, he brought the "goura" to a sudden stop. The panting ponies stood trembling in the sun and we concluded that he had stopped to give them a rest, so I told him in English to go over to a shade tree where it would not be so hot. But the beggar held out his hand saying, "Guilder, guilder!"

Frank then said: "Not by a damned sight. You won't get our money until you drive us back to the Kali Mas," which, of course, was not understood by the coolie.

After a few wild gestures with his hands and numerous "bargooses" from us, he again started but not in his mad drive. He was peeved at not receiving his money and let the ponies take their own gait back to the city. At every inter- section of streets he would stop and demand his money and we would tell him to drive on as we had done before. In this manner he sulked along and finally came to a stop, rolling a cigarette. He was persistent and so were we. We reasoned that if we should pay him on the other side of the city he might refuse to take us back and not having any too much money we wanted it to last as long as possible, so we sat still in the trap and when he rolled a cigarette we did the same. If he spit over the wheel we followed suit. When he got out of the "goura" to look at the ponies we did the same and were just as interested in the harness as he seemed to be.

On one of these times he suddenly jumped into the seat, thinking to whip up the ponies and leave us behind; but we caught them by the head and I jumped into the trap and took the reins away from him which was an easy matter. It amused us to think that he should try to outwit two sailors.

Imitating him as he drove along at last he came to the square where he got the second horse. There he jumped down and walked into the stable while we got down and walked down the street in the opposite direction as we reasoned that he would follow and ask for his guilder; but, instead, he found a policeman and sent him after us, who overhauled us some distance down the avenue. He spoke in broken English and said that the coolie told him he had agreed to take us across the city for one guilder and back to the Kali Mas for another. It was his word against ours and to save any further argument we paid the policeman the guilder and he said that he would see that the coolie received it.

On our way back through the native settlement almost every backyard exhibited a cock fight with a bunch of coolies gathered in small squads. They were great gamblers, throwing their money into a ring on the ground as the fight progressed.

Coming out into an open square we saw a travelling theater troup that went from one town to another giving open-air performances. It comprised a man, a girl and three musicians. The instruments were a xylophone, drum and flute. The music was weird and crude and the two dancers were dressed in highly-colored sarongs, decorated with beads of coral which hung from the hair. A mask was worn covering the face, while long ribbons, dangling from their shoulders and waists, were whipped out behind with a snap as they proceeded in their snakish dance. The masks were changed

at intervals and were in different colors denoting the characters they tried to represent. A striped mask denoting a bad
man. A red mask, a devil; while a white mask represented
an angel.

The dance was more of a contortion than anything else.
Legs, arms and body were twisted in all conceivable shapes.
We threw them some small pieces of money and the girl
slipped on her white mask and danced before us, throwing
her arms almost as far back as she could forward; then
twisting her body with her feet in one direction while she
faced the other; then in an upright position, she bent her
back till her head touched her buttocks while her arms swung
about until her sarong parted displaying a neck and breast
that one couldn't help admiring and as Frank said, "If it
wasn't for that bloody white mask over her face I would
have carried her off on the spot."

We wanted to see a Highland Fling or something lively
but they kept on throwing their feet about in the most awkward positions, prolonging the dance into a Dead March
which was entirely too tame for us and we moved on going
to the thickly populated district of the natives whose houses
or huts were of thatched bamboo roofs with sides of reed,
ferns, etc.

We didn't stay long for fear of vermin and the women
didn't seem to mind our curious eyes as they sat weeding out
each other's head. They would look at us with a black stare
as they placed the wiggling creatures on their tongues, with
the forefinger, no doubt wondering why we should have
such a troubled look on our faces.

The women were slight of stature, standing erect, and
were far better looking than the men who were a measly
dried-up production of human flesh and bones, lounging
about smoking cigarettes or chewing betel nut and watching
the little naked children play about the door while the
women seemed to be doing all the work, carrying water in
earthen jars on their heads, picking up wood and kindling
for the fire which is generally kept burning in a smudge

One Kind Turn Deserves Another—Luncheon Time at Sourabaya

KEDGING OVER THE FLATS NEAR SOURABAYA

throughout the day, for the mosquitoes swarm about in countless numbers.

The women dressed in a sarong of bright colors and wore a "slendang" or scarf of elaborate design draped over their shoulders to complete their dress. It was also worn over one shoulder, about the bust, protecting them from the sun, or was used to carry, at their side, their babies or bundles, when necessary. They wore their hair long and tied behind in a chignon. Both the men and women were very fond of cocoa-nut oil which was plastered on their hair on top of the head and on a hot day the rancid odor was far from refreshing. At sundown we were pretty well tired out and glad to get aboard ship where it was cooler and away from the mosquitoes ashore.

The next day we filled the lower hold and started on between-decks. The coolies gave us a chantey, below, in rolling the sugar in place, that was the same all day long. When a basket was lowered into the hold, instead of standing up as white men would work, about six coolies sat on the deck with their feet against the upper half of the basket, and bracing themselves behind with their hands on the deck, they shoved the basket over keeping time with their feet as they pushed it over to the following:

AH, HOO-E LA-E

Ah, hoo - e la - e. Ah, hoo - e la - e.

Ah - e, hoo - e, ah, hoo - e la - e, Ung!

Each accented note was a push with the foot and the basket was thus rolled over and across the deck or over skids on top of the sugar, while the coolies followed, never touching their feet to the deck until the sugar was in place.

In cutting or slewing the baskets they sang in a manner like our "Haul away, Joe!" All hands singing and keeping time with their feet, but pushing, until the final word "Ung!" Then all hands gave a violent shove and the big basket was cut into place nicely. Two white men with a handspike could do the work of the six coolies in half the time, but coolie labor was only twenty-one cents per day so the ship could well afford to pay it.

Both the port and starboard watches were allowed liberty every other Sunday. Bum-boats made their daily call and we indulged in all kinds of tropical fruits. On March 16, we took in our last three lighters of sugar and received the news that we were bound for New York for orders. This so filled our hearts with joy at the thought of getting away from this hot place that Williams started the old chantey that was always sung on all deep-water ships when leaving a foreign country and bound for home:

HOMEWARD BOUND (GOOD-BYE, FARE YOU WELL)

Andante

We're go-ing a-way to leave you now. Good-bye, fare you well,
good-bye, fare you well. We're go-ing a-way to leave you now,
Hur-rah, my boys, we're home-ward bound. Then give me the
girl with the bon-ny brown curl. Good-bye, fare you well,
good-bye, fare you well. Your hair of nut brown is the
talk of the town, Then hur-rah, my boys, we're home-ward bound.

We're homeward bound, I heard them say,
    We're homeward bound with nine month's pay.
Our anchor we'll weigh and our sails we will set,
    The friends we are leaving we leave with regret.

Oh, fare you well, we're homeward bound,
    We'll heave away till our anchor is found.
So, fare you well my Rosy Nell;
    Oh, fare you well, for I wish you well.

Oh, Rosy Nell, I'm under your spell,
   And when far away, I'll wish you well.
Your lips cherry red and your hair to your waist,
   Will long be remembered, though leaving in haste.

Then fill up your glasses for those who were kind,
   And drink to the girls we are leaving behind.
So, good-bye to Sally and good-bye to Sue,
   And those who are listening, good-bye to you.

We're homeward bound across the sea,
   We're homeward bound with sugar and tea.
We're homeward bound and the winds blowing fair,
   There'll be many true friends to greet us there.

Then, good-bye Sourabaya, our anchor's a-weigh;
   We'll sheet home the topsails before it's "Belay!"
We'll brace her up sharp and we'll board our main tack;
   'Twill be a long time before we get back.

This chantey is sometimes sung at the windlass with only the first half, but a good chanteyman can greatly improve the song, which is a rouser with good voices, by singing the double stanza as given above. Williams and Archie were both good chanteymen, never lacking in words, and seldom repeated a line, which is usually done in a long hoist, by inferior chanteymen.

We finished the sugar in the middle of the afternoon and waited for three hundred tons of tea and spices. The next day we bent the jibs and lighter sails and began painting the ship outside. The side ports were put in and the mate asked me to caulk them, thinking to save a little expense, but I refused for I told him I expected to go home in the ship and didn't want to go on record as a caulker. While no doubt I could have done the work as well as the coolies, yet I considered that it was out of my line and for the safety of all it was better that a regular caulker should do the work. He didn't insist and I kept busy with a paint brush over the side. The next day a couple of coolies did the work.

Monday, March 19, was a busy day. The captain came off

in the morning with a load of provisions and upon gaining the deck sang out in a disgruntled manner,

"Heave up your anchors and get under way!" and without another word walked aft, pacing the deck in a very excited manner. It developed that he was unable to get the spices and decided not to wait any longer.

With both anchors on the bottom, the ship, turning with the tide, had a number of turns in the cables which had to be taken out. Archie and Williams were in the captain's boat, putting a seizing around the cables as far as they could reach under water, while the port cable was unshackled, and Jim Dunn and I were over the bow taking out the turns, one by one. The mate watching proceedings from above, soon sang out:

"There are seventeen turns below. Damn it, don't waste so much time, down there! Dip it around seventeen times and shackle it up again! You work like a mess of coolies!"

We did as directed. The seizing below was cut and the cable slipped down in a tangled mess. Then with the order to "Man the windlass," the port chain began coming in. The thermometer registered 115 degrees, without a breath of air, and we wiped the perspiration from our faces as the work became heavier. The cable, coming in foul, wound about the starboard chain in a tangled mess and a bunch coming up to the water's edge, with both cables "up and down," would clear itself temporarily, slipping down only to be tangled in a tighter mess below.

The heaving was unusually hard and the old minor chanteys were resorted to because they are usually dragged out in slow time, being very appropriate for heavy heaving where it takes the force of the whole crew to bring down the windlass brakes that move none too quickly. Having sung all the words that could be thought of in "Lowlands," we started "Paddy Works on the Railway," a more cheerful chantey.

OH, POOR PADDY WORKS ON THE RAILWAY

Andantino

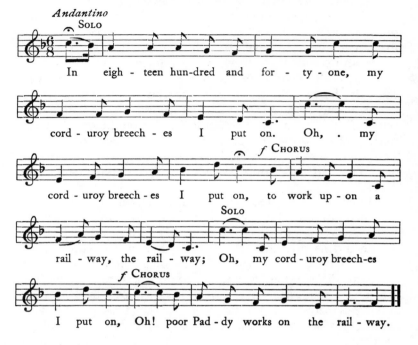

In eigh - teen hun-dred and for - ty - one, my

cord - uroy breech - es I put on. Oh, . my

f CHORUS

cord - uroy breech - es I put on, to work up - on a

SOLO

rail - way, the rail - way; Oh, my cord - uroy breech-es

f CHORUS

I put on, Oh! poor Pad - dy works on the rail - way.

In eighteen hundred and forty-two,
I found I could no better do.

In eighteen hundred and forty-three,
I thought I'd better cross the sea.

In eighteen hundred and forty-four,
I landed on Columbia's shore.

In eighteen hundred and forty-five,
I found myself more dead than alive.

In eighteen hundred and forty-six,
I found myself in a hell of a fix,
    From working, etc.

In eighteen hundred and forty-seven,
I wished myself from hell to heaven,
From working, etc.

In eighteen hundred and forty-eight,
My boys, I'm sorry to relate,
That I had worked, etc.

In eighteen hundred and forty-nine,
I then concluded to resign,
From working, etc.

In eighteen fifty, I soon found,
Myself shanghaied, for Frisco bound,
From working, etc.

The railway started me to roam,
But the sea is hell and I can't get home,
To work, etc.

Having no luck with the starboard chain we tried the port and the heaving was much lighter at the start but the farther we got the worse it came in. By the time we finished with "Fire down below," both anchors dragged together and refused to yield from the bottom. It took all hands at the brakes, on one side, to heave her down and the strain was so great that the windlass brakes were badly bent and had to be straightened with a top-maul. Then we lashed a boom on top of the handles, which kept them from bending, but it was very hard work in the hot sun and instead of chanteying we pulled and rode down the brake with cries of: "Heave and bust her! Heave and pawl!" etc., until we could do nothing more. The bow was hove down about eighteen inches and the mate at last said: "Avast heaving! We'll let the tide do the rest."

There was only two feet of tide rise in the bay, not much to count on, but it was on the flood and after waiting about an hour a squall from the west'ard came up and both anchors were tripped. Before we could clear them we drifted down towards the Dutch ship and to keep from fouling her we had to let go again much to the disgust of us all. We had had a strenuous day of it and the mates finally decided to knock off work and try it again the next day.

Joe's term in jail having expired he came off in a boat in the evening, unbeknown to the officers, and bid us all good-bye. He said that there would be no trouble in shipping, as nearly every ship in the bay was in need of men. He was in no hurry to ship, preferring to wait for an American ship that would take him to New York or Boston. Although he was confident of seeing me again in Boston I have never heard from him since. He said that most of the ships in the harbor had sent members of their crew to the hospital and as the fever was bad there I have always had my doubts if he ever got away for he may have taken the fever and died in the hospital.

On Sunday, March 25, with a light breeze from the westward, we were called to heave anchor again and with a good prospect of getting away, hove in the chain to:

BLOW YE WINDS IN THE MORNING

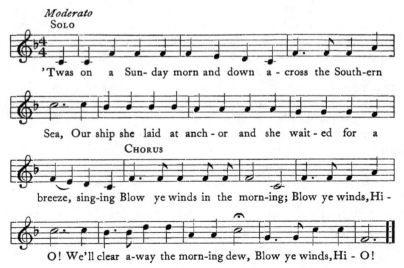

'Twas on a Sun-day morn and down a-cross the South-ern Sea, Our ship she laid at anch-or and she wait-ed for a breeze, sing-ing Blow ye winds in the morn-ing; Blow ye winds, Hi-O! We'll clear a-way the morn-ing dew, Blow ye winds, Hi-O!

The captain he was down below,
    And the men all laid about,
When under our bow we heard a splash,
    And then a regular shout, singing

"Man overboard!" the watchman cried
    And for'ard we all ran,
And hanging to the larboard chain
    Was an old bluff merman, singing,

His hair was blue, his eyes were green,
    His mouth was big as three;
His long green tail that he sat on,
    Went wigglin' in the sea, singing,

"Helloa!" cried our mate as bold as brass,
    "What cheer, mess-mate?" said he,
"Oh, I want to speak to your Old Man,
    I've a favor to ask, you see," singing,

"For I've been all night at a small sea-fight
    At the bottom of the deep blue sea.
Oh! 'twould break your heart to hear them groan
    And the fun they've had with me," singing,

The Old Man then he came on deck,
    And looked on the waters blue.
"Come tell me, my man, and as quick as you can,
    What favor can I do for you?" singing,

"Oh, you've dropped your anchor before my house
    And blocked up my only door,
And my wife can't get out, to roam about,
    Nor my chicks, who number four," singing,

"The anchor shall be hove in at once,
    And your wife and your chicks set free;
But I never saw a scale, from a sprat to a whale,
    Till now, that could speak to me," singing,

"Your figure-head is like a sailor bold,
    And you speak like an Englishman,
But where did you get such a great big tail,
    Come answer me that if you can?" singing,

"A long time ago, from the ship 'Hero,'
　　I fell overboard in a gale,
And away down below, where the seaweeds grow,
　　I met a lovely young girl—with a tail," singing,

"She saved my life and I made her my wife,
　　And my legs changed instantly;
Now I am married, to a mermaid,
　　At the bottom of the deep blue sea." Singing,

And now we are all loaded,
　　And I don't gave a damn,
With anchor weighed and hawser made,
　　We'll sail to Yankee land, singing,

We are bound for New York City,
　　In the good old ship *Akbar*,
The Old Man bought the consul out
　　With a barrel of Stockholm tar, singing.

With the anchor up and the gaskets off the sails we were in high spirits at the thought of at last getting away from port and although the morning had all the indications of a fair wind, by the time the sails were set it hauled ahead light and baffling from the eastward and soon we had orders to get ready for tacking ship.

The captain having bought, with other stores, a dozen or more hens for cabin fare, these fowl were running loose about the deck and with the orders "Tacks and Sheet," and later, "Mainsail Haul!" the big main yard swung around while the braces whizzed through the blocks in the rail accompanied by the cries of the men as they shouted in their different hauls, running from one place to another, and pandemonium seemed to break loose so that the chickens ran from under foot, flying to places of safety. Two unfortunately flew over the rail into the water.

After all had been made fast on the new tack, the ship having very little headway, the chickens were seen floating only a short distance astern and Frank jumped on top of the rail and dove into the water after them. The captain, seeing his intention, shouted to him not to attempt it but Frank was already in the water swimming after the two chickens which he picked up and brought back to the ship.

"You little fool!" said the captain. "It would have served you right if a shark had gobbled up all three of you."

In light, variable winds we only made about ten miles during the day and then anchored as the tide was on the ebb. Although we had a pilot aboard, the next day we grounded only ten miles from our former anchorage, in light, baffling winds which at times left us entirely. With favorable cat's-paws it was heave and chantey the greater part of the day. A fine breeze from the nor'ard springing up in the evening, being still aground, we hove up anchor and set all the sails, to no avail, for she was stuck hard and fast and wouldn't move. Finally we gave it up and furled the sails, letting go the anchor, awaiting for the morning tide which floated us; but there was no wind and we worked all day in a hot, boiling sun, kedging over the flats and singing all the songs at the capstan, I think, there were ever sung, among which were, "A Hundred Years Ago," "Johnny get your Oatcake Done," and a new chantey by Archie, "Roll the Cotton Down," and "The Song of the Fishes," in which each one took a fish in making up a verse, where we got a great deal of enjoyment from those who had no sense of rhyme.

A light breeze springing up from the nor'ard, about eight o'clock in the evening, we were called to make all sail again and soon the ship heeled over and we shook the mud from our keel and once more were afloat. Everybody was in good spirits and Archie said:

"Good-bye, Java! I hope I'll never see you again."

CHAPTER XVII

MAN OVERBOARD

THE pilot left us at nine o'clock and we steered a course southeast by south in light winds and calms. The following morning we took in the longboat and the kedge anchor. Early on the morning of April 7 we passed through and were outside of Lombok Strait and got our anchors in and the chains stowed below. The good weather held until May 5 when we were off the southern coast of Africa and sighted our first sail since leaving Java.

In the evening we saw lightning to the south'ard and the following day, at 2 P.M., furled the mizzen royal. The wind increasing we furled the topgallant sails and hauled up the mainsail in squally weather with heavy passing rain showers and heavy thunder and lightning to the west'ard. That evening all hands were called to shorten sail and we snugged her down to lower topsails and fore-topmast staysail. The gale was blowing from the west'ard and a heavy sea was following.

The sail sighted the day before proved to be an English ship bound for Liverpool and was only about three miles ahead of us, carrying the same amount of canvas that we were carrying. On account of the heavy sea, which was so short that we couldn't clear the next one, we pitched so much that we carried away the forestay but set it up temporarily with the fish-tackle.

The gale moderated the next morning and we set the reefed mainsail, main upper topsail and main-topmast staysail and jib. The English ship was still ahead on the starboard tack while we were on the port, steering "by the wind."

The next day the gale increased and we furled the maintopmast staysail and hove her to in a heavy head sea which required two men at the wheel. An English bark, to leeward, tried to signal us but we couldn't make out her number.

May 9 came in with fine weather and a steady breeze but with a heavy head sea that kept two men at the wheel. We saw three large sperm whales playing about the ship. The English bark was about two miles ahead. We tried again to make her but couldn't.

About the middle of the afternoon of the next day, while bending a new main spencer, we were carrying the main-topgallant sail expecting momentarily that the sail would have to come in for small dark clouds were driven by the wind across the blue sky leaving behind a scattering, grayish nebula which gradually spread into a haze foretelling an approaching storm. The noisy sea-gulls that had been following the ship all day for scraps of food thrown over the side by the cook, began flying to the nor'ard leaving behind a few Cape pigeons who flew swiftly across our stern and over the wake of the ship making that peculiar screeching sound heard only in a rising wind.

The mate, nervously walking the weather gangway on the poop, stopped occasionally to cast his eye to windward for any indication of an approaching squall and then with head thrown far back on his shoulders, watched the topgallant sail to see how much longer he could carry on before taking it in, as the wind steadily increased.

The wind whistled through the rigging and the yards creaked more and more as the ship rolled heavily to leeward and the man at the wheel watched the weather leech of the main-topgallant sail shiver and shake, doing his best to keep the ship straight while steering full and by on the port tack.

Old Dick, in his usual disgruntled frame of mind, began to swear, saying: "Damn hit t' 'ell! What's the use o' carrying on like this till somethin's carried away?"

A stately white albatross soaring high above our stern, breasted into the wind with long graceful wings spread far apart, scarcely moving. The bird also seemed to be watching the wind from its elevated position, loath to leave the ship, for it was motionless and apparently testing the strength of the wind.

At last the mate shouted, "Stand by the t'gallant halliards!" and the albatross evidently seeing that at last we were getting ready to shorten sail, turned its watchful eye and soared off to the south'ard leaving us to battle with the elements.

The squall was now upon us and the mate bellowed: "Let go your t'gallant halliards! Brail in the spencer!" The t'gallant yard was braced into the wind and the parral finally settled on the cap of the topmast head, while the flapping canvas above shook the whole ship.

"Clew up an' a couple o' hands jump aloft an' take in the t'gallan's'l!" immediately following with an order to "Lower away the mizzen tops'l! Call the watch! All hands on deck! Let go your fore-tops'l yard! Let go the main!"

The watch tumbled out of their bunks coming on deck half dressed, cinching up their belts as they ran in answer to the call of "Clew up the mainsail! Man the clew garnets!" from the "Old Man" who came on deck at this instant and seeing the strength of the wind determined to get the main-sail off of her before it was carried away.

The wind was now coming in great gusts and the gray haze deepened to a dark blue black shutting down all around us. Easing up the main-sheet the mate hobbled to wind'ard at the main tack, ready to let go when the buntlines and leechlines were manned. Then, with a "Haul away!" the tack was eased around the pin in the rail, through the hook in the water-ways, and the great sail was eased up. It thrashed and flapped in the wind, springing the big yard up and down like a reed in the wind, which settled into a quiver as the big sail was snugged up against the yard. The spilling-lines were manned and there was nothing more to be done on deck with the sail. Then we hauled up the foresail in like manner and the big green seas began pouring over the rail, sweeping across the deck, while the spray wet through to the skin those who were unfortunate enough in not having had time to put on oil-skins.

In handling the sails, all went well until we ran aloft to furl the foresail and while on the foreyard it was anything but a travesty, for all hands, running out on the foot-ropes,

were strung out along the yard where we picked up the sail
and tossed the bunt to "Paddy Doyle and his boots." Gaskets were passed and awaiting the men in the slings of the
yard to finish before getting off the yard, the mate, below, in
some manner let go the lee lift and the yard cock-billed.

It was easy for us who were on the weather side to slide
down the foot-rope into the top, but those who were on the
lee side had to shin up. While we were scrambling into the
top a cry went up from the men on the lee side, "Man
overboard!" Frank, who was the second man out from the
yardarm, had been knocked off the yard and fell into the
sea.

Shocked at the thought, for I loved him as a brother, I
hastened on deck with the others, determined to risk my life
for the man who had saved me from a shark in Sourabaya.

We all went aft in a body and I don't think there was a
man among us who hung back. All seemed anxious for
Frank's safety and willingly offered their services if the captain would permit lowering a boat. The ship had been
brought into the wind and we could see Frank astern, clinging to a life preserver which the captain had cut from the
taffrail, for he had seen Frank pitched into the sea. We all
knew Frank's ability as a swimmer to keep afloat and although the waves were mountains high and it was a dangerous undertaking to lower a boat, yet we implored the captain
to do so and give us a chance to rescue him.

"My men!" said the captain. "This is a dangerous undertaking with a hundred chances against you. Night is coming
on and it will be dark in a little while and you are liable to
be blown out of sight and all hands drowned. But if you are
willing to take the chance I am willing to lower the longboat."

A shout arose from the men who didn't wait for any further instructions and we ran forward to rig a tackle from the
foreyard which had been squared by the lifts in the meantime. The starboard longboat was slung and the lashings
cut and we soon had it on the rail where the second mate
threw in a half-barrel of pilot bread and a keg of fresh

water, not forgetting a flash-light. In those days boats were not provided with provisions as they are now and we waited impatiently for the equipment and it seemed hours to me before everything was ready.

The second mate was at a dozen different parts of the ship at once, in the right time, and finally shouted for four volunteers to go in the boat with him. We all signified our willingness and he quickly called for Jim Dunn, Williams, Archie and Tommy—leaving me out. I ran to his side and begged him to take me, for I knew my ability as an oarsman; telling him it was my duty to Frank who had saved my life in Sourabaya. He looked at Tommy and then at me. I read his thoughts and ran to Tommy, imploring him to let me go in his place. Overjoyed, I at last heard Mr. Sanborn say: "All right, Fred! You can go. Take the front thwart!"

We four then jumped into the longboat with the second mate and with our oars at our side, the ship rolling to leeward, we swung clear and settled nicely into the water. The tackle was unhooked and oars were immediately shipped while the ship rolled away from us to wind'ard. Rising far above us on the next wave, she pitched to leeward before we had time to gather headway. There seemed to be a suction towards her for the ship came down upon us and we were battered against her side which stove a hole in our port side that one could almost crawl through.

In an instant Archie pulled off his coat and stuffed it into the hole and called for another. I threw him mine and he kicked it in with the other which partially stopped the water from coming in. With over a foot of water in the boat, Jim Dunn began bailing. The wind drove us astern and there was not much need of rowing. In this condition we were adrift on the ocean with a rising wind and darkness coming on, hoping against hope that we would be able to see the object of our search before the night shut in.

Frank was nowhere in sight and the second mate stood up, pulling on the steering oar to keep the boat straight and searching the waves around for any clue as the longboat arose on every sea. We were about a mile from the ship

JAMES SANBORN,
SECOND MATE OF THE SHIP "AKBAR"

HARLOW, WILLIAMS, FRANK, ARCHIE, SPRAGUE (*alias* JIM DUNN)

when a huge wave lifted us up and I saw Frank clinging to the life preserver, about a thousand yards astern.

"There he is, astern!" I shouted.

We had actually passed him without seeing him. And yet, it is to be wondered that we saw him at all, for we in the boat were so low in the water that the seas breaking in white caps and the spray, flying far to leeward, was a turbulent mass of boiling, seething foam. It is nothing strange with two ships in company, hove to in a gale, for one to be completely out of sight when both ships are in the trough of the sea with a huge wave between them; and how much more difficult to observe an object in the sea from a longboat, with a choppy sea all around, as in our case.

On the next wave Archie and Williams both sang out simultaneously:

"There he is! I see him!"

The second mate also saw him and bellowed, "Give 'way t' port an' back water t' starboard!" and by the help of his steering oar we swung into the trough of the sea. The next wave was a comber which we met broadside and on an angle of 45 degrees. It was a close call, but the second mate was a sailor and with a quick sweep of his oar we took the white water over the port bow which completely drenched us and half filled the boat. There was danger of the coats washing out from the hole in the side and Archie braced his foot against them as best he could while we pulled away. Once into the wind, the port bow fell off as Mr. Sanborn steered for Frank.

"Pull in your oar, Jim, an' bail her out! Williams an' Fred have got all they can do t' keep the bow into th' wind!" shouted the second mate.

In pulling away from the ship Mr. Sanborn had favored the port side of our boat on account of the hole and naturally we drifted to leeward of Frank, but now we steered a course for him with the port bow to windward.

With all our strength at the oars our boat scarcely moved ahead in the wind, for we were tossed up and down like a chip in the water and commenting on the situation afterwards it was generally conceded that had the boat been free from water, with a high free-board, the gale would have swept us far away.

The wash in the boat was something awful. Rising almost perpendicularly, in going over a wave, the water rushed aft and slopped over the stern. The bow being high in the air, the wind swept us around to leeward where it took all our strength to keep the boat from falling off into the trough of the sea when going down the wave. The weight of the water rushing to leeward, on its way forward, nearly capsized us and we braced our feet to leeward, against the thwart in front of us, standing well to windward and pulling at the oars until the muscles of our arms stood out in big bunches and the trapezii muscles in our necks resembled bolt ropes in the luff of a lower topsail.

In all this time our one thought was of saving Frank and as long as we were afloat there was not a moment of anxiety on our part that the boat wouldn't weather the gale. But there was a question in my mind whether we could reach him before he was exhausted and to this end I pulled at my oar with supernatural strength not daring to turn my head to see what progress we were making.

My eyes were riveted on the second mate whose face, dripping with flying spray, I watched for any expression of hope. He stood at the steering oar, chewing tobacco. The juice oozing from the corners of his mouth flowed down his chin with the salt spray, for his lips were partly opened showing his teeth nervously chewing his quid, and without releasing his hold on the oar, occasionally he wiped his face with a hurried dip of his head into his shirt sleeve, above his elbow, all the while keeping an eye to windward.

At last the expression that I had been looking for came over his face. First a twinkle of the eye and then a smile broke out all over his face which settled in a quiver about the lips and his eyes filled with tears which flowed distinctly down that weatherbeaten face, in a channel of its own, through the salt spray.

I was alarmed, fearing Frank had succumbed to the inevitable, and with fear and trembling quickly turned my head in his direction expecting to see an empty life preserver floating in the water. But joy, indescribable! There he was, not fifty feet away, full of life and smiling at the prospect of being rescued. I gave a shout of joy which was followed by the others. The second mate tried to speak encouraging words to him, but his voice failed him and that rough, uncut diamond of the sea sobbed like a child. A lump came up in my throat that nearly choked me and we five men rowed and wept tears of joy in silence. It was a touching scene to watch those strong, husky men give way to their feelings and although rough and hardened in sin, yet their big hearts went out, as only a true shipmate's can, as they risked their lives for a shipmate in distress.

In a few minutes more we were alongside, where Archie and Williams caught Frank by the arms and rolled him into the boat. We were fortunate in that the boat didn't capsize and all hands be thrown into the sea; but it was done without shipping much water and Frank crawled into the stern-sheets nearly exhausted. The second mate had taken the precaution to fill a flask with whiskey, before going into the boat, and this he now handed to Frank, saying:

"Drink hearty, Frank! 'Twill do you a world of good."

It didn't take any persuasion on his part and Frank took a good-sized drink after which his head dropped on his shoulders while the whites of his eyes rolled from one to another in an expression of gratitude, and he said:

"I thought I was a gonner when you fellows passed me to lu'ard and nearly tired myself out trying to make you hear. But when I saw you turn, I knew you'd seen me and I had no fear that you wouldn't pick me up. But if anyone should ask you how it feels to be passed unseen in the water, just tell 'em for me, it's hell-a-poppin' for the man in the water. If it hadn't been for the life preserver I don't believe I could have held out." Then suddenly brightening up he asked,

"Who the bloody hell, let go the lee lift?"

The second mate broke in at that, saying: "Never mind

the lee lift, Frank. The mate spilled the beans, but you had better keep quiet and save your strength, for we're hell and gone to lu'ard and it will be hours before we get back to the ship in this sea."

Then, realizing that he was in the boat, with an uncommon amount of water in the bottom, and learning the cause, Frank became quite alarmed. We were making bad weather of it, at the oars, without Jim's help, who was still bailing out the water, when Frank suddenly realized that everyone was working but him. The whiskey had taken effect and his blood began to quicken in his veins, for he braced up and shouted:

"Give me that bailer, Jim. I can bail just as well as you. We'll never reach the ship without another oar and you are the one to pull it!" Notwithstanding we remonstrated, Frank seized the bailer and demanded that he be given a trial. "I'm feeling all right now and a little exercise will do me good," said he, laughingly.

With the help of Jim's oar we made better headway and Frank surprised us with his work, setting our minds at rest as to his strength for he seemed not to tire from his exertions. But other complications arose. It was rapidly getting dark and the ship, a long distance away, was gradually becoming more indistinct and finally disappeared altogether. Occasionally we could see her green light when we were on the crest of a wave, telling in which direction we were to pull, but finally it disappeared and there was nothing but the wind to steer by. Our strength was gradually getting weaker until it was with great difficulty that we could lift our oars without catching a crab. Then the second mate cautioned us to be careful or we would lose an oar.

Frank, in the meantime, ceased to keep up the bailing and finally gave up altogether. The second mate gave him another drink from the flask and at the same time exclaimed:

"It's no use boys! I can't see the ship any more and our only hope is to keep the boat's head into the wind and wait for them to pick us up in the morning."

Jim took his seat beside Frank, rubbing his hands and legs,

while Williams bailed and Archie and I worked the oars just enough to keep into the wind with the help of the steering oar. And so we spelled each other, every little while, through the night. About midnight the wind abated and our work was lighter and we were able to get a little sleep, when relieved, wet as we were. At sunrise the ship was nowhere to be seen, but in a couple of hours we raised a sail to windward, bearing down in our direction, and with the rise of her topgallant sails and then her topsails, finally showing her courses, we put out the oars and pulled in a direction to be in her course as she approached.

Williams pulled off his shirt and fastened it to an oar, which he held upright, hoping that it would be seen by the ship, but almost immediately she swung to starboard and our hearts almost stopped beating at the thought of her passing by without our being seen. We knew she was the *Akbar*, by the cut of her sails, and we laid to the oars pulling like mad to head her off. Then, joy! We saw the Stars and Stripes being run up to the monkey gaff and knew they had sighted us. She swung in a circle, rounding into the wind and laid her main topsail to the mast a half mile to windward of us.

What a glorious sight to us boys. And many were the expressions that she was the finest looking ship afloat while we pulled joyfully up to where we were greeted with a rousing three cheers from the men on the rail and in the main channels, all eager to lend a hand to assist us on deck, for we were so cramped from exposure to the wind and water and wet garments that it was with great difficulty we could stand.

The captain ordered a whip rigged from the main yard, in which we were to be hoisted, in a bo'sun's chair, to the deck above. Frank was nearly exhausted but we strapped him in the chair and he was the first man to leave the boat, after which we each took our turn. Then the boat was slung from the foreyard and we filled away with an order from the captain, "All hands splice the main brace!" It was a happy crowd that walked aft and many were the questions asked Frank as to how he felt while in the water.

"I wasn't scared while in the water," said he, "but when I got into the longboat and saw the big hole stuffed with coats and the water pouring in then I became frightened and lost my nerve."

The cook was ordered to give us a hot breakfast and we were told to change our clothes for dry ones and after breakfast we turned in until eight bells (noon). Frank was a great deal worse off than I and ate very little breakfast. He immediately turned in. Although I had lost a lot of sleep, I was hungry and did justice to the morning meal after which I rolled up in my blankets and was dead to the world. It seemed only a few minutes before I was awakened by the second mate, who shook me gently at noon, and gathering my scattered senses, upon seeing his face bending over me, I answered with a quick "Aye, aye, sir!" and jumping out of my bunk began to pull on my clothes in a hurry.

He cautioned me to be quiet, putting his forefinger to his lips and motioning that Frank was not to be disturbed. The noise I was making partially awakened him, however, and he rolled over on his side moaning incoherently: "I can bail! Give it to me, Jim! Don't let the ship go by!" etc., which told us that he was a little delirious.

It took me a few minutes to realize that it was eight bells and as Frank tossed from side to side the second mate shook his head alarmingly, saying: "He's a sick boy. The old man should see him." And with these words he went aft while I went to the galley for my dinner. When I got back, the captain was taking Frank's pulse and in a low tone he cautioned me to let him sleep, saying:

"Sleep is the best medicine we can give him. The poor boy is all in and he needs rest. You stay here and watch him. When he awakens, come aft and give me a call."

It was 4.30 P.M. before he awoke. His eyes wandered from side to side for some time with a puzzled look on his face and then he smiled. "Gee! Fred!" said he, "I thought at first that I was in the water again but I'm mighty glad to see those oilskins swinging back and forth from the bulkhead. Shake, old pard! Shake! We're safe aboard the old *Akbar*, ain't we?"

I assured him that we were and grasped his hand with a squeeze that told more than words could tell how glad I was to know that we were both safe. Then cautioning him to be quiet, for the Old Man wanted to see him, I ran aft to give him a call, while the watch on deck crowded about our room with inquiring eyes. The captain immediately came forward and as we reached the room we found Frank trying to dress, but the Old Man emphatically told him to get back into bed and stay there until he gave him permission to get up. Although Frank said he was all right, the captain had his way and he crawled into his bunk while the captain gave him some medicine that put him to sleep again.

CHAPTER XVIII

HOMEWARD BOUND

THAT evening I scanned the heavens trying to locate the "Big Dipper" on the horizon. It was in sight in 34 degrees South, but I didn't pick it up again until we were well into the Atlantic. Had we sailed in clear weather I believe it could have been seen nightly all the way around the Cape.

The bark and the English ship were again in sight. We passed the bark at noon but the English ship overhauled us, when we wore ship at 6 P.M., and parted company.

The following day Frank was feeling much better and turned to for work in fine weather with light winds and calms. That morning, with a northwesterly breeze, we could distinctly smell flowers to windward, indicating that land was not far off, and at six the next morning we sighted land off the starboard bow. Two sails were in sight, the one off the port bow showing her fore and mizzen topmasts carried away.

On May 13, Cape Agulhas was in sight about twenty-five miles off the starboard bow. That morning the wind increased to a gale and as we tacked ship the weather main brace fouled the guard rail, at the break of the poop, and carried it away. At the same time we also carried away the mizzen stay but no particular harm was done. Cape of Good Hope, at noon, bore N.N.W., about forty-five miles away.

The next day the gale, blowing from the nor'ard, hove her to at 1 P.M. under lower topsails, spencer and fore-topmast staysail. In furling the spanker, Fred was thrown off the boom but luckily landed on deck beside the wheel box, nearly breaking his leg. George was laid up with a sore foot and the second mate was troubled again with neuralgia and confined to his bunk. George had been troubled with a tape worm and the mate said he could cure it if George would follow his directions, by drinking a teacupful of turpen-

TABLE BAY, CAPE OF GOOD HOPE. From a colored aquatint by Huggins, in the Macpherson Collection.

SHIPPING NEAR BROOKLYN BRIDGE

From a photograph made about 1880. Courtesy of the Society for the
Preservation of New England Antiquities

tine. Confined to his bunk with his sore foot and laying the cause to the tape worm, he decided to try the remedy and hobbling to the cask of turpentine under the fo'c'sle-head he drew off a tin cup full and closing his eyes swallowed it in a couple of gulps and went back to bed again. With two men laid up and the second mate absent from duty, we were short-handed. The wind moderating the latter part of the day we set the topsails and courses in cloudy weather and passing heavy rain showers. The gale increasing we furled the foresail, lower fore and mizzen topsails and hove her to under lower main topsail, fore-topmast staysail and main spencer. The English bark was about a mile off the weather beam.

I shall never forget an incident that happened while shortening sail off the Cape, where, in a heavy head sea which was breaking over topgallant fo'c'sle deck, we were called to take in the jib. We ran on top of the deck, where a footing was next to an impossibility, but with a hold on the downhaul we managed to haul down the sail without slipping overboard, for we had no guard rail around the deck. Hauling the jib down "two blocks," Jim Dunn and I ran out to stow it. The sail and sheet-blocks were whipping over the boom, defying us on our way out, but we were soon masters of the situation by taking a turn with the gasket around the head of the sail, smothering the wind temporarily, notwithstanding we were pitching at a fearful rate.

The jib is one of the meanest sails to handle in a time like this. I have described the courses, bellying out and tearing away from our grasp, turning back finger nails and leaving blood stains on the canvas from bleeding fingers, because we were unable to hold the sail; and the jib is not unlike it, as any seafaring man could testify and who will at once say that the jib is the worst sail on the ship to stow, because of the ship's diving and pitching. Having gained our position on the jib-boom it was a good deal like the situation on the old-time ducking stool. You couldn't help yourself and you had to take your medicine and you'd be lucky to get back without a wetting. One moment you are high above the wave—the next instant, down you plunge with the same feeling under your ribs that you have in a high swing, going backwards, or in going down in a fast passenger elevator, not knowing the next minute where you are going to stop. If the ship is buoyant enough to raise over the wave, you are safe; but if the ship takes a dive—look out! and hold on, all! This was the situation Jim and I were in.

We had three or four turns of the gasket passed around the jib and were working in towards the bowsprit when up we were tossed high in air and the next second we were pointed down into a big sea that I thought would break over the jib-boom-end. Instantly Jim put his big, strong arm around me, hugging me up as a bear might hug a tree.

"Hold on Fred, for God's sake! She'll souse us under," said he.

Down, down, we went, until I thought she would never stop. The angry wave climbed up to meet us. The martingale was submerged and the quivering boom, held by the jib guys and back-ropes, told the fearful strain it was under as the ship stuck her nose into the wave. Down we went until our legs were knee-deep in water and as she raised again our feet were nearly pried off the foot-ropes. There was a seething, foaming mass of white water made from the plunge of the bowsprit into the wave. The spray flew high over the knight-heads across the deck and while we stuck like leeches we expected to be thrown from our perch into the sea.

Can you imagine a rough, uneducated sailor like Jim, forgetting all about himself at a time like that and thinking only of the safety of a shipmate? Ah!—They were the men that were true, uncut diamonds of the first water and coming to the surface they cast a beam of sunshine when you least expected it.

Just before noon old Dick was doing some work on the weather side of the booby-hatch and the captain coming out of the front door of the cabin asked him what he was doing. Dick, having a mouthful of tobacco juice, turned his head and spat over his shoulder on the deck. This so enraged the "Old Man" that before Dick had time to answer, he pounced upon him and taking him by the shoulder shook him violently, saying: "You Old Sailor! Where in hell do you think you are? I suppose you'd spit on your own parlor floor, if you had a home of your own, but being an Old Sailor, it's a damned sight easier to spit over your shoulder than to go to the lee scuppers!" Then he called:

"Mr. Burris! Send another man aft to take this man's job!" At the same time pushing Dick for'ard in no gentle manner. This was resented by Dick.

"Toik yer bloody 'ands off'n me!" shouted Dick, trying to shake loose from the captain's grasp. "Toik yer 'ands off, Hi says! Hi don't hallow hany man to put their 'ands on me!"

"Here's one man you'll see put his hands on you and don't you forget it!" exclaimed the captain. "You dirty Old Sailor, you forget that you are aft the mainmast! How many times have you got to be told that this is the captain's front yard? A boy would know better, but you being an Old Sailor, I've got to excuse you because you don't know any better!" By this time they were abreast the mainmast and the "Old Man" gave him a shove for'ard with parting instructions:

"Don't ever let me see you spit on the deck of this ship again—at any time or in any place! Humph! You Old Sailors will drive me crazy yet!"

Dick skulked for'ard and the "Old Man" walked aft, up the weather gangway steps and on the poop deck where he paced back and forth like a caged animal. Soon eight bells were struck and we were all surprised to hear the "Old Man" shout:

"Call the watch, Mr. Burris, and all hands lay aft to splice the main brace! This is my fifty-seventh birthday and we'll begin it right!"

He, no doubt, was thinking of his little fracas with Dick and determined to make amends by splicing the main brace. Williams exclaimed, "The Old Man's not such a bad fellow after all."

I was sent forward with a glass of grog to George, who, by the way, was a very sick man. There was no doubt as to the tape worm having been killed and the poor man nearly followed the tape worm. I never saw such a change in a man. Two days before he was the picture of health when I stopped at the fo'c'sle door to enquire about him.

Now, upon going into the fo'c'sle, I was startled at his appearance. The skin had shrunken tightly over his cheekbones and his complexion was a deep sallow color, bordering on green. The whites of his eyes loomed up like grommet holes for spilling buntlines in the courses. The light in the fo'c'sle was none too bright which added to the depressing scene. At first, I thought that he was dead and shrank back appalled at the sight. His eyes were closed but hearing me approach he slowly opened his eyelids until I thought they would never stop expanding. Not a word was spoken by either of us for sometime until I finally regained my composure and ventured to ask how he was feeling.

"Not so damned good, Fred," said he, staring at me without a smile with his mouth opened like his eyelids, his upper lip stretched tightly over his upper teeth and remaining there, exposing his teeth, and making him look more like a ghost than a thing of life. One hand rested on the bunk board and the skin was drawn tightly over the knuckles so that it resembled the talons of a vulture. I felt that I couldn't touch him and so stuck out the glass, saying:

"Here, George, is a drink for you. It's the Old Man's birthday and he's setting 'em up to the boys." Still that glassy stare without a move. "God! It smells like turpentine," said he, faintly, breathing through his lips drawn tightly over his teeth while great beads of perspiration stood out on his forehead at the thought of swallowing another dose.

Telling him that I would dilute it I ran to the water-cask for some water and on returning had quite composed myself and so helped him to raise his head so that he could drink. It tasted better than he imagined and gently dropping his head back on the pillow, the glassy stare vanished and his lips gradually resumed their normal state. He breathed a "thanks," as he settled back and I adjusted his blankets and pillow as best I could and with a few cheering words left him with a promise to come back and see him later.

The "Old Man" gave us a holiday for the afternoon and after finishing our dinner Frank and I went to the second mate's room where we found him suffering so much that we didn't stay very long, but told him that George was a very sick man. He advised us to go at once and see the "Old Man," which I did. The captain seemed alarmed, said it was the first that he had heard of the tape worm and immediately went forward to administer to George.

That evening the sun went down leaving us becalmed. The ship rolled back and forth slatting the sails against the masts so hard that it was necessary to clew up and lower away the upper yards. The heavy swell denoted wind not many miles away, but we thrashed about until 7.30 P.M. before we got any kind of a breeze.

The sky all around took on a golden grayish color which finally settled into a deep nimbus. The air was very sultry as the darkness came on and the lightning played back and forth in the distance, gradually coming nearer until we could hear the rumbling of thunder. The rain preceded the wind and the lightning became sharper, zig-zagging across the heavens, while the thunder followed, fairly shaking the whole ship.

The mate had been watching the approaching squall and for once he was right in not making sail with the first breath of air, as was his custom, and some of the sailors growled at the suspense, because we were not sent aloft, either to furl the sails that were clewed up or to set them again. Anything was better than standing idly by awaiting a call. It is the sailor's prerogative to growl.

The squall was stronger than we expected and the mate was not slow in giving orders to take in the mainsail, shouting in quick succession: "Tacks and sheets! Lower the topsails! Clew up the foresail! Down with the jib, etc. Call the watch! All hands on deck to shorten sail!"

The rain began to fall again and the cries of the men, in minor keys, at the ropes were anything but a joyful sound. The shrieking of the wind through the rigging drowned out the sound as the starboard watch came on deck in answer to the call and the ship heeled over, quivering in the squall, while the big white-caps came aboard again to make our acquaintance.

The mainsail was flapping over the yard at a terrific rate and the folds of canvas cracked and snapped as I had never heard them before.

"Jump aloft and take in the mainsail," thundered the mate, and away we ran up the rigging, knowing full well that it was important to get this sail off of her as soon as possible. When half way up the rigging an unusually heavy sea came aboard and the ship was nearly thrown on her beam-ends. The phosphorescent light below threw peculiar rays in the rigging above as we clung to the shrouds waiting for the ship to right herself again.

Staggering and shaking herself free, she rolled to windward with a jerk, and the big mainsail, which had blown over the yard, whipped back into place with the report of a cannon. The strain on the sail was too much, as it soared above like a big balloon, and there was a ripping and slatting of torn canvas. An old patch in the sail, near the weather head earing, gave way, making a start for an untimely finish and before we reached the yard the whole sail was a looking-glass, split from earing to earing, just below the jackstay. Whipping itself around the mainstay and blown clear out of the bolt-ropes, it was soon madly thrashing itself to pieces. The spilling-lines and buntlines kept the sail from blowing away entirely and it seemed hours before we made the sail secure.

The second mate being confined to his room, the mate thought he would take his place up aloft. It was the first time he had ever gone above the top. While on our way to take in the upper topsail, that sail, like the mainsail, was flapping over the yard to such an extent that no one ventured on the yard. Tommy and I were the first to run over the top and as he jumped on the foot-rope, the sail rolled over his head and he was thrown from the yard directly in front of me into the darkness below.

"Man overboard!" I shouted, as Williams came up.

It was a dangerous undertaking to attempt to run out on the yard with the sail whipping over it. Williams, who was one of the most powerful men in the ship, hesitated and commenting on Tommy's being thrown from the yard, said, "There's no such thing as saving a man overboard in this sea and the only thing to do is to get the sails off the ship as soon as possible."

Man after man was coming up from the mainsail and the first we knew the mate was up with us shouting, "Why in hell don't you lay out on the yard?" etc. At that instant the whole heavens were lighted by a flash of lightning followed by thunder that was deafening. There was a smell of burnt iron and I thought that the ship had been struck. We all clung to the rigging and many declared afterwards that the ironwork snapped off the rust spots of the chain tyes and runners about us.

The mate, finding his voice again, shouted: "Lay out on the yard, some of you! I would if I had my other boots on."

This was too much for Williams and he called back: "Boots, be damned! What do you take us for, a mess of damned fools? Why in hell don't you stay on deck and brace the yards so that it will be safe for us sailors to take care of your ship? Tommy was just knocked off the yard; if you want to know why we don't lay out!" Here, Archie chimed in: "Tommy's all right. I crawled over him in the top as I came off the main yard!"

"Thank God for that!" said Williams. "That's one sin the mate won't have to answer for," shouting at the top of his voice.

The mate evidently saw for the first time that the yard was pointed in too far and made his way down the rigging while Williams, instead of laying out on the yard, as Tommy had done, climbed above the sail and swinging on to the tye, rode down the sail, smothering it at the bunt where we took a temporary turn with the gasket and worked out and soon had the sail under control about the same time the mate reached the deck.

By the time we were through with the lighter sails everything on the fore had been taken care of. The starboard watch was sent below to get what sleep they could before eight bells while we in the port watch huddled about the main bitts where we could dodge the extra seas as they came aboard.

Tommy was the hero of the watch. He explained that when he was knocked off the topsail-yard he thought it was all off with him, but the next thing he knew he landed on all-fours in the maintop, instead of in a watery grave.

At 2 P.M. the gale came around to southwest and we made sail again setting the foresail, topsails and main-topgallant sail and jib. The next day we got down the mainsail. It was a wreck and so we bent a spare mainsail. The weather continued fair and Mr. Sanborn and George improved so much that they both reported for work.

We struck the southeasterly trades on June 2, in lat. 20° S., long. 7° 15″ W. In those steady trade winds it was the custom to overhaul all the rigging and we began by changing the braces end-for-end; setting up the bob-stays; refitting lifts and foot-ropes; setting up all standing rigging and getting ready for rattling down. Why it is called "rattling down," I could never understand for the work is started from the sheer pole, working up instead of down. The old ratlines were taken off and thrown into the junk barrel to be sold with other junk. The sailor's definition of "ratlines" is a ladder for rats to climb and we were the rats. The second day of rattling down, the mate, in an unusually pleasant frame of mind, said to me, "Watch me have some fun with 'Cockney,' " who, it will be remembered, was none too bright mentally.

"Here, 'Cockney'!" called the mate. "Go for'ard and get a slush pot."

"Get a slush pot, sir," answered "Cockney," at once off on the run and soon back with the pot.

"Do you see that royalmast up there?" pointing with his finger to the main royalmast. "Skin up aloft and begin at the sheave-hole and grease the after part of the royal, t'gallant and topmasts and mind you don't spill any slush on the sails. If you do, damn your heart! I'll skin you alive."

"Cockney" looked aloft and with a half-hearted sigh answered, "Skin you alive, sir," and throwing the lanyard over his head he climbed into the rigging with the slush pot dangling from his neck:

The ship was bowling before it at the rate of eight knots or more, rolling from side to side. The old ratlines were not all off on the lower shrouds, but from the maintop up, there was nothing for a footing and he must shin all the way. By the time he reached the royal rigging his strength was nearly gone and wrapping his legs around the backstay he started to slush the mast as directed. Holding on with one hand and using the other to grease the mast, he began shifting hands to relieve the one supporting his weight. As the royalmast is a short mast he got through fairly well and sat down on the eyes of the t'gallant rigging to rest before starting in on the t'gallant mast.

"What in hell are you doing up there!" shouted the mate, who was watching his every move. "Do you want me to bring you up a sofa to lie down on? Get t' work and don't be all day about it. Get a move on you!"

We heard "Cockney" answer, "Get a move, sir," and he was not slow in starting to work again, but his hands were both so greasy that he couldn't hold his weight and before he was halfway down the mast he was seen to shift his legs from one backstay to the other and with each shift, he lost ground and slipped below the spot he left off greasing and soon was down to the topmast cross-trees with several "holidays" above.

Instead of cursing "Cockney" as we all expected, the mate called to him in a pleasant voice, saying that he had missed several places. "Shin up and touch up those holidays, 'Cockney,' " said he. If any of my readers think that is any picnic, with a ship rolling from side to side, 40 degrees or more each side, just try it. Poor "Cockney" was a good deal like the frog jumping out of the well. For every two feet he gained, he fell back three. But he stayed with it and strange to say the mate didn't lose his patience but seemed pleased that "Cockney" was doing his best to do the work satisfactorily.

Strange it is that men in power cannot see their littleness at times. The Big Head shows itself on the land as well as on the sea and it is surprising how they get by with it.

After we finished rattling down we began scraping the dead-eyes and other bright woodwork. Nearing the Equator our fine weather left us and we ran into showers in which we caught enough rain water to fill our empty casks. Then began the scrubbing of paint-work which I liked no better than I did in this latitude when bound south.

On Saturday the twenty-third, we raised the Island of Ferdinando De Noronha and passed it at midnight, about five miles to the eastward. There are two principal islands in the group, the larger about seven miles long by one and a half wide. The moon was shining brightly and the rugged peak, with an elevation of 1,080 feet, shone out in all its glory. These islands serve as a place of banishment for Brazilian criminals and lie one hundred and twenty-five miles east of Brazil.

With fine weather and a good smart breeze we were nearing the Equator. "Cockney" began talking about "the Line," in the evening watch, and asked if it were possible to see it. He had crossed it a couple of times but didn't remember having seen it. I told him that we were expected to cross the Line at about 3 A.M., if the wind held as it was blowing.

"Pshaw," said he. "That's our watch below and I'll be asleep. Do you think we can see it in the morning watch?"

He seemed to be the foot-stool for us all and at this wide-open question I couldn't resist taking my turn. "I don't think you can see it with your naked eye," said I. "But you can look through the spy-glass of my sextant, at four bells, and if it isn't too dark, I think you'll be able to see it."

"Will you let me look through the glaus, Fred? You're a jolly good chap to do this for me," said he, and we walked the deck together while he kept up a continual conversation, tickled as a little child at the prospect of seeing the Line.

At eight bells and the call of the watch, I turned up the light in my room and unscrewing the lens in the glass, pulled a hair from my head and stretching it across the center, screwed back the lens so that the hair was horizontal. Before it was fixed, Frank came to the door and asked: "What are you doing, up at this hour? Why don't you turn in?" Explaining the *modus operandi*, he lost no time in spreading the news and the whole ship was acquainted with the procedure when the morning watch was called.

"Cockney" could hardly wait for daylight and before washing down I took him to the t'gallant fo'c'sle deck and handing him the sextant, after I had tried it, explained how to hold it, etc. One look was enough. "My God, Fred! I see it! I see it! I never thought there was a line there that could be seen. How did we jump over it? It must be mighty strong not to break wid all the ships jumpin' over it."

The crew stood by and enjoyed the fun. Even the mate came for'ard to join in the laugh, but "Cockney" was the most pleased of all and to the end of the voyage he still talked of how I let him take my sextant to see the Line. "Where ignorance is bliss 'tis folly to be wise," and I don't think there was one of us that undeceived him.

We crossed the Line in long. 35° 23′ W. and kept our fine breeze with occasional rain showers, picking up the northeast trades in lat. 11° 6′, long. 44° 00′ W. when we had fine weather and were employed in painting the ship.

We raised the ensign on July 4 and were given a holiday, and that day raised the first sail to windward since leaving the Cape—a brig, bound south.

At noon we ran into an unusual amount of gulf-weed. We had been sailing through short patches of it all the morning but now the surface was covered for miles around. It resembled in color the yellow rock-weed seen in the bays about home, but was very much different in size being much smaller and branching out more like Irish moss, with little bulbs or air bladders which grew very close to the stem like solitary grapes and were about the size of a buck-shot. It is also sometimes called "grape-weed." I put a bunch of it in a glass bottle filled with sea water and kept it for years. It acted as a barometer, rising and falling with the change of weather.

We lost sight of the Southern Cross on the evening of the fourth in lat. 24° 45' N. long. 58° 14' W. It had been plainly discernible up to that time.

A few days later the captain was taking his daily exercise, walking the poop and enjoying a smoke after dinner. The sun was sinking in the west and the ship was rolling quietly along under a free wind. A lone booby circled around the ship, evidently tired out from its long flight, and finally alighted on the port lower mizzen topsail yardarm. The slat of the sail in the light breeze seemed not to its liking, for with every roll and the flap of the sail it would raise its wings as if about to fly. These birds immediately go to sleep when resting and from the wheel I was watching with a great deal of curiosity to see how long it would be before it would be asleep. With a sudden pitch of the ship the booby seemed to have lost its balance and slipped off the yardarm, fouling the brace-pendant and turned a complete somersault before it regained its equilibrium. Then, returning again to the yardarm, a second time, and with no better success, it finally left its resting place, circled about the ship, and at last selected a roosting place on the port railing just abaft the mizzen rigging. The captain, who was also watching the movement of the booby, said: "Fred, that fellow is tired out and will soon be asleep. We'll let him alone till he is fast asleep and then we can catch him."

No sooner had he spoken than the mate came hobbling up the starboard gangway and bending over the binnacle to see if I was keeping the ship on her course, he raised his eyes and discovered the booby on the railing.

"Oh, captain!" said he. "There's a booby on the railing, asleep. I'll go and catch him." So saying he hobbled across the deck and made his way toward the bird, scuffling along and making enough noise to awaken the dead. When within ten feet of the booby it raised its wings and flew away, as much as to say, "This is no place for me," for it flew in a direct course away from the ship.

The mate turned and rounding the after corner of the cabin, met the captain who impatiently said: "Umph! Who ever heard of one booby trying to catch another!" It came so unexpectedly that I laughed aloud. The mate, of course, was chagrined at the captain's remark, but when he saw me trying to contain myself, he was furious. The captain abruptly left him and walked up the steps to the top of the cabin while the mate hobbled over to me and said:

"You laugh at me? Damn your heart! I'll fix you tonight!" And true to his word he had me running all over the ship from midnight till 4 A.M. Buntlines to stop, watch tackles to get, sweating up halliards, etc., in which the watch cursed again and again at the unreasonable things they were called upon to do. Outside of that he let me alone.

In light winds and very hot weather we sighted Wreck Hill, the westernmost part of Bermuda Island, and the following morning, while washing down decks, we raised a school of porpoises, off the port bow, about a half mile distant. The sea was glassy in the morning sun and they formed in two rows, one behind the other, about twenty feet apart, swimming in rank and file fully two miles in length and as straight as an arrow, rolling over and going under the water, in unison, at regular intervals. It was such an unusual sight that we all stopped work to watch them. Fully ten minutes went by before we turned to again. Finally the line was broken, the two schools separating, swimming as the geese fly and disappearing in the distance.

The ship was now as clean as a yacht and we were all ready for Sandy Hook, about three hundred miles distant. Three days later the "Old Man" gave us a course of northwest by west, and at 3 A.M. we wore ship on account of two lights ahead that puzzled the "Old Man."

At daylight we hoisted the jack for a pilot and a Delaware pilot came off, *Boat C*, but couldn't take us to New York. The two lights we had seen were Cape Charles and Cape Henry and when the "Old Man" found himself he stormed about the deck exclaiming: "Fool! Fool! The longer I go to sea the less I know. I gave the course N.W. by W. when it should have been N.W. by N. Four points would run any ship ashore. I'm no better than an Old Sailor! Ugh!"

I then thought of Dana's "Two Years before the Mast," in which he says,

> If the Bermudas let you pass,
> You must beware of Hatteras.

We sailed north all day, in light winds, and about nine that evening struck a shoal, off Egg Harbor, that shook us up. The second mate was not slow in ordering us to stand from under the yards, but we braced her up and in a couple of jumps we were in deep water again and on sounding the pumps found she was none the worse for bumping. The next morning the tugboat *A. F. Walcott,* of New York, came off to us at six o'clock and the pilot came aboard at eight. The *Walcott* then took our line. It was a happy moment for all to feel that "Blow high or blow low," it now could matter but little, as the towboat had us in tow, with a good hawser. At 11.30 a.m we were just inside Sandy Hook and dropped our port anchor, to await orders. The cargo being consigned, we might be ordered to England. Captain Lamson went ashore immediately. The runners from the sailor's boarding houses came aboard but were searched for any whiskey that might be concealed in their pockets before coming over the rail and those that had it were turned back.

The next afternoon the tugboats *E. H. Coffin* and *A. F. Walcott* came down with the captain, with orders to proceed to Brooklyn. This put us in better spirits and we hove up our anchor to "Heave away my Johnnies, we're all bound to go."

The Brooklyn Bridge was under construction at that time and we had to strike our main t'gallantmast before passing under. We were towed up to Harbeck Stores, the second dock from the bridge, where we made her fast, fore and aft, with enough sober men to sing the last chantey, "Leave her Johnny, leave her," as we pumped till she sucked.

Our ship was not different from hundreds of others arriving from a foreign voyage. We were well advertised among the sailor's boarding houses and the runners were on hand when we began heaving up anchor at Sandy Hook. Each runner had a pocket full of cards, advertising the good qualities of his hotel, which were thrust into our hands with promises of good treatment, plenty of whiskey, dance halls, pretty girls that were good girls and would look after their Jack Tar and take pleasure in steering him on a straight course should he be half-seas over, etc.

We were no exception to thousands of other sailors and by the time the ship was made fast to the dock, our men, who had sworn, time and again, that not another drop of whiskey should ever pass their lips again, threw their good resolutions to the wind at the smell of the "knock-out drops" and half of the crew were "three sheets in the wind" before we passed under the Brooklyn Bridge.

Frank and I stayed by the ship until we were paid off on Tuesday, July 24, 1877. Those who were able to change their clothes and go ashore in their Sunday togs, on the day of arrival, presented a sorry sight when we saw them again at the Exchange, awaiting the signing of the pay-roll. As our names were called we took what was handed us with instructions to immediately put it out of sight before some shark "lamped" it or it would be missing by the time we reached our hotel. The second mate, Jim Dunn, Frank and I, bought our tickets for Boston and took the steamer *Providence*, for Fall River, that evening. After parting company at Boston, I have never seen one of the crew since.

A CATALOG OF SELECTED
DOVER BOOKS
IN ALL FIELDS OF INTEREST

A CATALOG OF SELECTED DOVER
BOOKS IN ALL FIELDS OF INTEREST

CONCERNING THE SPIRITUAL IN ART, Wassily Kandinsky. Pioneering work by father of abstract art. Thoughts on color theory, nature of art. Analysis of earlier masters. 12 illustrations. 80pp. of text. 5⅜ x 8½.   23411-8 Pa. $3.95

ANIMALS: 1,419 Copyright-Free Illustrations of Mammals, Birds, Fish, Insects, etc., Jim Harter (ed.). Clear wood engravings present, in extremely lifelike poses, over 1,000 species of animals. One of the most extensive pictorial sourcebooks of its kind. Captions. Index. 284pp. 9 x 12.   23766-4 Pa. $12.95

CELTIC ART: The Methods of Construction, George Bain. Simple geometric techniques for making Celtic interlacements, spirals, Kells-type initials, animals, humans, etc. Over 500 illustrations. 160pp. 9 x 12. (USO)   22923-8 Pa. $9.95

AN ATLAS OF ANATOMY FOR ARTISTS, Fritz Schider. Most thorough reference work on art anatomy in the world. Hundreds of illustrations, including selections from works by Vesalius, Leonardo, Goya, Ingres, Michelangelo, others. 593 illustrations. 192pp. 7⅛ x 10¼.   20241-0 Pa. $9.95

CELTIC HAND STROKE-BY-STROKE (Irish Half-Uncial from "The Book of Kells"): An Arthur Baker Calligraphy Manual, Arthur Baker. Complete guide to creating each letter of the alphabet in distinctive Celtic manner. Covers hand position, strokes, pens, inks, paper, more. Illustrated. 48pp. 8¼ x 11.   24336-2 Pa. $3.95

EASY ORIGAMI, John Montroll. Charming collection of 32 projects (hat, cup, pelican, piano, swan, many more) specially designed for the novice origami hobbyist. Clearly illustrated easy-to-follow instructions insure that even beginning papercrafters will achieve successful results. 48pp. 8¼ x 11.   27298-2 Pa. $3.50

THE COMPLETE BOOK OF BIRDHOUSE CONSTRUCTION FOR WOOD-WORKERS, Scott D. Campbell. Detailed instructions, illustrations, tables. Also data on bird habitat and instinct patterns. Bibliography. 3 tables. 63 illustrations in 15 figures. 48pp. 5¼ x 8½.   24407-5 Pa. $2.50

BLOOMINGDALE'S ILLUSTRATED 1886 CATALOG: Fashions, Dry Goods and Housewares, Bloomingdale Brothers. Famed merchants' extremely rare catalog depicting about 1,700 products: clothing, housewares, firearms, dry goods, jewelry, more. Invaluable for dating, identifying vintage items. Also, copyright-free graphics for artists, designers. Co-published with Henry Ford Museum & Greenfield Village. 160pp. 8¼ x 11.   25780-0 Pa. $10.95

HISTORIC COSTUME IN PICTURES, Braun & Schneider. Over 1,450 costumed figures in clearly detailed engravings–from dawn of civilization to end of 19th century. Captions. Many folk costumes. 256pp. 8⅜ x 11¾.   23150-X Pa. $12.95

STICKLEY CRAFTSMAN FURNITURE CATALOGS, Gustav Stickley and L. & J. G. Stickley. Beautiful, functional furniture in two authentic catalogs from 1910. 594 illustrations, including 277 photos, show settles, rockers, armchairs, reclining chairs, bookcases, desks, tables. 183pp. 6½ x 9¼. 23838-5 Pa. $9.95

AMERICAN LOCOMOTIVES IN HISTORIC PHOTOGRAPHS: 1858 to 1949, Ron Ziel (ed.). A rare collection of 126 meticulously detailed official photographs, called "builder portraits," of American locomotives that majestically chronicle the rise of steam locomotive power in America. Introduction. Detailed captions. xi + 129pp. 9 x 12. 27393-8 Pa. $12.95

AMERICA'S LIGHTHOUSES: An Illustrated History, Francis Ross Holland, Jr. Delightfully written, profusely illustrated fact-filled survey of over 200 American lighthouses since 1716. History, anecdotes, technological advances, more. 240pp. 8 x 10¾. 25576-X Pa. $12.95

TOWARDS A NEW ARCHITECTURE, Le Corbusier. Pioneering manifesto by founder of "International School." Technical and aesthetic theories, views of industry, economics, relation of form to function, "mass-production split" and much more. Profusely illustrated. 320pp. 6⅛ x 9¼. (USO) 25023-7 Pa. $9.95

HOW THE OTHER HALF LIVES, Jacob Riis. Famous journalistic record, exposing poverty and degradation of New York slums around 1900, by major social reformer. 100 striking and influential photographs. 233pp. 10 x 7⅞. 22012-5 Pa. $10.95

FRUIT KEY AND TWIG KEY TO TREES AND SHRUBS, William M. Harlow. One of the handiest and most widely used identification aids. Fruit key covers 120 deciduous and evergreen species; twig key 160 deciduous species. Easily used. Over 300 photographs. 126pp. 5⅜ x 8½. 20511-8 Pa. $3.95

COMMON BIRD SONGS, Dr. Donald J. Borror. Songs of 60 most common U.S. birds: robins, sparrows, cardinals, bluejays, finches, more—arranged in order of increasing complexity. Up to 9 variations of songs of each species.
Cassette and manual 99911-4 $8.95

ORCHIDS AS HOUSE PLANTS, Rebecca Tyson Northen. Grow cattleyas and many other kinds of orchids—in a window, in a case, or under artificial light. 63 illustrations. 148pp. 5⅜ x 8½. 23261-1 Pa. $4.95

MONSTER MAZES, Dave Phillips. Masterful mazes at four levels of difficulty. Avoid deadly perils and evil creatures to find magical treasures. Solutions for all 32 exciting illustrated puzzles. 48pp. 8¼ x 11. 26005-4 Pa. $2.95

MOZART'S DON GIOVANNI (DOVER OPERA LIBRETTO SERIES), Wolfgang Amadeus Mozart. Introduced and translated by Ellen H. Bleiler. Standard Italian libretto, with complete English translation. Convenient and thoroughly portable—an ideal companion for reading along with a recording or the performance itself. Introduction. List of characters. Plot summary. 121pp. 5¼ x 8½. 24944-1 Pa. $2.95

TECHNICAL MANUAL AND DICTIONARY OF CLASSICAL BALLET, Gail Grant. Defines, explains, comments on steps, movements, poses and concepts. 15-page pictorial section. Basic book for student, viewer. 127pp. 5⅜ x 8½. 21843-0 Pa. $4.95

BRASS INSTRUMENTS: Their History and Development, Anthony Baines. Authoritative, updated survey of the evolution of trumpets, trombones, bugles, cornets, French horns, tubas and other brass wind instruments. Over 140 illustrations and 48 music examples. Corrected and updated by author. New preface. Bibliography. 320pp. 5⅜ x 8½. 27574-4 Pa. $9.95

HOLLYWOOD GLAMOR PORTRAITS, John Kobal (ed.). 145 photos from 1926-49. Harlow, Gable, Bogart, Bacall; 94 stars in all. Full background on photographers, technical aspects. 160pp. 8⅜ x 11¼. 23352-9 Pa. $12.95

MAX AND MORITZ, Wilhelm Busch. Great humor classic in both German and English. Also 10 other works: "Cat and Mouse," "Plisch and Plumm," etc. 216pp. 5⅜ x 8½. 20181-3 Pa. $6.95

THE RAVEN AND OTHER FAVORITE POEMS, Edgar Allan Poe. Over 40 of the author's most memorable poems: "The Bells," "Ulalume," "Israfel," "To Helen," "The Conqueror Worm," "Eldorado," "Annabel Lee," many more. Alphabetic lists of titles and first lines. 64pp. 5³⁄₁₆ x 8¼. 26685-0 Pa. $1.00

PERSONAL MEMOIRS OF U. S. GRANT, Ulysses Simpson Grant. Intelligent, deeply moving firsthand account of Civil War campaigns, considered by many the finest military memoirs ever written. Includes letters, historic photographs, maps and more. 528pp. 6⅛ x 9¼. 28587-1 Pa. $11.95

AMULETS AND SUPERSTITIONS, E. A. Wallis Budge. Comprehensive discourse on origin, powers of amulets in many ancient cultures: Arab, Persian Babylonian, Assyrian, Egyptian, Gnostic, Hebrew, Phoenician, Syriac, etc. Covers cross, swastika, crucifix, seals, rings, stones, etc. 584pp. 5⅜ x 8½. 23573-4 Pa. $12.95

RUSSIAN STORIES/PYCCKNE PACCKA3bl: A Dual-Language Book, edited by Gleb Struve. Twelve tales by such masters as Chekhov, Tolstoy, Dostoevsky, Pushkin, others. Excellent word-for-word English translations on facing pages, plus teaching and study aids, Russian/English vocabulary, biographical/critical introductions, more. 416pp. 5⅜ x 8½. 26244-8 Pa. $8.95

PHILADELPHIA THEN AND NOW: 60 Sites Photographed in the Past and Present, Kenneth Finkel and Susan Oyama. Rare photographs of City Hall, Logan Square, Independence Hall, Betsy Ross House, other landmarks juxtaposed with contemporary views. Captures changing face of historic city. Introduction. Captions. 128pp. 8¼ x 11. 25790-8 Pa. $9.95

AIA ARCHITECTURAL GUIDE TO NASSAU AND SUFFOLK COUNTIES, LONG ISLAND, The American Institute of Architects, Long Island Chapter, and the Society for the Preservation of Long Island Antiquities. Comprehensive, well-researched and generously illustrated volume brings to life over three centuries of Long Island's great architectural heritage. More than 240 photographs with authoritative, extensively detailed captions. 176pp. 8¼ x 11. 26946-9 Pa. $14.95

NORTH AMERICAN INDIAN LIFE: Customs and Traditions of 23 Tribes, Elsie Clews Parsons (ed.). 27 fictionalized essays by noted anthropologists examine religion, customs, government, additional facets of life among the Winnebago, Crow, Zuni, Eskimo, other tribes. 480pp. 6⅛ x 9¼. 27377-6 Pa. $10.95

FRANK LLOYD WRIGHT'S HOLLYHOCK HOUSE, Donald Hoffmann. Lavishly illustrated, carefully documented study of one of Wright's most controversial residential designs. Over 120 photographs, floor plans, elevations, etc. Detailed perceptive text by noted Wright scholar. Index. 128pp. 9¼ x 10¾. 27133-1 Pa. $11.95

THE MALE AND FEMALE FIGURE IN MOTION: 60 Classic Photographic Sequences, Eadweard Muybridge. 60 true-action photographs of men and women walking, running, climbing, bending, turning, etc., reproduced from rare 19th-century masterpiece. vi + 121pp. 9 x 12. 24745-7 Pa. $10.95

1001 QUESTIONS ANSWERED ABOUT THE SEASHORE, N. J. Berrill and Jacquelyn Berrill. Queries answered about dolphins, sea snails, sponges, starfish, fishes, shore birds, many others. Covers appearance, breeding, growth, feeding, much more. 305pp. 5¼ x 8¼. 23366-9 Pa. $8.95

GUIDE TO OWL WATCHING IN NORTH AMERICA, Donald S. Heintzelman. Superb guide offers complete data and descriptions of 19 species: barn owl, screech owl, snowy owl, many more. Expert coverage of owl-watching equipment, conservation, migrations and invasions, etc. Guide to observing sites. 84 illustrations. xiii + 193pp. 5⅜ x 8½. 27344-X Pa. $8.95

MEDICINAL AND OTHER USES OF NORTH AMERICAN PLANTS: A Historical Survey with Special Reference to the Eastern Indian Tribes, Charlotte Erichsen-Brown. Chronological historical citations document 500 years of usage of plants, trees, shrubs native to eastern Canada, northeastern U.S. Also complete identifying information. 343 illustrations. 544pp. 6½ x 9¼. 25951-X Pa. $12.95

STORYBOOK MAZES, Dave Phillips. 23 stories and mazes on two-page spreads: Wizard of Oz, Treasure Island, Robin Hood, etc. Solutions. 64pp. 8¼ x 11. 23628-5 Pa. $2.95

NEGRO FOLK MUSIC, U.S.A., Harold Courlander. Noted folklorist's scholarly yet readable analysis of rich and varied musical tradition. Includes authentic versions of over 40 folk songs. Valuable bibliography and discography. xi + 324pp. 5⅜ x 8½. 27350-4 Pa. $9.95

MOVIE-STAR PORTRAITS OF THE FORTIES, John Kobal (ed.). 163 glamor, studio photos of 106 stars of the 1940s: Rita Hayworth, Ava Gardner, Marlon Brando, Clark Gable, many more. 176pp. 8⅜ x 11¼. 23546-7 Pa. $12.95

BENCHLEY LOST AND FOUND, Robert Benchley. Finest humor from early 30s, about pet peeves, child psychologists, post office and others. Mostly unavailable elsewhere. 73 illustrations by Peter Arno and others. 183pp. 5⅜ x 8½. 22410-4 Pa. $6.95

YEKL and THE IMPORTED BRIDEGROOM AND OTHER STORIES OF YIDDISH NEW YORK, Abraham Cahan. Film Hester Street based on Yekl (1896). Novel, other stories among first about Jewish immigrants on N.Y.'s East Side. 240pp. 5⅜ x 8½. 22427-9 Pa. $6.95

SELECTED POEMS, Walt Whitman. Generous sampling from *Leaves of Grass*. Twenty-four poems include "I Hear America Singing," "Song of the Open Road," "I Sing the Body Electric," "When Lilacs Last in the Dooryard Bloom'd," "O Captain! My Captain!"–all reprinted from an authoritative edition. Lists of titles and first lines. 128pp. 5$\frac{3}{16}$ x 8¼. 26878-0 Pa. $1.00

THE BEST TALES OF HOFFMANN, E. T. A. Hoffmann. 10 of Hoffmann's most important stories: "Nutcracker and the King of Mice," "The Golden Flowerpot," etc. 458pp. 5⅜ x 8½. 21793-0 Pa. $9.95

FROM FETISH TO GOD IN ANCIENT EGYPT, E. A. Wallis Budge. Rich detailed survey of Egyptian conception of "God" and gods, magic, cult of animals, Osiris, more. Also, superb English translations of hymns and legends. 240 illustrations. 545pp. 5⅜ x 8½. 25803-3 Pa. $13.95

FRENCH STORIES/CONTES FRANÇAIS: A Dual-Language Book, Wallace Fowlie. Ten stories by French masters, Voltaire to Camus: "Micromegas" by Voltaire; "The Atheist's Mass" by Balzac; "Minuet" by de Maupassant; "The Guest" by Camus, six more. Excellent English translations on facing pages. Also French-English vocabulary list, exercises, more. 352pp. 5⅜ x 8½. 26443-2 Pa. $8.95

CHICAGO AT THE TURN OF THE CENTURY IN PHOTOGRAPHS: 122 Historic Views from the Collections of the Chicago Historical Society, Larry A. Viskochil. Rare large-format prints offer detailed views of City Hall, State Street, the Loop, Hull House, Union Station, many other landmarks, circa 1904-1913. Introduction. Captions. Maps. 144pp. 9⅜ x 12¼. 24656-6 Pa. $12.95

OLD BROOKLYN IN EARLY PHOTOGRAPHS, 1865-1929, William Lee Younger. Luna Park, Gravesend race track, construction of Grand Army Plaza, moving of Hotel Brighton, etc. 157 previously unpublished photographs. 165pp. 8⅞ x 11¾. 23587-4 Pa. $13.95

THE MYTHS OF THE NORTH AMERICAN INDIANS, Lewis Spence. Rich anthology of the myths and legends of the Algonquins, Iroquois, Pawnees and Sioux, prefaced by an extensive historical and ethnological commentary. 36 illustrations. 480pp. 5⅜ x 8½. 25967-6 Pa. $8.95

AN ENCYCLOPEDIA OF BATTLES: Accounts of Over 1,560 Battles from 1479 B.C. to the Present, David Eggenberger. Essential details of every major battle in recorded history from the first battle of Megiddo in 1479 B.C. to Grenada in 1984. List of Battle Maps. New Appendix covering the years 1967-1984. Index. 99 illustrations. 544pp. 6½ x 9¼. 24913-1 Pa. $14.95

SAILING ALONE AROUND THE WORLD, Captain Joshua Slocum. First man to sail around the world, alone, in small boat. One of great feats of seamanship told in delightful manner. 67 illustrations. 294pp. 5⅜ x 8½. 20326-3 Pa. $5.95

ANARCHISM AND OTHER ESSAYS, Emma Goldman. Powerful, penetrating, prophetic essays on direct action, role of minorities, prison reform, puritan hypocrisy, violence, etc. 271pp. 5⅜ x 8½. 22484-8 Pa. $6.95

MYTHS OF THE HINDUS AND BUDDHISTS, Ananda K. Coomaraswamy and Sister Nivedita. Great stories of the epics; deeds of Krishna, Shiva, taken from puranas, Vedas, folk tales; etc. 32 illustrations. 400pp. 5⅜ x 8½. 21759-0 Pa. $10.95

BEYOND PSYCHOLOGY, Otto Rank. Fear of death, desire of immortality, nature of sexuality, social organization, creativity, according to Rankian system. 291pp. 5⅜ x 8½. 20485-5 Pa. $8.95

A THEOLOGICO-POLITICAL TREATISE, Benedict Spinoza. Also contains unfinished Political Treatise. Great classic on religious liberty, theory of government on common consent. R. Elwes translation. Total of 421pp. 5⅜ x 8½. 20249-6 Pa. $9.95

MY BONDAGE AND MY FREEDOM, Frederick Douglass. Born a slave, Douglass became outspoken force in antislavery movement. The best of Douglass' autobiographies. Graphic description of slave life. 464pp. 5⅜ x 8½. 22457-0 Pa. $8.95

FOLLOWING THE EQUATOR: A Journey Around the World, Mark Twain. Fascinating humorous account of 1897 voyage to Hawaii, Australia, India, New Zealand, etc. Ironic, bemused reports on peoples, customs, climate, flora and fauna, politics, much more. 197 illustrations. 720pp. 5⅜ x 8½. 26113-1 Pa. $15.95

THE PEOPLE CALLED SHAKERS, Edward D. Andrews. Definitive study of Shakers: origins, beliefs, practices, dances, social organization, furniture and crafts, etc. 33 illustrations. 351pp. 5⅜ x 8½. 21081-2 Pa. $8.95

THE MYTHS OF GREECE AND ROME, H. A. Guerber. A classic of mythology, generously illustrated, long prized for its simple, graphic, accurate retelling of the principal myths of Greece and Rome, and for its commentary on their origins and significance. With 64 illustrations by Michelangelo, Raphael, Titian, Rubens, Canova, Bernini and others. 480pp. 5⅜ x 8½. 27584-1 Pa. $9.95

PSYCHOLOGY OF MUSIC, Carl E. Seashore. Classic work discusses music as a medium from psychological viewpoint. Clear treatment of physical acoustics, auditory apparatus, sound perception, development of musical skills, nature of musical feeling, host of other topics. 88 figures. 408pp. 5⅜ x 8½. 21851-1 Pa. $10.95

THE PHILOSOPHY OF HISTORY, Georg W. Hegel. Great classic of Western thought develops concept that history is not chance but rational process, the evolution of freedom. 457pp. 5⅜ x 8½. 20112-0 Pa. $9.95

THE BOOK OF TEA, Kakuzo Okakura. Minor classic of the Orient: entertaining, charming explanation, interpretation of traditional Japanese culture in terms of tea ceremony. 94pp. 5⅜ x 8½. 20070-1 Pa. $3.95

LIFE IN ANCIENT EGYPT, Adolf Erman. Fullest, most thorough, detailed older account with much not in more recent books, domestic life, religion, magic, medicine, commerce, much more. Many illustrations reproduce tomb paintings, carvings, hieroglyphs, etc. 597pp. 5⅜ x 8½. 22632-8 Pa. $11.95

SUNDIALS, Their Theory and Construction, Albert Waugh. Far and away the best, most thorough coverage of ideas, mathematics concerned, types, construction, adjusting anywhere. Simple, nontechnical treatment allows even children to build several of these dials. Over 100 illustrations. 230pp. 5⅜ x 8½. 22947-5 Pa. $7.95

DYNAMICS OF FLUIDS IN POROUS MEDIA, Jacob Bear. For advanced students of ground water hydrology, soil mechanics and physics, drainage and irrigation engineering, and more. 335 illustrations. Exercises, with answers. 784pp. 6⅛ x 9¼. 65675-6 Pa. $19.95

SONGS OF EXPERIENCE: Facsimile Reproduction with 26 Plates in Full Color, William Blake. 26 full-color plates from a rare 1826 edition. Includes "TheTyger," "London," "Holy Thursday," and other poems. Printed text of poems. 48pp. 5¼ x 7. 24636-1 Pa. $4.95

OLD-TIME VIGNETTES IN FULL COLOR, Carol Belanger Grafton (ed.). Over 390 charming, often sentimental illustrations, selected from archives of Victorian graphics—pretty women posing, children playing, food, flowers, kittens and puppies, smiling cherubs, birds and butterflies, much more. All copyright-free. 48pp. 9¼ x 12¼. 27269-9 Pa. $7.95

PERSPECTIVE FOR ARTISTS, Rex Vicat Cole. Depth, perspective of sky and sea, shadows, much more, not usually covered. 391 diagrams, 81 reproductions of drawings and paintings. 279pp. 5⅜ x 8½. 22487-2 Pa. $7.95

DRAWING THE LIVING FIGURE, Joseph Sheppard. Innovative approach to artistic anatomy focuses on specifics of surface anatomy, rather than muscles and bones. Over 170 drawings of live models in front, back and side views, and in widely varying poses. Accompanying diagrams. 177 illustrations. Introduction. Index. 144pp. 8⅜ x11¼. 26723-7 Pa. $8.95

GOTHIC AND OLD ENGLISH ALPHABETS: 100 Complete Fonts, Dan X. Solo. Add power, elegance to posters, signs, other graphics with 100 stunning copyright-free alphabets: Blackstone, Dolbey, Germania, 97 more–including many lower-case, numerals, punctuation marks. 104pp. 8⅛ x 11. 24695-7 Pa. $8.95

HOW TO DO BEADWORK, Mary White. Fundamental book on craft from simple projects to five-bead chains and woven works. 106 illustrations. 142pp. 5⅜ x 8. 20697-1 Pa. $4.95

THE BOOK OF WOOD CARVING, Charles Marshall Sayers. Finest book for beginners discusses fundamentals and offers 34 designs. "Absolutely first rate . . . well thought out and well executed."–E. J. Tangerman. 118pp. 7¾ x 10⅝. 23654-4 Pa. $6.95

ILLUSTRATED CATALOG OF CIVIL WAR MILITARY GOODS: Union Army Weapons, Insignia, Uniform Accessories, and Other Equipment, Schuyler, Hartley, and Graham. Rare, profusely illustrated 1846 catalog includes Union Army uniform and dress regulations, arms and ammunition, coats, insignia, flags, swords, rifles, etc. 226 illustrations. 160pp. 9 x 12. 24939-5 Pa. $10.95

WOMEN'S FASHIONS OF THE EARLY 1900s: An Unabridged Republication of "New York Fashions, 1909," National Cloak & Suit Co. Rare catalog of mail-order fashions documents women's and children's clothing styles shortly after the turn of the century. Captions offer full descriptions, prices. Invaluable resource for fashion, costume historians. Approximately 725 illustrations. 128pp. 8⅜ x 11¼. 27276-1 Pa. $11.95

THE 1912 AND 1915 GUSTAV STICKLEY FURNITURE CATALOGS, Gustav Stickley. With over 200 detailed illustrations and descriptions, these two catalogs are essential reading and reference materials and identification guides for Stickley furniture. Captions cite materials, dimensions and prices. 112pp. 6½ x 9¼. 26676-1 Pa. $9.95

EARLY AMERICAN LOCOMOTIVES, John H. White, Jr. Finest locomotive engravings from early 19th century: historical (1804–74), main-line (after 1870), special, foreign, etc. 147 plates. 142pp. 11⅜ x 8¼. 22772-3 Pa. $10.95

THE TALL SHIPS OF TODAY IN PHOTOGRAPHS, Frank O. Braynard. Lavishly illustrated tribute to nearly 100 majestic contemporary sailing vessels: Amerigo Vespucci, Clearwater, Constitution, Eagle, Mayflower, Sea Cloud, Victory, many more. Authoritative captions provide statistics, background on each ship. 190 black-and-white photographs and illustrations. Introduction. 128pp. 8⅞ x 11¾. 27163-3 Pa. $13.95

EARLY NINETEENTH-CENTURY CRAFTS AND TRADES, Peter Stockham (ed.). Extremely rare 1807 volume describes to youngsters the crafts and trades of the day: brickmaker, weaver, dressmaker, bookbinder, ropemaker, saddler, many more. Quaint prose, charming illustrations for each craft. 20 black-and-white line illustrations. 192pp. 4⅝ x 6. 27293-1 Pa. $4.95

VICTORIAN FASHIONS AND COSTUMES FROM HARPER'S BAZAR, 1867–1898, Stella Blum (ed.). Day costumes, evening wear, sports clothes, shoes, hats, other accessories in over 1,000 detailed engravings. 320pp. 9⅜ x 12¼. 22990-4 Pa. $14.95

GUSTAV STICKLEY, THE CRAFTSMAN, Mary Ann Smith. Superb study surveys broad scope of Stickley's achievement, especially in architecture. Design philosophy, rise and fall of the Craftsman empire, descriptions and floor plans for many Craftsman houses, more. 86 black-and-white halftones. 31 line illustrations. Introduction 208pp. 6½ x 9¼. 27210-9 Pa. $9.95

THE LONG ISLAND RAIL ROAD IN EARLY PHOTOGRAPHS, Ron Ziel. Over 220 rare photos, informative text document origin (1844) and development of rail service on Long Island. Vintage views of early trains, locomotives, stations, passengers, crews, much more. Captions. 8⅞ x 11¾. 26301-0 Pa. $13.95

THE BOOK OF OLD SHIPS: From Egyptian Galleys to Clipper Ships, Henry B. Culver. Superb, authoritative history of sailing vessels, with 80 magnificent line illustrations. Galley, bark, caravel, longship, whaler, many more. Detailed, informative text on each vessel by noted naval historian. Introduction. 256pp. 5⅜ x 8½. 27332-6 Pa. $7.95

TEN BOOKS ON ARCHITECTURE, Vitruvius. The most important book ever written on architecture. Early Roman aesthetics, technology, classical orders, site selection, all other aspects. Morgan translation. 331pp. 5⅜ x 8½. 20645-9 Pa. $8.95

THE HUMAN FIGURE IN MOTION, Eadweard Muybridge. More than 4,500 stopped-action photos, in action series, showing undraped men, women, children jumping, lying down, throwing, sitting, wrestling, carrying, etc. 390pp. 7⅞ x 10⅝. 20204-6 Clothbd. $25.95

TREES OF THE EASTERN AND CENTRAL UNITED STATES AND CANADA, William M. Harlow. Best one-volume guide to 140 trees. Full descriptions, woodlore, range, etc. Over 600 illustrations. Handy size. 288pp. 4½ x 6⅜. 20395-6 Pa. $6.95

SONGS OF WESTERN BIRDS, Dr. Donald J. Borror. Complete song and call repertoire of 60 western species, including flycatchers, juncoes, cactus wrens, many more—includes fully illustrated booklet. Cassette and manual 99913-0 $8.95

GROWING AND USING HERBS AND SPICES, Milo Miloradovich. Versatile handbook provides all the information needed for cultivation and use of all the herbs and spices available in North America. 4 illustrations. Index. Glossary. 236pp. 5⅜ x 8½. 25058-X Pa. $6.95

BIG BOOK OF MAZES AND LABYRINTHS, Walter Shepherd. 50 mazes and labyrinths in all—classical, solid, ripple, and more—in one great volume. Perfect inexpensive puzzler for clever youngsters. Full solutions. 112pp. 8⅛ x 11. 22951-3 Pa. $4.95

PIANO TUNING, J. Cree Fischer. Clearest, best book for beginner, amateur. Simple repairs, raising dropped notes, tuning by easy method of flattened fifths. No previous skills needed. 4 illustrations. 201pp. 5⅜ x 8½. 23267-0 Pa. $6.95

A SOURCE BOOK IN THEATRICAL HISTORY, A. M. Nagler. Contemporary observers on acting, directing, make-up, costuming, stage props, machinery, scene design, from Ancient Greece to Chekhov. 611pp. 5⅜ x 8½. 20515-0 Pa. $12.95

THE COMPLETE NONSENSE OF EDWARD LEAR, Edward Lear. All nonsense limericks, zany alphabets, Owl and Pussycat, songs, nonsense botany, etc., illustrated by Lear. Total of 320pp. 5⅜ x 8½. (USO) 20167-8 Pa. $6.95

VICTORIAN PARLOUR POETRY: An Annotated Anthology, Michael R. Turner. 117 gems by Longfellow, Tennyson, Browning, many lesser-known poets. "The Village Blacksmith," "Curfew Must Not Ring Tonight," "Only a Baby Small," dozens more, often difficult to find elsewhere. Index of poets, titles, first lines. xxiii + 325pp. 5⅝ x 8¼. 27044-0 Pa. $8.95

DUBLINERS, James Joyce. Fifteen stories offer vivid, tightly focused observations of the lives of Dublin's poorer classes. At least one, "The Dead," is considered a masterpiece. Reprinted complete and unabridged from standard edition. 160pp. 5³⁄₁₆ x 8¼. 26870-5 Pa. $1.00

THE HAUNTED MONASTERY and THE CHINESE MAZE MURDERS, Robert van Gulik. Two full novels by van Gulik, set in 7th-century China, continue adventures of Judge Dee and his companions. An evil Taoist monastery, seemingly supernatural events; overgrown topiary maze hides strange crimes. 27 illustrations. 328pp. 5⅜ x 8½. 23502-5 Pa. $8.95

THE BOOK OF THE SACRED MAGIC OF ABRAMELIN THE MAGE, translated by S. MacGregor Mathers. Medieval manuscript of ceremonial magic. Basic document in Aleister Crowley, Golden Dawn groups. 268pp. 5⅜ x 8½. 23211-5 Pa. $8.95

NEW RUSSIAN-ENGLISH AND ENGLISH-RUSSIAN DICTIONARY, M. A. O'Brien. This is a remarkably handy Russian dictionary, containing a surprising amount of information, including over 70,000 entries. 366pp. 4½ x 6⅛. 20208-9 Pa. $9.95

HISTORIC HOMES OF THE AMERICAN PRESIDENTS, Second, Revised Edition, Irvin Haas. A traveler's guide to American Presidential homes, most open to the public, depicting and describing homes occupied by every American President from George Washington to George Bush. With visiting hours, admission charges, travel routes. 175 photographs. Index. 160pp. 8¼ x 11. 26751-2 Pa. $11.95

NEW YORK IN THE FORTIES, Andreas Feininger. 162 brilliant photographs by the well-known photographer, formerly with *Life* magazine. Commuters, shoppers, Times Square at night, much else from city at its peak. Captions by John von Hartz. 181pp. 9¼ x 10¾. 23585-8 Pa. $12.95

INDIAN SIGN LANGUAGE, William Tomkins. Over 525 signs developed by Sioux and other tribes. Written instructions and diagrams. Also 290 pictographs. 111pp. 6⅛ x 9¼. 22029-X Pa. $3.95

ANATOMY: A Complete Guide for Artists, Joseph Sheppard. A master of figure drawing shows artists how to render human anatomy convincingly. Over 460 illustrations. 224pp. 8⅜ x 11¼. 27279-6 Pa. $10.95

MEDIEVAL CALLIGRAPHY: Its History and Technique, Marc Drogin. Spirited history, comprehensive instruction manual covers 13 styles (ca. 4th century thru 15th). Excellent photographs; directions for duplicating medieval techniques with modern tools. 224pp. 8⅜ x 11¼. 26142-5 Pa. $12.95

DRIED FLOWERS: How to Prepare Them, Sarah Whitlock and Martha Rankin. Complete instructions on how to use silica gel, meal and borax, perlite aggregate, sand and borax, glycerine and water to create attractive permanent flower arrangements. 12 illustrations. 32pp. 5⅜ x 8½. 21802-3 Pa. $1.00

EASY-TO-MAKE BIRD FEEDERS FOR WOODWORKERS, Scott D. Campbell. Detailed, simple-to-use guide for designing, constructing, caring for and using feeders. Text, illustrations for 12 classic and contemporary designs. 96pp. 5⅜ x 8½. 25847-5 Pa. $2.95

SCOTTISH WONDER TALES FROM MYTH AND LEGEND, Donald A. Mackenzie. 16 lively tales tell of giants rumbling down mountainsides, of a magic wand that turns stone pillars into warriors, of gods and goddesses, evil hags, powerful forces and more. 240pp. 5⅜ x 8½. 29677-6 Pa. $6.95

THE HISTORY OF UNDERCLOTHES, C. Willett Cunnington and Phyllis Cunnington. Fascinating, well-documented survey covering six centuries of English undergarments, enhanced with over 100 illustrations: 12th-century laced-up bodice, footed long drawers (1795), 19th-century bustles, 19th-century corsets for men, Victorian "bust improvers," much more. 272pp. 5⅜ x 8¼. 27124-2 Pa. $9.95

ARTS AND CRAFTS FURNITURE: The Complete Brooks Catalog of 1912, Brooks Manufacturing Co. Photos and detailed descriptions of more than 150 now very collectible furniture designs from the Arts and Crafts movement depict davenports, settees, buffets, desks, tables, chairs, bedsteads, dressers and more, all built of solid, quarter-sawed oak. Invaluable for students and enthusiasts of antiques, Americana and the decorative arts. 80pp. 6½ x 9¼. 27471-3 Pa. $8.95

HOW WE INVENTED THE AIRPLANE: An Illustrated History, Orville Wright. Fascinating firsthand account covers early experiments, construction of planes and motors, first flights, much more. Introduction and commentary by Fred C. Kelly. 76 photographs. 96pp. 8¼ x 11. 25662-6 Pa. $8.95

THE ARTS OF THE SAILOR: Knotting, Splicing and Ropework, Hervey Garrett Smith. Indispensable shipboard reference covers tools, basic knots and useful hitches; handsewing and canvas work, more. Over 100 illustrations. Delightful reading for sea lovers. 256pp. 5⅜ x 8½. 26440-8 Pa. $7.95

FRANK LLOYD WRIGHT'S FALLINGWATER: The House and Its History, Second, Revised Edition, Donald Hoffmann. A total revision—both in text and illustrations—of the standard document on Fallingwater, the boldest, most personal architectural statement of Wright's mature years, updated with valuable new material from the recently opened Frank Lloyd Wright Archives. "Fascinating"—*The New York Times*. 116 illustrations. 128pp. 9¼ x 10¾. 27430-6 Pa. $11.95

PHOTOGRAPHIC SKETCHBOOK OF THE CIVIL WAR, Alexander Gardner. 100 photos taken on field during the Civil War. Famous shots of Manassas Harper's Ferry, Lincoln, Richmond, slave pens, etc. 244pp. 10⅝ x 8¼. 22731-6 Pa. $9.95

FIVE ACRES AND INDEPENDENCE, Maurice G. Kains. Great back-to-the-land classic explains basics of self-sufficient farming. The one book to get. 95 illustrations. 397pp. 5⅜ x 8½. 20974-1 Pa. $7.95

SONGS OF EASTERN BIRDS, Dr. Donald J. Borror. Songs and calls of 60 species most common to eastern U.S.: warblers, woodpeckers, flycatchers, thrushes, larks, many more in high-quality recording. Cassette and manual 99912-2 $9.95

A MODERN HERBAL, Margaret Grieve. Much the fullest, most exact, most useful compilation of herbal material. Gigantic alphabetical encyclopedia, from aconite to zedoary, gives botanical information, medical properties, folklore, economic uses, much else. Indispensable to serious reader. 161 illustrations. 888pp. 6½ x 9¼. 2-vol. set. (USO) Vol. I: 22798-7 Pa. $9.95
Vol. II: 22799-5 Pa. $9.95

HIDDEN TREASURE MAZE BOOK, Dave Phillips. Solve 34 challenging mazes accompanied by heroic tales of adventure. Evil dragons, people-eating plants, blood-thirsty giants, many more dangerous adversaries lurk at every twist and turn. 34 mazes, stories, solutions. 48pp. 8¼ x 11. 24566-7 Pa. $2.95

LETTERS OF W. A. MOZART, Wolfgang A. Mozart. Remarkable letters show bawdy wit, humor, imagination, musical insights, contemporary musical world; includes some letters from Leopold Mozart. 276pp. 5⅜ x 8½. 22859-2 Pa. $7.95

BASIC PRINCIPLES OF CLASSICAL BALLET, Agrippina Vaganova. Great Russian theoretician, teacher explains methods for teaching classical ballet. 118 illustrations. 175pp. 5⅜ x 8½. 22036-2 Pa. $5.95

THE JUMPING FROG, Mark Twain. Revenge edition. The original story of The Celebrated Jumping Frog of Calaveras County, a hapless French translation, and Twain's hilarious "retranslation" from the French. 12 illustrations. 66pp. 5⅜ x 8½. 22686-7 Pa. $3.95

BEST REMEMBERED POEMS, Martin Gardner (ed.). The 126 poems in this superb collection of 19th- and 20th-century British and American verse range from Shelley's "To a Skylark" to the impassioned "Renascence" of Edna St. Vincent Millay and to Edward Lear's whimsical "The Owl and the Pussycat." 224pp. 5⅜ x 8½. 27165-X Pa. $4.95

COMPLETE SONNETS, William Shakespeare. Over 150 exquisite poems deal with love, friendship, the tyranny of time, beauty's evanescence, death and other themes in language of remarkable power, precision and beauty. Glossary of archaic terms. 80pp. 5³⁄₁₆ x 8¼. 26686-9 Pa. $1.00

BODIES IN A BOOKSHOP, R. T. Campbell. Challenging mystery of blackmail and murder with ingenious plot and superbly drawn characters. In the best tradition of British suspense fiction. 192pp. 5⅜ x 8½. 24720-1 Pa. $6.95

THE WIT AND HUMOR OF OSCAR WILDE, Alvin Redman (ed.). More than 1,000 ripostes, paradoxes, wisecracks: Work is the curse of the drinking classes; I can resist everything except temptation; etc. 258pp. 5⅜ x 8½. 20602-5 Pa. $5.95

SHAKESPEARE LEXICON AND QUOTATION DICTIONARY, Alexander Schmidt. Full definitions, locations, shades of meaning in every word in plays and poems. More than 50,000 exact quotations. 1,485pp. 6½ x 9¼. 2-vol. set.
Vol. 1: 22726-X Pa. $16.95
Vol. 2: 22727-8 Pa. $16.95

SELECTED POEMS, Emily Dickinson. Over 100 best-known, best-loved poems by one of America's foremost poets, reprinted from authoritative early editions. No comparable edition at this price. Index of first lines. 64pp. 5³⁄₁₆ x 8¼.
26466-1 Pa. $1.00

CELEBRATED CASES OF JUDGE DEE (DEE GOONG AN), translated by Robert van Gulik. Authentic 18th-century Chinese detective novel; Dee and associates solve three interlocked cases. Led to van Gulik's own stories with same characters. Extensive introduction. 9 illustrations. 237pp. 5⅜ x 8½. 23337-5 Pa. $6.95

THE MALLEUS MALEFICARUM OF KRAMER AND SPRENGER, translated by Montague Summers. Full text of most important witchhunter's "bible," used by both Catholics and Protestants. 278pp. 6⅝ x 10. 22802-9 Pa. $12.95

SPANISH STORIES/CUENTOS ESPAÑOLES: A Dual-Language Book, Angel Flores (ed.). Unique format offers 13 great stories in Spanish by Cervantes, Borges, others. Faithful English translations on facing pages. 352pp. 5⅜ x 8½.
25399-6 Pa. $8.95

THE CHICAGO WORLD'S FAIR OF 1893: A Photographic Record, Stanley Appelbaum (ed.). 128 rare photos show 200 buildings, Beaux-Arts architecture, Midway, original Ferris Wheel, Edison's kinetoscope, more. Architectural emphasis; full text. 116pp. 8¼ x 11. 23990-X Pa. $9.95

OLD QUEENS, N.Y., IN EARLY PHOTOGRAPHS, Vincent F. Seyfried and William Asadorian. Over 160 rare photographs of Maspeth, Jamaica, Jackson Heights, and other areas. Vintage views of DeWitt Clinton mansion, 1939 World's Fair and more. Captions. 192pp. 8⅞ x 11. 26358-4 Pa. $12.95

CAPTURED BY THE INDIANS: 15 Firsthand Accounts, 1750-1870, Frederick Drimmer. Astounding true historical accounts of grisly torture, bloody conflicts, relentless pursuits, miraculous escapes and more, by people who lived to tell the tale. 384pp. 5⅜ x 8½. 24901-8 Pa. $8.95

THE WORLD'S GREAT SPEECHES, Lewis Copeland and Lawrence W. Lamm (eds.). Vast collection of 278 speeches of Greeks to 1970. Powerful and effective models; unique look at history. 842pp. 5⅜ x 8½. 20468-5 Pa. $14.95

THE BOOK OF THE SWORD, Sir Richard F. Burton. Great Victorian scholar/adventurer's eloquent, erudite history of the "queen of weapons"–from prehistory to early Roman Empire. Evolution and development of early swords, variations (sabre, broadsword, cutlass, scimitar, etc.), much more. 336pp. 6⅛ x 9¼.
25434-8 Pa. $9.95

AUTOBIOGRAPHY: The Story of My Experiments with Truth, Mohandas K. Gandhi. Boyhood, legal studies, purification, the growth of the Satyagraha (nonviolent protest) movement. Critical, inspiring work of the man responsible for the freedom of India. 480pp. 5⅜ x 8½. (USO) 24593-4 Pa. $8.95

CELTIC MYTHS AND LEGENDS, T. W. Rolleston. Masterful retelling of Irish and Welsh stories and tales. Cuchulain, King Arthur, Deirdre, the Grail, many more. First paperback edition. 58 full-page illustrations. 512pp. 5⅜ x 8½. 26507-2 Pa. $9.95

THE PRINCIPLES OF PSYCHOLOGY, William James. Famous long course complete, unabridged. Stream of thought, time perception, memory, experimental methods; great work decades ahead of its time. 94 figures. 1,391pp. 5⅜ x 8½. 2-vol. set.
Vol. I: 20381-6 Pa. $12.95
Vol. II: 20382-4 Pa. $12.95

THE WORLD AS WILL AND REPRESENTATION, Arthur Schopenhauer. Definitive English translation of Schopenhauer's life work, correcting more than 1,000 errors, omissions in earlier translations. Translated by E. F. J. Payne. Total of 1,269pp. 5⅜ x 8½. 2-vol. set. Vol. 1: 21761-2 Pa. $11.95
Vol. 2: 21762-0 Pa. $12.95

MAGIC AND MYSTERY IN TIBET, Madame Alexandra David-Neel. Experiences among lamas, magicians, sages, sorcerers, Bonpa wizards. A true psychic discovery. 32 illustrations. 321pp. 5⅜ x 8½. (USO) 22682-4 Pa. $8.95

THE EGYPTIAN BOOK OF THE DEAD, E. A. Wallis Budge. Complete reproduction of Ani's papyrus, finest ever found. Full hieroglyphic text, interlinear transliteration, word-for-word translation, smooth translation. 533pp. 6½ x 9¼.
21866-X Pa. $10.95

MATHEMATICS FOR THE NONMATHEMATICIAN, Morris Kline. Detailed, college-level treatment of mathematics in cultural and historical context, with numerous exercises. Recommended Reading Lists. Tables. Numerous figures. 641pp. 5⅜ x 8½.
24823-2 Pa. $11.95

THEORY OF WING SECTIONS: Including a Summary of Airfoil Data, Ira H. Abbott and A. E. von Doenhoff. Concise compilation of subsonic aerodynamic characteristics of NACA wing sections, plus description of theory. 350pp. of tables. 693pp. 5⅜ x 8½. 60586-8 Pa. $14.95

THE RIME OF THE ANCIENT MARINER, Gustave Doré, S. T. Coleridge. Doré's finest work; 34 plates capture moods, subtleties of poem. Flawless full-size reproductions printed on facing pages with authoritative text of poem. "Beautiful. Simply beautiful."–*Publisher's Weekly*. 77pp. 9¼ x 12. 22305-1 Pa. $6.95

NORTH AMERICAN INDIAN DESIGNS FOR ARTISTS AND CRAFTSPEOPLE, Eva Wilson. Over 360 authentic copyright-free designs adapted from Navajo blankets, Hopi pottery, Sioux buffalo hides, more. Geometrics, symbolic figures, plant and animal motifs, etc. 128pp. 8⅜ x 11. (EUK) 25341-4 Pa. $8.95

SCULPTURE: Principles and Practice, Louis Slobodkin. Step-by-step approach to clay, plaster, metals, stone; classical and modern. 253 drawings, photos. 255pp. 8⅛ x 11.
22960-2 Pa. $11.95

CATALOG OF DOVER BOOKS

THE INFLUENCE OF SEA POWER UPON HISTORY, 1660–1783, A. T. Mahan. Influential classic of naval history and tactics still used as text in war colleges. First paperback edition. 4 maps. 24 battle plans. 640pp. 5⅜ x 8½. 25509-3 Pa. $12.95

THE STORY OF THE TITANIC AS TOLD BY ITS SURVIVORS, Jack Winocour (ed.). What it was really like. Panic, despair, shocking inefficiency, and a little heroism. More thrilling than any fictional account. 26 illustrations. 320pp. 5⅜ x 8½. 20610-6 Pa. $8.95

FAIRY AND FOLK TALES OF THE IRISH PEASANTRY, William Butler Yeats (ed.). Treasury of 64 tales from the twilight world of Celtic myth and legend: "The Soul Cages," "The Kildare Pooka," "King O'Toole and his Goose," many more. Introduction and Notes by W. B. Yeats. 352pp. 5⅜ x 8½. 26941-8 Pa. $8.95

BUDDHIST MAHAYANA TEXTS, E. B. Cowell and Others (eds.). Superb, accurate translations of basic documents in Mahayana Buddhism, highly important in history of religions. The Buddha-karita of Asvaghosha, Larger Sukhavativyuha, more. 448pp. 5⅜ x 8½. 25552-2 Pa. $12.95

ONE TWO THREE . . . INFINITY: Facts and Speculations of Science, George Gamow. Great physicist's fascinating, readable overview of contemporary science: number theory, relativity, fourth dimension, entropy, genes, atomic structure, much more. 128 illustrations. Index. 352pp. 5⅜ x 8½. 25664-2 Pa. $8.95

ENGINEERING IN HISTORY, Richard Shelton Kirby, et al. Broad, nontechnical survey of history's major technological advances: birth of Greek science, industrial revolution, electricity and applied science, 20th-century automation, much more. 181 illustrations. ". . . excellent . . ."–*Isis.* Bibliography. vii + 530pp. 5⅜ x 8¼. 26412-2 Pa. $14.95

DALÍ ON MODERN ART: The Cuckolds of Antiquated Modern Art, Salvador Dalí. Influential painter skewers modern art and its practitioners. Outrageous evaluations of Picasso, Cézanne, Turner, more. 15 renderings of paintings discussed. 44 calligraphic decorations by Dalí. 96pp. 5⅜ x 8½. (USO) 29220-7 Pa. $4.95

ANTIQUE PLAYING CARDS: A Pictorial History, Henry René D'Allemagne. Over 900 elaborate, decorative images from rare playing cards (14th–20th centuries): Bacchus, death, dancing dogs, hunting scenes, royal coats of arms, players cheating, much more. 96pp. 9¼ x 12¼. 29265-7 Pa. $11.95

MAKING FURNITURE MASTERPIECES: 30 Projects with Measured Drawings, Franklin H. Gottshall. Step-by-step instructions, illustrations for constructing handsome, useful pieces, among them a Sheraton desk, Chippendale chair, Spanish desk, Queen Anne table and a William and Mary dressing mirror. 224pp. 8⅛ x 11¼. 29338-6 Pa. $13.95

THE FOSSIL BOOK: A Record of Prehistoric Life, Patricia V. Rich et al. Profusely illustrated definitive guide covers everything from single-celled organisms and dinosaurs to birds and mammals and the interplay between climate and man. Over 1,500 illustrations. 760pp. 7½ x 10⅛. 29371-8 Pa. $29.95

Prices subject to change without notice.

Available at your book dealer or write for free catalog to Dept. GI, Dover Publications, Inc., 31 East 2nd St., Mineola, N.Y. 11501. Dover publishes more than 500 books each year on science, elementary and advanced mathematics, biology, music, art, literary history, social sciences and other areas.